D1507956

PROFILES
of Female
GENIUS

PROFILES of Female GENIUS

Thirteen Creative Women Who Changed the World

GENE N. LANDRUM, Ph.D.

 Prometheus Books

59 John Glenn Drive
Amherst, New York 14228-2197

Published 1994 by Prometheus Books

Photograph of Mary Kay Ash (p. 170) courtesy of Mary Kay Cosmetics. Photographs of Maria Callas (p. 188), Jane Fonda (p. 224), Golda Meir (p. 280), and Gloria Steinem (p. 312) courtesy of Archive Photos. Photograph of Liz Claiborne (p. 206) courtesy of *Vogue* (© 1986 by The Condé Nast Publications, Inc.). Photographs of Estée Lauder (p. 244), Madonna (p. 260), Ayn Rand, (p. 298), Margaret Thatcher (p. 330), Lillian Vernon (p. 346), and Linda Wacher (p. 360) courtesy of AP/Wide World Photos. Photograph of Oprah Winfrey (p. 374) courtesy of Harpo Productions.

98 97 96 95 94   5 4 3 2 1

Library of Congress Cataloging-in-Publication Data

Landrum, Gene N.
    Profiles of female genius : thirteen creative women who changed the world / by Gene N. Landrum.
        p.   cm.
    Includes bibliographical references and index.
    ISBN 0-87975-892-9 (alk. paper)
    1. Women in the professions. I. Title.
HD6054.L36   1994
331.4—dc20   94-7579
                                                                         CIP

Printed in the United States of America on acid-free paper.

To my mother, Charlotte Allen of Ft. Myers, Florida, who made this work possible through years of love, understanding, and support

Everyone is born with genius but most people only keep it a few minutes.
—Martha Graham

Some day there will undoubtedly be a science—it may be called the science of man—which will seek to learn about man in general through the study of creative man.
—Pablo Picasso

Contents

PROFILES OF CREATIVE GENIUS

8 CONTENTS

List of Figures

9

Acknowledgments

Many people helped with this book, not the least of whom were the subjects and their firms, who supplied much valuable information and detail. My wife, Diedra, continued to be my best critic, editor, and advisor on the personality of the female professional. She spent laborious hours reading the chapters on the females to ensure that my male perspective was not getting in the way of objectivity. Her input on the female viewpoint was invaluable. My mother-in-law, Fran Gansloser of California, was extremely supportive and helpful on various aspects of the book. The Naples Library staff were extremely helpful in obtaining the interlibrary research materials required of such an extensive research effort. Elizabeth Nagangast, Eric Bucher, Susan Mansfield, Jeanne Jemmott, and Ruth Schulze were especially helpful in the research. The most pervasive assistance came from Steven L. Mitchell, Editor-in-Chief for Prometheus Books, whose discerning analysis and probing questions helped make the book truly focused.

11

Preface

The selection process for the top female creative visionaries over the past forty years is extremely difficult at best and virtually impossible at worst. So many great women qualify who must be omitted and the criteria for selection can never be agreed on by any disparate group. Housewives wanted me to use Barbra Streisand or Dr. Joyce Brothers, career women preferred Dr. Ruth Westheimer or Helen Gurley Brown, intellectuals preferred Janet Reno or Ruth Ginsburg, and literary advisers pushed for Barbara Cartland or Indira Gandhi. I decided on a firm set of criteria which each subject had to meet regardless of her popularity or success in life or business. These women must *not have inherited or married into their profession*. They must have started with *nothing* and reached the very *top* of their field and stayed there for a minimum of *ten years*. They had to have had *international* influence and accomplished their major achievement within the past *forty years*. Even considering these difficult criteria many women still qualified for inclusion in the book. I became the final arbiter of their qualifications based on their contribution to society and the world. Many successful women were therefore left out, including Sandra Day O'Connor, Susie Thomkins (Esprit), Indira Gandhi, Sally Ride, Jenny Craig, Leona Helmsley, Sandra Kurtzig (Ask Computers), Mary Wells (Madison Avenue guru), Helen Gurley Brown, Rachel Carson, Frances Lear, and Barbara Walters among others. These women were researched and studied at length and in some instances are referred to within the text as examples of the characteristics of a creative genius. Validity factors prompted me to research three great historical female visionaries for comparison with the contemporary women selected. I elected to use three women who made enormous contributions to society and changed the world for the better.

The final criteria included the following parameters meant to ferret out eminent women who had reached the pinnacle of success regardless of their field of endeavor. These women are the crème de la crème of female accomplishment and are destined to be the role models for future generations. If a woman did not meet all of the following criteria she was not used regardless of her accomplishments:

Mother of the industry/field. The woman must have created her own success and not have inherited it from either a parent or a husband. Catherine Graham of *Washington Post* and *Newsweek* fame did not qualify because she inherited her position of power and influence and did not create it through her own efforts.

Ten-year dominating influence. The woman's concept, company, creation, or contribution must have proved dominant enough to have reached the top of that domain and had the staying power to remain in that position for a minimum of ten years. Sally Ride, as the first woman in space, achieved a remarkable accomplishment but it was of limited duration.

International in scope. The woman's success or achievement must have been multinational in scope with international influence, not just regional or national. Diane Feinstein and Margaret Chase Smith were dynamic leaders and successes but were not international in scope and influence.

Contemporary development. The woman's influence or achievement must have occurred during the past forty years. Babe Didrickson Zaharias, Maria Montessori, and Martha Graham are individuals who were giants in their fields but not within this time period.

The thirteen women finally selected are illustrated in the following figure with their most noteworthy achievements. Catherine the Great, Margaret Mead, and Mother Teresa will also be discussed as three eminent women of earlier success to further validate the findings on these thirteen. The thirteen female visionaries dominated and changed the world of business, politics, entertainment, and the humanities. All but three were chief executive officers of their own multimillion dollar enterprises. All were the masters of their own fate and achieved their mark in the world on their own. It was their drive and psychological need to become the very best that attracted me to these eminent women. Their backgrounds, family influences, psychological makeup and personalities are explored in depth in this book in order to discern precisely "what made these eminent women tick."

This book evolved out of a similar work on male creative genius, *Profiles of Genius* (1993), which was primarily aimed at business entrepreneurs who had become the symbolic fathers of their given industries. Those thirteen men had been instrumental in changing the way the world works based on their unique vision of reality. Most of the women in this work did not necessarily found their given industries or fields, but were almost always the most dominant and influential person in their field of expertise. They also changed the

Figure 1

Great Female Leaders and Their Accomplishments

Revolutionized Business

Mary Kay Ash — Created the largest direct-sales multilevel marketing cosmetics firm in the world, which allowed working mothers to earn excellent income at their own leisure.

Liz Claiborne — Fashion visionary who dominates the women's business-wear industry. First company started by a woman to make the *Fortune* 500 list.

Estée Lauder — Scion of the largest cosmetics empire in the United States created with her own hands, resulting in a personal family fortune of over $5 billion

Lillian Vernon — Undisputed matron of catalog sales with her distribution of 140 million catalogs annually. Created business from her kitchen table as mother of two.

Linda Wachner — First woman to acquire a *Fortune* 500 company via a hostile takeover. Heads the largest public company run by a woman. Highest-paid female executive at $3 million a year

Political Visionaries

Golda Meir — First Israeli foreign minister and first Israeli female prime minister

Margaret Thatcher — First Prime Minister of Great Britain and longest holder of that office in the twentieth century

Dominated the Entertainment Industry

Maria Callas — Greatest prima donna and operatic diva in twentieth century

Jane Fonda — Wrote largest-selling nonfiction book in United States and created largest-selling videotapes of all time. Two Academy Awards as best actress. Chief executive officer of video fitness business.

Madonna — Most successive #1 hit single records in music history music. Highest earning show business personality. Chief executive officer of Boy Toy, Inc., and other corporations.

Oprah Winfrey — Top talk-show hostess in the world, most revered TV personality, accomplished actress, and highest-earning TV personality as CEO of Harpo Studios at $98 million yearly.

Humanitarians Who Altered Societal Values and Ethics

Ayn Rand — Authored the world's first philosophical epic novel—*Atlas Shrugged*—which spawned a new philosophical movement, objectivism, and a new political party, the Libertarian Party

Gloria Steinem — Most visible and influential feminist in late twentieth century. Founder of *Ms.* magazine and other noteworthy female organizations.

world in just as significant a manner as the male visionaries. All but three of these women (Callas, Meir, and Thatcher) operated their own multimil-lion-dollar enterprises, including entertainers such as Winfrey, Madonna, and Fonda, who managed their own day-to-day business operations. Even author Ayn Rand ran her own newsletter and consulting-lecturing business. Two women who were not CEOs (Thatcher and Meir) achieved their success in profes-sions dominated by men. Margaret Thatcher, the first female prime minister of Britain, an awesome accomplishment in any society, stayed in that position longer than anyone in the twentieth century. Golda Meir's accomplishment was even more spectacular: she defied a male-dominated electorate and made it to the top of the Israeli government in a society where people normally place women on a pedestal within the home, but not in government positions of power. A Jewish newspaper confirmed this chauvinistic attitude by oppos-ing Meir's election based on a religious rationale: "It is difficult for a people whose religion assigns women a place of honor in the home to accept the idea of a woman at the head of a political department. With all due respect to women of good sense and diligence, a woman should not be placed at the helm of one of our central political bodies." Meir was not deterred and made it to the top.

One publisher told me he had difficulty "equating mere celebrity and financial success with 'genius.' " Au contraire! Too many people, including this particular publisher, confuse genius with IQ or some mysterious aptitude or talent. *Webster's Dictionary* defines "genius" as the ability to "influence another for good or bad." The word "creative," according to the same source means to "bring something new into existence." Therefore, when this book uses the phrase "creative genius," it refers to great female visionaries who had a "particularly strong aptitude for bringing new concepts into existence and influenced others for both good and bad." In fact, these women influenced others—and the world—for the good. One example is Madonna, who reached the top of her profession with only "average talent," a testimony to her creative and entre-preneurial genius. She, Winfrey, and Fonda, all CEOs, run their businesses much like all other entrepreneurial executives.

Liz Claiborne revolutionized the women's-wear fashion industry. This was an act of creative genius not a function of some test score. Ayn Rand created a new capitalist philosophy that spawned a whole new political party. *That* was creative genius. Gloria Steinem introduced the word "Ms." into our vocabulary and, in the process, changed legislation and the status of women. *That* was creative genius. Oprah Winfrey radically changed the nature of daytime talk shows, and is a creative genius for her role as America's pop psychologist. And consider Maria Callas. She was not a child prodigy, as is popularly thought. She worked diligently to become the greatest diva and prima donna of the twentieth century. Her voice was awesome but opera critics found her unacceptable since she did not meet their finite definition of operatic elegance. They therefore refused to listen to her because she did not meet their quantitative criteria for genius. But these men did not understand that her creative genius was not based on some esoteric voice quality; it was due to her imaginative and superlative execution on the stage. It was her charismatic portrayal of opera as art and entertainment that made her a creative genius. She was a consummate artist and actress and her voice was strictly a vehicle for her entertainment genius.

These women were selected because of their unique contributions to the world and their enormous accomplishments in their respective fields of endeavor. All reached the top of their given professions and stayed there for over a decade. All were true creative visionaries because they were qualitatively inspired as right-brain-driven spirits who had the guts and the courage of their convictions to achieve in spite of their limitations. They always disdained the quantitatively driven, left-brain-thinking people who questioned their right to create the new by destroying the old. Their self-esteem, intuition, and drive were their greatest strengths. These traits allowed them to accomplish the impossible and, furthermore, they did it with elegance and grace.

These women were paradoxes in that they accomplished enormous feats that should not have been possible. Paradoxes occur because the experts and industry leaders are arrogant, risk-averse, and resist all change. Most creative breakthroughs are accomplished by neophytes because the experts ignore the opportunity. Those who should be innovating for the future are preserving the past, thereby allowing the least likely individuals to pioneer innovations. Consider Darwin, a man trained to become a minister of the church who became the father of evolution. Albert Einstein was unemployable as a college instructor just a few years prior to his epochal discoveries of the theory of relativity. And imagine Sigmund Freud selling only 351 copies of his monumental work *Interpretation of Dreams* (1900), a book in which he formulated the breakthrough concepts of the ego, the unconscious, and repression, and effectively launched the field of psychoanalysis. How did Ayn Rand, a female Russian immigrant who could barely speak English, write the first great English philosophical epic novel? And what of Jane Fonda, a life-long anorexic/bulimic, revolutionizing the fitness video industry? It is almost axiomatic that those individuals "most unlikely to create the new and revolutionary, are usually the most likely to do it, and those most likely to do it, fall on their faces"! This is the great unwritten law of creativity. Here are some interesting paradoxes:

PARADOXES OF CREATIVE GENIUS!

What motivated a girl raised in a Milwaukee ghetto to become the first female prime minister of Israel?

Why was a shy introvert with a fear of public speaking able to become the world's most renowned feminist?

How could an ugly, insecure, two-hundred-pound teenager become the world's most beautiful and worshipped diva?

What drove an abused Mississippi farm girl to becc ne the most idolized talk show host in America?

How could a high-school dropout revolutionize the tradition-steeped female fashion industry?

Why was a young Jewish immigrant housewife able to create the largest Christmas mail-order gift catalog in America where personalized Christmas ornaments were the number one product?

What motivated a medically diagnosed bulimic ["I had a morbid fear of being fat" (Davidson 1970)] to create the largest-selling fitness videos in history?

How could a poor immigrant girl raised in a New York ghetto become the Queen of the cosmetics industry?

What inspired a girl who grew up without indoor plumbing to become Britain's first female prime minister and its longest-reigning prime minister in the twentieth Century?

Why was a Macy's bra and girdle buyer able to rise to the presidency of Max Factor by age thirty-three?

How could a Russian immigrant who barely spoke English write the first philosophical epic novel which created a new philosophical movement and a new political party?

Why was a middle-aged woman with no experience able to create the beauty titan known as Mary Kay Cosmetics?

What drove a twenty-two-year-old who ate out of garbage cans in 1980 to become the world's highest paid and most famous sex symbol by 1990?

It is the aim of this book to analyze why the above paradoxes were possible and why these thirteen creative geniuses were able to accomplish what others could not. An even greater paradox is how so many of these women could be simultaneously loved and hated. Most were not treated with indifference; they were adored or despised, especially Ayn Rand, Jane Fonda, Madonna, Gloria Steinem, Maria Callas, Linda Wachner, Golda Meir, and Margaret Thatcher. These women had that unique quality to spawn fierce emotion in everyone they touched, and it is this quality that made them great.

All were successful. Estée Lauder made the most money, Madonna became the most illustrious, Margaret Thatcher was the hardest working, and Linda Wachner was paid the highest salary. Maria Callas had the most emotional problems and Mary Kay was the most religious. Madonna is the least admired, and Oprah Winfrey the most loved along with the highest income. Liz Claiborne made the most money in the shortest period of time. Estée Lauder was easily the best dressed, and Golda Meir the worst. Sex drive was a tie between Madonna (as expected) and Golda Meir (unexpected). Thatcher has had the greatest influence on the contemporary world, and Ayn Rand is expected to have the greatest impact on the twenty-first century.

Their enormous achievements even surprised their families and friends. And these women often admitted that they themselves were surprised at the magnitude of their success. Even so, none of them ever doubted they would end up on top. They dared to go where others feared to tread, and were rewarded for their particular form of temerity. Their stories are profiled to delineate those personality and behavior traits found critical to success in entrepreneurship, creativity, and innovation. These factors are a function of both genetic (nature) and environmental (nurture) factors. These women appear to have mimicked the male power brokers in many of their operating styles, or possibly it is this particular style that is endemic to creative success. Their careers were placed ahead of their families and their aggressive/competitive/risk-taking styles are similar to those found in male creative genius. Their self-esteem was molded early and reinforced through adult successes. A "universal female" portrait or profile of "creative genius" can be drawn from the findings on these thirteen women including the three historical women: Catherine the Great, Margaret Mead, and Mother Teresa. Many exceptions exist but the following intrinsic and extrinsic profiles represent the most likely definition of the "universal female creative genius."

Intrinsic or Genetic Profile. First-born female with slightly above-average intelligence who had a self-employed father as the dominant influence in her life. Her parents were permissive, allowing a nonjudgmental outlet for her inquisitiveness. She moved or traveled extensively, which taught her to cope with unknown foreign environments. She was lonely or unhappy and lost herself in books. She faced an early crisis that instilled in her resilience and drive. Strong female role models or heroines or all-girl schools were a positive influence.

Extrinsic or Personality Profile. An obsessively driven intuitive-thinking Promethean spirit who had a renegade mentality and was comfortable with ambiguity and risk-taking. She had awesome self-esteem, which empowered her to be independent and self-reliant. Her excessive energy and work ethic labeled her "workaholic" by her peers. And an optimistic "will to power" attitude gave her a charismatic persona that attracted numerous disciples who assisted her in her maniacal drive to the top. Formal education was not a material factor in her success.

Introduction

Female Creative Genius

What distinguished Catherine the Great from the male leaders of the eighteenth century? Why did Madame Curie outperform most of the male scientists of her era? What motivated Florence Nightingale to sacrifice everything to create the nursing profession? What drove Margaret Mead to become the world's greatest female anthropologist, or Mother Teresa to risk her life with lepers and the diseased to create the Society of Charity? And what inspired Rachel Carson, a recluse turned revolutionary, to create a monumental work such as *Silent Spring,* enlightening an unsuspecting world to the dangers of pollution? The aim of this book is to answer these questions and query the nature and causes of creative and entrepreneurial genius in women. In doing this we will delve into the psyches and behavior characteristics of thirteen of the greatest female success stories of the twentieth century.

What behavior traits inspired a lower-middle-class grocer's daughter to become the first prime minister of Great Britain? How could a German-Jewish immigrant with zero training in business have created the largest gift catalog company in the world? What drove an illegitimate daughter of a Mississippi sharecropper to revolutionize television talk shows and become the highest-paid entertainer in America? And think of the moxie required of a Russian immigrant to write an epic philosophical novel in English, a language she spoke with difficulty. These women had temperaments strikingly similar to those of Catherine the Great, Margaret Mead, and Mother Teresa. Margaret Thatcher, Lillian Vernon, Oprah Winfrey, and Ayn Rand had been raised in dramatically different cultures—British, German, American, and Russian—yet they all idolized self-employed fathers, were innovator personality types (i.e., preferred doing things differently), and possessed a "psychic" energy level that was off the scale. These creative visionaries were quite similar in their behavior styles and traits but they thought, acted, and operated differently from the average person. How differently? The intent of this book is to answer that question—

to differentiate these eminent women from other women, to isolate character traits that appear predictive of great achievement and success, and to develop some generalizations about what makes the eminent female visionary tick.

Is Creative Behavior Cognitive or Imaginative?

I am convinced that these women became enamored with childhood fantasy images of reality found in books, role models, and fictional ideas from magazines and dreams, and buried them as wish-fulfillment in their unconscious. As adults they were able to tap into their unconscious reservoir of images and implement these fantasy dreams into their adult actions. In other words, their childhood imagination became their adult reality. Howard Gardner, the Harvard researcher on creative genius, says, "Creative geniuses tend to return to the conceptual world of childhood." (*Creative Minds* 1993) He used Einstein's childhood dreams of space and time to demonstrate his theory espoused in *Creative Minds*. I concur, but I am also convinced that these early childhood images are so imprinted that they become the untapped gems of adulthood. Our macro-visions in childhood allow us to see the big picture as adults and therefore no challenge is ever beyond our reach. A grandiose imagination begets eminent achievement. Creative geniuses are different. They build childhood castles in the sky and try to move in, while normal people *know* they can't move in and therefore never attempt such an outlandish action.

Ayn Rand envisioned larger-than-life heroes from French novels and saw herself in a "universal" or "macro-vision" sense as a great creator of epic-like characters. She saw herself from age nine as a person capable of world renown and success. She imagined herself impacting the world through writing, and she did. She unconsciously believed and was therefore able to implement those early dreams into an adult reality. Catherine the Great is another example of a woman who had visions of grandeur as a child and implemented them as an adult. She wrote in her memoirs of her teen years, "There was something within me which never allowed me to doubt for a single moment that I should one day succeed in becoming the Empress of Russia." As a child Margaret Mead was groomed and trained to view the world holistically. "Observation of others" taught her young mind to think in macro-vision "universals." She grew up viewing the world as her own personal laboratory and was therefore capable of altering the world of anthropology through "observation" techniques learned as an inquisitive child.

Martha Graham innovated in the field of dance, becoming widely acknowledged as the greatest dancer of the twentieth century, due to similar unconscious imprintings as a teenager. In a lecture to her on her personal behavior, Graham was told by her father, "Movement does not lie." This so impressed her that she adopted "movement" as her lifetime passion. She was obsessed with proving that "movement does not lie." Graham's mother encouraged her to "pretend" by setting up her own theater in her home. This make-believe theater became an adult wish-fulfillment exercise resulting in monumental success. Graham's father took his teenage daughter to see the exotic dancer Ruth St. Denis, featured as the God Krishna. Graham said, "From that moment on, my fate was sealed. I couldn't wait to learn to dance as the goddess did." Mother Teresa had a vision of her life's calling to help the poor while still in a crisis period after her father's premature death when she was eight. At age twelve she said, "It was then that I first knew I had a vocation to the poor."

It seems that all of these women had a vision bigger than life, which was indelibly imprinted on their unconscious at a very young age. The above stories confirm other research on eminently successful visionaries that *all* creative behavior emanates from the imprints of our youth—not our adult Eureka experiences. It appears we spend most of our lives fulfilling the prophesies of our childhood fantasies. They don't just pop up as instantaneous phenomena. Psychotherapist Carl Jung felt that the feminine side of our natures drives creativity. He said:

> The creative process has a feminine quality, and the creative work arises from unconscious depths. . . . Whenever the creative predominates, human life is ruled and molded by the unconscious as against the active will, and the conscious ego is swept along on a subterranean current, being nothing more than a helpless observer of events. . . . It is not Goethe who creates Faust, but Faust who creates Goethe. (*The Creative Process,* 1952)

Jung's theory and my research prompt the following hypothesis on the origin of creative concepts and behavior. Likening the mind to a newspaper the conscious is the headline and captions, the pre-conscious or unconscious is the detailed content or the essence of the story.

ALL BEHAVIOR IS UNCONSCIOUSLY DRIVEN

It is my contention that all behavior, creative and otherwise, originates in the unconscious*! Not the forbidden lust driven unconscious of Freud but the instinctive knowledge that makes us all unique in the world. Just as a computer is preprogrammed internally to operate in a certain way externally, so too is the human animal preprogrammed. Every human concept or idea emanates from an unconscious source within every individual, who then uses that information in a cognitive or conscious way to deal with the outside world. Based on this theory any cognitive action, such as selecting a best friend or a favorite food item, is not based on one's conscious reality but predetermined* *by an unconscious need for that particular choice. In other words, liking peanut butter is not a conscious choice, but an unconscious one predetermined by an internally driven desire for it. Likewise, the preference for a tall, dark, trim partner is a function of our internal need to fulfill some unconscious need created at some earlier time in our lives. The essence of this concept is that our conscious or ego-self merely speaks for the real controller of all our actions, namely, the unconscious self. Based on this theory every creative person is actually reaching back to some earlier vision of reality in order to create adult innovations. Thus, the creative women profiled here are successful because of their internal self-images, not their cognitive adult actions. And their self-esteem is the real catalyst for their innovative and creative success.*

Carl Jung believed the "unconscious" to be an enormous field of energy, much larger than the conscious mind. He equated the "conscious mind" to the tip of an iceberg with the unconscious representing the 95 percent area below the surface. He felt that our unconscious images were the real power behind all creative energy. Jung felt that some stored images were in fact universal imagery, something he labeled the "collective unconscious." He described this innate or universal knowledge as having been inherited from our ancestry. The active imagination *was Jung's equivalent of Freud's* free association *technique for probing into the unconscious for the purpose of modifying or changing the internally scripted message or repressed energies. This would make his active imagination concept (daydreaming or tapping into the unconscious) the creative visionary's tool for releasing childhood images for adult creativity.*

Extensive research on the creative, innovative, and entrepreneurial personality, in both males and females, has led me to the above conclusion. It appears that an intrinsic (unconscious) drive or motivation based on early imprinting and conditioning, is at the seat of all drive, behavior traits, needs, wants, desires, opinions, judgments, and other behavioral characteristics in the creative personality. These personal attributes emanate from an unconscious energy source within each individual. They are similar in nature to Jung's collective unconscious, *Sheldrake's* morphogenetic fields, *and Wilhelm Reich's* orgone, *all of which imply a universal knowledge innate in everyone.*

This theory of unconscious energy as the driving force for all conscious decision making is only intended as a concept relative to furthering the research on creative genius and will not be pursued further in this text. It has been discussed here because of its enormous impact on self-esteem, which appears to be the most critical variable in all creativity. No further attempt will be made to prove the hypothesis that all behavior emanates from the unconscious, but it is certainly the most pervasive influence on female creative genius.

The above concept gives credence to the findings on these creative and innovative women. They were all driven by some powerful internal force to pursue great achievements. In the case of these thirteen visionaries, success was predicated on their intrinsic not extrinsic, intuitive not sensory, covert not overt, and unconscious not conscious actions. They never knew what drove them, but they all knew they had a compulsion to excel, which they did better than most.

What Makes Them Tick?

These visionaries operate with a style and elegance not normally found in most people. Their behavior traits and energy levels are surprisingly similar to each other although they differ in many ways from the normal population. Contrary to popular belief, these women are living examples that the road to success is not paved with the classic Ivy League education, Mensa-level IQ, debutante progeny, super wealth, or *Fortune* 500 executive experience. None of these bromides were found to be critical in spawning great creative genius. However, many other factors are important to the creative process, many of which were not initially apparent prior to this research.

Some specific ingredients or characteristics of female creative genius (see figure 2) are predictive of entrepreneurial, creative, and innovative success. These behavioral and experiential factors were the primary influences in these visionaries' drive to the top. All-girl schooling and strong female mentors appear to be instrumental in the development of creative genius. Six of these women had such schooling: Margaret Thatcher, shockingly, went from kindergarten through college without ever sharing a school room with a male. As children, most were voracious readers and fantasized a great deal about larger-than-life heroines. These women were often the prima donnas in their families, a result of being first born, only children, or, in Thatcher's case, the center of the universe within the family. The father was the dominant parental influence for these female visionaries. In my study of male successes, the mother was the dominant influence. All of these women idolized their fathers and many disliked their mothers (Callas, Fonda, Winfrey, Meir, Rand). Most led early lives of transience, moving about a great deal and attending numerous schools (Margaret Mead attended sixty schools prior to high school and Callas had attended nine by age twelve). Most had self-employed fathers, which appears to have conditioned them to early feelings of self-sufficiency and autonomy. Self-employed fathers and early transience appear to have instilled a confidence that prepared them to survive in the new and unknown environments they would face as adults. It made them feel they were the masters of their own fate and gave them the confidence, at a very early age, to "know" that they could survive as independent entities without depending on a corporate organization for economic survival.

Figure 2

Behavior and Experiential Profiles of Female Creative Genius

1. **First-born females or father's favorite—Father the major influence**
   Demonstrates perfectionism, striving for superiority, and high need to achieve

2. **Transient childhoods—Leading to autonomous self-sufficiency**
   Ability to cope in foreign environments learned early in life through repeated movement

3. **Female mentors—Education in all-girls schools**
   Excellent feminine role models and mentors, larger-than-life fantasy heroines

4. **Self-employed father who became influential mentor**
   Father made his own way in the world as shopkeeper, carpenter, entrepreneur, or salesman

5. **Perfectionists—Willing to sacrifice everything for their goal**
   Strive for power and superiority through internalized "will to power"

6. **Persistently goal-oriented workaholics—Intransigent**
   Persevering prevails in entrepreneurship. Individuals who never give up never lose!

7. **Competitive drive and empowered to achieve**
   Aggressive behavior where winning is more important than playing

8. **Renegade "break the rules" mentality—"Kirton's Innovator Behavior Style"**
   Preference for "doing things differently" rather than "doing things excellently"

9. **Independent and indomitable personality**
   Intense and fearless with total self-sufficiency and self-assurance

10. **High self-confidence/self-esteem/self-image**
    Arrogance preferable to submissiveness for innovative success

11. **Charismatic, persuasive personality—A mystical aura**
    Enthusiastic, passionate, and inspirational leadership qualities

12. **Right-brain intuitive "gut" decision makers**
    Use macro vs. micro, long-term vs. short-term, qualitative vs. quantitative, analog vs. digital, inductive vs. deductive, and subjective vs. objective approach to problem resolution

13. **Psychic energy level—Sublimated libidinal drives of insecurity and inferiority**
    High need to achieve. Innate fear of failure sublimated into overachievement

Formal education, knowledge, and experience were also critical to their development, but not in the way most people would expect. Although the sample of thirteen is small, the results of this research would indicate that formal education is inversely related to great creative achievement. Formal education had little or no bearing on the success of these subjects—only five had college degrees and only Linda Wachner had a degree in the field in which she excelled. A Harvard MBA may open many important doors for an executive job, but having the degree appears to predispose a person to work for others—in a middle-management position of an existing organization—and not to pioneer in the gutters of entrepreneurial enterprise where all great creative endeavor originates.

Early life crises and trauma appear to prepare a young woman to over-achieve. Adversity enhances learning. It arms a woman with a desperate resolve to rise above misfortune. Five of these women lost a direct family member as a child and six had close brushes with death. Maria Callas and Linda Wachner were seriously incapacitated while young. The lessons they learned in coping with their early traumatic experiences appear to have armed them with exceptional resolve. These early crises appear to have armored and programmed them to deal effectively with calamity. It appears there is an appropriate amount of stress needed to develop strong character.

Charisma and superior communication skills were found in many of these women. Ash, Meir, Winfrey, and Thatcher were mesmerizing speakers. They became leaders by captivating their audiences and followers: many of their associates admitted that they would follow them anywhere. An associate of Margaret Mead said, "The sex appeal of that mind of hers was absolutely captivating. An exceptional man met her in 1973—was thirty years her junior—and said, 'If she had pointed to me and said, You! You're the one I choose! Come off with me. I would have gone with her. Anywhere.' " (Howard 1984)

The majority of these women were intuitive thinkers (possessed Promethean temperaments) with an innovator style of behavior (a preference for being different), with a right-brain macro-vision of the world and possibilities in life. These traits are analyzed in detail in the chapter on personality. Most had a "Type A" work ethic and were driven to be superior or perfect in everything they attempted. They were social renegades who broke rules and rebelled against traditional dogmas and the establishment. They were competitive risk-takers, not to the extent of an Amelia Earhart or of male entrepreneurs like Ted Turner, but to a far greater degree than the average female professional. They were as willing as any man to sacrifice their personal lives for their profes-sional lives.

These women all broke through that illusory glass ceiling, but in doing so paid the price of sacrificing motherhood (six had no children) or were required to choose between their maternal natures and their careers. This is such an important variable for the professional woman that one entire chapter has been dedicated to analyzing how these women dealt with the professional/ personal dilemma. These women resolved the career-family dichotomy in one of three ways: they either opted for a *serial* (family followed by career), *parallel* (family and career attempted simultaneously), or *sacrificial* (no marriage or children) lifestyle. Three of the women—Mary Kay Ash, Liz Claiborne, and Estée Lauder—opted for the *serial* approach, as did Margaret Mead. Four others—Margaret Thatcher, Golda Meir, Lillian Vernon, and Jane Fonda— chose the more difficult *parallel* route. Catherine the Great chose this route but was castigated by the world for her treatment of her son in order to maintain the top position in Russia. The majority of these visionaries—Gloria Steinem, Ayn Rand, Maria Callas, Linda Wachner, and to date Madonna and Oprah— have seen fit to "sacrifice" motherhood for their burgeoning careers. Mother Teresa also chose this route.

Self-esteem jumped out of the research at every turn. Self-esteem dominates every aspect of female leadership. Nothing great is ever accomplished without it. Because of its importance to the success of female visionaries, chapter one has been devoted to this critical element in female success. The other critical variables outlined in figure 2 will be examined throughout the book in order to determine which factors are most critical to the creative process. The primary objective will be to discover which personal characteristics are the primary ones for female creative genius, and what patterns are consistent with their success.

Nature or Nurture?

It is the opinion of this author that creative geniuses are bred not born. The Mozarts of the world exist but are the exception not the rule in great creative endeavor. The creative and entrepreneurial women in this work evolved into their successful personality traits, they were not born with them. Their exceptional achievements were not due to some isolated chance of birth but due to their early experiences in living. The traits found to be critical to their success were: *Self-confidence, comfort with ambiguity and risk-taking, renegade behavior, "type A" work ethic, intuitive vision, heuristic learning skills, and obsessive will.* While anyone can possess these traits in greater or lesser degree these women acquired these traits during their formative years through: *Unique birth-order, strong parental role models and mentors, permissive family environments, frequent transiency, self-employed parents, early crises, and slightly above average intelligence.* The above behavior characteristics and their apparent causal factors are the subject of this book. It is these factors that formed the strong Promethean temperaments found in these women. These particular characteristics were not evident in their youth but only became apparent as they matured often after they had experienced some truly memorable success. This research indicates that women with *impossible* dreams are the most likely to achieve *improbable* feats. Enjoy their trek to fame and fortune.

1

Self-Esteem, Self-Image, and Self-Confidence

The most creative people seem to be those with the easiest access to the unconscious.

—Nancy Napier, *Recreating Yourself* (1990)

Without this playing with fantasy no creative work has ever yet come to birth. The debt we owe to the play of imagination is incalculable.

—Carl Jung

The visions that we present to our children shape the future. They become self-fulfilling prophecies. Dreams are maps.

—Carl Sagan

Self-esteem is the most critical determinant for any success or endeavor in life. In creative, innovative, or entrepreneurial ventures it is pivotal. No one has ever accomplished anything worthwhile without an awesome self-confidence. Such confidence is not possible without an equally strong self-image and self-esteem. Female creative geniuses have both. They are unique in that they are also nice people considering that most high achievers are obnoxiously arrogant know-it-alls commonly referred to as egomaniacs. At a party such achievers tend to be self-absorbed boors, but in highly creative and breakthrough innovation domains, such dispositions are not only desirable but imperative.

How did these women become so self-confident? Some were driven to overcome early insecurities and thereby gained a pseudoconfidence in order to appear knowledgeable. Many were overcompensating for their fears. And, as we will discuss later in this chapter, mimicking eminent behavior can develop excellence, and thinking positively will in fact help to make positive things happen. Believing in something does in fact help to make it so, and many

31

of these women believed in the impossible and therefore achieved the impossible. Others, such as Golda Meir, Ayn Rand, Lillian Vernon, and Mary Kay Ash were optimistic women who lived their lives positively in the face of the greatest calamities. If Meir had ever allowed herself a negative thought, she would have been forced to give up because she was constantly faced with death and crises each day for over forty years. Ash has a similar disposition; she has denied herself any negative thoughts. Her favorite line is to ask a shoeshine or washroom attendant, "How are you?" "Fine," says the bootblack. "No," Ash answers, "you're great! Fake it till you make it." Such is the demeanor and attitude of the great. But most were action-oriented individuals willing to bet the farm on their dream. They had the temerity to "do" not just "talk." And having experienced success, they became energized by each ensuing success. Their confidence built with each success until they believed they were omniscient and could not lose. Success does beget success and self-confidence begets self-confidence.

What Motivated Them?

It certainly wasn't their formal education or intelligence, even though many of them were well educated, and all were bright. It had nothing to do with family heritage or economic status. In fact, there appears to be an inverse relationship between the so-called silver-spoon syndrome and creative genius. Every one of these women started with virtually nothing. They reached the top with almost *no* outside financial assistance. Their age at the time of achieving success was not a factor either: Maria Callas, Madonna, Jane Fonda, and Oprah Winfrey made it big in their twenties and thirties while Mary Kay Ash and Golda Meir were in their sixties and seventies before they reached the top of their professions. Common indices and other traditional barometers of success were not apparent in their accomplishments. It appears that something deeper was involved in their enormous success, something innate to their spirit. It was intrinsic in the personas of each of these subjects. It was their inviolable self-esteem.

Were They Different?

Yes, these great female creative visionaries were different. They marched to a different drum beat. But the beat they marched to was not audible in the sense that it could be heard by others. It came from deep in the subconscious as an internally generated energy. It did not come from any conscious, external, or cognitive source, nor from parents, peers, teachers, or mentors. As we will discover, teachers, parents and other early role models are critically important to forming positive internal images and high self-esteem. But once those internal images are formed, the creative genius ignores those original sources of support and marches to her own beat. She listens to her internal tunes and experiences imprinted on her unconscious at a very young age. This imprinting and conditioning has little or nothing to do with her educational training, parental influence, or peer pressure. It comes from deep within as an internally driven need to achieve and not from any external motivation to fulfill societal or parental values.

One example of this can be seen in Margaret Mead's independent and internal need for autonomy. At age nine she was inspired to pursue spiritual guidance and made the unilateral decision to become an Episcopalian in complete defiance of her agnostic parents. Conversely, Ayn Rand took it upon herself at age thirteen to become an atheist in opposition to her devoutly religious Jewish parents. Both Mead and Rand, in the likeness of Einstein, were rebels who held their teachers in contempt. These women were all masters of their destiny at a very early age. Meir decided to become a Zionist because of the Russian pogroms, which terrified her as a very young child. Steinem admits that she is exorcising her mother's nervous breakdown, caused by discrimination in the workplace when Gloria was a child. Winfrey admits to having decided on a career in speaking before the age of five. Each of these women were using an intrinsic, not extrinsic vision of the world in pursuing their adult success. That is, they listened to their own internal drum beat and cared little about what the rest of the world heard. Yes, they were different, but their differences were not discernible external qualities; instead, they were internally generated voices driving them to enormous achievement.

Early Self-Image and Adult Success

While a young girl Catherine the Great fantasized about becoming the idyllic leader of a great nation. These dreams led her to become the longest-reigning empress in Russian history. She became the most dominant, powerful, and feared female in the world despite the fact she was a full-blooded German with not one ounce of Russian blood. Her adult self-image had been created in childhood and led her far beyond her wildest expectations. Florence Nightingale heard a mystical voice (reminiscent of the findings on Joan of Arc and Mother Teresa) as a teenager. It was calling her to heal the sick, injured, and impoverished. Her aristocratic upbringing had prepared her for the salons of Europe with all the trappings of the advantaged. Yet she devoted her life to the sick and needy to create the nursing profession. When asked why, Florence said, "God spoke to me and called me to his service." Rachel

Carson was a severely introverted and fragile female, a lover of books and nature who just wanted to write and teach. Yet she became known as the "Nun of Nature" with her radical book *Silent Spring* (1962). She made ecology a household word, not by intent, but through her search for the truth and perfection in nature. Her work helped save the world from myopic governments and businesses. However, her greatest success was based on her search for redemption of her childhood dreams, and were not based on any overt attempt to discredit government and business.

Maria Callas told the magazine *Oggi* ("Memoirs," 1957) that she decided upon a career as a singer at the age of five and then proceeded to sacrifice everything in her life to that end. She even skipped high school in pursuit of her obsession to be a great diva. Mother Teresa, like Florence Nightingale, was raised in an upper middle-class European family but had visions of becoming a missionary and helping the weak and poor. Her nurturing temperament led her to devote her life to the poor and sick. As a teenager, Mother Teresa became so passionately absorbed with her identity as nurturer of the poor, she never saw any of the myriad opportunities for her future. She told reporters, "At the age of twelve I first knew I had a vocation to help the poor. I wanted to be a missionary." There was no other choice after that inspiration. These women were forming their internal self-images with these childhood visions.

Oprah Winfrey had a similar revelation at a very early age. She addressed a church congregation at the age of two and received accolades from the adults for her precocity. They said, "She is gifted," and she believed. She immediately announced that she would be "paid to talk" when she became an adult. By age twelve in Nashville she was known as "the little speaker" and earned $500 for a speech given to a church congregation. These early public speaking experiences made "talking" synonymous with adult achievement in her young mind. She imprinted "entertainment" and "public speaking" on her internal tapes. Her dreams of escaping rural Mississippi, a Milwaukee ghetto, and Nashville poverty became imbued with these images of talking success. Winfrey recently told the press that her "identity" and "psychological being," as Oprah the TV star, was no different than it was at the age of six when such thoughts were just childhood dreams of euphoria and escape to a better life.

Ayn Rand decided at the age of nine to write great adventure stories featuring epic heroes and heroines. She wrote constantly in journals from that day on. Howard Roark (her protagonist in *The Fountainhead*) and John Galt (the idyllic male hero of *Atlas Shrugged*) became the realization of her childhood dreams of success. She told reporters that her philosophy and life goals were no different at age sixty than they had been at age nine. Margaret Mead, the quintessential independent female, was writing poetry and a journal by age nine, and was a family renegade before the age of ten. Estée Lauder of cosmetics fame decided that the world of beauty was to be her life's work prior to her tenth birthday. There is a common pattern in all of these women— they were forming their internal self-images at a very early age. Adult visionaries appear to use their childhood images to create their breakthrough successes. They strive to live out early fantasy dreams, which more often than not become their adult "identity," resulting in great achievements.

Madonna devastated her tradition-bound and religious father when at the age of nine she came on stage in a Detroit St. Anthony's talent show almost nude. She wore a skin colored bikini and received a rousing ovation from the shocked but captivated crowd. This outrageous behavior was reinforced by the positive feedback she received from the audience. This conditioned Madonna that bizarre and exhibitionist behavior was an acceptable avenue to recognition and stardom. She has successfully used this method of shock and provocative behavior ever since. It is her socially acceptable means of attracting attention and satiating her enormous needs for love and adulation. It also happens to be financially rewarding. Her exhibitionist oriented videos and crotch-grabbing performances can be traced back to this early childhood incident aimed at seeking recognition and approval. This early experience satisfied her internal cravings and spawned a maverick entertainer. Madonna's childhood fantasy/reality episode is one more example of how childhood images can stimulate adult creative behavior.

Catherine the Great and Linda Wachner had similar childhood experiences that motivated them as adults. Catherine had a severe curvature of the spine that caused her to be bedridden for some time, during which she resolved to be a success. Then, when locked in her chambers as a teenager by an imbecile pretender to the throne, she methodically evolved the plan to take over Mother Russia. Linda Wachner became a compulsive overachiever in business as a result of spending a year and a half bedridden at age eleven. Linda was in a body cast with little hope of ever walking again when she vowed to be the master of her destiny and never allow a doctor, therapist, or boss to deter her from calling the shots. As she puts it, "The focus I have today comes from when I was sick." (*Ms.,* January 1987)

A study comparing boys and girls in kibbutz environments shows that freedom of exploration for Western and Middle-Eastern children can be a factor in their positive development. Alison Stallibrass in *The Self-Respecting Child* (1979) found that kibbutz-raised children had an edge in intellectual development. "Freedom to explore our environment and develop our bodily abilities is a link to intellectual development." This early freedom to explore and fail appears to be critical in developing creative individuals. These thirteen visionaries were all found to be raised in very permissive households, which appears to have been a factor in developing their freedom of spirit, resulting in adult achievement.

Fantasy Imaging Is Conducive to Creative Vision

Research shows that many women have been smarter, richer, stronger, better connected politically, with more natural talent than these thirteen creative geniuses. But one critical ingredient that appears to have made them different was their compulsion to "sublimate unconscious childhood fantasies into adult achievements." They often escaped into dream states or books and fantasized a more acceptable reality. Many of them dreamed of escaping into fantasy in order to cope with an unhappy childhood. As adults they tended to live out these fantasies, either subliminally or in reality, by making their images tangible goals. They had a unique ability to identify with super-heroine qualities in others. They were like "Alice walking through her looking glass" attempting to find their fantasy. These visionaries appear to have often confused their internal fantasies with the external world of reality. Many children fantasize, but these women so identified with their fantasies that they replaced reality with their dreams.

As a child, Gloria Steinem wanted to dance her way out of Toledo because she was so unhappy. She actually hoped she was adopted and another family would rescue her and take her away with them. She finally escaped Toledo, but as an independent feminist. Maria Callas dreamed of becoming a great diva and became one at the expense of everyone and everything in her life, including her own health. Golda Meir wanted to be a Milwaukee school teacher, but her need to exorcise the Russian pogroms led her to the world of Zionism and helped her found the state of Israel. Linda Wachner at age eleven dreamed only of walking again like a normal child. She promised that if she ever did walk again she would never get tired. She has since walked over most of the male power brokers of American industry with such boundless energy executives have quit her company out of sheer exhaustion. These women internalized their childhood visions which became the driving force behind their adult achievements.

Reading is one of the most common forms of fantasizing. Virtually all of these women were voracious readers as children. Ayn Rand admitted to spending her youth lost in her French novels instead of her textbooks. Others escaped through toys, daydreams, and other fantasies of a better life. Oprah Winfrey was one who escaped in books and envisioned herself a great actress. Gloria Steinem decided to be a Rockette dancer in Manhattan. Estée Lauder fantasized about creating beauty. Madonna just wanted to be famous and powerful so she never had to be hurt again. Lillian Vernon and Ayn Rand were insecure immigrants who just wanted to become an accepted part of the great American Dream. Playing "make-believe" is a universal trait of children. The difference with these women is that they somehow stored visions of superhuman accomplishment in their subconscious. As adults they used these fantasies to create and achieve. When faced with adversity they escaped into their own fantasy worlds—unconscious visions of reality. They stepped into a phone booth and stepped out as "superwomen," identifying with their secret heroines.

Self-Image = Self-Esteem = Confidence = Creative Genius

Self-image forms our *self-esteem,* which in turn determines our level of *confidence.* Without confidence no creativity can occur. The reason is that creativity and innovation never occur without breaking rules, and one cannot break rules without enormous amounts of self-confidence. Breaking rules, or what philosopher Joseph Schumpeter of Harvard labeled "creative destruction," is what innovation and creativity are all about. You cannot build a new house without destroying the old one. A new marriage or relationship demands the destruction of the existing one. Thus, creativity or innovation is dependent on destroying the status quo. And any rebellion requires super self-confidence in order to buck the system. Creative individuals, by definition, defy tradition, and had better come armed with an inviolable belief system and a resilient ego capable of braving assaults on their self-esteem. These thirteen women qualify on all counts.

Their strong internal self-images became the fuel for enormous self-confidence, which spawned their awesome hyper energy. This energy empowered them to their creative breakthroughs. High energy levels have been found in every great leader and entrepreneur. It becomes the driving force separating the exceptional from the ordinary. This life-force—an internalized drive of gargantuan proportions—is needed to overcome adversity and influence others to follow into the unknown reaches of innovation and creativity. But great achievement never occurs without a strong self-image which produces a high self-esteem making for enormous self-confidence. Creative success inevitably follows.

Mentors and Early Role Models Are Critical to Self-Esteem

First Lady Hillary Clinton told *Parade* magazine in April of 1993 that two of her early role models for success were Golda Meir and Ayn Rand. Mother Teresa and Ayn Rand selected spiritual and fictional characters as their role models. Mother Teresa's role models were the Virgin Mary and Christ. She identified with Mary from the age of eight, and by the time Mother Teresa was twelve she had decided to devote her life to Christ and pursue a life helping the poor. Ayn selected Catherine the Great as her female model to emulate and then chose a fictional role model—the warrior Cyrus—from a French novel. She idolized both Catherine the Great and Cyrus by age eight. Cyrus had made such an indelible impression on Rand that she spent her life writing and philosophizing about great heroes and heroines. She resolved to write about great epic heroes before she was ten; the philosophical movement known as objectivism became a realization of those dreams. Her objectivist philosophy ultimately became the credo of the Libertarian party, all devised because of her early need for fantasy heroes, which became her role models for life. Rand confirms this hypothesis with her quote in *Atlas Shrugged,* "I have held the same philosophy I now hold for as far back as I can remember."

Margaret Mead wrote in her autobiography (*Blackberry Winter,* 1972), "My paternal grandmother . . . was the most decisive influence in my life," because she allowed her to explore and observe people. Her grandmother treated her like an adult from a small child and Mead grew up seeing the world differently as a result. Lady Margaret Thatcher told her biographers, "I just owe almost everything to my father," who told her she should lead, never follow the crowd. Oprah Winfrey credited books with helping form her character. She said, "Books showed me there were possibilities in life. . . . Reading gave me hope." She used literature as her escape from the poverty of a Mississippi farm, and internalized her fictional role models. Books became her avenue to success and she admits, "for me it was the open door" to a better life. She walked through that door by creating fantasy visions for role models. Later her father and Barbara Walters would become real life role models for her. Later she was to say, "My father saved my life. He turned my life around by insisting I be more than I was and by believing I could be more." She then emulated Barbara Walters to that end.

Mary Kay Ash emulated her mother in creating her own positive self-image through successful performance. Her mother told her as a child that she could do anything, and she believed her mother's axiom, "Anything anyone else can do, you can do." Ash believed she could attempt the new and the different because she was forced to as a young child. Her inviolable belief system was further reinforced by Ida Blake—her first female boss—who made her believe she was invincible.

Positive Self-Image Overcomes Negative Environments

Positive self-image is the ticket out of a ghetto, a crisis, or an unhappy childhood. Female visionaries Gloria Steinem, Oprah Winfrey, Jane Fonda, Ayn Rand, Lillian Vernon, Maria Callas, Mary Kay Ash, Golda Meir, and Estée Lauder all overcame impoverished environments or great tragedies to reach the pinnacle of success. Their early environments were not idyllic, as is sometimes portrayed by the media. Golda Meir and Ayn Rand constantly defied death at a very early age in revolutionary Russia. Liz Claiborne and Lillian Vernon both fled the Nazi juggernaut to arrive as immigrants in depression-torn New Orleans and New York City respectively. Maria Callas survived near starvation in war-torn Greece. Margaret Thatcher survived the most bombed city in England as a teenager during World War II. These women learned how to take their early deprivations and crises and use them as motivational events. They were able to turn the negatives into positives in building resilient self-esteems. Their early experiences scarred them, but just as in physical scars, their damaged parts became stronger after the injury. They overcame their early tragedies to reach the top of their fields by sublimating their needs into a positive internal energy.

One of the factors that helped them overcome early problems was a strong internal belief in themselves. The Jewish people are notorious for indoctrinating their children with a strong self-image, telling them constantly they are great and wonderful (six of these women had one or more Jewish parents). Even those who were not Jewish had parents who followed the Jewish tradition of instilling their children with an omnipotent self-image. They were doted on, idolized, and constantly told that they were marvelous, magnificent, brilliant, beautiful, and superior to their peers. This indoctrination built resilient self-esteems that helped them overcome early deprivations and crises. Most of these women later confessed to believing they were special when growing up.

Many of these women were considered precocious or smarter than other children in school. Oprah Winfrey, Linda Wachner, Ayn Rand, Madonna, and Jane Fonda admit to having an innate knowledge of superiority. They just knew they were smarter or more talented than their friends. This personal knowledge empowered them to greater and higher achievement in school and later in life. It enhanced their self-image. They believed they were exceptional and operated with that mentality. Psychologists have recently demonstrated that we "become as we think" and "our images become our reality." They operated with a mentality of superiority that motivated them to excel.

These women often overcompensated (sublimated in Freud's vernacular) for their inferiorities and insecurities. Strong individuals are motivated by insecurities and overachieve in order to quiet their fears. Many of them were different. This conditioned them very early in life to view "different" as a positive not negative trait. Therefore, being told by their peers they were different was a positive reinforcement of their self-esteem. Being different augmented their self-esteem instead of inhibiting it. They always envisioned their differences as assets, not liabilities, and used them to bolster their self-image.

Negative Self-Esteem and Risk-Aversity

The converse of the ever-optimistic and self-confident Margaret Thatcher is the unfortunate gifted child whose dreams of utopia are often negated by a low self-esteem. Risk-averse parents who never allow a child to try and fail, to experience the new and untried, typically insist that their young conform to the stringent rules of the establishment. Such parents indoctrinate children with their own dogma, ethical and moral standards of good and bad, or right and wrong. To these individuals, any religious belief different from their own is bad and all opposing political beliefs are fanatical. Independent thinking is not tolerated and usually punished. Such an environment is counterproductive to any creative endeavor.

The book *You Can't Afford the Luxury of a Negative Thought* (1992) is an ideal philosophy for anyone who desires to become a creative visionary. Negative role models inhibit creativity and tend to spawn micro-vision personality types when the opposite, macro-vision, is critical to great creative endeavor. Negative role models produce disciples who base their belief systems on conforming to traditional doctrine and abhor "change," the "new," or the "unknown." Conversely, positive role models spawn great creators and innovators who worship change, the new, and the untried. While negative mentors teach how not to break the rules, positive mentors always preach the gospel of rule breaking.

Sam Walton, founder of Wal-Mart, said in his biography that his success was based on rule breaking. He said, "My first rule of business is 'Break the rules.' " Creative individuals typically break the rules thus gaining reputations as iconoclasts. Nonconformity and independence are strengths that make breaking rules an easier task. Jane Fonda, Maria Callas, Ayn Rand, Madonna, Lillian Vernon, Gloria Steinem, Golda Meir, Oprah Winfrey, and Estée Lauder were rule-breakers of the first order, with Madonna being the quintessential rule breaker of the group. She lives her life on the edge of acceptability, firing key employees, managers, and directors just because they were not inclined to violate the norms of society. Even the tradition-bound Margaret Thatcher broke the rules in her own way. During her term as prime minister of Britain, she would ask, "Is he one of us?"—meaning a believer in Thatcherism and its credo—when introduced to a new party member. This was her way of avoiding risk-averse individuals who were not part of her team. She was the personification of the creative leader who used a positive self-esteem to overcome her adversaries and did not want to spend any time with anyone who was not willing to bet the farm for her principles.

Intuition and Self-Image

The most common traits found in the creative genius are independence, high self-esteem, rebelliousness, egomania, risk-taking propensity, intransigence, and charisma. All of these traits have their foundation in an unwavering self-image. In fact, the self-confidence and image of great leaders often borders on arrogance; without it, though, they would have accomplished nothing worthwhile. Teresa Amabile in *Growing Up Creative* (1989) found that "creativity is impossible without an inner spark." She said "intrinsic motivation" is the crux of creativity and all creativity emanates from *within,* not from without. As psychiatrist Anthony Storr in *The Dynamics of Creation* (1993) described the process, "Creative people habitually describe their dependence for inspiration upon sources outside their conscious volition." He found a strong intuition to be the driving force in Einstein, Darwin, Mozart, and DaVinci. He says, "The creative person has easy access to his inner world" and it is in this inner world where the great creative geniuses find their inspiration.

Einstein is the perfect example of using intrinsic thinking in creating a new paradigm. He created his theory of relativity through intuitive thought processes alone. He then waited for the scientific community to empirically prove his theory through observation and experimentation, which took another fifteen years. He said, "A theory can be proven by experiment, but no path leads from experiment to a theory." Intuition researcher Daniel Cappon discussed "The Anatomy of Intuition" in the popular periodical *Psychology Today* (April 1993) and said Nobel Prize winners Linus Pauling, Lord Adrian, and Jonas Salk came to the same conclusion. They told him, "We know the answer before we work it out." Anthony Storr in the *Dynamics of Creation* said:

> The lack of satisfaction in the real world encourages the development of an inner world of phantasy; . . . sensitive, precocious, gifted children who may be presumed to possess a nervous system which is superior as a recording device . . . are more deeply affected and possibly "imprinted" by their whole experience of infancy.

Intuition or "inner knowing" is critically important to the creative process. Daniel Cappon corroborates our belief that all intuition comes from the unconscious and is a "vital part of human intelligence." He says, "Creative artists have always known that creativity is cradled in intuition" and therefore all creativity comes from the unconscious. He goes so far as to say that "intuition is responsible for the survival of the species" because it is "the product of all the processed ancestral instincts of the species, through which unconditioned reflexes become conditioned and organized into patterns of adaptive behavior called instinct."

Reality and Fantasy Are Inextricably Intertwined

Research indicates that great female visionaries are inspired by *unconscious images* of themselves. Paul Pearsall in *Making Miracles* (1993) insists that "our perceptions create our reality." His research on health has confirmed his belief that our observations determine our reality; ultimately our childhood and adult self-images preordain our success. Research on gifted individuals shows that their internal fantasies are inextricably intertwined with reality. They do not readily differentiate between their conscious and unconscious realities. Linda Schierse Leonard, a Jungian analyst and philosopher, characterizes such women as "visionaries." She found them to be highly intuitive as they "see into the future, reveal messages—sometimes dark prophecies, sometimes visions of light . . . [their] visions cannot be comprehended by rational thought." She goes on: "The Visionary receives knowledge directly from the unconscious through images, dreams, inner voices, words and titles, ideas, or bodily sensations that come to her suddenly, sometimes shocking her, sometimes inspiring her with ecstasy" (*Meeting the Madwoman,* 1993).

These thirteen female geniuses were preprogrammed as children to strive for superiority and overachievement in the Adlerian tradition. They possessed a kind of "psychic energy" or "internalized identity" that raised them to a state where they were never satisfied with mediocrity. The achievements of a Margaret Thatcher or a Golda Meir can be viewed as a function of these internalized energies. These women were driven to satiate their basic internal needs to succeed. Their unconscious childhood images became a kind of internal force driving them to the pinnacle of success—not necessarily knowingly or consciously— because of their preconditioned need to satiate internal visions of reality. Friedrich Nietzsche and Alfred Adler (Freud's disciple) described this drive as a "will to power" or "striving for superiority and perfection" (Adler 1979). Teresa Amabile (1989) found that, "Passion is that intrinsic motivation to do something for it's own sake, the motivation to undertake an activity because it is interesting, enjoyable, satisfying, or personally challenging. . . . It comes from within."

Psychic Energy (A Freudian Perspective)

These thirteen women possessed an awesome manic energy. Linda Wachner was a whirlwind of activity, causing disbelief from a business community dumbfounded by a woman with her prodigious productivity and energy. Lillian Vernon was a bundle of kinetic energy in her own understated way. Madonna is a prototypical example of a life-force. She runs her life with an electrically charged, libidinally driven need to control her reality. Golda Meir was so driven at the age of seventy that she never left her office for days at a time and slept only occasionally and often on her desk. Liz Claiborne worked eighteen-hour days for years and Oprah Winfrey has a schedule that would fatigue most men. These energies are a function of their enormous self-confidence and their need to achieve to meet those self-inflicted demands for perfection.

Conscious versus Unconscious Behavior: Scenes versus Movies

Abraham Maslow, Wayne Dyer, and other well-known psychologists have preached the gospel of "we become as we *think,*" prompting a teenage girl to say, "I should have been a boy by the time I was fifteen." Psychologists have now confirmed that our mental imagery determines our performance in most pursuits. The ability to ski down the face of a mountain has a lot more to do with a positive mentality than with skiing ability. Physicist Niels Bohr was the first to discuss how waves become particles depending on our *observations* of them. Medical researcher and writer Paul Pearsall says, "It is a profound truth that our perceptions create our reality." He means our actions are inextricably tied to our unconscious images of reality. Just try stepping on a nonoperating escalator and see what your mind has done to your body. It is difficult to maintain your balance because the mind has conditioned your body to adjust to the perceived movement of the escalator. Your mind thinks the escalator is moving, when it is not, and it is telling the body to adjust to that movement. Most nursing mothers have this same intuitive power. Mothers often experience breast milk emissions on hearing their baby cry with the milk flow initiated only by the baby's cries for food. Even more telling is a mother's ability to differentiate between her baby's cries of hunger and cries of discomfort caused by a dirty diaper. Hunger cries invariably elicit milk emissions while other cries do not. Stranger yet is when a mother experiences breast emissions from the cries of someone else's baby who has not been fed. In both adults and babies, every conscious movement or thought is governed by an "unconscious pre-knowledge" of what the mind perceives as real. That is the essence of self-esteem's importance to the creative process. It is the movie in the mind that dictates our behavior not the scenes.

Psychologists have found that those who *think positive* tend to perform positively and those who *think negative* usually perform negatively. New wave psychologists are now training people to condition themselves through positive imaging of success. Imaging success increases the chance for success as any world class athlete knows intuitively. Gregory Bateson gave credence to this in describing the hypomanic Margaret Mead: "It was almost a principle of pure energy. I couldn't keep up and she couldn't stop. She was like a tugboat. She could sit down and write 3000 words by eleven o'clock in the morning and spend the rest of the day working at the museum" (Howard, 1984). Thinking positively about skiing down a difficult ski slope conditions the muscles positively, which insures a high probability of success and euphoria. Conversely, negative thinking conditions the body to become tentative, and the muscles react accordingly, which virtually insures falling down the hill in preordained failure. The imaging school of psychology contends that "believing does make it so," a credo that has recently moved into the field of medicine and health.

Deepak Chopra, the world-famous doctor, lecturer, and writer is convinced that cancer and AIDS cures are a function of our belief systems. He argues that every cell in the body is replaced annually and the new ones are replaced with either positive or negative cells—some conditioned to sickness and others conditioned to health. Chopra believes that individuals who go into remission from cancer or AIDS have positive cells that "don't know" they are terminally ill. These cells become the positive agents that help destroy the disease. He makes the poignant observation that those who die first after diagnosis of a life-threatening disease like cancer are those who "know" their mortality probability. Doctors always die first because they "know" too much about their chances of success and about their limitations! The little old lady who has "no knowledge" of her mortality probability has the highest incidence of total remission because she is ignorant of her limitations. In other words, it is best *not* to know your statistical probability for health and sickness.

Conversely, it is best to "know" your potential for success but to leave your options open when pursuing new and unknown territory. Let your right brain (qualitative nature) explore the possibilities and get your left brain (quantitative censor) out of the way. People have an unconscious that is positively conditioned to succeed and the creative visionary will allow that to happen. They never allow their conscious reality to get in the way of their success. In other words, visionaries know where they are going and refuse to allow their minds to get in the way of their bodies. They are holistic in the sense that they utilize their minds, bodies, and unconscious together in one concerted effort aimed at their goals.

Women who program their internal movies to success become the creative achievers in society. The thirteen women in this book had complete control of their internal movies and allowed them to lead them to the promised land. They were holistic in that they never allowed the establishment or their own insecurities to get in the way of their performance. These women had the unique ability to operate under control of their internal (unconscious) mental states while resisting all external (conscious) distractions. In other words, they never let their minds get in the way of where their bodies were going.

Behavior and Success = Movie Scripts from the Past

It seems that the difference between a great author (e.g., Ayn Rand) and a drug addict, a prime minister (e.g., Margaret Thatcher or Golda Meir) and an unemployed secretary or a celebrated entertainer (e.g., Jane Fonda, Maria Callas, or Madonna) and a wretched prostitute has little to do with one's conscious image of themselves. The roles we live in our lives tend to be predicated on the movies being played in our unconscious and not the ones we play in our conscious minds. This doesn't mean that the unconscious movies can't be changed, but that the movies being played are beyond our conscious control unless we take steps to rewrite the original scripts stored in our unconscious. The internal image of our "self" is our self-image and is what we are continually in the state of becoming. Our *unconscious* mind is where that macro-image is stored and will dictate our performance on every stage of life. Our *conscious* mind only allows us to play individual scenes, such as going out on a date and selecting a partner. The physical and emotional qualities of the partner selected is always dictated by our unconscious needs. We select our partners based on our internal needs for security and fulfillment, and not what our conscious mind desires. That is, if our unconscious demands a submissive partner who is introverted, it is highly unlikely that our conscious self will select a dominant personality type with extraverted behavior.

Our unconscious dictates who we marry and whether we become president or prime minister. Our internal belief in our "self" as prime minister is critical to making it a reality. Whether one becomes a prime minister or a prostitute is not based on talent or some conscious wish, but on this critical *unconscious* image or belief system. In other words, our unconscious has stored on its internal tape the destiny of our lives. It has nothing to do with any *conscious* desire to be this or that. The prime minister type is not only preconditioned to attain that position in the real world but probably has believed it to have been her destiny since very early in life. The psychotic also believes she is the prime minister, but that is a departure from cognitive reality. The prostitute could *never* envision herself in such a lofty role and therefore could never accede to it. Shirley MacLaine's *Sweet Charity* role is a prime example of this mentality, especially when she sang, "If They Could See Me Now." It was her internalized admission that she was living a dream and tomorrow she would return to her role as dance-hall girl.

The prostitute unfortunately has a negative self-image which conditions her to that role very early in life. Her unconscious image of herself is imprinted on her mind and she can never see herself as anything else. Until she can change that internal image she will have difficulty rising above that gutter instinct and will be destined to live out her internal movie of herself. These images are indelibly imprinted until changed. They *cannot* be changed by any conscious thought processes which say, "I would like to be prime minister." "Prime minister" has to be indelibly stored on the master tape of the self-image or the person never has the ability to attain the position. Many women have the talent and the internal scripting to become prime minister but will never rise to the position for myriad other reasons: timing, chance, political party, etc. But if one doesn't have the correct internally imprinted imagery that says "prime minister," then neither the fates nor any other force can intercede to move the person to such a position of eminence.

The only way to change our macro-unconscious image of ourselves is to rewrite our internal script or identity of who "we" are. The great female innovative geniuses in this book were programmed early to strive for great things and had an internal belief system that identified them with success. Everyone who has underachieved in life is also living out their own preconditioned imprint for failure. To be trite, "Think big and you will be big—think small and you will be small!" The thinking is what reinforces the unconscious. The quintessential female geniuses of the world all thought big and ultimately reached their lofty goals and fully believed they were deserving of their success. Newsweek said of Margaret Mead, "The most impressive thing about Mead is not that she has become the world's most famous anthropologist, but rather that it never occurred to her that this wouldn't happen." Unfortunately, life's failures have also reached their idealized levels of achievement and fully believe they are deserving of their lowly stations in life. An executive reminiscing about Linda Wachner in her twenties said of this human dynamo, "Either they are going to run this girl right out of here or else she's going to be running this place." She not only ran the place, she now owns it!

Summary

These thirteen visionaries are different from traditional females but quite similar to other successful males and females. Their behavior characteristics are very similar to those found in the great women of the world like Catherine the Great, Margaret Mead, and Mother Teresa. These women march to a different drummer, but the drummer is their own internalized belief system imprinted in their psyches at a very early age. These imprints conditioned their unconscious to desire great things, and as adults they went out to search for and move toward those things. As previously stated, "Their unconscious became the master controller for their conscious behavior and cognitive drives."

All of these women were blessed with abnormally strong self-esteem, which enabled them to transform their childhood dreams into an adult reality of professional success. Their achievements were fostered by an inviolable self-confidence based on enormous self-esteem evolving out of an awesome self-image. They so believed in themselves that what appeared as a risk to others was not a risk to them, since they felt comfortable dealing with life's ambiguities. They saw risk as a mere necessity in pursuing their goals. Therefore, they approached new opportunities with abandon, as if a new venture was just another opportunity along the highway of life.

It appears that female creative genius does not possess any genetic pre-disposition for success other than a slightly higher-than-average IQ, high energy, and an indomitable self-image. These women tended to be bright, assertive, internally empowered to achieve, and blessed with a higher-than-normal proclivity for risk-taking. They were independent people who were proud of being different. They tended to pursue their internalized dreams despite parental disagreement, peer pressure, or derision by so-called experts. Margaret Thatcher was told by an elementary school teacher (as a compliment) that she was lucky to have won a debating contest. Margaret in her inimitable style said, "I was not lucky, I deserved it." This example of an indomitable spirit defines most female creative geniuses. Margaret's father instilled in her the importance of "leading the crowd" and not following it.

These women possessed an inexhaustible spirit and energy that made them special. Their "superwoman" personae gave them an edge on others, including most males, within their sphere of influence. Their personalities give credence to Adler's prophecy that all men (and women) strive for superiority and perfection. The female visionary appears to realize Adler's prediction more often than most. These supersuccessful, innovative, creative, and entrepreneurial women strove to be superior and to pursue excellence at whatever cost. This determination emanated from their unconscious belief system, formed between the ages of five and thirteen. It appears that those with the best access to their unconscious well of energy (see the remarkable findings on Margaret Mead) are the ones who optimize their achievements in life and become the most creative.

2

Birth Order, Childhood Transience, Role Models, and Mentors

The childhood shows the [wo]man as morning shows the day.

—John Milton

Creative vision in adulthood is clearly tied to early life experiences. Birth order, childhood transience, role models, mentors, the father's influence and employment, and family interrelationships are clearly instrumental in the formation of individuals capable of breakthrough creativity, entrepreneurship, and innovation. Overprotective mothers, authoritarian fathers, and mimicking the behavior of superior individuals are other factors important to the creative process.

Birth order appears to be an important variable for anyone attempting to achieve at high levels. Parents and other family members place a lot of pressure on a first-born to carry on the family heritage and to become more successful than the parents. Only and first-born children have a built-in need to overachieve and be perfect. Early transience and travel have also been found to be factors in the success of female visionaries. Moving a lot appears to teach a child how to cope in foreign and unknown environments. It teaches her self-sufficiency at a very early age. Another important variable is the relationships with the fathers. These women had unusually strong relationships with their fathers. These were the first men they loved and the most important early role models in their lives. Most of these women idolized their fathers. And their fathers were very strong personalities who were especially close to their daughters.

The father's influence went beyond their interpersonal relationship. His profession while the daughter was young influenced the professional life of each woman. The Institute for Personality Assessment and Research at the University of California found a correlation between the father's occupation

48

and the career path of creative personalities. The findings on our thirteen female geniuses was similar. Eleven of these visionary women had fathers who were self-employed. My previous work (*Profiles of Genius* [1993]) showed that 100 percent of male creative geniuses had fathers who were self-employed. Having a father outside of the corporate mainstream appears to instill the confidence that they can survive outside the corporate womb. Another important factor for molding female visionaries is the family environment. Most of these women were raised in permissive households where they were allowed the freedom to explore, to err and fail without fear of punishment. This type of environment enhances adult risk-taking propensity in a child and builds independence. Such children are virtually never afraid of the new and unknown when they get older—a fact that enhances their risk-taking ability.

Sibling interrelationships and parental guidance are two more important variables in molding creative genius. Many of the women featured in this book were either lonely or unhappy or both and often lost themselves in books or other fantasy activities. They were doted on and knew they were loved, but were often left alone to create their own images of reality. Their independence was encouraged by parents who were often iconoclasts themselves. Being alone and fantasizing in books gave them more reason than most to choose larger-than-life heroes or heroines as friends. These individuals liked their imaginary heroes better than their siblings. The permissive household appears far more conducive to molding creative genius than highly structured households where overprotective mothers and authoritarian fathers dictate all the rules. In fact, the overprotective parent is counterproductive to the development of creative visionary personalities.

Strong female role models appear critical to developing female leaders. The thirteen women in this book had strong female role models and mentors. They often emulated their role models to get through difficult periods and to achieve success. An example is Oprah Winfrey, who was frightened to death when asked to handle her first TV news show as an anchor. She imagined she was Barbara Walters, her professional mentor, and mimicked how she felt her hero would have handled the story. It worked. This instilled confidence in her for future shows where she could mimic the behavior of a recognized professional. The scientific name for such mimicking behavior is neuro-linguistic programming (NLP), which will be discussed in some detail at the end of this chapter.

Birth Order

Kevin Leman in *The Birth Order Book* (1985) says, "Your birth order—whether you were born first, second, or later in your [parent's] life—has a powerful influence on the kind of person you will be, the kind of person you will marry, the type of occupation you will choose, even the kind of parent you will be." Leman goes on to say that first-borns and only children are preconditioned to a life of "superachievement." Psychologist Alfred Adler found that first-born and only children tend to reach the very top of whatever they attempt. *The Encyclopedia of Sociology* confirms that first-borns are predestined to greatness. They say that more than half of all U.S. presidents were first-borns, 75 percent of teachers are first-borns, and 90 percent of all astronauts were first-borns. First-borns score the highest on intelligence tests and are most often found in positions of eminent leadership. Research shows that first-born females are disproportionately represented in virtually every profession.

First-borns and only children are different. They become "little adults" with very mature and aggressive natures. They see themselves as the "center of the universe" because they are. Strong organizational skills, structure, and perfectionism describe first-born and only children, and they are "super" at whatever they pursue, to the point of being intolerant of less driven individuals. Catherine the Great and Margaret Mead are prime examples of great women who were first-born. They became very independent and dominant women within their families at a very early age. Both were the dominant members of a family and had siblings die young. They were left to their own destiny and grew up as independent spirits. These thirteen women were the pivotal individuals within their families and grew up strong and independent. Virtually all were treated as "little adults" and therefore grew up with a very mature outlook on life and potential opportunities (see figure 3).

It is important to understand the subtle difference between order of birth and the psychology of family interrelationships. What is important, and apparently highly correlated to creative genius, is how one is raised within the family unit. Eminent female leaders are developed as a function of *being raised as* first-born or only children, not necessarily being literally born as such children. In other words, *order of birth is not as important as the expectations and subtle interrelationships which exist within every family.* For example, Margaret Thatcher was a second-born daughter, but was raised as the "one and only" superstar child and groomed in the likeness of her father's surrogate son. Margaret captivated her father with her aggressive and competitive demeanor. She became the son he never had; he responded by grooming her into his image of greatness. Margaret emulated his every move and was later to espouse his fundamental philosophy in Parliament. Her father, Alfred Roberts, chose Maggie as his favorite child and she responded by making him her favorite parent. His constant adulation and encouragement helped groom her for the highest position in Britain. If the nearest sibling is over seven years older, it appears the individual is raised almost like a first-child as she is given all of the attention and has inordinately high expectations placed on her. First-

Figure 3

BIRTH ORDER AND SIBLING STATUS

ONLY CHILDREN

Oprah Winfrey	Illegitimate with two younger half sisters. Raised alone by grandmother for first six years and alternately by mother and father

FIRST-BORN CHILD OR FIRST-BORN FEMALE

Liz Claiborne	Oldest daughter, born in Brussels, Belgium; older brother, Omer
Jane Fonda	One younger brother, Peter
Madonna	Oldest daughter, two younger half sisters and two older brothers
Ayn Rand	Two younger sisters, Natana and Elena
Lillian Vernon	Oldest daughter, born in Leipzig, Germany; older brother killed in war

RAISED LIKE FIRST-BORN (OVER 6 YEARS BETWEEN SIBLINGS)

Mary Kay Ash	Fourth child but eleven years younger than nearest sibling; raised as first child
Golda Meir	Sister Shana nine years older (mother figure); one younger sister, Clara (five brothers and sisters were born and died between Shana and Clar)
Gloria Steinem	One sister ten years older; raised like only child
Maria Callas	Sister Jackie six years older; brother died just prior to Maria's conception and mother desperately wanted a son
Linda Wachner	Older sister eighteen years her senior; raised as only child

SECOND OR LAST BORN

Margaret Thatcher	Older sister, Muriel, was mother's favorite; Maggie was doted on by her father
Estée Lauder	Last of nine children, only one of which was a blood sister due to multiple marriages

born children have the greatest pressure to strive for perfection followed by first-born daughters.

Another example of this principle at work is Linda Wachner, who was a second-born daughter, as was Margaret Thatcher. Her sister was eighteen years her senior, allowing Linda to be raised as an only child. She was indulged just like Margaret. This appears to be the most critical factor in the development of great creative individuals. Being born an only child is not nearly as important as being raised as an only child. However, early environmental influences tend to indelibly imprint "only child" characteristics and powerful self-esteem on the first and/or most important child in the household.

Only one of these visionary women was an only child (namely, Oprah Winfrey) and even she had two younger half sisters. She only lived with her sisters for brief periods in her life and they were never a factor in her development. Five others were the first-born, or the first-born female (Ayn Rand, Jane Fonda, Liz Claiborne, Madonna, and Lillian Vernon). Another five were raised as if they were first-born due to having much older siblings (Mary Kay Ash, Golda Meir, Gloria Steinem, Maria Callas, and Linda Wachner). Only Margaret Thatcher and Estée Lauder were raised in a position normally not considered preeminent within the household. Thatcher was "the child" in the family. Estée Lauder was the last child and the favorite of her uncle, who became her role model and mentor. He gave her the special attention and privileges usually offered by the parents. Eleven of the thirteen were born into a preferential station within the family unit, and all of them appear to have been the kingpins within their respective family units.

Notice from figure 3 that Maria Callas was born shortly after the untimely death of a brother, an event that had a major impact on her upbringing. Her mother refused to look at or hold Maria because she was not a boy. This experience had a lasting effect on Callas, according to both her godfather and father. Golda Meir's parents lost five sons between the births of Golda and her old sister, which caused the parents to idolize Golda and give her a great deal of love and affection, consequently her given name Goldie. Golda's sister Shana was ten years older and more of a surrogate mother than a sister.

Eleven of these thirteen women were effectively raised as only children by doting parents who were often very permissive and treated them more as adults than children. This built strong self-esteem and self-sufficiency in them. Thatcher and Lauder received their strong self-esteem from mentors and other internally generated sources. They were all adored by doting parents, a trait they share with most male creative geniuses. Their parents gave them the feeling they were special, and sure enough this imprimatur became a self-fulfilling prophecy.

Childhood Transience

There is strong evidence that early transience is highly correlated to great achievement in most creative, entrepreneurial, and innovative pursuits. The University of California at Berkeley studied the creative personality for over thirty years and found that architects tend to have unusually high transience during their early lives. Research on male entrepreneurs indicate that moving often and early in life predisposed them to great achievement. Albert Einstein moved at age one and then three more times including a different country prior to age twelve. Thomas Edison was a virtual vagabond during his early life and actually worked on a train at age eleven. Pablo Picasso also lived in various cities prior to his teenage years.

Catherine the Great moved to Russia at age fourteen, after having followed her father around Germany as a very young child. Margaret Mead lived in sixty homes prior to high school. She always considered home where she was at the given moment. This early transience conditioned her with unusual coping skills and independence. She unhesitatingly went off to the jungles of Samoa and New Guinea as a young single scientist—not the behavior of someone with a security-based background. She could never have accomplished her pioneering research without the unique independence developed at a young age moving about with her vagabond parents, which she saw as the essence of her success. In her autobiography *Blackberry Winter* she described herself as: "Being able to be at home anywhere in the world, in any house, in any time band, eating any different kind of food, learning new languages as needed, never afraid of the new." Mother Teresa traveled with her father as a child and visited religious shrines, which helped condition her to the task of a missionary. She signed on for training in Ireland and India as a teenager.

Childhood transience appears to teach the young important survival instincts, especially in new, unknown environments. Five of these women (Callas, Claiborne, Meir, Rand, and Vernon) were actually raised in a different country from that of their birth. This meant they encountered a new culture, language, friends, and school while quite young. This turns out to be excellent training for future entrepreneurs, creators, and innovators as they are constantly pioneering in new worlds. This experience grooms children in coping skills and builds resilience and self-sufficiency. These females all faced conditions as children almost identical to the conditions they faced as adults in breaking through the glass ceiling.

Oprah is an excellent example of such early transience. She attended over a dozen different schools in Milwaukee and Nashville. She moved between Mississippi, Milwaukee, and Nashville at least five times before starting high school. Maria Callas was conceived in Greece, born in America, and then moved nine times within New York City prior to the eighth grade. She then moved back to Greece with her mother and sister at age fourteen. Gloria Steinem actually lived a gypsy existence traveling with her salesman father throughout the Unites States in a trailer home. She was such a vagabond that she never spent more than a few months in any school until age thirteen. Jane Fonda lived a bicoastal existence for years following her actor father, Henry Fonda, to his show-business engagements. She finally ended up in a succession of boarding and prep schools not dissimilar to the early life transience of her current husband Ted Turner, who ended up in a succession of military academies during his youth.

Seven of our famous subjects (see figure 4) lived in a different country prior to coming of age. Five of the seven actually moved to a different continent—from Europe to America or from America to Europe. Golda Meir wins the prize for continent jumping, having moved from Russia to Milwaukee, Wisconsin, at age eight; to Denver with her sister at age fourteen; to Israel at age twenty-two; back to the United States at age thirty for two years; and then to Moscow as ambassador. Out of our thirteen women only Margaret Thatcher, Mary Kay Ash, and Linda Wachner were born and raised in the same city. The rest were moved from school to school and often city to city, and in some instances to a whole new culture. Gloria Steinem attended schools in Toledo, Ohio; New York, New York; and Washington, D.C. She spent a year in Switzerland as an exchange student in college, followed by a year in India on a fellowship. It appears that these early transient experiences are important to great achievement in creativity, entrepreneurship, and innovation.

Father's Profession

The occupation of the father appears to be another important variable for great creative visionaries. As I have said, having a self-employed father appears to mold children with the belief that they can function in the world outside of the organized work force. It demonstrates to the young that it is acceptable to be self-reliant which opens up myriad career opportunities outside the corporate womb. Entrepreneurial ventures or political careers are considered very tenuous and risky to children of nine-to-five fathers. The women profiled in this book never had such reservations, because of their self-employed fathers. They never saw their fathers in a reliant posture, having to punch a time clock at the so-called company store.

Notice in figure 5 that all of these women had self-employed fathers with the exception of Madonna and Liz Claiborne. And in Claiborne's case her father was a wealthy expatriate banker who was not punching any time clock. Eleven of the thirteen had fathers who were the master of their economic destiny, and did not have to depend on others for their livelihood. The "company"

Figure 4

TRANSIENCE AS CHILDREN AND ADULTS

Individual	Born	Raised	Adult Operations
Mary Kay Ash	Houston, Tex.	Houston, Tex.	Dallas, Tex.
Maria Callas	New York City	Athens, Greece	Western Europe
Catherine the Great	Stettin, Germany	Germany and Russia	Russia
Liz Claiborne	Brussels, Belgium	Brussels and New Orleans	New York City
Jane Fonda	New York City	Los Angeles, New York, Connecticut	New York, Paris, Los Angeles
Estée Lauder	New York City	Milwaukee and New York	New York City
Madonna	Bay City, Mich.	Detroit, Mich.	New York City and Hollywood
Margaret Mead	Philadelphia, Penn.	All over Pennsylvania	Far East/New York City
Golda Meir	Kiev, Russia	Milwaukee, Wisc.	Tel Aviv, Israel
Ayn Rand	Petrograd, Russia	Leningrad, Russia	New York City and Hollywood
Gloria Steinem	Toledo, Oh.	Various cities Florida to California, Ohio, and Washington, D.C.	New York City
Mother Teresa	Skopje, Yugoslavia	Skopje	Ireland and India
Margaret Thatcher	London, England	London	London
Lillian Vernon	Leipzig, Germany	Mt. Vernon, N.Y.	New York Metro
Linda Wachner	New York City	New York City	New York City, Houston, California
Oprah Winfrey	Kosciusko, Miss.	Milwaukee, Wisc., and Nashville, Tenn.	Baltimore, Md., and Chicago, Ill.

Figure 5

FATHER'S PROFESSION

SELF-EMPLOYED

Mary Kay Ash	Father invalid, mother (a nurse) owned and operated a restaurant
Maria Callas	Owned a pharmacy in Athens and later in Manhattan (entrepreneur)
Jane Fonda	Actor (Henry Fonda)
Estée Lauder	Hardware store owner
Golda Meir	Carpenter; family-owned and -operated grocery store in Milwaukee
Ayn Rand	Owned pharmacy until Russian Revolution
Gloria Steinem	Owned Ohio resort; was also an antique trader/broker all over the United States
Margaret Thatcher	Grocery store owner/operator; Methodist minister and mayor of Granthem
Lillian Vernon	German industrialist, garment manufacturer, and salesman
Linda Wachner	New York fur salesman
Oprah Winfrey	Owned barber shop and retail store; church deacon

OTHER VOCATION

Liz Claiborne	Expatriate banker
Madonna	Automotive engineer

or "organization" was not the only option in their adult career choices. Their self-employed fathers appear to have instilled in these women a high tolerance for uncertainty. Independence and self-assurance are just two of the traits that have their origin in economically independent fathers. Since the father is the dominant influence in the life of great female visionaries (see next section), their careers and their work ethic have to be considered critical factors in building character in the creative visionary female. It seems to have taught these women very early in life that there is no need to rely on others for survival; it was okay to earn their own way.

Gloria Steinem often said she learned her love of freedom from her vagabond father. She quoted his aphorism "My office is my hat" to show that he was not constrained by the establishment like other men. Her father's influence has been very strong on Steinem, who spent her life avoiding any permanent job or personal commitment. She free-lanced for years while turning down many attractive permanent job opportunities. This behavior was based on her need for freedom obviously gained from her father's sense of freedom and independence. Figure 5 shows that nine of the thirteen women had fathers who were entrepreneurs, actors, or self-employed sales representatives. Their fathers' independent spirits led these women to careers in which they desired control and mastery over their destiny.

The Father as the Dominant Influence

The father is the major influence in the lives of most creative women, at least according to this sample. In *The Managerial Woman,* Hennig and Jardim studied twenty-five female managers and found the women were either only children or first-born females, and *each woman had a close relationship with her father.* The father was even the dominating influence when they were absent. Jane Fonda spent much of her life attempting to gain the love of a cold, withdrawn father. According to an interview in *Ms.* magazine, she said, "My only major influence was my father." Fonda's biographer quotes her, "I was in awe of my father" (Davidson, 1990). She told the press, "It's tough growing up in the shadow of a national monument," adding that as a child she wished Katharine Hepburn were her mother because she believed that her brother, Peter, was her mother's favorite. Madonna, like Fonda, had the same almost messianic adulation for her father, or "Electra complex," and spent much of her youth fighting for his love and affection. She said, "My father was very strong. He was my role model."

Catherine the Great idolized her father. She said, "My father thought I was an angel." She was distraught over his constant absence, sought his approval, and hungered for his affection and love, a recurring theme among these women. Psychotherapist Joan Minninger (*Father-Daughter Dance,* 1993) says, "A woman's relationship with her dad—not her mom—is probably the most influential in her life . . . because fathers are the first men that daughters ever love." This finding is certainly corroborated by these thirteen female visionaries. Margaret Mead said, "It was my father who defined for me my place in the world." And Margaret Thatcher said, "I just owe almost everything to my father." Maria Callas was even more emphatic in saying, "My father I adored. . . . I was his favorite when I was a child . . . or maybe always."

Ayn Rand's father wanted to be a writer and she emulated him in this regard. She adored him and decided on a writing career at age nine. Ayn held the opposite emotion for her mother, saying, "I disliked her quite a lot." Gloria Steinem said, "Being with my father felt so much safer than being with my mother." And Oprah Winfrey has given her father all of the credit for her success. She says, "When my father took me, it changed the course of my life. He saved me." Even Estée Lauder was influenced by a father figure; it happened to be her uncle John, who introduced her to the world of skin creams. It was he who influenced her to spend her life in the pursuit of beauty.

Findings on male creative visionaries showed that the mothers were the dominant influence in their lives and inspired them to greatness by telling them they were wonderful. The opposite is true of female visionaries. The only women in this work who were not gushingly supportive of their fathers were Mary Kay Ash, Liz Claiborne, and Linda Wachner. Ash's father was an invalid whom she had to care for as a child in lieu of play. But she has little to say about his influence on her life. Liz Claiborne states that her father gave her the ability to separate form from function in her design work. Linda Wachner says that her older father gave her the freedom to explore and achieve. There is no doubt that the fathers are the dominating influences for these women and these men appear to have been critically important in the grooming of females capable of great innovative achievement.

Early Relationships and Creativity

"Sibling experience is crucial to the development of 'Woman Power' and women's leadership," according to *Women in Power* (1992) by Dorothy Cantor and Toni Bernay. These psychologists studied such prominent U.S. politicians as Diane Feinstein and Barbara Boxer and found that top female politicians had childhoods that contributed to their success. Many other studies on successful women have found early family interrelationships to be crucial to their eventual success. Allowing a child to explore and err appears very important to their development as creative adults. Treating them in a mature manner, like an adult, also appears to be conducive to adult vision.

Creative geniuses are byproducts of their early family upbringing. Wolfgang Amadeus Mozart was encouraged to start composing at the age of four and knew his destiny even earlier. Pablo Picasso drew before he talked and his first spoken word was "piz" for pencil or drawing. This same finding on early precocity is confirmed by Rosamond Harding in *An Anatomy of Inspiration:* "Technical skill is built up from childhood. The future poet scribbles verses as a child, the future artist begins to draw as soon as he can hold a pencil."

Catherine the Great, Margaret Mead, and Mother Teresa all realized their calling at a very early age. They knew they were destined to some great station in life and began preparing themselves during their youth. Catherine was told by Russia's British ambassador as a teenager, "You were born to command and rule." She took his advice literally and started forming her plans to rule Russia long before anyone thought there was any chance she could or would rule the nation. She wrote in her memoirs, "There was something within me which never allowed me to doubt for a single moment that I should one day succeed in becoming the Empress of Russia" (Troyat 1980). In *The Dynamics of Creation* (1993), research psychiatrist Anthony Storr found that George Eliot did not really begin her writings until middle age although she had the vision of her need to create in early childhood. Storr makes the point that much of this is due to what he calls the "Divine Discontent," which is based on a "prolonged and unsatisfactory infancy which spurs him [the creative genius] on to creative achievement."

Many of the women featured in this work have demonstrated the same propensity for childhood precociousness. Maria Callas was listening to opera at the age of two and was critical of New York Metropolitan Opera singers before she was ten. Oprah Winfrey started making speeches at age two and was rewarded with a $500 prize for a church speech at age five. Thereafter she told everyone she would earn her living talking and entertaining. Ayn Rand decided on a writing career at age nine and ended up implementing her dream on a different continent in a different language. Golda Meir decided on a career in Zionism as a young child in Russia because of the extreme influence of her older sister, Shana, who was a radical revolutionary. Madonna was dedicated to the world of dance and entertainment before she was nine. Linda Wachner vowed at age eleven to become a great overachiever. She had decided to own her own business and control her own destiny.

Unhappy or Lonely Childhoods

Many of these female visionaries had unhappy or lonely childhoods, where they were forced to escape in books, music, or solitude. Catherine the Great wrote of herself, "Eighteen years of boredom and loneliness caused her to read many books." Jane Fonda told her biographer that she was unhappy until she was thirty. Maria Callas hated her childhood and detested her mother's indulging of her older sister. Ayn Rand told Barbara Branden (her biographer) "I was desperately alone as a teenager." Golda Meir had an unhappy and adversarial relationship with her mother, which ended in Golda running away from home at age thirteen.

Many of these women were born to families who would have preferred a son. Thatcher, Callas, Fonda, Steinem, and Meir were daughters of mothers who desperately wanted a boy, and accepted their daughters in a less than cheerful way. Oprah Winfrey was unwanted as the illegitimate child of a brief romance between an army man and his girlfriend. Many of these creative women spent time alone fantasizing about escaping to mythical castles in the sky. They escaped through books and other fantasies. Psychologists since Freud have agreed that creativity is a form of wish-fulfillment manifested through fantasizing. Writers of fiction often enter the world of fantasy to realize their internal needs to create. Freud called these excursions into fantasyland *daydreams,* which he viewed as a motivating force based on being unhappy. He said, "A happy person never phantasizes, only an unsatisfied one. The motive forces of phantasies are unsatisfied wishes, and every single phantasy is the fulfillment of a wish, a correction of unsatisfying reality." (Storr 1993)

When children are unhappy they typically retreat into literature or movies and other forms of make-believe. Winfrey said books were her salvation. She said, "I grew up loving books. . . . It was a way to escape to another person's life." She added, "In Milwaukee, I would hide in the closet and read by flashlight." Virtually every one of these women were voracious readers as girls. Maria Callas read about music and opera and fantasized about a future as a great diva. Ayn Rand had heroes from French literature in books her mother bought for her. Gloria Steinem got lost in *Little Women* and Louisa May Alcott became her early heroine. Golda Meir was an inveterate reader of fiction and revolutionary novels, such as *War and Peace.* Margaret Mead both read and wrote poetry as a very young child. Margaret Thatcher spent her early years in the library reading everything she could find. Linda Wachner while incapacitated at age eleven focused on her recovery and reading. These women were lonely and unhappy as children and found their redemption in books and fantasy characters who were often larger than life. These fantasy heroes and heroines were then emulated when they became adults.

Overprotective Mothers, Authoritative Fathers: Bane of Creativity

Underachievers tend to fulfill a negative childhood self-image in much the same way that creative geniuses fulfill a positive self-image. Children raised in over-protective or hostile environments perform to their preprogrammed images of failure just as overachievers satisfy their positive images of success. The unemployment rolls are full of cases of "security-driven" and "risk-averse" individuals who are the byproducts of overprotective or risk-averse parents. The intent of such parents is to protect the child from harm, but such security-oriented conditioning is actually counterprotective to the healthy development of a child's long-term ability to cope in a competitive world. Children can never learn to survive in hostile or foreign environments if not allowed to experience anything negative. They never learn how to try and fail or to understand the difference between winning and losing. Teresa Amabile, who studied childhood creativity, says, "Give children choice wherever possible." In other words, give them direction and then get out of the way so they can experience life and break new ground.

Amabile (1989) found that "parents of creative children don't make a lot of rules." Margaret Mead's childhood is a prime example of direction without indoctrination, experimentation without control, and autonomy without restriction. Mead is a superb example of an independent spirit who grew because of early freedom to explore and err. These thirteen contemporary women are classic examples of how great creativity and innovation is spawned from permissive households. It is important to keep in mind that unconditional love is still a factor in permissive households. Overprotective mothers tend to negate risk-taking behavior by instilling fear of the unknown in the name of love. They build fear of unknown ghosts into the unconscious minds of the child in order to shield and protect them. Individuals from these environments believe "security" is safe when early "risk-taking" is the only safe way to prepare for life. Virtually all creative learning is inversely related to safety since creativity is highly correlated to risk-taking. Parents who do not allow their children to take risks as children are conditioning them to resist risk-taking as an adult. And risk-taking is probably the single most important characteristic in great creative and innovative achievement.

Authoritarian fathers can have an equally devastating influence on creativity, but in the exact opposite way from the mother. Macho, belligerent, and abusive fathers tend to control their offspring through aggressive and physically threatening methods. Such techniques condition the child to submissiveness and avoidance of conflict. Children raised by authoritarian adults tend to avoid the new and unknown as a means of protecting their fragile egos from the violent, reactionary behavior implanted by a strict, disciplinarian parent.

Adolf Hitler is an example of a child with a sadistic and abusive father. He had his early mental images of success and power twisted due to beatings by a cruel father. Hitler wad almost beaten to death by his father for trying to run away and was often treated with inhumanity. Children of such environments have such a negative self-image that monsters such as Hitler are sometimes born. They live their adult lives getting retribution for their early abuse. Hitler's personal retribution was sadistic tyranny against an unsuspecting world. Hitler's negative self-worth is just one more example of a child's early abuse resulting in a noncreative adult. The "getting even" mentality of such people is not just counter to the creative process but very destructive in the world. Both self-esteem and self-image are destroyed, and without these there can be no creativity.

Visionaries Were Treated as Adults

Most of the women we have been discussing were treated in a very adult manner as children. Many were the only children around the house or were with older parents. Linda Wachner says she was always treated as an adult and Mary Kay Ash was forced into adulthood at age seven, nursing an invalid father. Gloria Steinem had the same experience. Oprah Winfrey was making speeches before she attended school. Ayn Rand was a leader within the family unit and part of the decision-making process. Golda Meir ran away from home and was on her own after age fourteen. Margaret Mead, herself an anthropology expert on cultural influences, attributes being treated as an adult to her later success. In her autobiography she says: "In my family, I was treated as a person, never as a child who could not understand. . . . It was never suggested that because I was a child I could not understand the world around me and respond to it responsibly and meaningfully" (*Blackberry Winter,* 1972).

Most of these women were little adults who accepted unusual responsibility and learned to function at an inordinately young age. It certainly appears that treating children as a mature part of the family group is a major contributing factor in developing creative genius.

Role Models and Mentors: Crashing the Glass Ceiling

Early mentors and role models are critical to building self-confidence and self-esteem in potential creative female geniuses. Strong models of success appear critical to helping the visionary crash the proverbial "glass ceiling." Hillary Rodham Clinton was asked by *Parade* magazine in its April 1993 issue who her role models were. She picked eminent women including Golda Meir and Ayn Rand. Margaret Mead wrote in her biography, "My paternal grandmother . . . was the most decisive influence in my life. . . . She gave me my ease in being a woman." Mead's grandmother was her teacher until age ten, when Margaret finally attended regular school. She taught Margaret to be independent, to write poetry, and to think holistically. While attending Barnard College Mead became entranced by anthropology professor Franz Boas, who influenced her to change majors from psychology and journalism to anthropology. During that same period another mentor/role model came into her life in the form of Ruth Benedict. Benedict was an instructor at Barnard and became her mentor, confidante, lover, and friend for the rest of her life. Such role models were invaluable to these women, who readily admitted that they owed most of their later success to the influence of such important persons.

As we know, Mother Teresa's role models were spiritual. She identified with the Virgin Mary from the age of eight, and by the time she was twelve had decided to pursue a life of devotion to Mary and Christ. By the age of eight Ayn Rand had selected as role models Catherine the Great and Cyrus, a fictional character from Victor Hugo's novels. Cyrus made such an indelible impression on Rand's psyche that she spent her life writing and philosophizing about great heroes and heroines. They became the basis for her own philosophical system of thought, objectivism, before the age of ten. She said "I am a hero worshipper," which became the essence of her philosophy, the credo of the Libertarian political party. Rand's role models in adulthood ranged from such intellectual giants as Nietzsche and Dostoyevsky to mystery writer Mickey Spillane.

Golda Meir became a passionate Zionist as a teenager due to the enormous influence of her revolutionary sister, Shana. In her biography Meir wrote of her older sister's influence: "For me, Shana was perhaps the greatest influence on my life . . . a shining example, my dearest friend and my mentor." Another idol and mentor was Theodor Herzl, a turn-of-the-century Jewish leader. He was her ideological mentor. She adopted his famous aphorism, "If you will it, it is no fairy tale," which became her guiding light through years of adversity. First Lady Eleanor Roosevelt was Meir's female role model. She called Mrs. Roosevelt the "first lady of the world." Meir also had many powerful male mentors with whom she worked, played, and fought. Her most influential male mentor was Zalman Shazar, who captivated her as well as others on his way to the presidency of Israel. She was so attracted to him she agreed to get a divorce and marry him, but he backed out at the last minute.

Gloria Steinem adopted Gandhi and Louisa May Alcott as her early role models. Later she would say that politicians Robert Kennedy and Bella Abzug and author Alice Walker inspired her. Margaret Thatcher's childhood role model was her father, Alfred Roberts. As she grew older she was drawn to Katie Kay, a female professor at Oxford, then Tory leader Edward Heath, followed by her hero/mentor Airey Neave. Linda Wachner married her mentor, Seymour Applebaum, a man thirty-one years her senior, whom she described as the one who taught her "focus and self-esteem," and who taught her "to hold on to my dream." Madison Avenue's queen of advertising, Mary Wells, was Linda's mentor after she arrived in Manhattan. Wachner admired Wells for her "bright, tough, and aggressive demeanor." Wachner describes Wells as "one of the first shining stars in my life, one of the first to believe in me." Oprah Winfrey, like Margaret Mead, gives much of the credit for her early development to her authoritarian grandmother. Her father then became her role model during her teen years, to be followed by her career idol and mentor, Barbara Walters.

For Madonna, Christ and the Catholic nuns were her early role models prompting her to want to become a nun in elementary school. (Can you imagine a convent with Madonna orchestrating the entertainment? Just think of the possibilities for weekend retreats.) Madonna's influences began with her father. She says of him, "My father was very strong. He was my role model." Madonna as a teenager became enchanted with Chris Flynn, a dance instructor. He took her under his tutelage and became her mentor. She told *Newsweek* (March 4, 1985), "I latched on to him like a leech and took everything I could from him." Madonna's unconscious fantasy role model-mentor-idol has always been Marilyn Monroe, whom she emulates in her videos, movies (*Dick Tracy*), and tours. As discussed previously, Estée Lauder worshipped her uncle, Dr. John Schotz, who introduced her to the world of beauty in a jar. She reminisced about her uncle's influence in her biography: "I believe today that in my uncle John was my true path." Her adult heroes were the Duchess of Windsor (Wallace Simpson), Princess Grace (Kelly), and Begum Aga Khan, all elegant ladies whom Estée has emulated.

Jane Fonda had a childhood obsession over her father's lack of affection to such a degree that he was her role model without her ever admitting to it. He was the "monument" of maleness in her eyes. Lee Strasbourg, her teacher at the New York actors studio, became her mentor, as did virtually every male lover and husband including, but not limited to: Alexander Voutsinas, Roger Vadim, Tom Hayden, and Ted Turner. It appears Vadim was her sexual mentor, Hayden her ideological mentor, and Turner her power mentor. She needed men and used them to fulfill the needs her father never had. Maria Callas says that Elvira de Hidalgo was her mentor from the age fourteen. She says of Hidalgo, "I owe all my preparation, my artistic formation as an actress and musician to Elvira." She then married a father figure, twenty-seven years her senior, Giovanni Meneghini, who became her lover, friend, and mentor for ten years.

Mary Kay Ash was inspired by her mother. She constantly encouraged with "Honey, you can do it" when Mary Kay was very young. This early motivation built her self-esteem to the point that she believed in her own ability. In her first job Ida Blake, her sales manager, became her role model and stimulated her to greater success. As an adult Ash selected God as her hero and the bumble bee as her role model because "a bee shouldn't be able to fly. . . . But the bumblebee doesn't know it and it flies very well." This latter role model is so ingrained in Ash's psyche that she uses it as a sales motivation device in her company and gives diamond-encrusted bumblebees to her top performers as a symbol of their success along with her world-famous pink Cadillacs.

Early fantasy heroes, role models, mentors, and idols are critical to grooming women to get to the top. They are critical in helping them break through that glass ceiling, which restricts many women through subtle duplicity. Picking role models who have made it through that elusive barrier is very important. Science has recently shown that emulating greatness is the quickest path to greatness, which makes it incumbent upon aspiring young women to pick a winner and follow her everywhere. Creativity is contagious and these women are ideal candidates for such associations—you might just catch some of their success.

Creativity Is Contagious: Neuro-Linguistic Programming (NLP)

Success mimicking success lends credence to the neuro-linguistic programming (NLP) or "imaging" theories of John Grinder and Richard Bandler of the University of California at Berkeley. These two research psychologists created the NLP theory by demonstrating how modeling and mimicking great creative talent can improve performance for a neophyte. They successfully demonstrated in the laboratory how imaging successful talent can actually improve the talent of someone less skilled. In other words, find superstars and emulate their actions and your performance at that given task will be enhanced. Assuming this is true then "creativity is contagious." Everyone should follow around after great leaders, mimic their behavior, study them, and find out what makes them tick, so they can also be successful leaders. NLP research supports what many already knew: that talent is transferable between teachers and students, leaders and followers, that is, within certain limits. Associating with eminent people will improve performance and offer a greater chance for achieving eminence. Conversely, associating with prosaic and unimaginative people can prove counterproductive to the creative process. One formula for success in life is to find someone who is best at what you desire and emulate their performance. Spending time with or studying any one of our thirteen female wunderkinds would be a good place to start.

The above also appears to work in sports activities. Anyone scrutinizing professional teams will have noticed that the "superstar" on a team tends to have an inordinate influence over the performance of the other members of that team. A miraculous improvement typically occurs in the average talent surrounding that superstar. Cite the great basketball stars—Larry Bird and Michael Jordan—who brought success to their high schools, colleges, and pro teams, or Wayne Gretsky in hockey. When these stars graduated or left their teams, the teams continued to achieve far beyond the talent level of those remaining, due to some kind of osmosis or collective unconscious—the residue of their mere presence. This strange anomaly occurs far beyond chance occurrence. Just ask any avid sports fan who has followed the eminently successful woman's basketball teams at Stanford and Tennessee universities. These teams remain at the very top of the national rankings year after year, not necessarily because of the existing talent but due to the mystique of past superstars who brought them to that level of excellence. A superstar aura seems to surround the program due to a heritage from the past. This theory would indicate that success does breed success, and reading about creative genius is preferable to reading a novel for enhancing one's performance potential.

The Collective Unconscious

Winning role models are the pathways to excellence, based on the NLP theory. Bandler and Grinder worked with Milton Erikson, Virginia Satir, and Gregory Bateson to demonstrate how modeling excellence can dramatically improve performance of the neophyte. If you want to become successful in a given field, find those who are excellent in that field and model their behavior. Emulating creative and innovative behavior imprints the disciple with many of the qualities of the leader. Numerous examples of this exist in the world of business, politics, and science. It certainly is not a coincidence that Freud spawned disciples the likes of Alfred Adler, Carl Jung, Otto Rank, and Wilhelm Reich. Or consider the case of Notre Dame football teams being cheered on to great heights due to the Knute Rockne image of "Win one for the Gipper." Notre Dame appears to conjure up some magical elixir of success seventy years after Rockne's death. This implies a kind of creative collective unconscious for winning.

Carl Jung originated the concept of this "collective unconscious," an innate or universal knowledge passed on genetically by a kind of osmosis from generation to generation. His theory is that universal knowledge permeates all beings and is pervasive in the universe. John Bell has more recently proved a similar concept scientifically. His theory is that "there are no isolated systems: every particle in the universe is in 'instantaneous' communication with every other particle." Applied to creative success in life, Bell's theory would presuppose that superachieving influences everyone in its path even if they are only briefly touched by that creative genius.

Recent brain research has shown similar results at Berkeley and the University of Southern California. Sheldrake in 1981 theorized that a rat in Australia could "know" something taught to a rat in America. He bred smart rats separately from dumb rats for twenty-two generations; not only were the smart rats smarter but all the rats were smarter—*even the dumbest breeds*. In other words, science has finally confirmed that "success breeds success."

This would also presuppose that early *enhanced* or *impoverished* environments will be highly predictive of creative and noncreative achievement later in life.

Summary

The prototypical female creative genius is either a first-born female or was raised as one. She is doted on in a permissive household where she is the prima donna. She has a self-employed father who is both her idol and role model. Early moves and travel or attending many different schools have provided her with self-sufficiency and strong coping skills. An unhappy or lonely childhood prepares her to deal with uncertainty and allows her to fantasize an idyllic life. Not all of these family characteristics are necessary for a female to become creative, but at least two of them appear critical for anyone to have the predisposition to become a great creative genius.

Eleven of these thirteen visionaries were either first-born or raised as first-borns. The other two were indulged and idolized as if they were only children. Most were treated as little adults even when quite young. Eleven of the thirteen had fathers who were self-employed. Having a self-employed father appears to have conditioned these women to believe in the freedom of a laissez faire way of life. All but three of these women lived in many cities prior to adulthood. Ten of the thirteen lived in different cities prior to age ten and five actually lived in a different country. Most moved prior to attending school, which appears to have predisposed them to learn how to effectively deal with new and unknown environments.

The father is the dominant influence for these creative visionaries. He was typically their first male role model and the one they loved and admired most. Most found themselves alone or unhappy and turned to books, movies, magazines, and fantasizing to cope with reality. Most had decided on the career of their ultimate choice prior to age ten and all but Jane Fonda had their careers well in mind before high school. Most were fortunate to have had indulgent parents who allowed them to risk and fail very early in life.

These women's role models and mentors were eminent real-life successes or larger-than-life fictional or historical figures. They fantasized about fictional heroic characters while they were young. These real or imagined early mentors and role models led them into successful achievement, proving the aphorism "Creativity can be contagious." NLP theory says to find great leaders or superstars in your given field and mimic their behavior. This is a quick and sure way of improving an existing skill level. Recent scientific discoveries now indicate that this could have some universal implications, which Carl Jung has described as a collective unconscious, or universal creative knowledge. These creative visionaries offer an idealist model for young women everywhere to emulate.

3

Education, Intelligence, and Knowledge

It is nothing short of a miracle that the modern methods of instruction have not entirely strangled the holy curiosity of inquiry.

—Albert Einstein

To know is to be ignorant; not to know is the beginning of wisdom.

—J. Krishnamurti

Knowledge is critical to the creative process. Formal education is not. The above quotes from Einstein and Krishnamurti (a world-renowned philosopher on education and truth) state that formal education is not the sacrosanct path to success and power we once thought. And it certainly is not the key to successful innovation, creativity, or entrepreneurship. Although it must be emphasized that complete in-depth knowledge and understanding is critical to success in any endeavor, formal education is not. Educational institutions have a way of compartmentalizing life, thus putting everyone and everything in a box to fit their system. The result is the idolization of mediocrity and the rejection of nonconformity; but nonconformity is what creative endeavor is all about.

An example of this thesis is the educational background of Thomas A. Edison, the most prodigious inventor in history, who had only three months of formal schooling yet he innovated in a field requiring technological expertise even in his era. Albert Einstein's experience was more bizarre considering he was repeatedly turned down for a teaching position and forced to work as a clerk in the Swiss postal service because he did not fit the rigorous mold of the educational institutions. Only after submitting his world-renowned papers on the theory of relativity was he offered a university teaching position. Einstein was never accepted as an academician, because he did not follow the academy's regimen for formal research: he intuited many of his great ideas and was always content to leave proofs to his colleagues.

Distinguished critic and historian Jacques Barzun in "Paradoxes of Creativity" said, "Being too good a student can limit creativity." In other words, too much emphasis on the details in life does not allow room for universal insights. Playwright George Bernard Shaw said geniuses are "masters of reality," a reference to the importance of simple solutions for complex problems. The most elegant solutions have always been the simplest. Heuristic trial-and-error solutions are always quicker and more practical than cumbersome experiments. Edison was saying the same with his famous aphorism "Genius is 1 percent inspiration and 99 percent perspiration." Soichiro Honda, the founder of Honda Motors, gave even more credit to trial-and-error creativity by saying, "My success represents the 1 percent of work—resulting from the 99 percent that is failure." Economist George Gilder was more cynical, saying, "Nothing has been so rare in recent years as an Ivy League graduate who has made a significant innovation in American enterprise." He went on to berate our educational system, saying, "Business schools tend to turn out cynical manipulators of existing values rather than entrepreneurial creators of new values."

Females, Education, and Knowledge

Catherine the Great reached the pinnacle of success with little or no formal education, but cherished knowledge and intellectual inquiry. After her marriage to the imbecile Peter III, she spent eighteen years buried in books in the pursuit of pure knowledge. She became the patron of eighteenth-century intellectuals, including Voltaire, Diderot, Grimm, and Potemkin. Catherine's dedication to philosophy and knowledge made Mother Russia an unlikely seat for intellectual inquiry during the seventeenth century. She was responsible for funding the first encyclopedia and entertained philosophers and intellectuals at her salons. Catherine revered knowledge, philosophy, and world history, which helped elevate her to become one of the great world leaders in history. Mother Teresa, steeped in the Edison tradition of heuristic inquiry, went to people in the streets to gain knowledge, and founded the Sisters of Charity. She then used her street knowledge to help the poor and dying and in so doing changed history. Her efforts resulted in gaining her a Nobel Peace Prize in 1979. Mother Teresa had little formal education but had the universal knowledge of truth and wisdom.

Margaret Mead was the first American female anthropologist to receive her doctorate. Mead was a pioneer in field research, which had little to do with her formal education but it motivated her to pursue culture through heuristic observation techniques. Ironically, she had no formal education until high school: her academic parents did not want her contaminated by the structure of a school system. They taught her holistically and thereby armed her to deal with life pragmatically. She learned to "observe" nature and behavior as a young child and ultimately used "observation" to show that culture affected personality and with that penetrating insight she changed the world of anthropology. Mead had a wonderful formal education from Barnard College and New York University, but resorted to the jungles of the world to search for the real truth. She traveled into remote Samoa and New Guinea to investigate the nature of various cultures and find out what made them tick.

All thirteen visionaries in this book were extremely knowledgeable in their fields, but even those with excellent formal educations never allowed their education to limit their ability to search for truth. The essence of the truly educated is not their pedigree, but their ability to seek truth and knowledge in the trenches of life. This has never been articulated better than by the great educator and philosopher J. Krishnamurti, who said, "Why do you want to be students of books, rather than students of life? Find out what is true and false in your environment with all its oppressions and its cruelties and then you will find out what is true." Ayn Rand told her biographer Barbara Branden, "I did not learn my values from school." Gloria Steinem also agreed, believing her time at Smith College equally useless in preparing her for her professional life.

Formal Education

The formal educational backgrounds of these female wunderkinds were diverse. Four never completed high school, four had some college, and four graduated from college (see figure 6). Only Margaret Thatcher went as far as graduate school, earning a masters degree in chemistry in 1950 and a law degree from Oxford in 1953. Neither chemistry nor law were fields in which she made her mark in the world. It appears that those women with a business and/ or entrepreneurial bent were the least dependent on formal education. Mary Kay Ash, Estée Lauder, and Liz Claiborne have been eminently successful by any barometer of business, yet none finished high school. Lauder's net worth in 1992 was estimated by *Fortune* magazine at $5.2 billion, and both Ash and Claiborne are worth hundreds of millions, yet none of these women made it to college. It would certainly have been different had these women not started and controlled their own firms. It is likely that they would have been just another employee or executive had they acquired more formal education. Ted Turner once quipped, "I couldn't even get an interview at CNN if I didn't own it." The other two business gurus, Linda Wachner and Lillian Vernon, were a bit more educated than Lauder, Ash, and Claiborne. Wachner had a business degree from Buffalo State College and Lillian Vernon attended New York University in psychology but dropped out to get married.

Formal education is more important for anyone pursuing careers in the

Figure 6

FORMAL EDUCATION

High school or less

Maria Callas	Eighth grade in New York City and voice lessons in Greece
Liz Claiborne	Tenth grade in New Orleans. Studied art and painting in Europe
Estée Lauder	Eleventh grade in Queens, New York
Mary Kay Ash	Straight A student in high school in Houston, Texas

Some college

Golda Meir	One year at Milwaukee's Normal Teacher's College
Madonna	Straight A student in Michigan. One year at Michigan University on dance scholarship. Dropped out in second year for New York career
Jane Fonda	Two years at Vassar (women's college), dropped out to study art in Paris. Two years at Lee Strasberg's Actors Studio in New York City
Lillian Vernon	High school in New York. Three years at NYU in psychology

College graduates

Ayn Rand	Bachelor's in history, St. Petersburg University, Russia, 1924
Gloria Steinem	Bachelor's in political science, Smith College (women's college), 1956, Phi Beta Kappa, cum laude and one year in Switzerland as exchange student
Linda Wachner	Bachelor's in business administration, Buffalo State College, 1966, at age of 20
Oprah Winfrey	Bachelor's in drama, Tennessee State University, 1976 (1988 degree granted)

Graduate school

Margaret Thatcher	Bachelor's in chemisty, Somerville (women's college), 1947; master's in chemistry, Oxford, 1950; law degree, Oxford, 1953

humanities or politics. These fields demand a pedigree in order to appease the constituency or the established hierarchy. In this way they are similar to entering the corporate hierarchy, where a requisite formal education is the price of entry. The entry fee for creativity, innovation, and entrepreneurship is hard work, a high risk-taking propensity, and no preconceived ideas as to what can be accomplished. These traits are not found in the job descriptions of most corporate organizations. In politics a degree, preferably from a prestigious institution, is the price of entry. The women who opted for a political career (Meir, Thatcher, and Steinem) felt a degree was important, although Meir never bothered to get one. Margaret Thatcher matriculated at the finest women's college at Oxford (Somerville) in chemistry and then received her law degree after working as a research chemist for three years. Gloria Steinem received a cum laude degree from Smith College in political science but insists that it was not helpful in her career and in some respects counterproductive. Golda Meir aspired to be a teacher but left Milwaukee's Normal Teacher's College after one year.

Four of these female visionaries made it big in the world of entertainment: Maria Callas, Jane Fonda, Madonna, and Oprah Winfrey. Maria Callas was the least educated of this group, making it only through the eighth grade. She quit school in New York City after junior high to pursue voice lessons and an operatic career in Athens, Greece. Both Fonda and Madonna left their respective colleges in their sophomore years to pursue their entertainment careers and coincidentally part of their "street" education was acquired in Paris. Oprah Winfrey attended Tennessee State University, but didn't actually finish all of her course work for a degree until 1987. She had been offered a job as a TV anchor and resisted until her professor told her, "Look, job offers from CBS are the reason people go to college." Oprah has the most formal education of the entertainers in this book but mainly due to her father's insistence that she would be a failure without a college degree. She owned her own entertainment company and earned $25 million a year prior to receiving her degree.

It is apparent that any of these women could have had a college degree had they been so motivated. They were not, and it appears they are better off for having avoided formal education.

Male/Female Educations

My research on thirteen male creative geniuses indicates a pattern similar to those of the women profiled in this book. Soichiro Honda of Honda Motors and Arthur Jones of Nautilus made it only to the eighth grade, yet both made significant contributions in the world of technology. Bill Gates of Microsoft and Steve Jobs of Apple Computer fame had only one year of college even though they made it big in the high-technology world of computers. Gates, whose estimated $7 billion net worth makes him the richest person in America according to *Forbes* and *Fortune,* left Harvard at age nineteen to pursue a career in software. Tom Monaghan, founder of Domino's Pizza, attended only one semester at Michigan State. Fred Smith, the father of overnight package delivery and founder of Federal Express, said, "I was a crummy student" while at Yale, where he graduated in economics. Bill Lear revolutionized the business jet aircraft industry with his Lear jet; he accomplished this with a ninth grade education.

"Heuristic Knowledge = Creative Power"

George Gilder has been especially outspoken on the subject of formal education. As noted above, he criticizes business schools for producing graduates who can only perpetuate the status quo rather than "entrepreneurial creators of new values." Professional educator Warren Bennis succinctly describes the problem with the maxim "Teaching homogenizes both its subjects and its objects." One reason for this pessimism is that highly educated people feel they should start at the middle or top of an organization instead of at the bottom, where all creativity begins. The well educated never want to start in the sweatshops or grovel in high-risk, treacherous environments where true innovation and creativity usually take place. Almost everyone who has a great idea wants to reap an easy dividend by selling the idea to some large company and simply collecting royalties. This is not possible. The only way to get rich is to take the idea to market to prove its merit, and *then* sell it off. Most people are not willing to pay that dear price.

The college diploma is really a pedigree for entrance to an executive position in an established organization. Creative visionaries, entrepreneurs, and innovative geniuses are never looking for a corporate position and therefore do not hold sheepskins in high regard. In addition, they are usually so confident in their own ability, they do not believe they need a diploma to prove themselves. Many of the creative geniuses in this study overachieved because they did not have the requisite pedigree for an executive position, which forced them to start at the bottom. Therefore, not having a degree appears to be doubly advantageous in the favor of great creative endeavor. "If you are totally confident in your ability you don't need the pedigree, and if you don't have it, you overachieve to such a degree you wouldn't have needed it anyway."

"Knowledge is power," but it is not attained by acquiring a piece of paper. These creative visionaries proved this axiom by learning more about their profession than anyone with any kind of degree. They did it in the trenches. Most would agree that a thorough knowledge of their field was critical to their success, but it would be misleading to assume that their knowledge came from books or classrooms. Formal education is often the easiest and least expensive way to obtain knowledge, but it is not the *only* way, especially when attempting something never before tried. Learning on the street, in the classroom, or through personal trial-and-error research are all acceptable methods for mastering any task or career path. More often than not these women took the more time-consuming and costly "street path." They all started at the bottom with little knowledge of their field and rose to the top without much help from others. The trip was more time-consuming and costly but, as in most things, the more difficult path is often the more financially and psychologically rewarding one.

These thirteen female visionaries operated in a heuristic fashion through trial-and-error pursuit of their concepts and careers. Madonna continually rehearsed new routines and refined them to perfection until they worked. Estée Lauder would try a new sales promotion and discard it if it did not produce the expected results. Linda Wachner worked her way to the top, becoming president of Max Factor at age thirty-three, and promptly quit at age forty, when she was not allowed to acquire the company. Her goal was to own and operate her own firm so she resigned and risked everything to realize her dream. Both Mary Kay Ash and Lillian Vernon began their firms from their kitchen tables with nothing more sophisticated than a yellow tablet and an idea. Even Oprah Winfrey began at the bottom of the talk show industry and worked her way to the top. Her unparalleled success has come from being different. She throws caution to the wind and says what she thinks and that "humanness" is contagious. Her guests are motivated to bare their souls since she has. This unique but fundamental strategy has made Winfrey eminently successful and created her own particular niche in the talk show business.

Gloria Steinem literally started on the street, marching with her sisters. She has often risked life and limb walking through Harlem to get a story of racial or sex discrimination. After toiling as a freelance writer she created her own communication vehicle—*Ms.* magazine—in order to preach her gospel to the multitudes. No one had ever attempted such a thing, but she was not deterred, doing it with the financial backing of Warner Communications. All of these women experimented with new concepts and ideas, never departing far from their ultimate trajectory. They tried an approach, refined it, and then changed it in an inextricable march toward their goals.

These visionaries used a "qualitative methodology" to resolve "qualitative problems." They never resorted to the use of "quantitative analysis" as preached in academia. Modeling is fine as an MBA instructional routine to better understand something that already exists. It is useless, however, in attempting to resolve new technological, marketing, or societal problems. Quantitative analysis, which is succinctly referred to as "analysis paralysis" by entrepreneurial types, is inappropriate for breaking new ground in almost any profession. Any concept can be proved or disproved by quantitative analysis, depending on the assumptions. The only true technique for achieving breakthrough innovation is through repeated trial-and-error experimentation in the very bowels of the creative process.

Thomas Edison, the most prolific inventor in history, believed only in trial-and-error experimentation. He felt that all discoveries resulted from the heuristic approach to creativity, not the classroom approach. "Do you think I would have amounted to anything," he said, "if I went to school? University trained scientists saw what they were taught to look for and thus missed the great secrets of nature. . . . Discovery is not invention, it is more or less the nature of an accident" (Josephson, 1959).

Learning Comes from Doing!

A Hollywood lawyer for the opposition in one of Madonna's litigations with Sean Penn said of her: "Her lack of formal education is made up in street smarts. I would take her street-smart business sense over someone with a Harvard MBA any day." This is a repeated finding in creative success, which is also prevalent in sports. Learning how to properly serve a tennis ball is important to becoming an accomplished tennis player. But studying the theoretical points of serving a tennis ball from a textbook has little chance of success. Only practicing the tennis serve ad nauseam has any chance of reaching perfection in the art of serving a tennis ball. Trial-and-error learning is preferable in any endeavor and the repetitive drudgery of "doing it," not reading about it, is the ultimate way to "becoming proficient." An interesting example of experience being *the* preeminent factor in success comes from the tiny country of Malaysia, which is producing literally millions of the products used daily in the United States. On a recent trip I received a business card from a highly successful executive who had no formal education. Behind his name were the letters QBE where the Ph.D. was shown on my card. On enquiry I was delighted to find QBE stands for Qualified By Experience.

The above analogy is true of all creative endeavor. Knowledge and skill are a function of getting into the depths of creativity with dirty hands, battered egos, ravished finances, and destroyed self-confidence. True knowledge (or skill in the tennis-serve example) only becomes a reality, as Edison said, through perspiration, not inspiration. To sum up, learning to serve tennis aces or mothering a great creative breakthrough concept is the result of "doing it" rather than theorizing about it. The "how to" knowledge acquired in a textbook can only be perfected on the court of life through repeated practice and failure.

Consider the example of selecting the finest doctor for performing your life-threatening triple-bypass heart surgery. A formal education from a prestigious Ivy League medical school is nice, but that education, without vast amounts of hands-on experience, is useless, as any doctor of medicine will tell you. Formal education teaches students which books to study for the proper medical procedure, it does not teach the nuances of what to do in an actual situation. Consider the choice of having an operation by a newly graduated doctor who had never performed the difficult surgery, or by an uneducated practitioner who had performed 10,000 such procedures in the jungles of South America. Common sense dictates opting for the uneducated doctor with the experience.

The creative females we've been discussing typically acquired their knowledge through empirical methods and applied it in a qualitative way to reach their goals. They acquired knowledge wherever they could—in the streets, in factories, and in libraries—and applied it in a creative way to make their mark in the world. Consider Madonna, who did not get to the top of her profession because she was an accomplished dancer, had a wonderful voice, or was a gifted actress. Actually, she is very mediocre in all these skills. Her talent is what this book is about. Madonna was able to take her mediocre skills and mold them into a world-class phenomenon known as the "Material Girl." She persevered, took enormous risks, was obsessively driven, and walked over many bodies in her march to the top. She did so by pioneering in unknown vistas and working very hard to perfect her knowledge of pop entertainment. Madonna sought "knowledge" on the street of life. She emulated great entertainers like Marilyn Monroe and Jean Harlow. Her trial-and-error experimentation has paid off in a big way and has made her rich and famous. These women prove Edison's aphorism about perspiration, not inspiration, being the key to the creative process. They were eminently successful but it was only because they were willing to work eighty-hour, seven-day weeks for many years to reach their goals.

Knowledge, Creativity, and Power

Marilyn Ferguson, the brilliant scientific writer who authored *The Aquarian Conspiracy,* says that our educational systems emphasize being "right" at the expense of being "open." She stresses that learning "is where you find it," which is a sentiment not found in traditional textbooks and classrooms. Ferguson cites Margaret Mead's home education as an example of a child not being contaminated by the school system, which apparently allowed her to think openly without traditional, boxed-in parameters of thinking. This mentality contributed to Mead's monumental breakthroughs in cultural anthropology. Educator and writer Warren Bennis (1989) confirms Ferguson's hypothesis by saying, "Every time we teach a child something, rather than helping him learn, we keep him from inventing it himself . . . or from reinventing himself."

Educational institutions are administered by bureaucrats who automatically presume that everyone must be put in the box of mediocrity. What then becomes of the gifted or the iconoclasts, who by definition are destined to be our creative geniuses? In most schools they find themselves in an environment contrary to their temperament. Researchers have found the gifted to be "intolerant of useless conformity." Unfortunately, most schools are nothing but useless conformity based on learning by rote. It is no wonder Einstein, Edison, and Picasso hated school and that Margaret Mead and Ayn Rand were contemptuous of school and their teachers. Visionaries are not well suited to inflexible and sterile environments. Forcing them to operate in such domains will only stifle their creativity and force them to rebel.

Author Alvin Toffler has made a strong case for a shift from financial power to knowledge power in his book *Powershift* (1990). Here he paints a picture of our evolution from the muscle power of the Middle Ages to the money power of the Industrial Age and finally to the knowledge power of the Information Age. Toffler idealizes knowledge power as the ultimate self-actualizing power that will bring its users the ultimate rewards of physical, financial, and political power. He predicts that knowledge power will become the catalyst of all great leadership and creativity. He says, "The control of knowledge is the crux of tomorrow's worldwide struggle for power in every human institution," and then proceeds to confirm our findings that "mass education systems are largely obsolete." Each of the females in this work are examples of Toffler's knowledge power at work in their professions. Most were not steeped in philosophical or intellectual knowledge but nevertheless utilized the power of superior knowledge to dominate their fields of interest.

Liz Claiborne was a high school dropout but intuitively knew more about what the working female demanded in clothing than all of the formally educated Seventh Avenue garment gurus put together. She revolutionized women's clothing because of her intuitive knowledge, which was totally lost on the educated experts. Oprah Winfrey had little or no training in the broadcast media or talk show hosting. Yet she intuitively knows just what to say and when to say it. Golda Meir had no training in statesmanship but became Israel's first ambassador to Russia, and did a commendable job, because she knew more about intercultural problems than any other person in the world. Mary Kay Ash created an organization that women identify with because she created a job she herself wanted. She violated all of the corporate rules for starting a business: insisting on no rules, sales quotas, or work hours for her consultants. Mary Kay Cosmetics is now a billion-dollar operation admired and idealized by other organizations.

Maria Callas never even watched the conductor when performing her great arias. She was myopic and therefore forced to memorize all the routines and lines of an opera, and consequently became a sensational success through her innovative technique. Ayn Rand violated all of the rules of writing and publishing and has sold twenty-five million books in the process. Jane Fonda admitted that her only reason for making fitness videos was that she knew more about women's exercise than anything else in life since she had exercised to stay fit every day for over twenty years. She revolutionized the video fitness business overnight. All of these women were as knowledgeable in their given fields as anyone in the world, even though they weren't necessarily armed with sheepskins to flaunt their knowledge. Their success confirms that "knowledge is power."

Knowledge Power

Margaret Mead trailblazed the field of anthropology: she pioneered because there were no precedents for her to follow. She went off to the jungles of the South Pacific and in her words, "I created my field work and approach as I went." Catherine the Great's power was even more subtle. Dressed in a colonel's uniform for psychological affect, she mounted a great white stallion full stride like a man (unheard of in those days) and rode to confront her weak husband. He had never seen military action until confronted by his assertive and committed wife. He capitulated immediately, turning over Mother Russia to her. Mounting a horse full saddle was just not done in the eighteenth century by proper ladies, who always rode side saddle. This ploy not only had psycho-sexual implications, according to her biographer (Alexander, 1989), it also demonstrated Catherine's passion and "desire for mastery, personal autonomy, sensual gratification, and power."

Estée Lauder was not nearly so conversant with the nuances of power but used knowledge power to succeed in cosmetics. She had no formal education but knew all there was to know about her field, since she had been giving facials to women since grade school. She had *no* technical education in body chemistry or face creams, but she has earned billions by knowing more about women's facials than anyone in her business. Golda Meir knew nothing of political science but was instrumental in creating the state of Israel because of her intimate knowledge of Zionism and its adherents. She took pains to learn everything she could about her mortal enemies, the Arabs, which is why she was made prime minister of Israel. Madonna has never taken a course in business, but *Working Woman* in 1991 acknowledged her superior business acumen by labeling her "the consummate entrepreneur." She earned the label because of her adept handling of a huge corporate operation which she runs herself with little or no staff. Madonna is an unlikely CEO who has learned every nuance of the entertainment business and landed a $60 million contract with Warner in 1992. Liz Claiborne was called "America's greatest female entrepreneur" by no less an authority than *Fortune* magazine for her phenomenal success in revolutionizing women's clothing. In ten short years Claiborne came to dominate women's clothing like no other company in history. Without making it to high school, she knew her field better than any man or woman alive. Lillian Vernon "knows" what mail-order shoppers want. She says her market research entails "testing it on yourself." Margaret Thatcher knew what Great Britain needed in terms of reducing the unions' power and creating a more laissez faire business environment. Her insight lifted her to the top of the government for over ten years.

Even the women who had spent a great deal of their time pursuing formal education were not necessarily assisted in their professions by their degrees. Oprah Winfrey majored in drama, but when faced with anchoring a radio and TV show, admitted that she had to learn from scratch how to perform in these mediums. She says, "I had no experience and no classes that gave me any feel for the reality of the job." No education could have helped Lillian Vernon create her world-famous catalog. She created it because it was something she could do as a pregnant young mother who needed to supplement the family's income. She sat at her kitchen table and learned as she went. Margaret Thatcher had the most formal education and the vast majority of her classroom time was spent in learning to become a research chemist. This training assisted her in the knowledge of the industrial sector of Great Britain but it certainly had no bearing on her rising to position of prime minister. Ayn Rand had a degree in history, which gave her little or no help in writing her first great epic philosophical novel.

Intelligence: Help or Hinderance?

First-borns have higher IQs (7 points higher) than their younger brothers and sisters, according to a recent study by United States psychologists. However, too much intelligence has also been found to be detrimental to great innovation and creativity. All of the females in this work were bright. Ayn Rand, Oprah Winfrey, and Linda Wachner had superior intellects. Gloria Steinem, Mary Kay Ash, and Margaret Thatcher were honor students. Virtually all females in this study were straight-A students in their elementary and high schools. Even the "Material Girl," who unabashedly displays her physical assets at the expense of her mental attributes, recorded a 140 IQ in a high school intelligence test. Oprah Winfrey skipped kindergarten and the second grade. She was an articulate debater in school as were Thatcher, Steinem, and Rand.

Educator, psychologist, and writer Frederick Herzberg found that IQ was not critical to innovative success. "There is no denying that an above-average IQ is a prerequisite to innovation," he said, but "innovative people are not necessarily brilliant people." He reiterates, "An extremely high IQ can be a detriment to innovation because they are too highly correlated to educational achievement" (1989). Frank Barron, in his book *Creative Person and Creative Process* (1969), found that "for certain intrinsically creative activities a specifiable minimum IQ is probably necessary to engage in the activity at all, but beyond that minimum, which is often surprisingly low, creativity has little correlation with scores on IQ tests." A prime example of Barron's theory is Maria Callas, the universally acclaimed genius of modern opera who made it through only eighth grade. Opera critic John Ardoin described her in 1994 as "no intellectual, but she was wiser than anyone else when she began to sing. Music transformed her into another being, one who knew and felt things more deeply than others" (*USA Today,* February 1994).

The female geniuses considered here appear to confirm the above findings, since these thirteen women were bright but not endowed with Mensa-level intelligence. Other traits, such as persistence, intuition, charisma, persuasion, and a renegade disposition were the vehicles they used to reach the top. They were bright, but far more important than their mental acuity was their need to achieve through exorcising past ghosts of insecurity and fear of failure.

Gifted Children and Their Role Models

Overprotective parents tend to be negative role models for gifted children; they impede potential creativity by restricting risk-taking. Conversely, permissive parents tend to be very positive influences for gifted and precocious children because they encourage risk-taking. Gifted children need to have role models who allow them to err often without rebuke and encourage spontaneity at an early age. And according to gifted counselor Linda Silverman, Ph.D., "Gifted girls need role models of women who successfully combine marriage, raising children, and a career." It appears that a tolerant environment for young children is critical for building their self-esteem and grooming them for great achievement. It trains children to win *and* lose, and not to fear playing any game for the fear of losing. The gifted have been found to be intolerant of conformity, which often gains them the "renegade" label but makes them ideal candidates for creative genius. They learn to risk and lose without personal denigration and therefore become the movers and shakers of the world. Role models who condone this freedom of action ferment creative behavior.

Avoid Experts: They Know Too Much!

Experts have an ego investment in the past and present. They always know all the reasons why anything new will not work. These individuals resist change because their expertise is at stake. It is this mentality that caused the Inquisition and caused Copernicus, Galileo, and Columbus such difficulty. Experts always believe the new and unknown are preposterous, which is why innovative visionaries have an opportunity to become rich and famous. New Age writer Anton Wilson describes experts as arrogant "know-it-alls": "The authoritarian personality is "Always Right" and tends to seek positions of power. [Such people] are obsessed with facts and figures. . . . I think it was men of this type who killed Socrates" (*Prometheus Rising*, 1983).

Market research does not work. You cannot research something that never existed. Do you think Darwin checked with the church prior to developing his evolutionary hypothesis? Or did Einstein checked with Newton's laws prior to formulating his relativity theory? No way! Only pioneering in the unknown land of creativity can establish a new concept. Not one of these women listened to an expert before launching into her successful achievement. If she had she would not be in this book.

Paradoxical Intention: Don't Be Too Smart

Female creative geniuses have a reality map that gives them permission to pioneer in obscure areas. They succeed because they do not know that they can't. It is all right to be ignorant of something and admit it and move on through the learning cycle. The people who are dangerous in the world are those who don't know, but don't know they don't know. These visionaries knew what they didn't know. In other words, they were not too smart. Schools teach us what can be accomplished and innocuously teach us our limitations in life. Great visionaries ignore such instruction and are seldom constrained by the unknown. They do not know they can't, therefore they can. This is another way of saying they have eliminated their ego in pursuit of their life's goal. With the ego removed, talent can take over and move the person toward success. Allowing "gut" instincts to take over increases the chance of success in most ventures in life. Allowing the "ego" to get in the way tends to inhibit achievement.

Victor Frankl defined this concept as "paradoxical intention." He found that "fear brings about that which one is afraid of, and hyper intention makes impossible what one wishes." More simply put, this theory tells us not to try too hard or we cannot attain our goals. Setting goals is imperative to great success, such as winning a tennis match, but once the goal is set, it should be forgotten, with all energies directed toward hitting the necessary strokes to win. Thinking about winning is normally counterproductive to winning because the ego gets in the way of the body's natural instinct toward performance. In sum, one can only win by not thinking about winning. The harder one tries to do anything, the more difficult it is to accomplish. Try signing your name three times *exactly* the same. Impossible! Seeking love and romance is the worst possible way of finding it. The only way to find love and romance is *not* to seek it. Paradoxical intention teaches us to win not by concentrating on winning the war, but by concentrating on winning the battles. That is the essence of creative genius.

Paradoxical intention also demonstrates that cognitive wishing is counter to effective achieving. We become, "not what we consciously wish to become in life" but "what we unconsciously believe our destiny in life to be." That is, we need to relax our conscious minds enough to allow our unconscious minds the freedom to explore new and unknown territory. The ability to holistically operate with all our faculties, both conscious and unconscious, is critical to the creative process. Margaret Mead is the consummate example of this point. Her parents ignored her formal education and trained her in the ways of the world until she was a teenager. They trained her holistically in all aspects of life—the arts, music, poetry—and encouraged her to experiment and fail. She was taking notes on the behavior of other children at the age of eight and writing poetry by age nine. Writer and psychologist Jean Houston says Mead's early holistic education eliminated her "either/or" mentality. She says Mead's "dualisms were discouraged; she was trained to accept unity of mind and body, thinking and feeling." Houston feels that Margaret's early training allowed her to "move in and out of her unconscious with ease." Most of these women had this ability but not to the degree of a Margaret Mead, who was in a class of her own in tapping the power of the unconscious to achieve the impossible.

Mead was unique, but we can all utilize our internal (unconscious) belief systems to assist us in our daily performance. The important thing is to make sure that our unconscious imprintings are positive and desirable images. If they are not, it is critical that we change our internal scripting to fit the positive model needed to reach our goals. Creative, visionary women like Margaret Mead have a programmed, unconscious tape that tells them to be limitless in all things. They live their lives fulfilling childhood images of great opportunities. They have a reality map totally open to whatever opportunities come along. This ability makes these women unique and facilitates their great creative achievement.

Single-Sex Schooling

All-girl schools, parochial schools, and boarding schools appear to be a significant factor in grooming females for later creative achievement. It creates an advantageous setting for them to experience early female role models. Many of these women had early female role models who appear to have been instrumental in their later success. A study called *Women in Power* (1993) found that great female political leaders in America were ten times more likely to have attended all-girl schools. One-half of all women in Congress and one-fourth of all female board members of *Fortune* 500 companies were found to have been educated in all-girl schools. *Women in Power* concluded that all-girl schools offer women better female role models since "girls defer to boys in coed groups." One successful female politician said, "Girls in coed schools don't succeed. Don't excel. You want the boys to like you, not to be the class brain."

Margaret Mead said much the same in her biography, *Blackberry Winter* (1972), when describing her move from a coed college to an all-girl college. She felt strongly that her all-girl schooling optimized her potential for empowerment as a female. She attended DePauw University in Chicago for one year at the behest of her father and then transferred to all-girl Barnard College in New York City because at DePauw "it became perfectly clear both that bright girls could do better than bright boys and that they would suffer for it." She went on to say, "As long as I remained at DePauw, I felt I was an exile." Mead was convinced that females competing for the attention of males in the college environment were incapable of being successful due to the pressure to allow the boys to be superior. At Barnard College she could run for office and be as competitive as she liked without hurting her chances for dates. She made lifelong friends at Barnard who came to be known as the "Ash Can Cats." Mead was their leader and Ruth Benedict became their role model and ultimately Mead's friend, confidante, and companion.

Six of these women attended all-female primary, secondary, or college institutions (see figure 7). Maria Callas, Liz Claiborne, Jane Fonda, Madonna, Gloria Steinem, and Margaret Thatcher benefitted from having female role models in these all-girl school environments. Four of the nine who attended college for any period of time matriculated at all-girl colleges.

Only Ayn Rand, Oprah Winfrey, and Linda Wachner graduated from co-educational institutions. Those who graduated from all-female schools were Gloria Steinem (Smith) and Thatcher (Somerville). Jane Fonda spent two arduous years at Vassar and saw many female role models but their influence is questionable since her sorority sisters said she was seldom there. Margaret Thatcher benefitted the most from female role models in school as she had the unique distinction of having never attended class with a boy until graduate school. She had gone through elementary, secondary, and college in all-female institutions.

Figure 7

SINGLE-SEX SCHOOLING

Maria Callas	Parochial and public school in New York City until eighth grade
Liz Claiborne	Parochial schools in Belgium and New Orleans
Jane Fonda	Boarding schools in California and Connecticut; all-girl prep schools (Greenwich Academy, Connecticut; Emma Willard, New York), and Vassar, an all-girl college in Poughkeepsie, New York
Madonna	Parochial schools through high school with nuns as role models
Gloria Steinem	Various schools all over the United States. No school for one full year until sixth grade. New York and Washington, D.C., schools. Smith College, a women's college
Margaret Thatcher	All-girl elementary and secondary schools and then on to Somerville College, Oxford—a women's college. Graduate school was her first education experience with males.

Summary

Formal education appears not to be a factor in the success of great females. Eight of the thirteen women in this study did not have a college degree and only one—Margaret Thatcher—had graduate training. In spite of their lack of formal education these women were well educated in their fields of expertise. They gained their knowledge through a heuristic, trial-and-error approach to problem resolution earned at the grassroots level of innovation. These women learned by doing. Their knowledge was their power and they tended to know more about their given profession than anyone, including those who had superior educations in the field.

Intelligence or IQ does not appear to be a factor in the success of female creative genius. Ironically, Madonna probably has one of the highest IQs of any of the women. All of them were bright, but other personal traits such as perseverance, risk-taking propensity, charisma, self-esteem, and work ethic were greater factors in their success than intelligence. However, they were all gifted, and as such were intolerant of useless conformity. This made them dislike bureaucrats. Their intolerance made them nonconformists, which tends to be a positive trait for successful creative endeavor. These women were not overly endowed with knowledge of their fields prior to entering it. They succeeded in spite of not knowing their limitations. The experts predicted their early demise because they were operating in a man's world or in an area unfamiliar to them. They proved the experts wrong.

Single-sex schooling appears to have been another positive contributing factor to their success. Half of the women attended schools where they saw female role models in action at a very early age. This experience instilled the knowledge that a woman can reach the top and be successful without relying on their feminine mystique or gaining approval from a male mentor. These successful visionary women are now role models for other young women around the world to admire and emulate. They have proved that knowledge is power and can be tapped by anyone willing to pay the price.

4

Creative Renegades Go Where Others Fear to Tread!

We should fear the "known" far more than the "unknown."
—Deepak Chopra, M.D.

Break all the rules. Swim upstream. Go the other way. Ignore the conventional wisdom. If everybody else is doing it one way, there's a good chance you can find your niche in exactly the opposite direction.
—Sam Walton

Experts are people with an omniscient belief in their own view of reality—and consequently they never discover anything new or worthwhile in life. They are fundamentalists who are *always* right! Conversely, neophytes are those who do not know their limitations, what is attainable, or which product will sell—and therefore are destined to become the innovators and creators of new, breakthrough concepts. Such neophyte visionaries "know" intuitively that there is no *absolute* right or wrong path to reality and therefore move toward their goals with incisive accuracy and surprising haste. They are not mired in someone else's reality map; they devise their own guide to the promised land. Their vision, if on target, destroys the old maps. Experts are always fearful of the new and unknown and label novel concepts preposterous, allowing the innovators and entrepreneurs an opportunity to move unfettered into the creative void. Creative geniuses are usually paid handsomely for pioneering and taking risks. Their resulting wealth and acclaim are small remuneration for the immense contributions they make to society. These thirteen visionaries ignored experts and changed the world through their divergent behavior. They refused to follow the crowd and therefore became the acknowledged leaders in their given areas of expertise.

Macro-Vision: Creators See the Forest—Not the Trees

A holistic, macro, big-picture view of the world was critical to success for these women. They were able to resolve complex problems with "simple" solutions. Lillian Vernon knew that women wanted unique, personalized items not available in traditional catalogs, so she created her own distinctive direct-marketing approach to reach these people. She knew she had no chance of success going head to head with Sears or Penney's catalogs. Her intuitive vision was right on target as the Sears catalog is now out of business and Lillian Vernon catalogs are experiencing record sales.

Creative women see the big picture but implement their solutions with a simple vision. They understand that too much knowledge is counterproductive to creative achievement. They ignore micro-vision "experts" who protect their ego investment in the known. Experts know the world is flat. They are wrong! The Wright brothers' flight was a hoax, according to many newspaper accounts of that first flight. But the so-called hoax revolutionized the world of travel. CNN was a stupid idea, according to the networks. But Ted Turner's innovation has changed television and is now the primary competitor of the same networks that predicted his demise. The experts told Ayn Rand that her writing would never sell, but she has sold over twenty-five million copies of her three major books. Experts knew that videotapes could never sell: they could only be rented. But Jane Fonda proved them wrong and in the process sold more videos than anyone in history. The political power brokers in Britain saw Margaret Thatcher as an anomaly of the times, not a serious threat. She believed in her destiny and acceded to the pinnacle of British politics. The lawyers and accountants for both Mary Kay Ash and Estée Lauder told them they would fail. Both women ignored the advice and now could buy these lawyers out of their petty cash. These female visionaries had macro-vision: they made decisions based on long-range possibilities, which enabled them to outperform the world's micro-vision experts.

Self-Confidence: The Catalyst of All Creativity

A potent self-confidence is the most important attribute of creative genius, especially when the objective is to break new ground on innovative, large-scale projects. Pioneers are always faced with fighting the system and the so-called industry experts. This can only be done with an awesome self-confidence. Some people confuse insecurity with lack of confidence. These women had many insecurities but overachieved in their drive to excel and overcome their feelings of inadequacy. Their performance anxiety became a positive motivation in their pursuit of excellence. Psychologists such as Rollo May have demonstrated that notable performance requires a minimal amount of anxiety. In fact, anxiety enhances performance. These women overcame their insecurities with moxie and daring. To the outside world their behavior looked much like self-confidence, even when it was a pseudoconfidence based on angst. Whatever it's called, it worked.

Virtually no one believed in these women or their concepts before they made it to the top. They had to believe in themselves along the way in order to overcome the enormous skepticism of their adversaries and friends. Marilyn Ferguson, the brilliant visionary writer, discusses the problem of cynical experts in her book *The Aquarian Conspiracy* (1976). She says self-confidence is critical for overcoming the cynical traditionalists when creating new paradigms: "New paradigms are nearly always received with coolness, even mockery and hostility. Their discoveries are attacked for their heresy. . . . Our fear of conformity has been due in part to our fear of ourselves, our doubts about the rightness of our decisions."

Ayn Rand gives substance to this same thesis. "I submit that any man who ascribes success to *luck* has never achieved anything and has no inkling of the relentless effort which achievement requires." Both Ayn Rand and Linda Wachner have said that most women have had a problem with success because they have been groomed to cherish "approval" when young. Mary Kay Ash, Linda Wachner, and Oprah Winfrey have been quite vocal in criticizing women for an unwillingness to risk disapproval or violate the prevailing paternalistic society. It takes great confidence to proceed in the face of adversity, especially when the advice comes from those you have been trained to respect. These women were willing to ignore the experts. That is not to say they didn't pay a terrible price for their iconoclastic behavior. But they subjugated their female needs to their obsession for achievement. They fought the so-called experts every day, and prevailed. They utilized their extraordinary self-esteems and resolute self-confidence in accomplishing their objectives in the face of their detractors. Only their self-confidence prevailed when the going got rough. Golda Meir faced death and devastation for the better part of her life but remained confident and optimistic. That confidence was instrumental in the creation of a free Israeli state, which may not have happened without her resolute self-confidence.

Cellular Knowledge and Creativity

Deepak Chopra's quote at the beginning of this chapter about the known being more deadly to creativity than the unknown is pertinent for aspiring creative geniuses. Chopra contends that we tend to limit our potential opportunities in life based on our preconceived idea of what can or cannot be accomplished.

We often know too much about what "is" to grasp what "can be." Chopra preaches this gospel relative to mental and physical health. He illustrates in his lectures how every cell in the body is replaced every year. When asked why the cancer and AIDS victims are not then cured each year with the new cells, he explains that the "experts" continually reproduce deadly cells because of their intellectual arrogance. He goes on to explain that the body replaces every cell with a new cell each year. But the mind becomes the limiting link as it has sixty thousand thoughts a day and 90 percent of them are conditioned to be just like the old cells in their genetic makeup. Therefore, a dogmatic mentality can cause the sick to stay sick since they replicate their cells with negative cells and conversely the healthy stay healthy for the very same reason. The negative thoughts of the sick (preprogrammed cells) contaminate the new healthy cells, resulting in no change in the medical prognosis of the patient. Cancer and AIDS patients preordain their own health by replicating their "sick cell" thoughts, which are then imprinted daily into their brain cells, defining the character of the new cells in their body.

Chopra is preaching that our internal knowledge of being sick is what keeps us sick. We kill ourselves based on too much knowledge that we "are sick." Studies have shown that cases of spontaneous remission virtually all occur in "little old ladies" who are not steeped in too much knowledge. They have a high incidence of recovery only because they don't know they should die. Statistics show that early fatalities in cancer and AIDS tend to be doctors and other experts who "know" the probability of their mortality. Creativity, entrepreneurship, and innovation are much like our health. Knowledge is critically important (see chapter 3); however, it is very important to have an open mind when it comes to new concepts and not to "know too much." Preknowledge of *how* something is accomplished is important, but preknowledge of *what* can be accomplished is counterproductive to the creative process. In other words, our internal visualizations of reality will dictate our creative potential. One of the interesting findings in the research on both male and female creative geniuses is that they virtually never got sick even though they abused their physical and emotional systems as total type-A workaholics (the subject for another book).

Intellectual Arrogance and Creativity

Unsuccessful people know *everything*, successful people know *too much*, and geniuses know *very little!* A paradox? No! Experience teaches us all too well what doesn't work, what not to try, and what cannot be done. In fact, the sacrilege of our school systems is that that is exactly what they attempt to do. They teach students their limitations incarnate. Columbus was taught that the world was flat, but he didn't buy it. Almost everyone else did. Professor Silvanus P. Thompson said that Edison's electric light bulb project was "doomed to failure and showed the most airy ignorance of the fundamental principles both of electricity and dynamics." The professor was not alone in this thinking as Dr. Henry Morton of the Stevens Institute called Edison's findings on the electric lamp "absurd claims attributed by sheer ignorance." These two educated men were deriding a man with but three months of formal education who just happened to be right. The poor, uneducated Edison was not so constrained by what was possible and what was not—so he did the impossible. He created the truth. True creative genius, like that of Edison, emerges out of the admission of ignorance. These creative women had the same simple intuitive mentality that led them to ignore the establishment and the experts. Margaret Mead said it very eloquently in *Blackberry Winter*: "It was clear to me that I was a deviant in the sense that I had a much greater interest in the kinds of things in which most women, not committed to careers, were interested."

Excess Knowledge Can Kill!

Numerous studies have shown that the great innovators of the world had open minds, allowing them to explore virgin territory. History has given numerous examples of how experts, in their zeal to protect tradition, have stifled creativity. Even Edison refuted the alternating current theory of Tesla because it was not compatible with his concept of reality and mostly because it violated the logic of his own direct current innovation. Examples abound where too much knowledge has proved deadly to those who steadfastly believe what they are told by experts. (Thomas S. Kuhn theorized in *Scientific Revolutions* that no new paradigm can gain universal acceptance by the masses until the influential experts of the old paradigm die off.)

Consider the man who was accidentally locked in a refrigerated railroad car. He knew he would die of the cold if not rescued within hours. He kept notes and scribbled on the car walls as he was nearing death saying, "It is getting colder and colder. It's almost over." When the dead man was found the next day, the car's refrigeration unit was investigated and found to be inoperative. The temperature was 58 degrees. The man "knew" too much and it killed him.

Medical science has recorded an even more bizarre story. Eight men were trapped in a cave and knew they would die unless rescued within days because of their lack of food and water. Only one man had a watch so he was assigned the responsibility for announcing the elapsed time to the others, so they would know their chances of living. The man lied to keep up the spirits of the others. He told them 30 minutes had elapsed when an hour had gone by. He kept up this fabrication for days. The group was rescued a week later, far too long for any of them to have lived without water. Everyone was alive except the time keeper, who knew the truth. Too much knowledge had killed him and too little knowledge had saved the others.

Psychologists have shown that thinking "it" does make it so. If a baseball manager says to the pitcher, "Don't throw the ball high and inside," all that is recorded in the pitcher's unconscious mind is the exact opposite of the manager's intent: "high and inside." The only appropriate communication should have been the pertinent information necessary for recording on the unconscious. In this example, "low and outside" should be the only language communicated. Visualizing the positive is the only way to imprint the appropriate image on the mind for successful behavioral response. The two criteria for this are: limiting knowledge to what is pertinent, and imprinting new positive knowledge. Our thirteen female visionaries never allowed old dogmas to delude them into thinking about anything other than their ultimate goals.

Creative Genius Goes Where Others Fear to Tread

Madonna told her producer to break the rules, to go where no one else had been. She insisted that they try the "different," even if it was nontraditional. That philosophy helped her break the Beatles' all-time record for number one hits during the eighties and made her wealthy along the way. Margaret Thatcher, in her very first position of power as minister of education, stopped free milk for kids in an attempt to get control over the education budget. She was criticized by the press and the opposition party promptly gave her the not-so-endearing title, "Thatcher the Milk Snatcher." The negative press said "Ditch the Bitch" and was adamant about her demise. Had she committed political suicide? She ignored the flack and became immersed in the future and proceeded inextricably toward her long-range goals. This daring act was just one of many that ultimately led Thatcher to the highest office in the land. She stepped up as the leader of the Conservative Party when no man had the temerity to take the impossible position. She was not afraid to step into the direct fire and take the heat, and it paid off for her in a big way.

Author Ayn Rand broke all the rules of writing novels with *The Fountainhead* and *Atlas Shrugged*. Her publisher begged her to recant and rewrite these epic novels, which were thought to be far too intellectual to ever sell to the average consumer. Rand knew nothing of publishing or demographic profiles for readership, but defiantly refused to change one word of her manuscripts, causing much animosity between herself and her publisher. History has proved her right, with more than twenty-five million sales of two books that had no future according to the experts. *The Fountainhead* became a highly acclaimed movie starring Gary Cooper.

Break the Rules

The ability to break the rules is a critical behavior trait for the creative visionary. When Sam Walton wrote his rules for successful entrepreneurship he said, "I always prided myself on breaking everybody else's rules, and I always favored the mavericks who challenged my rules." This philosophy made him the world's richest man by the mid-eighties. In his 1990 biography, Walton said, "First of all break the rules. . . . Everybody who knew I was going ahead with the discounting idea really did think I'd just completely lost my mind. Nobody wanted to gamble on that first Wal-Mart. . . . We pledged houses and property, everything we had."

Like Sam Walton, Mary Kay Ash was told by her lawyer, "Liquidate the business right now and recoup whatever cash you can. If you don't you'll end up penniless." Her accountant told her she was destined to fail after her husband suddenly died of a heart attack just thirty days before opening her first store. Ash was not deterred by these doomsayers. She went on to create a billion-dollar cosmetics empire. Ironically, Estée Lauder had been told the exact same thing about fifteen years earlier by her accountant and her lawyer. They told her to refrain from competing in a cut-throat business in which she had little chance of success. She ignored their advice and built a multibillion dollar cosmetics empire.

Golda Meir went where most males would have refused to go. She crawled across a desert at night to meet with her mortal enemy, King Abdullah of Jordan in a last-minute quest for peace prior to Israeli statehood. She carried hand grenades in her bra to protect her countrymen and ensure the preservation of the Israeli state. She also spent much of her life living an ascetic existence on subsistence wages. She slept on a couch for almost thirty years without complaining. And most women would never have been able to cope with wearing two cotton dresses for many years, which she alternated by wearing one while the other was being washed. These material things were not important to this passionately driven woman, not even makeup. She broke most rules of femininity but was ironically considered ravishing and sensuous up to age fifty.

Iconoclastic Females

Many female visionaries are considered rebels because they defy the establishment. Jane Fonda, Maria Callas, Lillian Vernon, Madonna, Ayn Rand, and Gloria Steinem were particularly recalcitrant female visionaries. They had strong self-esteem and self-confidence, which allowed them to challenge tradition without threatening their egos. Their eccentricities resulted in considerable rejection and hostility from their peers and adversaries. They were prone to off-the-wall decisions, which made them interesting but different. Consider immigrant Ayn Rand (alias Alissa Rosenbaum) taking her name from a typewriter logo, marrying her "hunk" Hollywood extra so as not to be deported, and then demanding to keep her borrowed name, Rand. Or imagine Maria Callas telling her Roman Catholic husband, Batista, to cancel an audience with the pope: "I don't want to see the pope this morning. It's rainy, it's a grey day and wearing black would irritate me. We'll go some other time." Batista went crazy in a vain attempt to explain that no one stands up a pope because it's raining. Callas stood her ground, and the pope—a great opera fan—granted her another visit, at which time the volatile maverick Callas proceeded to get into a heated argument with him over operatic ethics.

Steinem told one all-female audience, "Do one outrageous thing in the cause of simple justice during the next twenty-four hours." Hanoi Jane followed Gloria's advice for over five years. She declared, "I'm a revolutionary" in 1969, and by 1972 was sitting on a North Vietnam howitzer broadcasting live to GIs pleading for them to stop fighting, in the tradition of Tokyo Rose of World War II fame. These outrageous acts and behavior were not without cost. Most women would have been devastated by the continual mental flagellation these visionaries faced almost daily. Catherine the Great proved to be one of the more iconoclastic females in history. She reversed the accepted gender roles in society by riding her stallion like a man and kept a stable of handsome young men for her pleasure. Mother Teresa could be equally renegade. The pope, on a trip to India, donated a new Cadillac to Mother Teresa for transportation. Most women would have followed political decorum and used it, at least ceremoniously. But the nonconforming Mother Teresa ignored etiquette, sold it, and gave the monies to the poor. Margaret Mead even went so far as to describe herself and husband Gregory Bateson as "deviants."

Many of these nonconformists were given less-than-attractive labels by their adversaries. Thatcher endured the "Iron Lady" sobriquet and it actually worked to her favor. Callas was labeled the "Diabolical Diva." Even Mother Teresa was called a "religious imperialist" by Germaine Greer. Madonna became synonymous with the "Bimbo of Babylon" and the "Material Girl." She endured the reputation as the most arcane and sexually perverse female of the twentieth century, to her delight. She said, "I saw losing my virginity as a career move," which gives some insight into her renegade nature. She enraged 20,000 Puerto Ricans in late 1993 by passing their flag between her legs as only Madonna could do. Rand earned the label "Epistemological Conscience" by castigating Kant, Skinner, Sullivan, and Sartre. Wachner was labeled "Fire and Ice" and the "Hatchet Lady" for her cold-blooded approach to the bottom line in business. She was infamous for a business philosophy of "my way or the highway." Winfrey is known as "America's Psychiatrist" for her empathic and sympathetic guest interviews. Ash acquired the title "Queen of Queens" bestowed by her adoring consultants. These images often became inextricably immersed in the personalities and behavior of these women and they usually lived up to their reputations (we all have an innate propensity to do so).

All thirteen of these female mavericks constantly rebelled in one way or another against the establishment and tradition. Estée Lauder rebelled, but not as vocally or antagonistically as others. She learned to live with the harsh realities of her early life, but determined to change it or bury it as an adult. In developing her company she never allowed the harsh "realities" of life to interfere with her objective. She characterized herself in her autobiography as "a woman on a mission." Margaret Thatcher and Golda Meir gained reputations as indomitable personalities. They minced no words in telling it the way they saw it. Lillian Vernon, Liz Claiborne, and Mary Kay Ash were far more submissive in their struggle to the top and are admired for their efforts as being tough but nice. All were independent spirits who never feared marching to their own drummer even when it differed from the band.

Experts: Purveyors of Self-Indulgence

The January 1906 *Scientific American* rejected the Wright brothers' flight as a hoax. J. P. Morgan, the financial genius of his time, wrote to Alexander Graham Bell and told him his phone invention "had no commercial applications." Admiral William Leahy, an expert in explosives, announced in June 1945, one month prior to the bombing of Hiroshima, "the Manhattan Project is the biggest fool thing we have ever done. The bomb will never go off, and I speak as an expert in explosives." An expert is someone with a belief in their own omniscience. They never discover anything new or worthwhile because they are too busy protecting their own turf. Their ego is at stake and they must protect it at all costs. Henry Ford came face to face with the experts in building his empire in the early twentieth century and coined the most succinct and accurate description of an expert as "someone who knows all the reasons an idea will not work." Mark Sheppard, the president of Texas Instruments in the seventies, was asked how he beat out the giants of industry (Westinghouse, GE, Raytheon, RCA). His eloquent response was, "Those companies knew all the things that weren't possible. We didn't. We were stupid."

Marilyn Ferguson, author of *The Aquarian Conspiracy* (1976) said, "Our fear of conformity has been due in part to our fear of ourselves, our doubts about the rightness of our decisions." Conformity was not one of the traits found in any of the women in this work, although the women tended to be less demonstrative and blatantly outrageous in their eccentricities than their male counterparts. Margaret Mead confused her adversaries, "I was accused of antifeminism by women, of rampant feminism by men."

Expertise Is in the Gut

All of these women ignored expert opinion. Liz Claiborne launched a line of women's professional clothes that appealed to her particular tastes. This was in complete defiance of the expert garment manufacturers of the 1970s. Madonna continually broke with all tradition as the most rebellious of any of the women in this work, or possibly in this century. Her book *Sex* (1993) and banned videos are testimony to her iconoclastic nature. Lillian Vernon has always expressed a preference for being "different"; she claims it is what made her successful. She ignores traditional market research methodologies in lieu of her own "Golden Gut" approach to market analysis. Jane Fonda, one-time leader of the New Left and foe of capitalism, became the consummate capitalist. She founded a chain of workout studios and launched the best-selling fitness videos of all time, which made her, paradoxically, an eminent capitalist. This woman then added to the anomaly by donating all the monies (estimated at over $100 million) to her husband Tom Hayden's left-wing causes. The coup de grace was when Fonda married the consummate capitalist and antithesis of all her left-wing political causes, Ted Turner. Turner had spent his career as an accomplished womanizer, the titan of capitalism, and was of the political right. Fonda not only defied the experts she has manifestly confused them.

Even the passive and seemingly docile Mother Teresa defied the experts in her desire to help the poor. She broke the rules of her order, asking the pope for permission to leave her order and live in the ghettos of Calcutta. This was unprecedented but she was able to gain papal approval and used her position of power to make extraordinary gains with the poor and dying of Calcutta. Her success earned her a Nobel Prize for her herculean efforts. These women are living testimony that there is far more creativity in the "gut" than in the head.

Fear the Known, Not the Unknown

We are our worst enemies since we "know" what our limitations are. These female visionaries were capable of ignoring their own internal self-talk and functioned on a higher plane of optimistic euphoria. They had enormous visions of their self-worth and defied anyone to refute their internal belief systems. They did not know their limitations and therefore had none. They did not know they couldn't achieve so they did. Margaret Mead didn't know that a twenty-five-year-old unaccompanied female should not be wandering alone around the jungles of New Guinea and Samoa. Margaret Thatcher did not bother to ask whether a female prime minister of Great Britain was acceptable to her constituency. She had virtually no chance of acceding to that lofty position, but she did. Oprah Winfrey was not deterred that Phil Donahue owned the daytime talk show market; it took her all of six months to surpass him in the ratings. None of these women could have succeeded based on the common belief by the establishment. They never asked the question and therefore moved into their castles in the sky as if it was their right to do so.

Risk-Taking Mentality: Confidence versus Fear

All children and employees should be given the opportunity to risk and fail, or no knowledge, self-confidence, or self-worth are ever acquired. Creative ability is a function of early experiential activity and if children are not allowed to risk and fail, they will never learn the critical ingredients of creativity. Catherine the Great told one of her ministers of state, "There is no woman bolder than I. I have the most reckless audacity." It was this attitude that led her to become the most famous woman in Russian history, and she wasn't even Russian. Mother Teresa actually took greater personal risks than the other women in this book. She worked and slept among the terminally ill for fifty years. She lived in a leper colony and defied medical science in her trek to help the indigent and poor of the world.

The risk-taking propensity of the average woman is less than that of the average male for two major reasons. *Biologically,* the female has significantly lower levels of testosterone, the hormone responsible for male aggressiveness, competitiveness, risk-taking, and high sex drive. *Sociologically,* the female has historically been trained to revere "security" not "risk." Females have a heritage of securing the household and protection of the children. In the minds of females risk-taking has been the province of males. However, the visionary females in this book were found to be far more risk oriented than the average female. It appears they were blessed with higher levels of testosterone in addition to having been raised to be self-sufficient and competitive, and to risk and fail without loss of self-esteem. The thrill of the chase was probably the dominant factor in their ultimate success.

Most risk-taking behavior is formed in childhood. Parents must allow their children the chance to risk and fail if they are to develop into adults willing to risk achievement. Mary Kay Ash's mother left her to tend to an invalid father and would be gone for fourteen hours at a time while Mary Kay stood on chairs to cook food for her bedridden dad. She would call her mother twenty times a day to get the encouragement on how to function as an adult. Mary Kay was forced to risk at the age of seven and never forgot the experience. Risk was not a negative word in Mary Kay's vocabulary.

Just like parents, corporations must allow their employees the opportunity to risk and fail if they are to build self-confident, risk-oriented capable employees. The same risk/reward training found in child-rearing must be tolerated in business. This mentality is built by the leader in every organization. Most organizations are static; consequently, they seldom innovate.

I have found that management types fall into three distinct categories in most organizations. There are *risk-takers,* who are necessary for all entrepreneurial or innovative organizations; *care-takers,* who inhabit most static or mature organizations; and *under-takers,* who are usually found in organizations in decline or in chaos (see *Profiles of Genius* [1993]). All of these women were risk-oriented.

Risk and Intuition

Risk-takers are the management types who found start-up companies or who break new ground, like the females in this book. These intuitive types are necessary for any creative endeavor and therefore have a higher proclivity for gambling than the norm. Traditionalists preach the preservation of the asset base. Older people and organizations tend to take less risks. They have more to lose and therefore become more risk-averse since more is at risk and they are more mature in their stage of life. However, removing all risk from anything in life eliminates all the potential and opportunity. The potential for opportunity is always in direct proportion to the risk. Only great risk offers great achievement. Children locked in living rooms will never skin their knees, but will also never accomplish anything worthwhile. Is the elimination of risk worth the cost? Not usually, considering the limited life span we have to achieve our goals. The child who is never allowed to risk pioneering is unlikely to ever contribute anything worthwhile to society because they are constrained by self-preservation motives.

Employees who are never allowed the opportunity to make risky decisions will likely freeze at the first opportunity to do so. The only way to groom an employee capable of successfully functioning in a dynamic environment is to train them to operate in a dynamic environment. The logical conclusion of this argument is that if risk-taking and creativity are highly correlated then no creative adult can ever be spawned in a risk-averse environment. Children must be allowed and encouraged to risk and fail in order to build creative and innovative adults. These thirteen women had that opportunity due to having been raised in permissive environments that encouraged risk-taking rather than security. Self-preservation was never high on their list of need. Opportunity is never possible without substantial risk.

Risk and Parental Guidance

A prime example of the positive aspects of instilling a risk mentality in your child is the story told by Richard Branson's mother. Branson is the English entrepreneurial genius who built Virgin Records and Virgin Airlines, the third largest conglomerate in Britain. While he was in grammar school Richard's mother decided to teach him the art of self-reliance and the ability to cope with risk. She dropped him in a field five miles from home and challenged him to find his way home. She told "60 Minutes" that this risk-oriented learning experience was instrumental in "developing his highly successful entrepreneurial behavior." Branson's mother could have practiced psychology with a specialty in self-image. Her son has won many air balloon races and is the consummate entrepreneur in a normally risk-averse society. This high school dropout, who has defied the establishment in every business venture he has attempted, became a billionaire before the age of forty. He did it with little more than a risk-taking mentality formed in childhood.

Unsuccessful individuals are often blessed with even greater talents than Richard Branson or the overachieving women in this work. These risk-averse individuals usually have an internal need to fulfill a negative self-image or revere a risk-free lifestyle. Their intrinsic fear of failure typically makes them afraid to pioneer in the unknown areas of creativity, innovation, and entrepreneurship. While the risk-averse person is afraid to fail, the successful entrepreneur typically is driven by a fear of not succeeding. Bill Gates at age thirty-seven is the richest man in America and admits that fear drives his performance every day. Oprah Winfrey has repeatedly admitted that she fears failure most of all and it is this fear that drives her to achieve. This innate fear of failure ironically is the driving force for both the creative genius and the noncreative—the former is positive, the latter negative. Creative individuals worry about how to win and the noncreative worry about how not to lose. Most world-class athletes know this axiom intuitively.

Female leaders and innovators groom themselves in a kind of survival training. They know intuitively how to survive and succeed in a world of uncertainty. They learn very early in life that risk-taking is more a function of the preparation for risk and not dependent on the nature of the risk. It is only a gamble if not treated as a risk. Mary Kay Ash said of her venture, "I didn't see it as a risk. I saw it as an opportunity. . . . I just never even thought about the fact it would fail. That was not a possibility." The risk taking propensity of these women is summarized in figure 8.

The Greater Risk Is Not Risking

Psychiatrist and writer David Viscott in his book *Risking* says that the most likely person to be killed in a traffic accident at an intersection is not the one who acts but the one who hesitates. Risk-taking in this instance is dangerous because of fear and has nothing to do with preparation. Not acting or taking the appropriate risk is often more dangerous than taking it. Ted Turner often said that the greater risk to him was in *not* buying MGM, not *buying* it. Had he not bought MGM he would not have had the movies necessary for the vast amount of airtime for his numerous cable channels. Nevertheless, the industry experts said he was crazy. Just five years later they said he was a genius. He said, "No I wasn't. I was just taking the lesser of the risks."

In most instances risk-taking tends to be an invigorating and exciting experience. At the amusement park, the most exciting ride is the roller coaster, which appears risky but is not, yet generates fear and thrills to those not comfortable with the ride. Confidence is built in taking risks and overcoming the innate fear of the unknown. When we get very old, it is not the risks we took on the way that we will regret, but those risks we never had the temerity to take. The subjects in this book all would have said the greater risk in their lives would have been not having taken the risk. No one has ever regretted the risks they took, only those they never had the guts to take.

These female visionaries learned early on to risk and fail. Their early training contributed to building strong self-images and molded them into creative and innovative adults. They typically viewed risk as a positive "opportunity" to pursue their dreams. As they conquered each new milestone along the way they became stronger for the experience and more prepared for the next great challenge or risk. They became more confident and conditioned to view each new risk as less dangerous than the previous one. They built stronger and stronger risk-taking personas, becoming more comfortable in hazardous environments. The result was divergent and nonconformist behavior, that appeared risky to the media and their peers. To them it was just another walk in the park.

Standing on a podium in front of five thousand people is only considered a risk if people are afraid of failing or making fools of themselves. To the person with tremendous self-assurance and confidence such an experience is not a risk but a unique challenge. That is not to confuse risk with anxiety. Anxiety is good up to a point, but it has nothing to do with risk. It is okay to worry about succeeding and doing the very best job. That is different from worrying over the decision to risk. This same mental process is at work in most business ventures. Examples abound. These thirteen women had a high propensity for risk, which has set them apart from most women who have been reticent about taking risks.

Figure 8

Risk-Taking Propensity of Visionary Women

Visionary	Risk Nature and Propensity
Mary Kay Ash	"I didn't see it as a risk. I saw it as an opportunity. . . . I just never even thought about the fact it would fail. That was not a possibility."
Maria Callas	Ran through a barrage of machine gun fire during the war, and sailed alone to New York City and a new career after the war. Risked career, husband, and everything for her true love, Aristotle Onassis.
Liz Claiborne	Put her $50,000 life savings on the "come-line" at age 47 and would have been broke had Liz Claiborne, Inc., not made it.
Jane Fonda	Fearless competitor in spite of opposition or the odds against her beliefs. She sued the FBI, President Nixon, the U.S. Congress and government for $2.8 million and won.
Estée Lauder	"Risk taking is the cornerstone of empires." She built hers in a constant display of gutsy moves around or through her competitors.
Madonna	Former manager Camille Burbonne said, "Madonna lived on the edge always and was not afraid of anything." She purposely violated all traditional approaches to dress, entertainment, and stage props.
Golda Meir	She had no fear of failure. "I can honestly say that I was never deflected from doing something because I thought I might fail." She carried hand grenades in her bra and crawled across a desert in the middle of the night to meet her mortal enemy, King Abdullah.
Ayn Rand	Purposely came to America from Russia on a six-month visa never intending to return and got married to avoid deportation. From then on she led a life of risk by opposing the leftist establishment prevalent during the thirties and forties.
Gloria Steinem	Risked her esteem and life in cause after cause and participated in many militant marches that often turned violent. She would roam the streets of Harlem doing stories others would never consider.
Margaret Thatcher	"Fearless and indomitable spirit" according to more than one biographer. The Iron Lady was resilient, intransigent, and always willing to risk to obtain the result necessary for her government.
Lillian Vernon	"Be prepared to take risks. . . . I take chances relying on my 'Golden Gut.' "
Linda Wachner	An avid downhill skier and competitive spirit, she bet everything she had ($10 million) in a hostile takeover of Warnaco.
Oprah Winfrey	Always willing to risk everything for what is right, she's a very vulnerable lady who bares her soul in order for others to do the same. Her restaurant, named "Eccentric," tells the story of her risk-taking propensity.

Female Fear of Risk

Females, as the nurturers of civilization, have been trained for millions of years to be risk-averse. They have been protected, conditioned, and encouraged to value security and avoid taking chances. Stone Age females bore the children and were then relegated to the cave (household) to protect them. This heritage groomed them to become nurturing and securing individuals, protecting the family against any outside intrusion or disruption. Women were not inclined to venture far from the safety of the cave or the home. Conversely, males evolved as risk-takers in the relationship, and were expected to forage for food in the unknown wilds outside the safety of the home. This heritage has given the male and female unique perspectives on risk-taking. Males traditionally explore new territory and are more comfortable taking greater risks while females are more comfortable maintaining and securing the household against outside risk. Females on average are far more risk-averse than males due to this heritage.

Females are less likely to bet the farm since the farm is family security. Conversely, males are far more at ease dealing with uncertainty and tend to opt for the riskier path than the typical female. The female need for personal security and for the safety of children is greater than for the typical male. Our thirteen women were not so steeped in security, and in fact had a higher propensity for taking risks, pioneering, and living on the edge than the average female. It appears that their tolerance for risk and ambiguity was even greater than that of most males. Their indulgent households taught them freedom to explore and risk without fear. This early grooming appears to have programmed them to be more content in risk-oriented environments. Research has shown that "freedom" to explore and fail in trial-and-error situations develops venturesome individuals who make excellent innovators. One study in Israel compared boys and girls in kibbutz environments relative to both Western and Middle-Eastern environments. Alison Stallibrass in *The Self-Respecting Child* (1979) found that kibbutz-raised children had the edge in intellectual development based on an early environment allowing them the freedom to explore. She says, "Freedom to explore our environment and develop our bodily abilities is a link to intellectual development." This early freedom to explore and fail appears to be critical in developing creative risk-taking adults.

Female Intuition

According to Albert Einstein, "The really valuable thing is intuition." He relied on intuition more than any other trait in his quests for the truths of the universe. Golda Meir intuited the Yom Kippur War but her prediction was ignored by her cabinet of males, who "knew" better. If she had listened to her intuition, many thousands of lives would have been spared. Catherine the Great had a similar intuitive insight with her prediction of the French Revolution and the coming of Napoleon. Note her comment dated 1788:

> When will this Caesar come? Oh! Come he will, make no doubt about it! If revolution takes hold. . . . If France survives, she will be stronger than she has ever been. . . . All she needs is a superior man, greater than his contemporaries, greater perhaps than an entire age. Has he already been born? . . . Will he come? Everything depends on that. (Troyat, 1980)

What vision. The superior man she described in 1788 had already been born in Corsica in 1769 and her vision would come to fruition within a few years. The French Revolution occurred just one year after her great insight, and Napoleon, arguably the greatest military leader in history, would assume the leadership of France in 1799. He proceeded to confirm her prediction of his destiny by conquering much of Europe, only to be denied total success by her country, Mother Russia.

Artists and musical prodigies are usually associated with the intuitive process, not entrepreneurs, innovators, politicians, and entertainers. However, there is little difference in the process of thinking out unique and novel concepts in any of these fields. The process entails having the intellectual freedom to explore new, disparate ideas without being constrained by existing norms. Not knowing where to go in exploring the truth is far more important than having a map, since the map is someone else's perception of reality, and it only outlines where someone else has been. In order to go where no one has been it is important to throw away the maps and create your own. These thirteen women threw away all maps and paved their own roads to their goals.

Female intuition has been found to be more than a figure of speech. Women tend to be more right-brain driven than men and have been allowed to express their emotions more freely. Western society has always been more tolerant of women openly expressing their feelings. Unlike men, women have therefore had far more cultural permission and freedom to experience self-awareness and to allow their right brains to explore the unknown. Doreen Kimura of the University of Western Ontario studied the human brain's right and left hemispheres and found that females apparently spread verbal tasks throughout both hemispheres, whereas males use only the left hemisphere. This substantiates the speculation that women are the more intuitive individuals in our society, which most empathic males already know.

Creativity is a qualitative rather than a quantitative process. Therefore, intuitive (right-brain) women tend to be more qualitative than men, which is one reason why they generally value relationships more than men. The male establishment typically operates by the numbers in a quantitative manner. This highly predictable environment lends itself to stability. But it also becomes a survival instinct for the establishment and "good old boy network" as they opt for maintaining the status quo at all costs. That is okay for the static organizations of the world, since they rely on stability and quantitative reliability. However, this quantitative mentality is diametrically opposed to what is necessary for success in the world of creativity and innovation. Dynamic societies and creative and innovative achievement demand a qualitative approach dependent on intuition. Therefore, females with an intuitive bent, highly tolerant of ambiguity and risk, are best suited to lead dynamic organizations. They will become the preeminent leaders in creative and innovative organizations if allowed to perform.

Right-Brain Thinking

Robert E. Ornstein's book *The Psychology of Consciousness* made the observation that our schools were training students in left-brain traditions to the detriment of their creativity. He found that schools emphasize analytical training over nonverbal training at the expense of creativity. "The artist, dancer, and mystic have learned to develop the nonverbal portion of intelligence" and therefore have become creative individuals. Fritjov Capra in *The Turning Point* (1982) sees the problem as a function of the Western world following an obsolete Copernican/Newtonian vision of man as a mechanical being. Capra accurately depicts the world as qualitative, not quantitative, as Descartes had described it. Ivy League colleges teach MBA students to model existing business in order to understand the vagaries of operating in a dynamic environment. This is good for static organizations and the absolute worst way to train students in the new and unknown world of entrepreneurship. You cannot research the existing to learn about the new. This methodology is the personification of obsolete Cartesian thinking, which produces mechanical models of perfection that are out of touch with the real world. The great innovators and creative geniuses have somehow escaped this worship of the *numbers*. The right-brain-driven innovators have learned to use the qualitative problem-solving techniques necessary for operating in a dynamic society. Mother Teresa, with her simple approach to achievement, saw this better than most: "If we wait until we get the numbers, then we will be lost in the numbers."

  Scientists have long since found that the left hemisphere of the brain controls the *verbal, sequential, digital, and logical thinking processes.* This Western approach is the left-brain orientation around the organized and predictable. Conversely, the right hemisphere of the brain is responsible for the *nonverbal, visual-spatial, perceptual, and intuitive,* which is more Eastern in nature. The right-hemisphere thinking is where our spontaneous and divergent ideas come from. Einstein knew this well. When disembarking from a ship in New York a young reporter asked him the distance from the Earth to the Moon. Einstein said he didn't know, causing the reporter to pontificate that any high school student knew this simple fact. Einstein said, "If I need to know such trivia I know where to find it. I need to devote my mental energies to more important subjects." He knew that his right-brain intuitive powers would be inhibited by the useless dedication to left-brain quantitative facts. He was not about to deflect his right-brain thinking with an abundance of left-brain trivia.

Scientists have also shown that the left brain is dominant in the sense that when one is in the process of counting numbers it is virtually impossible to be having spontaneous and intuitive or creative thoughts. That is why great insights occur on airplanes, in the shower, or just prior to waking. The mind is not burdened with quantitative problem solving at these times, leaving the right brain, the intuitive brain, open to creative insight. How then can we put ourselves into this creative state? Relaxation, meditation, sensory deprivation chambers, and sleep are the ways to get there. You cannot be creative while sitting behind a calculator or typewriter, for at these times the left brain is in charge of your thinking and until it is dormant the right brain has no chance of operating effectively. Put the left brain in neutral by taking a walk on the beach and the right brain will be allowed to perform its magical, intuitive powers. Lillian Vernon uses this approach in her new product selection. She never uses formal market research techniques but relies on what she calls "my Golden Gut," which is her way of saying, "I only sell a product I would buy myself."

Visualization

Anton Wilson, the popular New Wave writer, says very accurately, "The future exists first in imagination, then in will, then in reality." Carl Jung preceded Wilson's view, saying in 1933, "Visualization is the mechanism of creation." Visualization and imagery are not constrained by what "is"; they pursue what "might be." Therefore, listening to one's own inner feelings allows for new, unknown revelations to cross the mind. It allows an individual the freedom to err, to remove the ego, and to disregard peer influence. Internally imprinting the scripts of success is the only way to accomplish breakthrough creativity, and visualization is the process to effect such imaging. Whether it is accomplished via meditation, relaxation, sensory deprivation, hypnosis, or a personal methodology is irrelevant. People must be unconsciously programmed to believe in themselves. This power can only be built through relaxed concentration. Many of our female subjects never heard of Anton Wilson or Carl Jung, but they certainly operated with a keen sense of these scientists' sense of intellectual creativity.

Dogmatic Thinking Is Contrary to Creativity

Golda Meir was associated with an Orthodox religious movement her whole life. Ironically she was not religious. Golda was married in the Jewish faith by a rabbi, but only because her mother insisted on it, since Golda had decided that the dogmatic ceremonies were unnecessary. Ayn Rand created her own dogma. She was a devout atheist by the age of thirteen, but her writings were spiritually passionate to the point that they spawned a new political movement in the United States, libertarianism. She wrote *Atlas Shrugged* because of a confrontational phone call. A friend told her, "It is your duty to write a nonfiction treatise on your philosophy." Ayn was furious and said, "What if I went on strike? What if all the creative minds in the world went on strike?" This in a nutshell is the story line and moral philosophy of *Atlas Shrugged*: "One of the most destructive anti-concepts in the history of moral philosophy—Duty!" Rand philosophized, "Duty destroys reason; Duty destroys values; Duty destroys love; Duty destroys self-esteem (It leaves no self to be esteemed); Duty destroys morality."

Most creative geniuses are in search of truth and in doing so are forced to destroy the old dogmas that tend to limit the new and novel. Joseph Schumpeter's "Creative Destruction" defines the essence of the innovative process. Anything new must come at the expense of the old. Dogmatic thinking is one trait that must be eliminated for anyone to become truly creative. All the females in this book have kept their perspective on dogmatic rituals and were the first to destroy such icons to the past.

Summary

A rebellious "break-the-rules" mentality is essential to the creative process, as demonstrated by the females in this work. Each was willing to go where others feared to tread and used a macro-vision to get there. Their feminine intuition was a big factor in their success. They operated with an inductive, macro, qualitative perspective in everything they did. They had intuitive vision, with a big picture of life and a long-range attitude. These women ignored all dogma and used their vision and imaginative insights to accomplish their goals. They reached the top of their individual careers and industries via a rebellious and renegade attitude.

These thirteen creative visionaries were renegades in the sense of traditional female roles. They were their own women no matter the consequences. These iconoclasts were armed with a resilient self-confidence not often seen in business, politics, or entertainment. They were not programmed to please the world but to please their own internal needs and dreams. They accomplished their objectives in an elegant yet rebellious way. They did it in a fashion that philosopher Arthur Schopenhauer would have approved. "All truth goes through three steps," he said.

First = It is ridiculed
Second = It is violently opposed
Third = It is accepted as self-evident

Schopenhauer went on to show that only 3 percent of the people ever get involved in the first two stages. Ninety-seven percent wait for the self-evident stage, when it is too late for any major opportunities to occur. The female creative geniuses are willing to be ridiculed and consequently are in the 3 percent group and therefore typically earn with the top 99 percent group. Their comfort level with ambiguity makes them both rich and famous.

5

Professional versus Personal Dichotomy

Gifted girls need role models of women who successfully combine marriage, raising children, and a career.

—Linda Silverman, counselor of the gifted

If we are to have a world in which women work beside men . . . women must learn to give up pandering to male sensitivities.

—Margaret Mead

Male success is typically achieved by effective competition; female success, by *relationship*.

—Carol Gilligan, *In a Different Voice*

Aspiring female entrepreneurs, creative geniuses, and innovative leaders have but three choices relative to their personal/professional interrelationships. *Choice one is to forego any restrictive personal relationship* such as husband and children (Mother Teresa, Maria Callas, Ayn Rand, Gloria Steinem, Linda Wachner). *Choice two is to attempt both in serial fashion*—marry and have children, then, when they are old enough to be independent, move into a career path (Mary Kay Ash and Liz Claiborne), or reverse the process by going for the career while delaying a family life with children until the late thirties (Margaret Mead, Oprah Winfrey, and Madonna). *Choice three is to attempt both in parallel,* which appears the most difficult (Catherine the Great, Jane Fonda, Estée Lauder, Golda Meir, and Lillian Vernon).

Notice that out of sixteen women studied in this book, an equal number (five, or 33 percent) fall into each of the above categories. It appears no one approach is better than another. The proper path depends on the family/career preferences of each individual. The findings for these female visionaries was similar to the findings on male creative genius in that the family always appeared to end up in second place relative to the career.

The media loves to extol the virtues of the woman who has it all. Such superwomen are eminently successful housewives, mothers, and career women. Based on my research, such triple-threat success is somewhat of a myth. Having two masters is difficult and three is impossible without a great deal of sacrifice in one or more of the areas. Devoting the necessary time required for becoming an excellent wife and mother while simultaneously managing a demanding professional career is very difficult if not impossible. The dichotomy between personal success and professional success lies in the desire to attain "creative genius" stature in both. Everyone can have both, as is seen in America today, where 59 percent of females with children under six work outside the home. Only 31 percent of these women, in a 1990 Gallup Poll, rated themselves an A in parenthood, while 65 percent rated the relationships with their children "excellent." However, this book is not about the average woman. It is about creative geniuses who reached the very top of their professions and were able to change the world in the process. This kind of monumental achievement comes with a much higher price than just working from nine to five and coming home to the husband and children. The thirteen women profiled in this book give an interesting perspective to each of the three choices facing women who want it all. They can sacrifice one or attempt both serially or in parallel.

Gender-Based Attitudes: Career versus Family

Various controversial but endemic attitudes prevail in Western society. Males have been considered the titular heads of families. Within the household the female is queen and predominates. U.S. Sen. Diane Feinstein of California was surprised by a question from Marian Burros of the *New York Times,* about keeping house: "Of course. I think women always keep house. It comes with the gender. Every career woman with a family does the wash, the laundry, scrubs floors, cleans the bathrooms, changes the beds. The man generally does not." She added, "My daughter could run for district attorney and win, but she'd still have to go home and clean."

Males generally place career ahead of family because they have been molded to believe that that is their primary responsibility as "breadwinner" within the family unit. His role model is similar to the female role model as house cleaner. It isn't necessarily right or the way creative visionary women can be the most effective, but it is the way the genders have been conditioned to see the two responsibilities. Diane Feinstein evidently cleans her own house. Margaret Mead never did nor did Jane Fonda, and it is hard to imagine Madonna with a mop and broom in hand. And Gloria Steinem and Linda Wachner detest domestic chores. Margaret Mead's husband, celebrated anthropologist Gregory

Bateson, said, "I have never seen her perform a domestic task."

Based on gender conditioning, males often feel within their rights to call up without notice and announce they will not be home for the weekend due to a job-related problem. They also feel comfortable (as the titular head of the household and the primary breadwinner) with announcing that the family is relocating to another city because of a new job opportunity. They assume such an omnipotent role due to centuries of imprinting and breeding. In other words, the male has been conditioned to place career first and family second.

Women have been trained with the opposite set of priorities. The female assumes a more submissive role within the family unit (even when she is a CEO). She still assumes the responsibility for the children and the household in the absence of the father (even if she works outside the home), and she is expected to quit her job in order to follow her husband to a new city. Dual-income families are changing contemporary households in a dramatic way—the family was always the highest priority for most females. In other words, average females always place the family first and career second in the priority of importance. This is changing. Did our thirteen visionary women possess the typical female mentality on professional versus personal roles within the family unit? No. They gave lip service to the family but were so goal oriented their careers always took precedence.

In many respects, these female superstars emulated the prototypical male. These women were invariably dominant in the familial relationship. They were the ones to call (e.g., Rand, Fonda, Callas, Lauder, Meir, and Thatcher) and say, "I'm stuck on the West Coast; see you next week." Or, "I've signed a contract for six months in Europe; are you coming?" These female visionaries invariably placed their careers ahead of their husbands or children and assumed the "power" within the family unit in the fashion of Nietzsche's "will to power" (power accedes to those who assume it). These women took the power needed to achieve success whether that power was within the family or in their field of endeavor. They operated with a "male-like" mentality, as Beatrix Campbell of Great Britain so eloquently put it in describing Margaret Thatcher: "Femininity is what she wears, masculinity is what she admires." Many others said of the Iron Lady, "She's not a real woman." Or as Jimmy Carter's national security adviser said, In her presence you pretty quickly forget that she's a woman. She doesn't strike me as being a very female type." Margaret Mead's best friend and mentor, Ruth Benedict, told her, "You'd make a better father than mother." Similar conclusions were reached for virtually every one of the females in this book, with Ayn Rand openly admitting she preferred maleness to femaleness.

The Price of Pursuing Multiple Masters

Every successful creative genius is dedicated to the pursuit of perfection; however, it is very difficult to have multiple masters. The consensus of this research is that a woman can be wife, mother, and professional, but not without a price. A successful career and fulfillment as a wife and mother take time and each will exact a price. Attempting both simultaneously appears to be all but impossible if excellence is expected of each endeavor. Vice President Al Gore's wife, Tipper, told *Redbook* (February 14, 1994), "I don't think you can have it all." She added, "If I had pursued a career, we would have had two separate lives and I don't even known if we would have stayed married." Both Mary Kay Ash and Liz Claiborne chose the serial approach and resisted their entrepreneurial venture until after raising their respective families. Having two masters in this case caused them to start a new business venture after the age of forty-five. Those attempting both simultaneously (Fonda, Lauder, Meir, Vernon), were forced into sacrificing family time for career time. Their careers were eminently successful but their families paid the price. Attempting a family and career simultaneously appears to prejudice the woman into dedicating most of her energies to the one with the biggest psychological and financial payoff. Six of these women did not have children and one, Gloria Steinem, never married. It is not surprising to find that almost half of these superachieving women did not have children. They chose to pursue another master and it caused them to sacrifice the family opportunities.

Can Female Leaders Have It All?

Catherine the Great bore Paul I by lover Serge Saltykov in her twenties. He was the heir apparent to the throne of Russia and was spirited away from Catherine at birth by Empress Elizabeth. This not only infuriated Catherine but gave her an even greater resolve to become the empress of Russia with control over her destiny. In her determination, she had both her husband Peter III and his cousin Ivan VI assassinated and considered the same for her son. She was content in keeping him "in her shadow, an educated but docile child— a possible successor, not a disguised rival." But as long as she lived she was adamant that no one else would rule Russia. When Margaret Mead married Luther Cressman they agreed not to have children; later, when she married Reo Fortune she committed "to do field work as a way of life." Margaret had a number of miscarriages while doing field work in the South Pacific with husband Gregory Bateson. By this time she was committed to motherhood and said, "I decided that I would have a child no matter how many miscarriages it meant." She had Cathy Bateson at age thirty-eight but continued working two jobs, as an instructor at New York University and as curator of the New York Museum. Mead hired a nanny at birth, and when her daughter was two she moved in with another couple, Larry and Mary Frank, in order to have a home for her daughter. She and Bateson were immersed in international conferences and pursuing successful careers; their daughter was an adored treasure in their lives but had to play second to their number one passion, work. Both Catherine the Great and Margaret Mead were eminently successful professionals but less than nurturing mothers and wives.

Five of the thirteen contemporary women chose a parallel path to having it all. They elected to have their children and pursue their careers at the same time. It is quite apparent that their families paid the price for having talented and career-oriented wives and mothers. Those who attempted to do both in parallel were Jane Fonda, Estée Lauder, Golda Meir, Margaret Thatcher, and Lillian Vernon. These women never denied that they could have been better mothers. In their defense, a world-class career places enormous demands on family life. Being the very best and reaching the top demands a total and unrelenting commitment that precludes virtually all else in one's life. The high-stakes area in which these women operated typically allows for no other masters. Barbara Walters has been quoted as saying, "A woman must choose between being a wife, mother, and having a career. She can have two of these but not all three." Mary Kay Ash agrees with Walters' assessment. In describing her marriage to Mel Ash after she was already a successful founder and executive at Mary Kay Cosmetics, Ash says, "I had to make some drastic adjustments in order to be the person he wanted as a wife. He did not want a chairman of the board for a wife. He did not want me telling him what to do in any way, shape, or form. When I came home, he wanted me to be his wife, period." Based on the feedback from these successful women, it is clear that you can have it all, but not without a price.

These successful female leaders subjugated all else to their careers and in many cases the sacrifices were their families. (There are probably thousands of great women who could never qualify for this work because they were not eminently successful in their careers; they opted for family over career when a critical choice had to be made). Margaret Mead was an internationally renowned celebrity before she finally decided to become a mother at age thirty-eight. She had awaited the event with trepidation and great delight only to relegate her daughter to a nanny and step-home so she could immediately return to her lecturing and research. It appears she became so immersed in her professional lifestyle that she was unable to adapt to the new role of motherhood. The other women in this book had similar experiences in trying to adapt and juggle both family and career. Margaret Thatcher sat for the bar just four months after the birth of her twins, Mark and Carol. Then she started a law practice when they were one year old and became a member of Parliament when they were but six. Her obsessive need to fulfill her career goals apparently overwhelmed her natural nurturing instincts. Liz Claiborne likewise worked as a New York City fashion designer up until her son Alexander's birth and then went back to her design work two weeks later.

Golda Meir adored her daughter and son but preferred spending her time in pursuit of Zionism than as a full-time mother. She left her children in the care of others and placed them in a kibbutz while pursuing her dream for an Israeli state. Meir admitted in her biography to having sacrificed her marriage and children for Zionism. She said, "Whatever I was asked to do, I did. The party said I should go, so I went." Margaret Thatcher's twin children attended a boarding school once she started her move up the political ladder in England. A long-time friend of the family describes her attempt to handle both tasks simultaneously; "Margaret Thatcher is an unbelievably successful politician but an unsuccessful mother and she knows it." Similarly, Jane Fonda left daughter Vanessa with Roger Vadim in 1971 to pursue her social and antiwar causes. Later, she left Vanessa and a newborn to pursue various social causes or to pitch her videos, books, or exercise studios when not making a movie. She certainly had far too many masters to have been an effective parent. She admits that if she had not had the money for professional babysitters, she could never have accomplished what she did professionally. Estée Lauder's marriage was an early casualty of her need for a career. During the four years when she and Joe Lauder were divorced the children were placed in boarding schools and flitted between New York and Miami Beach. After starting her cosmetic empire she attempted to do both but the call of beauty and skin care took precedence over the family in virtually every instance. She was on the road throughout the United States building Estée Lauder Cosmetics into the dominant firm in its field.

All of these women became titans in their given fields, but their children suffered from having overachieving mothers. They were often away on business trips and the children suffered the consequences of not having an available mother. Although this research indicates early isolation and independence is a positive influence for adult success, the children of these creative visionaries never received the same nurturing they would have from "normal" parents. The husbands of these women often suffered even more than the children as they were relegated to third place on the priority list. The major point here is that the women were so obsessed with reaching the top that they were willing to sacrifice virtually everything. Men have long been castigated for this very behavior but these women appear to have had a malelike propensity for trading off the personal for the professional.

Serial Family/Career Interrelationships

Two women resolved the career/family issue serially—Mary Kay Ash and Liz Claiborne. They were parents before initiating their entrepreneurial ventures. The price they paid was waiting until their mid-forties before starting their companies. Ash was in her late forties and Claiborne was forty-six before the launch of their breakthrough business enterprises. Ash had been faced with supporting and raising a family of three under the age of eight from the time she was twenty-seven and her husband deserted her. Claiborne also worked but more out of desire for a profession than need, since she had a husband during her son's early life. Claiborne's first marriage became a casualty of her career in a roundabout manner: she met the man who would be her second husband in Milwaukee on a design assignment. They fell in love and married after divorcing their respective spouses.

Working nine to five in contrast to owning and operating your own firm or pursuing your own professional career are miles apart in terms of stress and responsibility. Mary Kay Ash and Liz Claiborne worked full time while their children were small and gained valuable knowledge toward their ultimate business ventures. But working for another organization is not nearly so draining as developing your own operation. New ventures typically require an eighty-hour work week with constant pressure and stress. Ash and Claiborne avoided that by electing to wait until their children were out of the house to start their companies. The price they paid was multiple marriages. Ash was married three times and Claiborne twice. Ash is not convinced that you can have it all. She says, "I don't think there is time in the day to have it all at once. How can you be a mother to three children, have those cares and worries of a large corporation, and a husband and all the other things at once? I don't think you can!"

Sacrificing the Personal for the Professional

Those who sacrificed family for career were Madonna, Maria Callas, Ayn Rand, Gloria Steinem, Linda Wachner, and Oprah Winfrey. Of these only Madonna and Oprah have not yet fallen to the immutable march of their biological clocks, although Oprah is close at age forty. Madonna had one of many reconciliations with Sean Penn in the late eighties and promised to work less and to have his baby. However, when the opportunity to play Breathless Mahoney in *Dick Tracy* arose, Madonna not only forgot her promise about working, but began a passionate affair with Warren Beatty, and the remarriage became history. She had sacrificed her maternal instincts for her career, an occurrence that would be often repeated during her drive to the top. Melinda

Cooper, a friend of Madonna, says, "she doesn't have a maternal bone in her body." Cooper says that Madonna has had at least three abortions on her way to the top.

Linda Wachner purposely never had children but feels that her decision was a mistake. Now in her mid-forties she says, "I would really love a child," but admits that her career may have taken precedence. "I don't think I would have had the time to raise a child and deal with the quality of male chauvinism I was dealing with then." Gloria Steinem always thought she would get married and have children when she was young. She felt she had to marry to feel whole, yet, in retrospect, she says, "I'll definitely get married, I kept thinking, but not right now." Steinem kept adopting one feminist cause after another until she finally ran out of biological time. In 1984 she used her marital status as an Equal Rights Amendment motivational ploy, by vowing, "I will not get married until the ERA is passed." It never passed, and Gloria is still single in her sixties and cynically rationalizes her status: "I cannot mate in captivity."

Oprah Winfrey is engaged and living with Stedman Graham, who already has children. She has unconsciously delayed their marriage long enough that her child-bearing period is now in serious jeopardy. Could this have been an unwitting choice to forego motherhood? She turned forty on January 29, 1994, and has been seriously involved with Stedman since 1986. Winfrey's reticence to marry and have children has cost her many years of male companionship and potential children, although her career has never been better. She told *Redbook* in 1993 that "she couldn't marry Stedman because she couldn't imagine putting him—or anyone—ahead of her career." Winfrey's eminent success as the consummate talk-show hostess has been at the expense of a personal life. She has always vacillated on the children issue, as indicated by this quote to *Good Housekeeping* in 1991:

> Do I want to have a child of my own? Sometimes I think yes, I do want to have that experience, and other times I must admit having a child is not a deep yearning at this time. Maybe I'm afraid. Raising a child is a serious business. You have to be emotionally mature and responsible, and I'm not sure I'm describing me when I say that, at least not yet.

Maria Callas, like Linda Wachner, married a much older man (in fact he was twenty-seven years her senior). Why? One reason was her deep-seated insecurities, which demanded an older, experienced mentor to lead and guide her. Her biographers have often described Callas as a "child woman," which gives some insight into her selection of an older spouse. Batista Meneghini functioned as her tutor, mentor, lover, and manager. Callas needed constant public adulation to satiate her deep-seated insecurities. Her husband, Batista, was an important factor in quenching her internal fires and satisfying her needs for security. Batista's adulation and tutelage were solace for her basic insecurities and manic-depressive nature, allowing her to sacrifice her desire for children (Meneghini, 1982; Stassinopoulas, 1981).

Then Callas met Aristotle Onassis and her long-suppressed maternal needs and romantic inclinations were instantly resurrected. She spurned her career, husband, and everything for Ari. To her delight, he promised her marriage and a baby, but then he welched on his promise. When she accidentally got pregnant in 1966 with "Aristo's" baby, he ordered her to have an abortion. She was devastated but complied, justifying her decision with, "I was afraid of losing Aristo" (Stanicoff, 1987). She lived out her life with two poodles as her surrogate children in a Paris apartment.

Ayn Rand never had time to have children, subjugating all to her writing. Rand was oblivious of all else, and maternal she was not. She was rational to a fault, causing her to approach her fifteen-year affair with Nathaniel Branden in a philosophical manner. Ayn informed her husband and Branden's wife of the liaison by describing it as an intellectual and spiritual relationship unworthy of any emotional upset. Rand's brutal honesty and rationality were admirable traits, but they never left room for the maternal. Rand was always willing to sacrifice everything in her life for the redemption of her writing career and ultimately the objectivist philosophy.

Husbands of Creative Visionaries

Empowered women tend to dominate their marital relationships in a manner normally associated with male power brokers. Female visionaries—based on the findings for our thirteen female subjects—tend to treat their spousal relationships much like their powerful male counterparts. The husbands of these female leaders were often relegated to the background reminiscent of the classic female "wallflower" stereotype. Female spouses of eminent leaders are often depicted by the media as little more than window dressing for their more famous mates (Hillary Rodham Clinton being an obvious contemporary exception). In fact, Frances Lear constantly referred to herself as the "wife-of" in a cynical justification of her split with Norman Lear. She felt so strongly about her subordinate role to Norman that she founded *Lear's* magazine with the divorce monies in retribution for her servile position in the relationship. The findings for these women indicate little or no difference between great females or males in the treatment of their spouses. Both genders of power brokers tend to operate with their spouses walking five paces behind.

Catherine the Great not only deposed her husband, Peter III of Russia, she had him assassinated. She then proceeded to spend the present day equivalent of $1.5 billion dollars maintaining a stable of young lovers, according to the

British ambassador at Catherine's court. Margaret Mead maintained an ardent independence through three marriages to powerful men, but insisted on keeping her own name through all three. (This practice was not quite in vogue during the twenties and thirties). Mead married Luther Cressman at the age of twenty-two, and kept the name Mead for the less than timorous reasoning that "I'm going to be famous someday." She married twice more and each time kept her maiden name, even when married to the world-famous anthropologist Gregory Bateson.

Frances Lear also kept her maiden name, Loeb, through two husbands and then took the name of Lear with her last. Then she defied logic and the feminists by using her ex-husband's name in her launch of *Lear's* magazine in the mid-eighties. After getting out of her "wife-of" role, Lear assumed an empowered woman role, which she cynically described as, "I have a man for every reason." Barbara Walters was another female visionary researched for this book. She kept her maiden name, Walters, through three marriages and each husband always took a deferential role in their relationship (Oppenheimer, 1990). Lillian Vernon finally changed her name to the name of her company after her last (her third) marriage. Vernon had long since assumed the identity of her world-famous Lillian Vernon catalog company and took that name as her own identity in lieu of Katz or her maiden name Menasche.

Ayn (Rosenbaum) Rand kept "her own name" even though it was a pseudonym taken from a typewriter logo. Everyone knew of Frances Lear's world-famous husband, Norman Lear. But who was Ayn's husband? He was an ever-faithful and wonderfully understanding man named Frank O'Connor, who was as much the wallflower as any male autocrat's wife. Rand had an affair for fifteen years with a man twenty-five years her junior, Nathaniel Branden, and asked the devoted Frank to take a walk while she consummated her libidinal needs with her lover. She actually married Frank O'Connor for spurious career and personal reasons. She was a young Russian immigrant, a neophyte writer, and a part-time waitress. She had to be married to keep her American visa and to acquire American citizenship. The marriage lasted a lifetime and Frank ultimately became her editor and "go-fer" during an era when that was an unheard of role for a handsome and talented male.

Jane Fonda also kept her maiden name through her three marriages, although it was a far more recognizable name, with the possible exception of that of her current mate, Ted Turner. Fonda also maintained her own identity through her marriages and relationships. She used these men to fill a psychological need for a father figure, but she never lost her own identity. In her inimitable way, Fonda remained the dominant person in each of her relationships.

Morris Meyerson, the lifelong mate of Golda Meir, was a nonentity in both her political and family life. Meir's biographer, Ralph Martin, described her husband's role this way: "Morris was a mild nothing compared to Goldie's life force." He said, "Golda was the power behind the throne." An example of their dominant/submissive relationship occurred shortly after their marriage. Meir unilaterally decided to live and work in Israel for Zionism, and invited her husband along for this sojourn into a different part of the world. She told Morris point blank that she would have gone without him had he declined to accompany her.

Dennis Thatcher was another infamous husband fortunate enough to have a famous wife use his name but who was otherwise an invisible force in her career, and a nonfactor in her success. He was just there when needed and was classy window dressing for formal functions. Likewise, the name Joe Lauder would have little recognition in the board rooms of industrial America had he not been married to the queen of cosmetics, Estée Lauder. And who was the husband of opera star Maria Callas? Everyone is conversant with her twenty-year romance and affair with Aristotle Onassis, which continued even after he married Jackie Kennedy. Callas's husband of ten years, Batista Meneghini, was a titan of industry in his native Verona, Italy, but was little more than a puppet to the volatile opera diva. She used and then discarded him when the charismatic Onassis appeared on the scene. Linda Wachner has been married once but never remarried after her mentor husband died in 1983. One reason for remaining single has been her public position that her profession is more important than her personal relationships. She told *Cosmopolitan* in 1990, "I would like to be married again, but it's very hard to meet people with the patience to understand that my business comes first." Her other problem in finding appropriate relationships is her intimidating personality, which exudes power. Wachner is not comfortable around weak people and can be an over-whelming force for someone making overtures. She strikes fear into the hearts of most male employees and would be a disarming combatant in any marital relationship.

Nurturing and Children

Highly focused creative women tend to deny themselves their maternal natures. Ayn Rand, Gloria Steinem, Maria Callas, Oprah Winfrey, Madonna, and Linda Wachner were all childless even though all were quite vocal in expressing their desire for children. Their desire for motherhood evidently was not nearly so strong as their professional obsession. Six of these thirteen visionaries—46 percent of the total group—did not have children. This appears typical for females with an entrepreneurial bent. Joanne Wilkens, in her book *Her Own Business* (1987), found that 43 percent of the 117 entrepreneurial women she interviewed were childless. This contrasts with the American average of 11 percent. It is evident that a professional career is antithetical to motherhood.

Madonna has said, "I think about having children all the time," but she hasn't seen fit to take the time out from her career to become a mother. Gloria Steinem and Maria Callas both had abortions, Steinem as a very young woman just out of college, and Callas in her early forties at the behest of a tyrannical Aristotle Onassis. Oprah Winfrey had a disastrous experience as a fourteen-year-old when her baby was born prematurely and died shortly after birth. She has never totally recovered from the trauma of this devastating experience (Bly, 1993). Both Steinem and Madonna were disenchanted with diapers, cooking, and nurturing others during their childhoods and have unconsciously avoided assuming the maternal role as adults. The nurturing instinct appears to take a distant second place to career in the priorities of the female creative leader.

Relationships: A Female's Real Power

Carol Gilligan has very poignantly described the female as hearing *Different Voices* (1982), causing her to be "care focused" in contrast to the more "justice focused" male. Gilligan feels the female's ethical value system is centered around a network of "relationships, responsibility, and caring" in contrast to the male's primary focus on "separation, autonomy, principles and rights, and pyramidal hierarchy." Psychologist David Barash confirms Gilligan's hypothesis by saying, "Male success is typically achieved by effective competition; female success by relationship." Fundamentally women would prefer to be nice in most leadership roles and men prefer power.

The research on creative genius indicates that females focus on inter-relationships while males focus on intra-relationships. The female tends to be more personal, the male more impersonal. Females are into caring, while males are into bottom-line functions. The female attempts to nurture her operation toward success; the male will attempt to lecture or legislate toward success. When faced with conflict the female will attempt to negotiate a solution, while the male tends toward an aggressive or intimidating resolution. Emotional gratification of libidinal drive is resolved by the female through romance; the male, on the other hand, prefers a sexual solution. The female prefers a secure approach to business enterprise; the male prefers a risk-oriented approach. Females ask for advice and males give advice. The female's approach to confrontation is through compassion and understanding, the male's via aggressiveness. The female seeks respect in all new relationships; the male seeks ego gratification. Females try to be nice; males attempt to be powerful. In gamesmanship, the female is content to play the game while the male prefers to win the game. The female's decisions are based on how they feel; males decide based on how they think. Power tends to liberate the female, and corrupt the male. The female uses her beauty and sex to gain power; the male uses his power to get sex. In summation, the female places the *relationship* above all else in all personal interactions; males place the *individual* at the apex of all human interactions.

Paternalistic societies have always used force and physical power to resolve their conflicts because males in those societies were in positions of power. Aggression was the solution to all problems, physical power their master. Conversely, females value a relational not aggressive solution to problems and have a compassionate not physical power approach to conflict. That is, females prefer talking, males prefer fighting (a function of testosterone levels). This simple difference in the solution of conflict legislates in favor of a female leader for any society faced with confrontation. The female leader will more likely opt for resolution through mediation, negotiation, and securing a compassionate solution through verbal communications. Females will be dedicated to keeping the society or organization rationally intact due to their internal need for nurturing and security. The male is always more willing to destroy the society or organization for redemption of the ego and the individual. The female's greatest strength has also been her greatest weakness: she has had a history of talking too much when attempting to avoid conflict. The chance for resolving the issue sometimes passes before a woman has finished talking. Her greatest strength has become her greatest weakness which happens to be true of everyone (most just are not aware of this dichotomy).

A Revelation—Men and Women are Different

Christine De Lacoste at Berkeley found she could differentiate between male and female brains (physical examination of corpus callosums), saying they were as different as the arms and legs of males and females. Robert Ornstein in *The Psychology of Consciousness* says, "The hemispheres in males are more specialized than those in females. The representation of analytic and sequential thinking is more clearly present in the left hemisphere of males than in females, and spatial abilities are more lateralized in the right hemispheres of males than females." In other words, female brains have a more "generalized" orientation and males a more "specialized" orientation. Which is testimony to why the average male scores higher on math tests* and why females have a better holistic view of the world, more popularly referred to as "female intuition."

Figure 9 shows the above concept in matrix form. Notice most females

---

*A study of 100,000 teenage boys and girls by Benbow and Stanley (1985) showed a 13:1 ratio of math aptitude for boys over girls based on SAT testing of samples in excess of 700.

Figure 9

Qualities of Female and Male Leadership

Variable	Female Solution	Male Solution
Brain orientation	Generalized	Specialized
Ethical values	Interrelationships	Intrarelationships
Morality Issues	Care focused	Justice focused
Behavior styles	Attachments	Separations
Personal needs	Relationships	Individuality
Perceptions (overview)	Visual approach	Spatial approach
Under stress	Verbalize (talk it out)	Physically aggressive
Leadership approach	Nurture	Lecture
Decision-making	Feeling	Thinking
Communications	Negotiate	Intimidate
Libidinal drives	Romance/love	Physical sex
Confrontations	Compassion	Aggression
Disposition	Security orientation	Risk orientation
Gamesmanship	Enjoying the game	Competing to win
Nurturing nature	Giving	Taking
Power	Liberating	Corrupting
Seductions	Use sex to get power	Use power to get sex
Emotional needs	Respect	Ego power

are "relationship" driven and most males "individual" or "ego" driven, which are specific examples of their "generalized" and "specialized" orientations. You can also discern that women strive to be nice and that men are more desirous of power which becomes the driving force behind their interrelationships and often becomes a handicap to effective communication between the two.

Libidinal Drives

Golda Meir and Madonna hold the distinction of being the most libidinally driven of our female subjects, with Jane Fonda and Maria Callas close seconds.

Sex drive has often been associated with success because it is highly correlated with risk-taking, competitiveness, and creativity (according to Frank Farley's research on the creative personality). All of these traits are a function of high testosterone and overachievement. From this study it does not appear that female genius is as libidinally driven as male genius. The research on males shows the subjects had an abnormally high libidinal energy and abundant need for sex. This is not true of these women although some had a higher sex drive than males. Meir's career aspirations were improved by her many sexual liaisons with the great creative leaders of Israel. Her exploits caused her enemies to label her "Meir the mattress." Madonna is infamous for her sexual liaisons and Fonda and Callas have made many headlines with their sexual dalliances. Most of the others were not so libidinally driven. In fact the biographers of both Margaret Mead and Margaret Thatcher indicated they were virgins at marriage in their twenties.

The marriage and child-bearing instincts of these dynamic women are listed in figure 10. Notice that two (Gloria Steinem and Oprah Winfrey) never entered the state of matrimony, although Oprah's marriage is planned in 1994. Ayn Rand, Madonna, Maria Callas, and Linda Wachner were married once but with no children. Ayn Rand's marriage lasted a lifetime despite her fifteen-year affair with Nathaniel Branden. Rand had an open marriage arrangement with her husband, who accepted Ayn's indiscretions. Madonna's relationship to Sean Penn lasted only months, but due to numerous reconciliations and Sean's prison time the marriage lasted four years. Callas married a man twenty-seven years her senior, a union that was destined to fail even though it lasted ten years until she met Aristotle Onassis. Oprah Winfrey has had a long-term relationship and engagement with Stedman Graham.

Never Married

Gloria Steinem and Oprah Winfrey are the only subjects who have never married. Steinem is fast approaching the time when she will not marry. Winfrey is engaged at the time of this writing but appears to be hesitant in taking that final walk to the altar.

Married Once with No Children

Linda Wachner, Maria Callas, Ayn Rand, and Madonna were each married once but remained childless. Wachner married a much older man, who died just prior to her takeover of Warnaco. She refused to have children because of his ill health and his age. She later said that her decision was a mistake.

Figure 10

Marriages, Motherhood, and Sex Drive

	Marriages	Children	Libidinal Drive
Mary Kay Ash	3	3	Moderate
Maria Callas	1	0	Occasional affairs
Catherine the Great	1	1	Maintained a stable of young lovers
Liz Claiborne	2	1	Moderate
Jane Fonda	3	2	Active
Estée Lauder	2	2	Average
Golda Meir	1	2	Excessive
Madonna	1	0	Excessive and bisexual
Margaret Mead	3	1	Varied and sublimated
Ayn Rand	1	0	One long-term affair
Gloria Steinem	0	0	Several serial committed relationships
Mother Teresa	0	0	Vows of chastity
Margaret Thatcher	1	2	Below average
Lillian Vernon	2	2	Average
Linda Wachner	1	0	Sublimated in work
Oprah Winfrey	0	0	Moderate

Maria Callas also married a much older man and never had children for much the same reason as Wachner. She divorced her husband for Onassis, who had promised her marriage and children. By the time the Catholic Church granted Callas an Italian divorce Onassis had become enamored of Jackie Kennedy and Callas was left with only memories. Ayn Rand married once but children were never in her plans. Her long affair with Nathaniel Branden did not begin until she was in her forties. Madonna's marriage to Sean Penn ended in a much-publicized divorce. She has had many lovers of both sexes and has remained single and without children, according to Camille Barbone, a former agent (Anderson, 1991). Madonna's cynical attitude is summed up with this quote to *USA Today* in 1992, "I think everyone should get married at least once so you can see what a silly, outdated institution it is." She also said, "I think about having children all the time. . . . It's important to have a father around, so when you think about that, you have to think, 'Is this person the right person?' " She went on to say in January 1993 that she intends to have a child but not in marriage.

Once Married With Children

Two of these visionaries, Margaret Thatcher and Golda Meir, ironically both prime ministers of their respective countries, were married once with two children each. Thatcher was blessed with twins, a boy and a girl, born during her stint in law school. Golda's children, also one boy and one girl, were born during her early years in Palestine. Thatcher spent her whole life with Dennis Thatcher, who had been married once previously. Thatcher never had time for more children since she was to become immediately involved in the bar and a political career after the birth of her twins. Meir's marriage legally lasted her whole life but effectively ended after the first few years of marriage. The harsh life of the kibbutz and the open sexuality of that period in Israel encouraged open relationships. Meir experienced more than her share: she had affairs with two Israeli prime ministers, David Ben-Gurion and Zalman Shazar (Martin, 1988). Her "love of a lifetime" was David Remez, who also was her mentor. She was intimate with Berl Katznelson, known as the Socrates of Israel, and lived out many fantasies with another romantic liaison, Zalman Aranne. A brilliant American fund raiser, Henry Montor, was also a dynamo who fell under the spell and into Meir's bed. She actually agreed to a divorce and marriage to her passionate lover Zalman Shazar, but he refused to divorce and the affair ended.

Multiple Marriages and Liaisons

Five of the thirteen subjects were married more than once: Mary Kay Ash (three times), Jane Fonda (three times), Estée Lauder (twice), Lillian Vernon (twice), and Liz Claiborne (twice). Lauder's two marriages were to the same man, her late husband, Joe Lauder. Two of Ash's husbands died; the first deserted her (Ash, 1987). Liz Claiborne was married to a Time-Life art director and divorced him to marry her present husband, design executive Arthur Ortenberg.

Sex and Power

Michael Hutchinson in *Sex and Power* (1990) says that, "Power is the ultimate aphrodisiac" and concludes that, "Sex equals power." He was speaking about how women use their sex to gain power and how men use power to get sex. Golda Meir's political adversaries would have agreed; they were convinced that she got to the top by sleeping with the most powerful leaders of Israel (Martin, 1988). Gloria Steinem's sisterhood and her enemies believed she used her sexuality and feminine mystique to achieve her rise to the top of the feminist movement. Even those who didn't believe she used sex believed that she used her femininity to further her career (Levitt, 1971).

According to biographer Bill Davidson (1990), Jane Fonda had an "insatiable nymphomaniac drive" during her two years at Vassar and the ensuing seven years in Paris and New York City. He says she was in a desperate search for the love and affection she never received from her father. Madonna had numerous liaisons, reportedly in excess of one hundred casual lovers between 1979 and 1983 alone, according to her former manager and lover Camille Barbone. Madonna never limited herself to one sex, race, or creed, or even to any combinations. She met her needs anywhere and with whomever happened to wander across her path, according to Barbone. Frances Lear shocked the world with an off-the-wall, sexually perverse autobiography, *The Second Seduction* (1992). This matronly woman was in her sixties when she candidly described her life of seduction and success. (I must admit that she was a strong candidate for one of the thirteen subjects of this book.) The above women were more libidinally driven than most women and not quite as provocative as the thirteen creative men I studied. This suggests a possible case of higher testosterone in many of these women. They were not only sexual but highly competitive and risk-oriented.

Masculine versus Feminine

Psychologist Carl Jung devised a psychological model for both men and women, which he labeled "anima" and "animus." He suggested that every man has an internalized and intensely erotic feminine force, and every woman has a similar force which connotes maleness. He felt this internalized "animus" or maleness in women was responsible for their innate creativity. This "maleness" is quite evident in much of the life force found in these thirteen female innovators. As described earlier in this chapter, these women made personal and professionally oriented decisions in a very "malelike" manner.

These women also exuded a maleness that often irritated feminists, who felt they were not true to the feminist ideal of their gender. Margaret Thatcher was constantly castigated for her lack of sensitivity to women's issues. She said, "The home should be the center but not the boundary of a woman's life," but went on to say, "I hate those strident tones we hear from some women's libbers." Feminists looked to this "Iron Lady" as a supporter of their causes to correct inequities. Her response to the feminists was, "The feminists have become far too strident and have done damage to the cause of women by making us out to be something we're not. You get on because you have the right talents." She gave her perspective on her own place in history to the *Daily Mirror* (March 1, 1980), "I don't notice that I'm a woman. I regard myself as the prime minister." These quotes demonstrate her philosophical belief that women should be willing to fight the political wars on the grounds laid out by men and not to attempt to change the rules of the game. She was unsympathetic to those wanting more favored treatment than she had been given. However, Thatcher had her detractors. Her biographer, Hugo Young, said, "She's not a real woman."

Ayn Rand was also castigated by the feminists for her constant idealization of maleness. She built icons to the male as consummate hero, much to the chagrin of feminists. This brilliant and articulate female was more independent than any feminist ever thought of being; many in the women's movement saw in her a potential leader of enormous influence. But it was not to be, since she considered man to be a superior being and said so to anyone who would listen. When she said, "man is a heroic being" she was referring to her epic heroes, Howard Roark of *The Fountainhead* and John Galt of *Atlas Shrugged*. These two fictional characters represented the personification of her "idyllic man." John Galt, her alter ego, was the consummate epic hero and the personification of all that was right in the world of free enterprise. It is no wonder that Rand upset the feminists of her day. Both Rand and Margaret Thatcher had an inordinate share of Jung's "animus force" in their makeup, which helped them achieve beyond the norm.

Most of these thirteen women exhibited male-oriented traits and behavior. Almost all of them were extremely aggressive, competitive, ambitious, and possessed a gambling spirit. This is not to say they were unfeminine. They were very interested in their hair, clothes, and appearance. They were sensuous women who used their personal appeal to get action as they would any other instrument in their arsenal of power tools. These women used their maleness to satisfy their own ends, a potential trend in Western society according to Patricia Aburdeen and John Naisbitt. They agree with Jung's "animus" concept as indicated by the following quote from their classic work, *Megatrends for Women* (1993):

> Successful human beings possess a combination of masculine and feminine traits. The most creative are a hybrid of supposedly conflicting characteristics: competitive and compassionate; goal-oriented and nurturing; intuitive and risk taking. Cardboard, one-dimensional females and males alike are doomed to failure.

Interestingly, most of the thirteen females studied in this work had far more male friends than female friends, with the exception of Maria Callas, Mary Kay Ash, and Oprah Winfrey. These three women are the only ones with "feeling" personality types. They have nurturing dispositions, causing them to identify with the "feeling" feminine more than the "thinking" masculine. Their feeling dimension inclines them to gravitate more to the sensitive and caring females in their private lives. Women like Catherine the Great, Margaret Mead, Ayn Rand, Margaret Thatcher, Jane Fonda, Golda Meir, Lillian Vernon, and Linda Wachner felt more comfortable with males as friends. Estée Lauder, Liz Claiborne, and Gloria Steinem were so engrossed in their own female-oriented careers (beauty, design, and sisterhood) that they functioned quite successfully within their own female (anima) mentality and were not inclined to the animus parts of their persona.

One of the possible reasons most of these women had such a strong "animus" identity has to do with their early childhood role models, who were virtually all male. Almost to a woman these female superstars idolized their fathers or surrogate father images. Thatcher said, "I just owe almost everything to my father." Winfrey told a reporter, "When my father took me it changed my life. He saved me." Madonna was in awe of her father and cooed, "My father was very strong. He was my role model." Jane Fonda spent her life attempting to please her famous father, Henry. She told a reporter, "It is very difficult having an icon for a father." Gloria Steinem admits to a much stronger attachment to and influence from her father than her mother. Maria Callas had a lifelong affection for her father and hated her mother. Ayn Rand emulated her father's dream of being a great writer. Lillian Vernon's role model was her father, whom she admired for his perseverance through crisis after crisis. Estée Lauder found her inspiration in her uncle John. At least four of these women married powerful father figures—Callas, Fonda, Thatcher, and Wachner.

The one poignant fact is that men and women are different. The 1993 box office smash *Indecent Proposal* was titillating and exciting as entertainment because Robert Redford offered $1 million—an indecent proposal—to sleep one night with the married Demi Moore. Consider the interest in this movie if the roles had been reversed. If Demi Moore had offered Robert Redford $1 million to sleep with her there would have been *no* movie. Why? Fundamentally because no one would have cared and if they did the price for the liaison would have been twenty-five dollars due to the accepted role models of men and women in our society. We unconsciously label the female as the seductress (valued asset) in such a proposal and the male as the aggressor. The woman is expected to use her sexuality to gain power and the male to use his power to enlarge his sexual prowess. This observation is not necessarily nice in these cold terms, but it is the reality of Western society, if not all other societies. Males and females are treated differently and interact differently due to the perceived nature of their roles in life, and all creative achievement will be conducted within those parameters.

"Big T" Personalities

High testosterone levels have been shown to be the reason males have a typically higher sex drive and are more aggressive than females, causing University of Wisconsin researcher Frank Farley (president of the U.S. Psychological Association) to label the aggressive risk-taking males with high sex drives as "Big T" personalities. These personality types tend to be "more creative, more extraverted, take more risks, have more experimental artistic preferences, and prefer more variety in their sex lives," according to Farley. The "T" stands for thrill-seeking and/or testosterone. Conversely, Farley labels the classic female personality as "little t's," since they are typically far less prone to risk-taking, competitive behavior, and high sex drive. Studies have shown that when females are injected with testosterone they tend to emulate the male and "mate more frequently with a wider variety of males, are less selective in sexual partners and are more likely to become pregnant by inappropriate males" (*Sex and Power,* 1990). The level of testosterone appears to be a major variable in both the drive for career success in both males and females. Many of the subjects in this book appear to have been blessed (or cursed) with a much higher than average amount of testosterone based on their creativity, risk-taking propensity, competitive spirit, and aggressiveness. Only five of them had a higher than normal sex drive, according to the findings but they all were competitive, aggressive, and more inclined to risk than other females. This made them more malelike.

Camille Barbone, a former manager for Madonna, has said, "There's a strong maleness in Madonna. She seduces men the way men seduce women." Golda Meir was labeled "meshugge"—Yiddish for wild and crazy—when she was young. David Ben-Gurion said of her, "She is the only man in my cabinet," referring to her aggressive and risk-taking propensity ("gutsy approach") when faced with resolving a difficult problem. Ayn Rand's hero in *Atlas Shrugged,* John Galt, was her alter ego ideal for mankind. He was the heroic "superman" who exemplified her truth for all men (and women). Men were the quintessential being in her scheme of things, which is shown by her response to whether she preferred men or women: "I was always in favor of tomboys, and of intellectual equality, but women as such didn't interest me." Further to this argument, Golda Meir and Margaret Thatcher were labeled "intransigent" by the world's politicians because of their malelike zeal, an uncommon label for effeminate women, even if they are in power.

Communication and Emotion in Creative Genius

John Gray, in his 1993 book *Men Are from Mars, Women Are from Venus,* writes, "Men and women are from different planets, they are so different." He was referring to the vast differences in the way men and women communicate and handle stress. Gray's consensus is that the old ways of communicating are counterproductive to a successful solution. He feels the genders approach disagreements incorrectly. I agree (see figure 10) that the genders are different and the basic "feeling" versus "thinking" approach discussed in the personality chapter is critical to the creative process. Visionaries need to eliminate their emotional responses (typically female) and utilize a more rational approach to decision making. The Myers-Briggs (largest test on personality preferences) "thinking versus feeling" scale shows that. Seventy-five percent of American females make decisions based on how they "feel" about a subject and only 25 percent make decisions predicated on how they "think" about it. Conversely, 75 percent of American males typically make decisions based on how they "think" about a subject rather than how they "feel" about it. No wonder Gray concluded that the two genders have trouble seeing solutions in the same way.

The male personality preferences of feeling over thinking inclines the female to be more sensitive to resolving conflict than the male. Females prefer to talk through the process. Males are far more rational, unemotional, and impersonal in resolving conflict. Women prefer to think through the process. Neither approach is right or wrong but the data suggest that this is significant since all but three of these visionary women employ a "thinking" approach to problem resolution. The three exceptions are Mary Kay Ash, Maria Callas, and Oprah Winfrey, all of whom have been famous for their "feeling" approach to life as well as their decision-making. All the rest utilize the more "male-like," thinking approach to decision-making.

Summary

As Sophocles so eloquently said, "Once a woman is made equal to a man, she becomes his superior." These women were given, or at times took, the power to compete on the same level with men, and rose to the same heights as their male counterparts—in many instances surpassing them. This research indicates that if a woman expects to achieve like a man, she must adopt male-like characteristics such as placing her professional goals above all else, including the family. The female normally chooses between the personal (family) and the professional (career) based on which she chooses as her master. However, no one can successfully serve two masters, therefore her decision is always a perilous one. If she chooses the family over the career, it is highly unlikely she will ever achieve great eminence as a creative visionary. But that is okay; not everyone can be a creative genius. Those who are so inclined must be prepared to sacrifice the personal for the professional. The female creative visionaries in this book invariably chose: career over family, dominance over submissiveness, candor over coyness, strength over weakness, performance over appearance, and the rational over the emotional.

Many women who choose profession over family never achieve eminence in either even though they pay the same price these women did. Only a few make it to the very top and become tremendously successful. The only people in society who never fail are those who never attempt anything new. These thirteen women did, but their achievements came at a cost. Some paid the price of their femininity, like Margaret Thatcher and Golda Meir who wore the malelike mantel because of their intransigent behavior. It is what made them great, but it also made them less feminine and brought them many enemies. These women were loved and hated but this is part of playing in the big leagues of entrepreneurship and innovation. Many of these women sacrificed any chance for children (namely, Maria Callas, Ayn Rand, Gloria Steinem, Linda Wachner, and Oprah Winfrey). Others like Mary Kay Ash, Liz Claiborne, Jane Fonda, Estée Lauder, and Lillian Vernon sacrificed valuable years with their children. Only they can say whether the sacrifices were worth the rewards. It is apparent from this research that the sacrifices were critical to their extraordinary achievements. These women achieved great things because they were willing to place their professions above their personal lives. Their decisions paid big dividends, but not every female is willing to play such a high-stakes game. For our female creative geniuses it was a wonderful and lucrative journey.

Working Woman (April 1994) featured "trophy husbands" on its cover and ranked *brains, beauty, bank account, star power,* and *husbandry* as key attributes for "high-powered" women. Ted Turner headed this list with high ratings by his power-mate Jane Fonda. Success and sex certainly play pivotal roles in the personal and professional pursuits of powerful women. Their holistic (generalized) view of the world sets them apart from the more one-dimensional (specialized) males.

6

Crisis, Mania, and Creativity

Life emerges out of entropy [chaos]—not despite it.

Every artistic or scientific creation implies a transition from disorder to order.
—Dr. Ilya Prigogine, *Theory of Dissipative Structures*

Our protean selves are products of the dislocations of history, the confusions of rapid change whether brought about by war and disaster, or by the constant press of changing technology, or by radical shifts in political and cultural ideas.
—Dr. Robert Jay Lifton

Is Crisis the Mother of Creativity?

If crisis is not the mother of creativity then it is the godmother. Trauma and crisis have been shown to spawn great creativity in people who survive the experience. All superachievers have been found to be obsessively driven. In fact, of all the variables discussed in this book, an obsessive drive is clearly the most important criteria for achieving greatness. What is the derivation of such obsessive drive? Is it genetic? Not according to the research. Adler said we are all driven to seek perfection and superiority. But simple observation shows that great individuals are driven by a maniacal need to achieve while others are content to live a more normal life. Working in excess of a hundred hours a week is not the province of ordinary drive, but the compulsion of people who are driven. It appears this obsessive drive emanates from some childhood or early adult experience that instills the need to get even or to show the world they are special. Many factors probably coincide to instill such obsessive energy in some children, although unique behaviors often emanate from unique experiences. Crises and trauma qualify as unique experiences.

Sometimes obsessive energy and drive come from a manic-depressive personality. In 1931 Ernst Kretschmer published *The Psychology of Men of Genius,* in which he identified mania as a contributing factor for most genius. He said there was a "resemblance between mania and periods of creative productivity." Anthony Storr studied creativity in artists and scientists and found that "many of the world's great creators have exhibited obsessional symptoms and traits of character. . . . Perhaps the most striking feature of the obsessional temperament is the compulsive need to control both the self and the environment" (1993). The thirteen women we've been discussing fit these descriptions. They had an obsessive need to overachieve, which appears to have resulted from some traumatic event or crises in their lives. These events appear to have instilled in them a strong need to prove something to themselves and to society.

Other researchers have uncovered similar findings. Hershman and Lieb in *The Key to Genius* (1988) point out, "The hypomanic individual driven by impulse, insists on getting his needs or desires satisfied immediately and has a 'will of iron.' . . . Many high-ranking executives and people successful in politics are hypomanics. Their drive, imagination, charisma, and other hypomanic virtues are known, their problems hidden." The composer Tchaikovsky claimed, "Without work life has no meaning for me." All of these quotes have validity for our thirteen women. Catherine the Great was an empress who could have lived a life of leisure. Her biographer Troyat (1980) characterized her obsession with work: "She herself was up at five in the morning and worked twelve to fourteen hours a day. She scarcely took time to eat, and around nine o'clock in the evening, after spending a brief moment at the table with intimate friends, she would collapse on her bed in exhaustion. She fired off drafts at a speed that surprised and even vexed the copyists."

Linda Leonard, a Jungian psychologist, describes how crisis and trauma can cause an obsession with work and creative achievement. She said in her book *Meeting the Madwoman* (1993), "Out of inner chaos and emotional upheaval can come creative, energizing visions that bring new life to the individual and the culture." Ilya Prigogine, a Nobel Prize winner, said it even more eloquently: "Psychological suffering, anxiety, and collapse, can lead to new emotional, intellectual, and spiritual strengths." The research on these women gives some evidence that their overachievement could have been related to childhood events that traumatized them.

A prime example is Catherine the Great, who was confronted with multiple crises—personal, political, physical, psychological—and survived them all to become one of the most celebrated rulers in Russian, European, and world history. She had siblings die and was bedridden with a curvature of the spine at age seven. A similar malady afflicted Linda Wachner at age eleven. Margaret Mead had a sister die, a very traumatic event for her. Golda Meir had five siblings die and three (Callas, Fonda, and Steinem) had mothers committed to mental institutions, one of whom killed herself. Each one had her own particular trauma to overcome and many faced the prospect of death at an early age. These events often made them distraught or unhappy, as has already been discussed. Unhappiness is an important factor in trauma. Psychiatrist Anthony Storr, who spent years investigating the creative personality, concludes that a "divine discontent" tends to spur individuals on to creative achievement. He theorized, "The discontent thus engendered might itself be adaptive, since frustration encourages the formation of an inner world of the imagination; . . . this in turn promotes the creative discovery of symbolic achievements and satisfactions" (1988).

Unhappy/Lonely Childhoods and Creativity

Most creative and innovative personalities seem to have had unhappy childhoods, which appear to have been instrumental in their driven natures and enormous contributions to society. Sir Isaac Newton, Charles Dickens, Beethoven, and Van Gogh are examples of creative men who experienced unhappy childhoods filled with rejection and crises. The German writer Goethe remarked, "I have always been regarded as a man specially favored by fortune. . . . But . . . I might go so far as to say that in my seventy-five years I have not known four weeks of genuine ease of mind."

The early life traumas and crises of these thirteen females appear to have had a similar influence in their rise to the top. They had experienced a "worst case" scenario, after which it was much easier to deal with the mundane, day-to-day rituals of living. When a person experiences bankruptcy they are never again so worried over money. After falling on the ski slope and not breaking a leg, it is far easier to ski without fear itself. The fear of the unknown is much worse than the unknown itself. Therefore childhood trauma and crises tend to develop coping skills and self-sufficiency in those who have experienced such fortunes. They learn how to deal with intolerable obstacles without panicking, which is a requirement for every entrepreneur/innovator. Such skills endow a certain street-smart resiliency to those who survive crisis. Such resiliency is not often found in those who have had a smooth and uneventful life. Crisis survivors have learned how to effectively cope in a competitive world.

Gloria Steinem's early bouts with crisis (a severely emotionally disturbed mother) gave her the strength and resolve to face adversaries in the feminist movement. Her rebellious appeal to her constituents—"Do one outrageous thing in the cause of simple justice during the next twenty-four hours" (*Outrageous Acts and Everyday Rebellions,* 1983)—is testimony to a resilient psyche conditioned by her past experiences. It is evident that Steinem felt she could buck the system without being destroyed by it. Most people learn early not to fight the system because it has the power to bury them. For those who have been close to being buried, the threats of annihilation are not so dire. Most kids learn early that the only way to disarm a bully is to be a bully. Bullies do not want to fight, they just want to intimidate. Only those who have survived great crisis and trauma have learned all about reaching the bottom and are no longer afraid of it. They are survivors of worst-case scenarios and feel comfortable operating in less than congenial environments. It appears that crisis is often the mother of creativity because it conditions the person to deal effectively with ambiguity in a positive manner.

Crisis and Superlearning

Freudian Wilhelm Reich and biofeedback expert Thomas Bulzynski of the University of Colorado Medical Center have shown that great crisis enhances superlearning because it puts the person into a *theta* state (trance or dreamlike state with very slow brainwaves) where learning, memory, and creativity are enhanced. When people experience a crisis or trauma their brain wave activity shifts into this theta state. In other words, a person's behavior is often modified just after a traumatic event. In a traumatic state everyone learns and remembers events and information far more quickly. When Maria Callas was struck by a car and lay in a coma for twelve days at the age of six she was in great trauma. When she came out of the coma she emerged an addicted, almost obsessed prodigy, determined to get to the top at all costs. She became a perfectionist and an overachiever in her chosen profession of voice and opera. These dreams became her passion. How important was the crisis to Callas's passionate obsession to be the greatest diva in history? It is hard to tell, but there is certainly some evidence in those who have experienced similar crises and have become similarly driven to succeed. Catherine the Great, Golda Meir, Ayn Rand, Linda Wachner, Oprah Winfrey, Mary Kay Ash, and Madonna had very serious crises and the others had very traumatic events in their lives. If not causal, the experience of a crisis is certainly correlated, in my opinion. Passionate drive and extraordinary energy, at the level found in Maria Callas, is unusual and often the result of a crisis or traumatic event.

Traumatic or "shock" states of learning are not new. These devices of behavior modification were used extensively in brainwashing POWs during wartime. Sensory deprivation (confinement to black holes or dungeons) was used to lower brain waves to condition the vulnerable prisoners to change their views. Another, more acceptable device to enhance superlearning is transcendental meditation, which has been successfully used prior to exams, speech making, or other demanding intellectual accomplishments. Whatever the ploy, superlearning appears to have been an influential factor in creative achievement.

Crisis and the Creativity of Female Visionaries

Catherine the Great fashioned mountains out of ant hills. She was on the verge of losing everything, including her freedom, her son, and her life, when she mounted a stallion and took the reigns of Mother Russia, which led her to unprecedented heights. Two centuries later, Ayn Rand as an eight-year-old chose Catherine as her mentor. She was threatened with death at the hands of the Bolshevik revolutionists. She survived near-death experiences only to be confronted by the horrors of World War I at age nine, the revolution at age twelve, and near starvation while just a teenager during the last year of the war. Then the interminable Russian Revolution seized her home, the family business, and her self-respect. Rand endured these crises to emerge as the most vocal capitalist author since Adam Smith. Her early bouts with calamity had inspired her to create her epic philosophical novels. She became the most vocal, crusading capitalist of this century (attested to by the giant dollar sign on her coffin in 1982), and spawned the philosophical movement known as objectivism, which became the theoretical cornerstone of the antigovernment Libertarian Party.

Margaret Mead was a precocious child of nontraditional parents. They let her name her newborn sister (Katherine) when she was four. Margaret was devastated six months later when Katherine died unexpectedly at Christmas. Not much was mentioned of this obscure event in biographies about her, or in her autobiography *Blackberry Winter* (1972). But thirty-five years later Mead named her own daughter Catherine. Losing a loved one at such a critical stage of her development appears to have been one of the factors in her compulsive drive to the top of the world of anthropology.

Jane Fonda lost her mother to suicide at age twelve, which launched her into a twenty-three-year bout with bulimia. Her mother had experienced a turbulent life of nervous breakdowns and obsessions, all of which affected little Jane, who had a love/hate relationship with her mother and had secretly wished that Katharine Hepburn were her mother. All of this contributed to her guilt and ultimate obsession with perfection and overachieving. Her mother had been obsessed with her weight and figure and this ultimately drove Fonda into eating disorders. Fonda admits the bulimia resulted from her internalizing the guilt over her mother's death. Her obsessive and manic-depressive behavior started shortly after she learned of her mother's tragedy, which induced horrible nightmares all through Fonda's school years. Brooke Howard, a college roommate, said, "Wild screaming went on for hours." Jane had treated her mother badly just prior to the suicide; she and her brother, Peter, had hidden from their mother, who was desperately attempting to communicate with them. Mrs. Fonda called out to Jane but her daughter refused to respond. Mrs. Fonda went back to the sanitarium and two days later slashed her throat from ear to ear. Jane's guilt over the traumatic event left an indelible mark on her psyche.

Even in her seventies, Golda Meir still recalled the nightmarish pogroms in Kiev, Russia. She was only four years old when she first heard the accusation "Christ killer." The rabble-rousers instilled such fear into this innocent little girl that she reminisced about the trauma and fear in her mid-seventies while penning her biography. These traumatic experiences led Meir to Zionism and a lifelong struggle for a permanent home for the wandering Jew. A free state of Israel became her unconscious dream, which would extract every ounce of her energy her whole life. Meir would face many traumas and crises in her march to the office of prime minister of Israel. Life had been so difficult in Russia at the turn of the century that five of her brothers and sisters died before reaching their second year. Golda grew up knowing hunger and fear and thereby built such an awesome and resilient self-esteem and iron will that she was never lost. During her late twenties she almost starved to death in Jerusalem, and later became a truly "fearless woman" in order to survive the harsh life of a trail-blazing colonist. At age fifty she was still confronted with death every hour of every day. She experienced death and annihilation virtually every day of her life and it never daunted her spirit. She experienced far more crises than any other female in this book but never allowed them to effect her attitude. Her first crises in Russia evidently conditioned her for almost anything that could happen later in life.

Madonna, like Fonda, faced the loss of her mother at a very impressionable age. Madonna's mother died of cancer when she was five years old and her unconscious psyche has never let her forget the trauma. Madonna's lifelong scars have been sublimated into every bizarre and rebellious act imaginable, both personal and professional. She admits the experience is still haunting her: "My mother's death left me with a certain kind of loneliness, an indelible longing for something. If I hadn't had that emptiness, I wouldn't have been so driven." She would later talk about the hurt of being left alone by saying, "No one's going to break my heart again." Madonna has kept that promise in her intense and obsessive drive to the top by rejecting everyone who attempts to get close to her emotionally.

Gloria Steinem's early trauma and crisis revolved around her manic-depressive mother, who had a nervous breakdown prior to her birth and was institutionalized when Gloria was twelve. She had been dismissed from a job as a journalist at a Toledo, Ohio, newspaper. This contributed to her problems and Gloria was told her mother's problems were related to female emotionalism, when it was really manic-depression. Gloria was required to nurse and care for her mother throughout her youth and was tormented for having to play nursemaid while her friends were playing and partying. This early trauma has been a major factor in Steinem's rejection of both marriage and family. She has gone through serial relationships in a very orderly manner, and when they get to the point of permanence she disappears. Steinem's past has given her the psychological energy and persistence necessary to become a leader of the feminist movement in the United States. She would have preferred a more normal childhood but probably would never have overachieved if that had been the case. She would probably now be a grandmother in Toledo, Ohio.

Lillian Vernon was just five when her family was forced to flee anti-Semitic Germany for Holland. Five years later the family had to flee once again to the United States when the Nazi juggernaut invaded Western Europe. A second trauma occurred when Vernon's brother was killed in the resulting conflagration. She had to learn new languages, learn new cultures, and find new friends— not nice as a child but great training for a future entrepreneurial genius.

Margaret Thatcher stood firm against the Nazis, having grown up as a teenager in Grantham, the most bombed city in England. More than thirty thousand British subjects died in the Battle of Britain. The experience molded her into the invincible Iron Lady.

Linda Wachner had a chair pulled out from under her at age ten and at age eleven was in a body cast for nearly two years. She was not sure she would ever walk again and vowed that when she did, she would never get tired. Ever since that childhood trauma she has been a driven woman. She admits, "I have an unrelenting need to do the right thing, to be as close to a goal as possible." She says, "Sometimes when I'm very tired, I still dream about that silver traction triangle over my head." Because of the crisis, she says, "I have enormous energy. I'm a morning person and an afternoon person and an evening person. And I will stay up for two or three days in a row to get it done." Past employees and company executives, who could never keep up with this human dynamo, will attest to the fact that she has kept her childhood promise to never tire.

Maria Callas lived a life surrounded by crisis and trauma, which very probably had a major influence on her volatile personality as well as her incomparable talent. Callas's mother never wanted her and refused to look at her or touch her for the first four days of her life. Then, when she was five, Maria was hit by a car in Manhattan and dragged a block. The doctors told her distraught parents that it was hopeless. She was in a coma for twelve days and in the hospital for twenty-two days. She emerged with a determined commitment to become the world's greatest singer. Callas's mother then attempted suicide when Maria was eight because of the family's financial problems brought on by the Depression. Her mother was committed to Bellevue Hospital for a month. At the age of seventeen Callas was in Athens when World War II erupted and the Nazi war machine invaded her country. Athens was occupied for four years and there were times when she was forced to eat out of garbage cans to survive. After the war, during a Red occupation, she was almost killed when running through a barrage of bullets. These crises shaped her manic-depressive personality, which molded Callas into an impatient, impulsive perfectionist and the volatile prima donna that audiences around the world grew to love and hate. Callas never really got over her mother's early rejection and returned the favor when at the age of thirty she bought her a fur coat and said goodbye to her forever. She never saw her mother again.

Mary Kay Ash faced three major crises in her life. Her father was stricken with tuberculosis when she was two and she had to nurse him from age seven while her mother worked two jobs to support the family. Then her husband deserted her at age twenty-seven, leaving her with three children under the age of eight. Her most devastating crisis occurred a month before the launch of Mary Kay Cosmetics. Her husband, who was to be the administrative and financial advisor for the new company, dropped dead of a heart attack. These crises appear to have instilled in Ash some marvelous ability to ignore the negatives in life and pursue the positives. She went on to revolutionize multi-level marketing sales in the United States with a Norman Vincent Peale brand of zeal and confidence.

Oprah Winfrey was born carrying crises on her back like a cross. She was illegitimate and was without a father or mother for the first six years of her life. At age nine she was raped and later sexually assaulted and molested by three different family members. For eight years she was shuffled between mother and father, attending numerous schools in three different cities. Oprah repressed much of the guilt over these experiences and after experiencing still more rejection in Baltimore, she attempted suicide. These events all appear instrumental in her rise to become America's premiere talk-show host. Her supersensitivity and empathy have evolved out of her own childhood traumas. Oprah gave credence to the view that such trauma can have positive effects by saying that her sexual abuse "was not a horrible thing in my life. There was a lesson in it." However, she has since admitted that her weight problems and her inability to commit to marriage have been a function of not entirely dealing with that early trauma. She admits that her early traumas did have something to do with her great success and driven nature. In her words, "I was trying to make myself loved. And the way I could receive what I thought was love was through achievement."

Much like Lillian Vernon, Liz Claiborne had to flee Brussels in 1939 when the Nazis were invading. Estée Lauder's major life crisis was growing up in a ghetto and never wanting to admit it. A summary of these crises and traumas is listed in figure 11.

Figure 11

Crises and Early Adversity

Individual	Crisis or Trauma
Mary Kay Ash	Nursed invalid father from age seven, functioned as adult when but a child. First husband left her with three children under age eight when she was twenty-seven. Second husband died thirty days prior to launch of Mary Kay Cosmetics.
Maria Callas	Involved in terrible car accident at age five. In coma for twelve days. Mother attempted suicide when Maria was seven and was committed to a New York mental hospital. In Athens at age seventeen when Nazis occupied city, she lived in constant fear of death and starvation.
Liz Claiborne	Nazis invaded Belgium when she was ten causing her family to flee to the United States.
Jane Fonda	Mother committed to sanitarium with nervous breakdown when Fonda was eleven. Committed ghastly suicide when she was twelve, initiating Fonda's struggle with bulimia for next twenty-three years.
Estée Lauder	Sister had polio as a child.
Madonna	Mother died of cancer when Madonna was five. Her "everything" father betrayed her by marrying the baby sitter, who became the wicked stepmother.
Golda Meir	Pogroms in Kiev, Russia, from birth to age eight during which she was branded as "Christ killer." Trauma drove her to life of Zionism during which she faced death daily for fifty years. Almost starved to death in the 1920s in Jerusalem.
Ayn Rand	Lived through horror of World War I at age nine, Russian revolution at age twelve, near starvation in Russia as teenager. Had near-death experiences constantly during teenage years.
Gloria Steinem	Mother had nervous breakdown prior to her birth, which left her permanently disabled and mentally disturbed throughout Steinem's childhood. Parents divorced when she was ten. Mother relapsed when she was fourteen.
Margaret Thatcher	More bombs hit Grantham, England, than any other British city during World War II, while Margaret was a teenager.
Lillian Vernon	Anti-Semitism forced family to leave Germany for Holland when Hitler took power and then forced them to flee the Nazis for the United States. Vernon's brother was killed fighting in the war.
Linda Wachner	Bedridden at age eleven and never expected to walk again. In body cast for almost two years. Vowed to become great and never tire if able to walk and be normal.
Oprah Winfrey	Illegitimate child. Five moves by teen years. Raped at age nine, molested by three family members. Pregnant at fourteen and had child die at birth. Jilted relationship in Baltimore drove her to attempt suicide.

Female Crises and Creative Endeavor

Notice that the women in this work experienced several major crises during their lives but these traumas seem to have prepared each woman for a life of creativity and innovation. Lillian Vernon feels that all entrepreneurs need to be prepared for crises on a daily basis. She contends, "Every business has continual bouts with crises . . . but I learn from them and move ahead in a positive way." Bouts with trauma taught these women to deal with change as a positive rather than a negative experience. It allowed them to deal with ambiguity in a far more effective manner. Change became a catalyst for exorcising their personal ghosts of the past. They became empowered with the internal sense that they could bet the farm for the redemption of their dreams, since they had already seen the farm destroyed.

Paul Pearsall, medical doctor, writer, and philosopher, in his book *Making Miracles* (1993), describes crises as our evidence of survivability. "Crises are our experience of the chaos caused by the fifth energy constantly stirring things up to higher and more developed levels." This was his description of rebirth after reaching the precipice of death. Scientifically this is known as entropy, or the rebirth of a system after it reaches the point of chaos or self-destruction.

Dr. Prigogine's "Dissipative Structures"

The theory of *dissipative structures* was created by Ilya Prigogine, a Nobel Prize–winning theoretical chemist. He established that order arises out of disorder, and life emerges out of entropy. In other words, "artistic and scientific creativity" emerges out of chaos or entropy. Prigogine's hypothesis is illustrated by those females who turned a life of crises into creative endeavors. In Prigogine's words, "It is out of chaos, turmoil, and disorder that higher levels of order and wisdom occur." Applied to human behavior, Prigogine's scientific theories suggest that people hitting the very bottom—stripped mentally and physically and in a state of chaos—are the most likely to create breakthrough innovations. Prigogine makes an eloquent argument: "Many seeming systems of *breakdown* are actually harbingers of *breakthrough*." This apt description validates the ancient Greek pleasure/pain principle, which prophesies that true pleasure is unattainable without first knowing pain. It also suggests how both Germany and Japan could rise out of the devastation of World War II to become the two dominant powers in the world just thirty years later, and how these thirteen women who experienced such traumatic lives could become great creative visionaries as adults.

Crisis Is the Mother of Creativity!

The theory of dissipative structures offers scientific evidence for my hypothesis that "crisis is the mother of creativity." Prigogine said it more eloquently: "The more unstable an organization [or people] the more likely it is to change—to evolve." We find this process occurring in our bodies every day. When very ill we reach the crisis stage ending in a life-threatening fever or terminal condition. The body then goes to work and builds new antibodies and the "new cells" become more resistant to the disease than the "old cells." Likewise, a broken bone is always stronger at the break point than the original bone. According to dissipative-structure theory, the body either dies or emerges as something greater than it was prior to the crisis.

Further evidence that "crisis is the mother of creativity" comes from Donald Mackinnon (1975), who in a study on the creative personality, found that "persons of the most extraordinary effectiveness had had life histories marked by severe frustrations, deprivations, and traumatic experiences." Examples abound in history, such as the tragic lives of Abraham Lincoln, Theodore Roosevelt, and Mahatma Gandhi who rose above their crises to reach the pinnacle of success. As a law student Martin Luther was struck by a bolt of lighting and, fearing death, said, "St. Anne help! I will become a monk!" He lived and two weeks later became a monk, rather than writing law drafts. He went on to revolutionize religion. More recently, Arthur Jones, the creator of the Nautilus empire, narrowly escaped death at the hands of the Nigerian government, and this middle-aged crocodile hunter became an eminently successful entrepreneur. Ted Turner launched his empire shortly after his father committed suicide, and Fred Smith created Federal Express on returning from front-line action in Vietnam as a fighter pilot.

Virtually every great creative and innovative genius has been inspired by change, not inhibited by it. The weak are destroyed by crises, the strong are driven to greater heights as a result of trauma. As Prigogine has so eloquently said, "Life emerges out of entropy [chaos], not despite it." Crisis is the catalyst for achievement in the strong, not the insurmountable hurdle described by the weak. The thirteen visionaries in this book intuitively knew this and used their infirmities to further their careers. Societies have done the same.

Cultural Crisis and Creativity

An interesting example of crisis mothering great creative achievements can be seen in the meteoric rise of the United States from turmoil and chaos to the most powerful country in history. Even more enlightening is how both Japan and Germany rose from the ashes of defeat to become the most awesome economic titans the world has ever seen. Japan has since created an economy that dominates industry like no other. It has twenty-three of the top twenty-five banks in the world, dominates mass consumer electronics markets as well as automobile production, and leads in the production of semiconductors. Its worker productivity and yen value have overtaken that of the United States. In Germany, the Mercedes, the BMW, and the Porsche dominate the precision auto markets, and the Deutschmark is the strongest currency in the world as of late 1993.

Both Japan and Germany were virtually annihilated in 1945; their states were in utter chaos. Their economies could have perished, but instead they emerged stronger than before. These two nations took the *negentropy* path, transforming themselves into dynamic, innovative, creative, and resourceful nations. They are dominant on every postwar economic barometer because of an internalized psychological energy ingrained in their people—the same people who were decimated in the latter days of the war. They lost everything: jobs, families, futures, money, homes, and hope. Their losses stripped them of all self-esteem and broke their spirits. They were beaten people, but they picked themselves up and reconstructed their lives and their economies. Their wartime trauma appears to have spurred them on to greater achievement and creativity than they could ever have attained without the crises.

Prigogine clarifies this hypothesis with his aphorism, "Psychological suffering, anxiety, and collapse, can lead to new emotional, intellectual, and spiritual strengths—confusion and doubt can lead to new scientific ideas." The above theory, when applied to "social behavior, ecology, and economics" credits cultural crisis as the mother of economic creativity. According to Prigogine, terrible chaos appears to be a precursor for order and creative success in nations, cultures, and individuals as well as in biological systems: "With the paradigm of self-organization we see a transition from disorder to order. In the field of psychological activity this is perhaps the main experience we have—*every artistic or scientific reaction implies a transition from disorder to order.*"

Prigogine's "bifurcation point" is the critical point in a crisis where a system either dies or is reborn. It is at this point that a person or system moves on to greater creative endeavor or is destroyed by the crisis. These thirteen women were inspired to greater performance after having reached their bifurcation point. They emerged stronger than ever from their negative experiences using their crises to move mountains instead of hills.

Summary

Crisis is a concomitant of creativity. Mohammed attempted suicide more than once. Martin Luther had depressions and hallucinations and states of manic confusion. Manic depression, obsessive-compulsive behavior, and other forms of hypomania are found in most great creative geniuses. Maria Callas is a good example in this work. Oftentimes these psychological problems are a direct result of some childhood trauma or crisis. These behavior traits are not necessary for all great creativity, but they appear to help. It is not necessary for a person to have been afflicted with some great tragedy as a child to become an eminent entrepreneur, creator, or innovator. But an inordinate number of people who experienced such crises have gone on to exceptional accomplishments.

Crisis also appears to mold a person with a special resiliency and prepares them to operate in dynamic environments. The women in this book had an inordinate amount of childhood trauma and crisis in their lives. Half of them had an immediate family member die or become seriously incapacitated. Many had near-death experiences themselves. These traumatic events seem to have imprinted them with a tenacity and willpower not found in the average female.

Prigogine found that when a system reaches the point of bifurcation (chaos) it will then die or reemerge as something greater than before. That is apparently what happened with the women in this book. They faced adversity but were able to overcome it and reach the top. Children reaching Prigogine's state of disorder or entropy end up in a traumatic or theta state, in which they are capable of "superlearning," which imprints them with a highly resilient personality. Their early traumas and crises indelibly imprinted them with an exceptional determination to succeed, which helped them reach the top of their fields later in life. Crises, transience, and unhappy childhoods play a large role in creative and innovative achievement. Many of these female visionaries experienced childhood dysfunctions, relocations, and depressive states, giving credence to Prigogine's "bifurcation point" theory.

Facing a terrible crisis early in life appears to be a positive force for developing individuals into creative adults. Such experiences evidently condition the child to cope in similar environments as an adult. Creative endeavor, breakthrough innovation, and great entrepreneurship are nothing more than learning to cope with daily crises and overcoming them. Overachievers seem to have learned these lessons early in life. These women experienced more crises in their lives than the normal population and consequently learned to deal with them better than others. It was this factor that appears to have been instrumental in their creative genius.

7

Personality Traits and Temperaments

The extroverted intuitive personality fits many of today's leading innovators.
—Carl Jung

Nine of the thirteen innovative geniuses in this book were extroverted intuitive personality types, thus validating Carl Jung's prophetic quote. This type personality is classified visionary. Those who have it see the possibilities and opportunities in life and pursue them in a grand and eloquent manner. They have a macro-vision, allowing them a clear view of the forests in life rather than the trees. This vision gives them a broad perspective and permits them to circumvent the many roadblocks along the way to great achievement. Problem resolution is more a function of definition than any other single factor and these personality types are able to reduce complex problems to simple solutions.

Great creative visionaries have the talent to see the big picture, the self-confidence to attack it, and the temperament to risk everything to prevail in the struggle. They believe in their own ability to make the right decision even when everyone else disbelieves. They are not deterred by negative thinking or naysaying adversaries, which is why "Mary Kay" elicits an image of pink Cadillacs; "Thatcherism" now defines a definitive political concept; Oprah is "Everywoman"; Liz Claiborne means fashionable women's wear; John Galt evokes antibureaucracy and "Enlightened self-interest"; Steinem is equated with the feminist movement; Estée Lauder implies skin care; and Madonna connotes sex. Whether you love them or despise them, you cannot deny their enormous impact on society, and the fact that they have materially influenced the way the world thinks, looks, works, and functions.

Visionary Behavior Characteristics

There is a strikingly similar pattern in the way visionaries perceive the world and interact with their peers. There is universal agreement that "the creative genius is different." Many are eccentric and most have renegade mentalities. They dream on a fantastic scale and have the temerity to make dreams come true, while the rest of us look on in total disbelief. According to personality researcher David Keirsey, "Intuitive-thinkers are compelled to rearrange the environment." In other words, they thrive on change while most other people resist and/or fear it.

The personality traits for these women are very similar as a group, but quite different from noncreative types. The creative visionary tends to operate holistically, with a propensity for intuitive decision-making. Mozart commented that his work "did not come to me successively . . . but in its entirety." Einstein's monumental special theory of relativity was conceived through the sheer force of intuitiveness. He would later reflect on the intuitive process as the only viable approach to the creative process by saying, "A theory can be proved by experiment, but no path leads from experiment to the birth of a theory."

Creative individuals often characterize their work as spontaneous, seren-dipitous, and shocking. They are intolerant of error and inefficiency in people. Acquiring knowledge and competence are very important to them and they typically demand more of themselves than others. Intellectual stimulation is their forte, and optimism their deity. They are the architects of change with a higher-than-normal proclivity for risk-taking. Maria Callas, Mary Kay Ash, and Oprah Winfrey share the above traits but have another dimension missing in the others. These three women score high in empathy and sensitivity. All thirteen were charismatic leaders with insatiable energy and drive. They were competitive to a fault and highly focused in their drive toward long-term objectives. Most were physically strong and worked longer hours with less fatigue than the average person. Any one of them could have been labeled a "Type A" personality. No one trait defines them all as none had just one of the above traits. In this work each has been assigned one trait that best defines them, but they all had a number of the following thirteen traits: self-confidence, charisma, perseverance, maverick mentality, impatience, drive, auto-cratic tendencies, intransigence, optimism, intuition, rebelliousness, competi-tiveness, risk-taking propensities, workaholic tendencies, persuasiveness.

Dominant Personality Traits

Catherine the Great, Margaret Mead, and Mother Teresa are historical exam-ples of the female visionary personality. They had many of the identical personality traits assigned to these women. Note Henry Troyat's 1980 description of Catherine the Great's personality:

> She was a relentless worker, and at the same time a charmer who combined the graces of her sex with a virile authority. Everything that she desired she obtained by patience, intelligence, toughness, courage, taking incredible risks when necessary, suddenly changing course in order to reach the goal more surely.

Catherine was arrogant and rebellious even as a teenager, causing King Frederick of Germany to say, "The child is impertinent." She wrote in her memoirs, "I was sustained by ambition alone. There was something within me which never allowed me to doubt for a single moment that I should one day succeed in becoming the Empress of Russia." Margaret Mead had the same independent and almost arrogant self-confidence. Her biographer, Jane Howard (1984), said, "She was goal-oriented when there wasn't any goal" and "her need for adulation and approval was boundless." Mother Teresa was less overt in her approach but certainly was an independent spirit who also overachieved by refusing to take no for an answer.

The Confident Charismatic: Mary Kay Ash

Poet Alexander Pope said, "Self-confidence is the first requisite to great undertakings." Both confidence and charisma personify Mary Kay Ash, who has built a billion-dollar company because of these two qualities. Ash exudes a magnetic charm and a personal aura which are spellbinding to those around her. Her supreme confidence helped her launch the Mary Kay enterprise in the highly competitive cosmetics field. Her charisma attracted the largest multi-level-marketing female sales force in America and then motivated them to extraordinary heights. These two traits were critical in making Mary Kay Cosmetics the dominant force in the multilevel-marketing industry.

Charisma comes from the Greek for "gift of God" and the great leaders of the world have had it. Jesus, Napoleon, Gandhi, and John F. Kennedy had a power to inspire others to buy into their prophetic visions. These thirteen women all had this unique ability to inspire those around them. They attracted disciples who followed them toward their goals. Ash's favorite saying is, "If you think you can, you can. If you think you can't, you can't!" which is in tune with her favorite motivational metaphor, the bumblebee. Because the bee shouldn't be able to fly but does, Ash equates it to female overachievers. "It's just like our women who didn't know they could fly to the top, but they did." Self-motivation is Ash's forte and the reason for her enormous success.

Some of the other women profiled in this book had Ash's traits. Golda Meir mesmerized audiences throughout the world. David Ben Gurion said of her, "Golda could move people to tears." Ayn Rand was about to be castigated by a hostile TV newsman during a 1970s show because of her highly opinionated and controversial demeanor. Instead she so captivated him, he changed course during the interview and became her ally. Catherine the Great, Margaret Mead, and Mother Teresa all exuded an aura when entering a room. Powerful men and leaders of nations all bowed to their charismatic power. Mother Teresa used this power to save millions of lives. This woman is powerful while physically weak, commands respect though impoverished, and is rich despite being destitute. Strangers meeting her speak with reverence of her aura. She can move people and programs without so much as uttering a word. This was never so apparent as when she persuaded the Catholic Church to create the "Missionaries of Charity" as an adjunct group. This mindboggling feat surpasses logic since the church is notorious for apathy and nonperformance, even on meaningless issues. Mother Teresa was able to accomplish what others could not get accomplished over centuries of cajoling and persuasion. Anyone expecting to lead others must possess a confident and charismatic attitude because it attracts followers to their cause. Ash and Mother Teresa are prime examples of these critically important traits.

Competitive and Indomitable Spirit: Margaret Thatcher

The Iron Lady was a combative and indomitable spirit as Britain's prime minister. She was not one to equivocate even when cornered, and much of this resolve was due to a highly competitive nature nurtured during her early years by her doting father. He preached to her to "lead, not follow" and that it was quite all right to be "different." Margaret was competitive to a fault, which gave her the will to go head to head with her many adversaries in the British Parliament. Her iron resolve has remained intact as Lady Thatcher. *Forbes* magazine confirms this trait, saying in 1992, "You can't spend an hour with Margaret Thatcher without being aware you have met one of the world's most indomitable personalities."

Margaret had her own blunt but honest agenda. Her party members were either with her or they became the enemy. She asked of every new political prospect, "Is he one of us?" "Us" meant, did he agree with "Thatcherism" as a political platform. Thatcher was not about to spend time with those not in sync with her philosophical beliefs. The Iron Lady was never deterred by her political adversaries. Her fierce, competitive nature loved a fight. And it has been proved that competition improves everyone for the better. Her biographer Young (1989) characterized her as a "hardworking, single-minded, fierce antagonist in argument, and an uncrackable performer in the House of Commons." She approached every issue as if it were a game to be played out on a political battlefield. Political commentator Paul Johnson said of her, "Even her most venomous opponents will admit that she has bounteous reserves of truly Churchillian valour."

The other women in this volume had similar spirits and competitive mentalities. They never equivocated on issues regardless of the consequences, and were prepared to live or die with the consequences of their actions. Their internal strength was enormous and it carried them through to victory in most battles. The Iron Lady is the personification of the strong female leader. But Jane Fonda was equally strong, as illustrated by her successful 1973 lawsuit against the U.S. government, President Nixon and his Cabinet, and the FBI for $2.8 million. Golda Meir also was never one to back down from a confrontation. She riveted her attention on the goal of winning every battle. Mary Kay Ash, Linda Wachner, Lillian Vernon, Estée Lauder, and Liz Claiborne were all highly competitive or would not have survived as businesswomen in male-dominated industries. They never shied away from confrontations with competitors, although their feminine natures made them fight with more integrity than many of their male adversaries.

Empowered Independence: Lillian Vernon

Women political leaders are empowered and independent according to *Women in Power,* a volume published in 1992 focusing on twenty-five prominent female American politicians. This book analyzed the success factors for these powerful women and found that female political leaders are empowered through "enabling messages" from their parents and other early role models. The authors concluded that women's power and leadership is a function of a "competent self plus creative aggression plus woman power." In other words, powerful female leaders are not born, but molded through internalized competence (self-esteem), which instills creative aggression that empowers them to great success. Lillian Vernon personifies these traits.

Margaret Mead is another example of a woman who commanded great power manifested via an independent persona. At age four she gathered her siblings in a bedroom and in a rebellious act announced she was seceding from the family. This independence and nonconforming attitude were encouraged by her parents, who were responsible for creating one of the world's most independent women. Mead the anthropologist wrote, "The child who displays repudiated parental traits starts life with a handicap," which illustrates her belief that one should determine one's own destiny in spite of any parental belief systems. In accordance with this philosophy, Mead kept her own name in all three of her marriages. This was her way of maintaining her own identity, which, in her era, was close to heresy.

Lillian Vernon is a more contemporary visionary who personifies empowered independence. She utilized high self-confidence and independence in changing the world of direct-mail retailing. When a new product or concept is being formulated she has the self-confidence to rely on her "Golden Gut" to make the decision. When told the market research says otherwise, she has the temerity to ignore the computer's advice. She uses her personal empowerment as a "superwoman" to make the important decisions in her business. In other words she has the empowered confidence to follow her own instincts in operating her business. While Sears announced the closing of its catalog operations, this empowered and independent woman has never done better.

Power and independence typify the other women in this work. These traits are especially evident in the lives of Thatcher, Meir, Madonna, Rand, Fonda, Wachner, Lauder, and Ash. Catherine the Great told the French ambassador, "There is no woman bolder than I. I have the most reckless audacity." All of these women were powerful and independent individuals who often used their strength to attain their positions of eminence. Personal power and independence go together, especially when one is determined to reach the top.

Rebellious Femme Fatale: Gloria Steinem

Opening doors with feminine charm has long been a heritage of the beautiful people. Catherine the Great used her lover to overthrow her husband's political regime and take power. Mary Kay Ash admitted that she would walk into a room intent on captivating the men with her feminine charms until she could assess their weaknesses. Using physical beauty and talent to create societal good has been the province of few, however; Gloria Steinem is one such woman. Steinem was an attractive female leader in the early years of the 1960s feminist movement, even though her comeliness turned off many of her more zealous sisters. Beauty conjured up values opposite to the feminist movement in the eyes of some militant feminists. Many of her sisters, constituents, compatriots, and followers were confused by her role in the movement, since she dated and socialized with people they considered the enemy. *Esquire* called her an "enigmatic femme fatale" and quoted her ex-boss as saying, "Much of her success had to do with her effect on men."

Gloria fueled this argument with her first major journalistic accomplishment, donning a bunny outfit in order to accurately write an article on the Playboy Club called "A Bunny's Tale." Gloria often used her femininity, either knowingly or unknowingly, to open doors and to fight the paternalistic systems that denied equal rights to women. What was lost on the militant anti-feminine types within the movement was that her voice was heard primarily because she was the antithesis of the popular image of a militant female. This subtlety was lost on many of her feminist detractors; they felt she was not of their "identity." The truth is that her femininity is what helped the movement gain credibility, since it opened many doors for her to enter and preach the gospel of inequality.

Madonna, Estée Lauder, Mary Kay Ash, Ayn Rand, and Golda Meir were far more guilty of using their feminine allure to further their careers and causes than was Steinem. Consider Ayn Rand, who had a fifteen-year affair with her mentor, press agent, and objectivism publisher, Nathaniel Branden. Estée Lauder flirted her way through the department stores of America to launch the Estée Lauder line of cosmetics and skin care. She was purported to have had liaisons with a Hollywood mogul in the interest of furthering the Estée Lauder fortunes during the early days, according to biographer Lee Israel (1985). Golda Meir was an enchanting young zealot in Israel and a femme fatale of the first order. Her biographer, Ralph Martin (1988), characterized her as a "Femme Fatale without makeup and never more than two dresses at one time." Golda never denied the allegation that she used her personal magnetism to get to the top. She considered romantic liaisons a natural part of living, and passion a necessary part of a life faced with death at every corner. Jane Fonda had long affairs with her directors and leading men. One of these, Roger Vadim, became her first husband. Madonna is infamous for using men to help launch her to fame. She repeatedly used and discarded disc jockeys, directors, managers (of both sexes), and producers in her dizzying ascent from the bottom to the top (Anderson, 1990).

Many provocative and attractive women have a difficult time disassociating their sexuality from their careers. How to be attractive and not have it become an Achilles heel is not an easy task. Teenage girls have been trained through their role models and the media to use their allure to gain approval, get a date, or land a job. Changing this pattern as an adult becomes a difficult task. Even males like John F. Kennedy used their attractiveness to win elections, most notably his win over Richard Nixon in the famous 1960 TV debates. Female credibility for the attractive woman has been a problem since Cleopatra used her beauty to charm Marc Antony. I believe that it is incumbent on everyone to use all of their assets to achieve success as long as they are not abused or used in an unfair or inappropriate manner. Gloria Steinem used her charms to open doors in a totally appropriate manner. However, she was able to accomplish far more for the feminist movement because of her femme fatale nature than if she had been homely. Steinem had many other important traits. She was bright, articulate, independent, persuasive, and worked very hard. She will be remembered as an attractive feminist who changed the world for the better.

Impatient Hyper-Heroine: Estée Lauder

Patience is a virtue in some societies and cultures but not so in the world of creativity and innovation. Psychologist Alfred Adler propounded the theory that all people strive for perfection and superiority. Abraham Maslow built on that theory with his concept of self-actualization, which was based on excellence. The pursuit of excellence, perfection, and superiority are typically accompanied by impatience and intolerance. In fact, most gifted children have been found to be intolerant of useless conformity in school. Intolerance and impatience are what made many of these creative visionaries poor students, including Estée Lauder, who is the prototypical example of the impatient overachiever. This trait of impatience made her a tigress in creating the Estée Lauder empire.

As a "Type A" personality, Estée Lauder was quick to say, "I act on instinct quickly, without pondering possible disaster and without indulging in deep introspection." She pursued her dream of beauty in everything she did. When asked about her success she responded, "I was quicksilver and driven." Margaret Mead was notorious for her impatience and for her drive, as were Golda Meir, Madonna, Linda Wachner, and Maria Callas. Ayn Rand's biographer and lover, Nathaniel Branden, described her as "impatient, arrogant, dogmatic and visionary." Wachner is notorious for her impatient, "do it now" approach to business. Even though she operates in the New York garment district, which is notorious for its frenetic style and overt impatience, she is still considered unusual. Wachner requires every executive in the company to carry a notebook inscribed with "Do It Now" for recording all problems that require action. Wachner and Lauder are two New York visionary women who define the impatient, hyper, overachieving woman.

Intransigent Will: Golda Meir

Golda Meir and Margaret Thatcher epitomize women with intransigent wills. Both were labeled such by their political enemies and allies alike. Peggy Mann, a biographer of Meir, said of her, "She runs her cabinet like a front-line officer, thumping the table for order, and making blunt and rapid decisions. . . . When she makes a decision, it's made." The Russians tagged Thatcher with the label "Iron Lady" for her intransigent negotiating style. Thatcher's biographer, Young (1989), said, "Her style was built on domination. . . . Certitude was her stock in trade. . . . [In] her reluctance ever to lose an argument, she seemed so damnably sure of herself that nobody could suppose there lurked much uncertainty anywhere in her makeup." Meir had the strongest will of any of the women in this book, though all had strong will power and never vacillated from their cause despite enormous odds against them.

All female visionaries are armed with strong wills or they could never overcome the violent opposition that faces them daily. If they did not, the doomsdayers and so-called experts who predict their imminent demise would deter them from their goals. The intransigent will and spirit of these women tend to keep them on track. Their resolute demeanor becomes a shield from the left-brain-driven majority, who attempt to defeat them at every turn. Ayn Rand was another intransigent female who embodied what could be the motto for this section, "I have sworn eternal hostility to every form of tyranny over the mind of man." She was another woman who never backed down from her philosophical position of capitalistic self-interest no matter what the consequences.

Libidinally Driven: Madonna

Madonna is a libidinally driven female with an insatiable drive for more and more of everything in life. Her constant striving for sexual fulfillment and exhibitionism appears to be seated in an early unfulfilled need for love. This constant need for affection and adulation comes from a need to exorcise early feelings of rejection by her father (based on his marriage to the babysitter after her mother died). Madonna's behavior has all the signs of an Electra complex. She told *Vanity Fair* (1990), "I have not resolved my Electra complex." She appears to have a subliminal need to fill an unrequited father's love. She has turned her needs into a compulsion to overachieve to demonstrate to the world that she is worthy of affection and of being loved.

Napoleon Hill, writer of *Think and Grow Rich,* said, "Sex energy is the creative energy of all geniuses." He went on to say, "There never has been, and never will be a great leader, builder, or artist lacking in this driving force of sex." Hill's hypothesis is true of the women in this research even though his research was done on males only. Madonna is the prototypical model for excessive, sexually driven energy, although Meir, Fonda, Callas, and others were also passionate women. They were all blessed with a high libidinal energy, although in some cases the drive was sublimated into their work. This was certainly true of Mother Teresa, Margaret Mead, Margaret Thatcher, and Linda Wachner.

The quintessential example of a woman driven by sexual energy is Catherine the Great, probably the most prolific "man-izer" in history. Imagine spending the equivalent of $1.5 billion in today's dollars on male concubines. According to her biographer Troyat (1989), to her "men were instruments of pleasure." Catherine's debauchery is legend. Margaret Mead also led an active sex life— both in and out of marriage—to three different men. Mead did not limit her libidinal drive to men, as she had liaisons with various females throughout her life (Howard, 1984).

Golda Meir is often viewed as the grandmotherly type since she was seventy when she assumed the office of prime minister of Israel. As a younger woman Meir was probably more sexually active and seductive than Madonna or Fonda. A school friend said, "She was so vibrant and attractive" everyone fell in love with her. Golda admitted, "I was no nun" in a moment of candor. She was libidinally driven in much the way Napoleon Hill describes great leaders of the world. Sexual energy or vital force differs for various women and it was substantially different for these creative geniuses. Madonna, Fonda, Meir, Ash, Callas, Rand, and Steinem were passionate women with healthy sex drives, as demonstrated by their many relationships. The others were far more reserved about their sexual needs and probably channeled their energy into their work. It is apparent that the sexual needs of these women varied but all had driven natures, which appears critical to the creative process.

Macro-Oriented Intuitor: Ayn Rand

Psychiatric researcher Daniel Cappon has dedicated his life's work to the study of intuition. He created an "intuition quotient" test and, according to *Psychology Today* in 1993, he found that "intuition is like a very old whore . . . who is on her way to becoming a very respectable lady . . . the archetypal jewel in the crown of human intelligence." Cappon is convinced that all creativity is a function of intuitive ability. "Intuition is the 'secret' of survival and success in all human endeavors," he says. "Intuition is responsible for the survival of the species."

Ayn Rand, the acknowledged patron saint of Promethean temperaments, espoused rational objectivity in mankind. She hated psychologist B. F. Skinner's behaviorism, seeing it as the basis of communism and the potential destruction of both human freedom and creativity. She said, "Just listen to any prophet, and if you hear him speak of sacrifice—run. Run faster than from a plague. Where there's sacrifice, there's someone collecting." Rand was the thinking woman's woman. She worshiped qualitative issues rather than quantitative ones. She created her philosophy of life, objectivism, based on a nonstructured way of life with minimal government interference. Her philosophy of "enlightened self-interest" espoused by John Galt and Howard Roark (her fictional alter egos) was in absolute defiance of the pervasive socialistic trends popular during the thirties and forties. Ayn was writing the capitalist creed while the FDR regime was passing socialistic legislation and the British, French, and Italian governments were replacing capitalist leaders with socialists and fascists. Rand's intellectual defiance of worldwide trends was indicative of her macro world view and her intuitive mentality. No matter how hostile the opposition, she never backed down. She passionately believed in a laissez-faire society led by those with an "enlightened self-interest." Her philosophical model centered on reason and freedom, which ultimately became the philosophical platform for the Libertarian Party.

Eleven of these thirteen women are classified "intuitive" on the Myers-Briggs personality scale. They were leaders in their field because they knew where they were going based on their intuitive or "gut" feel. This made them powerful leaders, since people want to follow those who have a clear vision of their destination. No one wants to follow someone who is lost. They were not inclined to use market research to guide them, but instead used an internal vision or what Lillian Vernon calls her "Golden Gut." They intuitively knew it was impossible to do market research on something that had never been done. It must be felt with gut-wrenching insight and little or no validation. Only the intuitive-thinking visionaries of the world are comfortable operating in this zone.

Perpetual Perfectionist: Maria Callas

Alfred Adler described man as "striving for perfection; striving for superiority; striving for power." He believed that "striving for perfection was innate" and fundamental to a well-adjusted and successful life. Maria Callas is the ideal example of Adler's theory. She often said of herself, "I am impatient and impulsive, I have an obsession for perfection." She told one reporter, "I do not like the middle way. All or nothing is my way." Adler felt that all people have this innate drive, but it appears that the creative visionaries of the world are more driven to be perfect than most. They do not abide mediocrity in anything.

Madonna drives her employees crazy with her compulsive need to have everything perfect. Others were more tactful than Madonna but that desire for excellence characterized every one of the subjects in this book during their rise to the top. Ayn Rand was such a perfectionist that she spent two years writing John Galt's famous radio speech which ended up as 500,000 words. Considering that the whole of this book is approximately 150,000 words in length, her efforts were astonishing. Every great innovative leader is a perfectionist in some way. They never accept mediocre or inferior performance from themselves or from their subordinates. Their need to be the best drives them to live as examples of Adler's admonition that we are all "striving for perfection."

Persuasive Persona: Oprah Winfrey

"We are all salesmen. We must sell something in order to live. . . . You are selling your brains, your health, your vitality, your strength; you are selling your ingenuity, your resourcefulness, your originality, your initiative, your courage; you are selling your executive ability in some ways." This sage axiom was written in 1909 by Orison Marden, founder of *Success* magazine. Female visionaries all have an unusual ability to sell their concepts, even introverts like Mother Teresa, Ayn Rand, Liz Claiborne, Gloria Steinem, and Maria Callas.

Oprah Winfrey makes P. T. Barnum look like Mr. Peepers. She has the charismatic power to captivate an audience and sell them on her ideas and perspective. She has been the making of many authors. Marianne Williamson sold over 500,000 copies of *A Return to Love* (1992) because of her guest appearance on "Oprah." Winfrey's persuasive ability has made her talk show the number one show in the history of American television and made her the highest paid entertainer in show business. Winfrey has an uncanny feel for selling. She can empathize with diverse groups and can hone in on the exact feelings of everyone in her viewing audience. "Every woman," as she is sometimes called, can articulate the right question at the right time no matter how controversial. Oprah could have become a world-class teacher of salesmanship without any knowledge that she was selling because of her unique ability to empathize and honestly articulate her feelings. Winfrey's integrity is her strength, which has been found to correlate well with sales success. All of these women were able to sell their concepts but Winfrey is the consummate persuasive personality.

Mary Kay Ash and Estée Lauder made millions through the art of persuasion, and Golda Meir and Margaret Thatcher rose to the very top of their nation's political strata because of this ability. Gloria Steinem and Mother Teresa sold their ideas of better social systems to achieve their goals. Ayn Rand could never have published her books without having sold her publishers. Maria Callas, Jane Fonda, and Madonna had to convince directors to back them before they could go on stage for the general public. None of these women could have moved beyond mediocrity without their ability to sell. It is one of the most critical traits for the entrepreneur, innovator, and creator.

Persevering Pioneer: Liz Claiborne

Liz Claiborne personifies a female who persevered in an industry intolerant of outside influence. She was convinced that professional women's work clothes should be practical, affordable, flexible, and chic. She was convinced that a school teacher or designer should not have to dress in a formal business suit to emulate the males from Wall Street. Her employers at Jonathan Logan turned down her ideas repeatedly until frustration forced her to start her own firm to launch her products. Liz Claiborne now *owns* the career women's clothes market due to her inviolable perseverance.

Most of these visionaries had the same tenacity. They followed their dreams until they dropped and then got up and pursued them some more. Persistence and perseverance are critical to the creative process and these women were steeped in this talent. Maria Callas was turned down repeatedly to sing opera. She never accepted the criticism of her voice range and made herself into one of the world's greatest prima donnas based on her stage personality, not her voice. Linda Wachner quit Max Factor when the owners misled her into believing that if she raised the money they would allow her to buy the firm. Then she pursued an acquisition of Revlon. When the offer was presented another was accepted. She never quit and a year later was able to acquire Warnaco in a hostile takeover—the first such takeover by a woman in the history of Wall Street. These stories are rampant in the lives of the creative genius. They doggedly pursue their goals until they achieve them, no matter the cost.

Worldly Workaholic: Linda Wachner

Linda Wachner is the classic "Type A" personality—a workaholic. When queried by *Cosmopolitan* magazine on her reputation she confirmed her addiction by saying, "I don't bring work home anymore—I stay here until I get it done. Until nine, until ten, until whenever. . . .The problem is that sometimes I don't leave the office." She is not alone: Mary Kay Ash, Margaret Thatcher, Maria Callas, and Golda Meir admitted in their biographies to fourteen-hour work days as a norm, often for seven days a week. Prime Minister Meir, was in her seventies during the Yom Kippur War and slept but four hours a night for three years—and those four hours were often cat naps on her desk. Most of the other creative geniuses were compulsive workaholics with little regard for their health or their families. However, most would take issue with the workaholic label, primarily because they view work as enjoyment. It is their passion, and passion to them is fun, not work.

Work often has a negative connotation but not to these visionaries. They view work as enjoyable and more akin to play than a chore. They are prepared to spend inordinate amounts of time working for the realization of their careers and dreams. Catherine the Great's biographer characterized her work ethic:

> She herself was up at five in the morning and worked twelve to fourteen hours a day. She scarcely took time to eat, and around nine o'clock in the

evening, after spending a brief moment at table with intimate friends, she would collapse on her bed in exhaustion. She fired off drafts at a speed that surprised and even vexed the copyists. (Troyat, 1989)

Thomas A. Edison, like Catherine, was known to lock himself in his laboratory for days at a time in order to complete a scientific project. All of these women had that same inclination. Linda Wachner especially fits this profile; she spends every waking moment in a fanatical, driven pursuit of her dreams. She told *Fortune* in June 1992, "I know I push very hard, but I don't push anyone harder that I push myself. Last year I traveled two hundred days visiting stores and plants."

This workaholic mentality is evident in the life of every subject in this book. They are compulsive workers. Most were content to stay on the job until they dropped from exhaustion, even when it took eighteen-hour days, seven days a week. They typically sacrificed their sleep, their lifestyles, their relationships, and their health to realize their dreams. Their vision was their driving force and the need to redeem those dreams made them consummate workaholics, at least in the vernacular of ordinary people, if not their own.

Renegade Innovator: Jane Fonda

Jane Fonda returned to America from France in 1969 and announced to the press, "I'm a revolutionary woman." She was describing her new-found sensitivity to the killing in Vietnam. But her personality is not unusual: the creative visionary cannot be a true innovator in life without defying the establishment and the existing order of things. Innovation has been described as creative destruction, and if one is to destroy anything she must be prepared to become a maverick or renegade personality. Jane Fonda was a virulent rebel. If she had not been, she would never have been able to revolutionize the videotape industry in America. She was always prepared to confront the establishment, which is what makes her an innovative female.

Revolutionary spirits are needed to create the new by destroying the old or no innovation is possible. If an individual is not rebellious, eccentric, non-conformist, independent, and a complete individualist she can never accomplish anything worthwhile in the world of creativity and innovation. Jane Fonda, Maria Callas, Madonna, and Gloria Steinem are probably the most outrageously rebellious of the subjects in this book. These women were the most loved and hated of any of the visionaries studied here. They were willing to defy the established way of things and able to change the world for the better. Every one of these women was an independent-thinking maverick who tended to work outside the existing paradigms to create new concepts. Traditionalists look upon such women as creating havoc but without them nothing new would ever occur (see the next section of this chapter). Their ability to violate existing tradition made them special and at times made them mavericks, but that very trait is what made them innovative visionaries.

Innovator versus Adaptor Styles of Behavior

Both "creative destruction" and "breaking the rules" are concepts based on a preference for doing things differently. Therefore, being different is highly correlated to creativity. Unfortunately, conservative well-meaning, overprotective parents almost always prefer their offspring to perform "excellently" in contrast to performing "differently." And ironically those parents who allow their children to perform differently are grooming them to become excellent creative visionaries. Margaret Thatcher's father had virtually no formal education but knew the value of an independent identity quite well when he told Margaret as a young child, "You do not follow the crowd because you're afraid of being different; you decide what to do yourself and if necessary you lead the crowd, but you never just follow" (Murray, 1980).

People with a preference for operating with what Michael Kirton labeled the *innovator style behavior* prefer to do things differently. Those with *adaptor style behavior* prefer to do things excellently. He found both important for society with neither style being right or wrong. What he observed was that those who preferred "different" behavior tended to be more creative, and those who preferred "excellent" behavior were more inclined to resist change and protect the status quo. He found each behavior style optimally suited to a particular job classification or career path.

If doing things differently is best suited to the macro-vision innovator type who prefers to break traditional values and create new concepts, then doing things excellently is best suited to the individual who values security and prefers to maintain existing values. Adaptors resist any change that could jeopardize the existing system. Innovators pursue change with an attempt at destruction of the existing system. Neither behavior style is found exclusively in one individual; most people are endowed with some of each style. However, the creative visionary is typically biased toward the "innovator style."

Macro versus Micro Reality

Our thirteen women subjects were unique, with a self-image based on a larger-than-life vision of reality. Their self-image differed from the norm because they saw the "big picture" rather than their own narrow perspective. They operated with a macro view of the world which gave them a universal insight to know what decision was right in the long run. Linda Wachner scolds women who operate in too personal a fashion in business. She says, "A woman's definition of being successful in a working environment too often has too much to do with personal approval. You need to focus on quantitative and qualitative goals" (*Working Woman,* 1992).

Why were these women blessed with an omniscient and ontological view of the world? It appears that their early lives' imprinting and conditioning—early life-experiences—were the major influences. They were taught to see life holistically. They saw school in terms of an education, not as getting through sophomore English. And education was a function of learning a needed concept, not in getting a diploma. Rand, Winfrey, Madonna, Thatcher, and Meir wrote in journals as very young girls. In business they were concerned with the long-term implications of their decisions and were not afraid to sacrifice the present for the future. They lived their lives implementing these internal images of themselves in a macro-vision manner. They were able to discard the day-to-day micro images and problems and stay focused on the larger picture of where they were going. The trees may have been burning out of control, but these visionaries never lost sight of the potential for the forest.

Optimism: Critical to All Creativity

Most people believe children learn to ski or surf more easily than adults because of some physical skill innate in youth. This is not true. Certainly people over thirty start losing some physical ability, but the real reason children learn to ski faster than adults is because of their mental, not their physical abilities. Skill in these sports is more a function of mind than body. A positive mentality or optimism is more important than physical skill. Children are more naturally optimistic than adults. Think of the skiing example. A child typically pictures falling in the snow as a positive event and therefore has virtually no fear of falling and thus learns to ski quickly and superbly because of a positive mentality. An adult pictures falling as a negative event, imagining embarrassment, broken bones, and hospitalization. Because adults fear falling they learn to ski defensively, a much longer and less proficient process. Children, on the other hand, non-chalantly race down a hill almost hoping they fall in the snow as a cherished experience. No such mentality ever exists in the mind of ever-fearful adults. Adults have too much negative knowledge inhibiting their ability to perform.

Just as with children skiing, all thirteen of our visionary females had a positive belief system or optimism that permitted them to achieve beyond the norm. Margaret Thatcher believed in abolishing union power and she had followers who bought into her vision of reality. They believed she knew where she was going and they wanted to join the voyage. People prefer following leaders who know where they are going, a concept not lost on the great leaders of the world. Even when they don't know where they are going the masses have an attraction to those who profess knowledge of their destiny. This is the reason so many people followed Attila the Hun, Napoleon, Hitler, Jim Jones, and David Koresh to their deaths. It is also the reason these women have such devoted followers. Oprah Winfrey's producer said she would take a bullet for her and Mary Kay Ash's consultants long for a glimpse of her. People want to be with optimistic leaders who know where they are going. These women have a positive and optimistic belief system that is contagious. Creative visionaries always know where they are going, even when temporarily lost.

Creativity Philosophy: An Anti-Cartesian Mentality

Creative geniuses operate their lives in a right-brain, qualitative manner that contrasts with the operating styles of establishment-type personalities. Oprah Winfrey says what comes to mind and doesn't attempt to quantify it or make it fit the classic profile of her producers. Tradition-bound, quantitatively driven individuals still function by the Cartesian worldview that man and his systems are mechanistic in nature. Descartes defined man in his philosophical aphorism, "I think, therefore I am." This Enlightenment definition was very narrow— logical, deductive, proof oriented—and based on a Newtonian philosophical view of man as a machine. That is not the way female creative visionaries operate at the dawn of a new millennium. The establishment types bought into this worldview of man as machine. These risk-averse and unimaginative types are ruled by the numbers and cause/effect, stimulus/response, and other behavioristic determinations. These visionary women ignore such quantitative precepts.

The Industrial Revolution gave the mechanistic theory of the universe credibility and economic substance. This rationalist, Cartesian worldview became inculcated into our schools, institutions, and organizations. Industry knelt in compliance at this altar to the mechanical being. Quantitative modeling became the fashion for operating and creativity. The machine was king and the universe was its pawn, with all creative endeavor relegated to a left-brain, quantitative approach to problem resolution. No wonder twentieth-century personality testing confirms most Americans (75 percent) prefer operating in a detailed, quantitative, and micro way with a tendency to see the trees not the forest in problem resolution. The Western world has been obsessed with "science" and "facts" to the detriment of "creativity" and "vision." Liz Claiborne never heard of Cartesian logic but used a right-brain, qualitative mentality to give the working woman the clothing she desired.

Einstein awakened the world to the realization that man is not a machine. His intuitive insights proved to be far more momentous than any of his quantitative analyses, even though he is remembered historically as a great mathematical genius in physics. Einstein almost always utilized inductive logic to present a concept and then resorted to the math to find some truth in it. Edison did the same. He created the idea of the incandescent light bulb in his mind, told the press he had it solved and then retired to the lab to actually find a solution. This was Edison's approach to creative problem resolution as it was Einstein's, yet the world of education and business has continued to resort to the opposite approach. These visionary women used their feminine intuition to lead them to great innovative breakthroughs. They used a right-brain perspective to get to the top of their professions.

Right/Left Brain and Holistic Thinking

As already discussed, life is qualitative, not quantitative. The establishment operates by the numbers in a quantitative manner that is highly predictable and very stable. It is motivated by a survival instinct to protect the given order of things and maintain the status quo at all costs. This is necessary for a smoothly functioning system in a nondynamic world. However, it is diametrically opposed to what is necessary in a world of creativity and innovation. The only way to create anything new is by destroying present methodologies. A new romance is destined to destroy an old one just as a new dress relegates the old one to the back of the closet. This doesn't mean there isn't a place for both mentalities. It does mean that to be innovative and creative one must be prepared to destroy traditional value systems and to defy the establishment.

In 1970, Robert Ornstein published a book entitled *The Psychology of Consciousness.* He insisted that our schools were training students in left-brained traditions, and the analytical training far exceeded the nonverbal, to the detriment of creativity. Ornstein demonstrates his theory saying, "The artist, dancer, and mystic have learned to develop the nonverbal portion of intelligence." He explained how our inability to think holistically is based on our education systems: "All knowledge cannot be expressed in words, yet our education is based almost exclusively on the written or spoken word. One reason it is difficult to expand our ideas of education and intelligence is that as yet we have no way of assessing the nonverbal portion of intelligence." Fritjov Capra in *Turning Point* (1982) describes the world as a qualitative place, not a quantitative one. Scientists have long since found that the left hemisphere of the brain controls the verbal, digital and logical and is Western in nature. It is the way organized and predictable people think and operate. In contrast, the right hemisphere of the brain is responsible for the nonverbal, visual-spatial, perceptual, and intuitive, which is more Eastern in nature. Right-hemisphere thinking is where our spontaneous and divergent ideas come from.

Creativity in the East versus West

The Western world became enamored of left-brain thinking during the Industrial Revolution. It was a male-dominated mentality that caused this. This romance with behaviorism and man as machine has hurt innovative and creative behavior. The adulation of quantitative management to the detriment of qualitative management made the West vulnerable to anyone who did not worship the existing (quantitative) ways. Consider the television, videocassette recorder, and compact disc industries, all of which were invented or innovated in the United States but commercialized and dominated by the Pacific Rim nations. Eastern nations were not inclined to maintain the status-quo and operated in a qualitative, inductive style intent on providing the consumer the best product at the expense of the existing ones. This revolutionary type of thinking allowed the Pacific Rim nations to exploit U.S. inventions, which turned into Eastern Rim jobs and profits. They took a qualitative view of what the world needed (low-priced, high-quality products that everyone could afford) while the West was busy preserving existing markets. This quantitative (Cartesian) mentality so prevalent in Western society is what I call the "self-preservation mentality" (*Profiles of Genius,* 1993). It is eliminating the ego and subjugating the individual for the perfection of the process (products). The status quo is a necessary objective for governments and many other parts of society, but if growth, creativity, and innovation are to occur, both organizations and individuals must adopt a holistic and right-brain qualitative mentality conducive to such activity. The women we are concentrating on operated in absolute defiance of the above. They are creative geniuses because they were prepared to use their feminine intuition to drive their professional careers and companies.

Female Intuition

Females throughout history have been blessed and cursed for possessing a keener sense of intuition than men. The reason is that they have had free reign to express themselves emotionally without fear of retribution. This ability has put them ahead of most males in effectively dealing with the "rightness" and "wrongness" in things. Lillian Vernon calls this her "Golden Gut." Jane Fonda says she just knew more about fitness than anything else so she went for it. This same talent was pervasive in all thirteen female visionaries. They were not inclined to follow the mechanistic approach to management so often endemic to our large, bureaucratically driven organizations. This mechanistic mentality has tended to produce noncreative individuals. The bureaucratic organizations tend to produce left-brain-driven number crunchers who are into what *is* to the point of never considering what *might be*. They follow the "book" as an operating style. Real solutions to difficult problems are never found in the "book." The creative women in this volume typically cared about what *might be* and less about what *is* and consequently were able to innovate and create via their female intuition and never referred to the "book." They were comfortable operating outside the system and did it with elegance and style.

Number Crunchers versus Risk-Takers

Deductive-thinking, noncreative people are valuable for any organization since these individuals ensure continuity for those institutions demanding constancy. However, many of the deductive antichange managers have been promoted to the top and continue to maintain the status quo at the expense of change. They employ many workers who fulfill these important functions. They ensure budgets are met and values kept, but are counterproductive to the innovative process, so necessary to a firm's growth via competitive products and markets. In contrast, visionary women are not the ideal personality types to put in charge of budget control. Control of the numbers is not the strength of the right-brain driven; these individuals are more concerned with the symbolic growth and possibilities of what "might be" and not what "is." The two types of individuals are either adaptive (deductive thinking) or intuitive (inductive thinking). An organization should utilize these personality types in accordance with their respective talents. The success of dynamic societies and institutions is dependent on their ability to place each human resource in its appropriate niche. The Promethean personality types, like these visionary women, are better suited as leaders than followers.

Psychological Types

Sigmund Freud believed that we are all driven by an erotic force from within, which he labeled "psychic energy" or "life force." Freud's disciple Alfred Adler saw this driving force to be power and a striving for superiority and perfection. Carl Jung felt everyone was different but patterned in a structured way. He created a system of instinctual attitudes labeled "Archetypes," that he believed drive us from within, causing us to function in unique ways. Jung called these

Figure 12

Universal Personality Preferences
(Myers-Briggs Personality Types)

How You Are Energized	Extroversion	vs.	Introversion
Energy source	External		Internal
Functional	Sociable		Territorial
How You Gather Information	**Sensing**	**vs.**	**Intuiting**
Perceptions	Micro/trees		Macro/forrest
Functional	Quantitative		Qualitative
Decision-Making System	**Thinking**	**vs.**	**Feeling**
Decisions	Rational		Emotional
Functional	Impersonal		Personal
Life You Adopt	**Perceiving**	**vs.**	**Judging**
Life Style	Spontaneous		Structured
Functional	Open-ended		Closed-ended

personality categories "functional types" or "psychological types." Abraham Maslow and the existentialists went on to describe the human condition as oriented around the "self" and considered success to be a function of the degree the self can be actualized. Jung's system has evolved into the most clearly refined scheme of behavioral classifications and has gained the broadest support from the scientific and business communities. His psychological types have been refined into the Myers-Briggs personality types, which were further refined into temperaments by David Keirsey. The preferences everyone has for functioning in the world are illustrated in figure 12.

Catherine the Great is a classic extroverted, intuitive, thinking judger or Promethean temperament. Margaret Mead had the same behavioral preferences. Mother Teresa differed in that she was an introvert and preferred a feeling and spontaneous approach to life. Like the other two she was an intuitive. All thirteen of these visionaries have been classified into personality types on the Myers-Briggs (Jungian) scale, as shown in figure 13.

Figure 13

Personality Profiles of Visionary Subjects

Individual	Temperament	Dominant Behavior Traits	% Pop.
Catherine the Great	Promethean (Visionary)	Extrovert-Intuitive-Thinker-Judger	5%
Margaret Mead	Promethean (Visionary)	Extrovert-Intuitive-Thinker-Judger	5
Mother Teresa	Apollonian (Catalyst)	Introvert-Intuitive-Feeler-Judger	5
Mary Kay Ash	Apollonian (Catalyst)	Extrovert-Intuitive-Feeler-Judger	5
Maria Callas	Dionysian (Artisan)	Introvert-Sensor-Feeler-Perceiver	5
Liz Claiborne	Promethean (Visionary)	Extrovert-Intuitive-Thinker-Judger	5
Jane Fonda	Promethean (Visionary)	Extrovert-Intuitive-Thinker-Judger	5
Estée Lauder	Promethean (Visionary)	Extrovert-Intuitive-Thinker-Judger	5
Madonna	Promethean (Visionary)	Extrovert-Intuitive-Thinker-Judger	5
Golda Meir	Promethean (Visionary)	Extrovert-Intuitive-Thinker-Judger	5
Ayn Rand	Promethean (Visionary)	Introvert-Intuitive-Thinker-Judger	1
Gloria Steinem	Promethean (Visionary)	Introvert-Intuitive-Thinker-Judger	1
Margaret Thatcher	Epimethean (Traditionalist)	Extrovert-Sensor-Thinker-Judger	13
Lillian Vernon	Promethean (Visionary)	Extrovert-Intuitive-Thinker-Judger	5
Linda Wachner	Promethean (Visionary)	Extrovert-Intuitive-Thinker-Judger	5
Oprah Winfrey	Apollonian (Catalyst)	Extrovert-Intuitive-Feeler-Perceiver	5

Myers-Briggs Type Indicator: Personality Types

The mother and daughter psychologist team Isabel Myers and Katheryn Briggs refined the Jungian archetypes into the most widely used personality test, now known as the Myers-Briggs Type Indicator (MBTI). This system pairs everyone into bipolar preferences for dealing with life. Everyone is either an "extrovert" or "introvert"; "intuitor" or "sensor"; "thinker" or "feeler"; and "perceiver" or "judger." A person is then classified as one of sixteen distinctly different types who operate in the world in a distinctive manner. The sixteen different types of action classify individuals into their particular preference for dealing with life.

Seven of these thirteen female subjects—Claiborne, Fonda, Lauder, Madonna, Meir, Wachner, and Vernon—are Extroverted-Intuitive-Thinker-

Judgers. This personality type is energized externally, perceives the world in an intuitive manner, makes decisions by rational thought processes, and lives a very structured life in a judgmental manner. Gloria Steinem and Ayn Rand are identical to the above six with the exception of their introverted natures, which make them unique indeed in that only 1 percent of the population has this particular behavior preference. Therefore, nine of the thirteen subjects have the Promethean temperament: seven extroverts and two introverts. Notice the two catalyst temperaments are Oprah Winfrey (Extrovert-Intuitive-Feeler-Perceiver) and Mary Kay Ash (Extrovert-Intuitive-Feeler-Judger). These women prefer to make decisions based on how they feel, in contrast to how they think and are visionary in that they are still very intuitive in their thought processes. Both Margaret Thatcher (Extrovert-Sensor-Thinker-Judger) and Maria Callas (Introvert-Sensor-Feeler-Perceiver) have wholly unique personality typologies as traditionalists and artisans, which fits their societal image. By any barometer they represent a minority of the population.

Keirsey's Temperaments

David Keirsey compared Greek mythological gods to the temperaments shown in figure 14. Those personalities with great spirit he labeled Apollonian after the god Apollo, commissioned to give man spirit. Dionysus taught man joy, Prometheus brought us science, and Epimetheus conveys a sense of duty. These four temperaments are different in fundamental ways and correlate well with the Myers-Briggs personality types. There is no right or wrong temperament or personality type. What is important to know is which one best fits a given organizational role. A good fit of personality and career is like a good fit for a dress. It is critical for optimal effectiveness and happiness. For example, a "guardian" temperament (Sensor-Judger) enjoys controlling numbers and would not be happy, nor very effective, working in the mysterious world of the long-range planning. Conversely, a "visionary" would be ill-suited to sit behind a desk controlling budgets. This is self-evident to most but graphically seen when analyzing the preferences for these thirteen women as shown in the chart. Creative visionaries definitely have different personality preferences than the general population. The four potential temperaments are described in figure 14.

Promethean

The Promethean types are Intuitive-Thinking personalities who are the vi-sionaries of the world with a proclivity for innovation and scientific inves-tigation. These personality types strive for opportunity and always see the

Figure 14

Keirsey Temperament Types

Promethean NT (Intuitive-Thinker) Visionary who works on ideas with ingenuity and logic and focuses on possibilities

Apollonian NF (Intuitive-Feeler) Catalyst, spokesperson, and energizer who works by interacting with people about values. Is imaginative and nurturing

Dionysian SP (Sensor Perceiver) Troubleshooter and negotiator who works via action with cleverness and timeliness. Is pragmatic and values freedom

Epimethean SJ (Sensor-Judger) Traditionalist, stabilizer, and consolidator with sense of responsibility and loyalty. Values the present order of things

possibilities in life. They work with ideas and live by the motto "Be excellent in all things." A rational and macro vision of the world drives them. Ayn Rand is often used to describe this personality type in psychological manuals. Examples in history are Socrates, Catherine the Great, Madame Curie, and Margaret Mead. In this work, Ayn Rand, Liz Claiborne, Jane Fonda, Estée Lauder, Madonna, Linda Wachner, Lillian Vernon, Golda Meir, and Gloria Steinem are Promethean personality types. They represent 69 percent of all the subjects. These personality types lead by developing strategies and have fraternal or mentor-type relationships. They have an internal and abiding need for competence. They tend to think quantitatively but operate qualitatively.

Apollonian

The Apollonian personality types are Intuitive-Feelers, the idealists of the world who tend to be catalysts. They work by interacting with people and have a motto of "To thine own self be true." Examples in history are Joan of Arc, William Shakespeare, Gandhi, and Mother Teresa. The individuals in this work who best fit this temperament are Mary Kay Ash and Oprah Winfrey. These women lead by giving praise, are maternal in nature, and have a need for authenticity.

Dionysian

Dionysus gave us joy and Sensor-Perceivers become the artisans of the world with a propensity for troubleshooting, fire-fighting, and negotiating. They tend to work with cleverness and timeliness and live by the motto "Eat, drink, and be merry." Examples in history are St. Francis of Assisi, aviator Amelia Earhart, Gen. George Patton, and comedian Jack Benny. These types need freedom, which epitomizes Maria Callas, the only subject in this work who fits the Dionysian temperament.

Epimethean

Epimetheus gave us a sense of duty, which is why the Sensor-Judger personality types become traditionalists, consolidators, and the stabilizers of society. They tend to work with a sense of loyalty, responsibility, and industry and have the motto of "Early to bed, and early to rise." Examples in history are nursing advocate Florence Nightingale, George Washington, philanthropist Andrew Carnegie, and artist Norman Rockwell. These types have a need for belonging. The only subject among our thirteen women innovators fitting this type is Margaret Thatcher, who earned her nickname the "Iron Lady" from her sense of stability.

Cultural Diversity in Personality

People have unique personality preferences, as do organizations and cultures. All of these preferences vary depending on the needs, locations, and history of the person. The Finnish have decided that the "extroverted" personality is unusual and they consider such people mavericks. In Finland the "introverted" personality is considered normal, which is just the opposite from the findings in the United States, where 75 percent of the population is thought to be extroverted. Italy also has the opposite opinion of the idealistic personality. The "extrovert" is considered normal and the "introvert" eccentric in Italy. Consequently, more Italians work as salesmen and maitre d's in restaurants; Finns are more often found as accountants and analysts. Neither preference is right or wrong but it is important to understand the differences if we are to understand the proper placement of each within an organizational group. The dynamic Pacific rim nations of Japan, Malasia, Taiwan, and South Korea (China is emerging) have a disproportion of intuitive-thinker (Promethean) temperaments, which is why they have been so innovative at the commercialization process.

Summary

The thirteen creative geniuses in this work are different. They operated and thought differently than the general population. These women prefer to operate with an "innovator" or "different" style of behavior. Where the "adaptor" style prefers to operate "excellently" these thirteen women were comfortable with ambiguity and functioning in a pioneering environment. These visionaries functioned in a holistic manner with a predilection for using the right hemisphere of their brain in planning and decision making. Most were Promethean spirits who made decisions in macro, long-term, qualitative, inductive, and intuitive ways. They were driven by enormous energy and pursued their goals in an aggressive and competitive fashion. Patience was not their virtue, perfection and perseverance were. They often used their female charms to further their causes and were fanatical workaholics. Eleven of the thirteen were classified as Extroverted-Intuitors on the Jungian scale of psychological types.

A composite set of personality traits for these visionary women would be: confident, charismatic, perfectionist, persevering, unconventional, impatient, hypomanic, empowered, driven, independent, intransigent, intuitive, passionate, workaholic, rebellious, competitive, sensual, indomitable, and persuasive. They have obsessively driven, break-the-rules mentalities due to an indomitable self-esteem. Their temperaments were their strength, which allowed them to change the world without being changed. These personality types are the change masters of the world because they value knowledge and are insensitive to authority. Personal competence is their only criteria for success and achievement. They are the quintessential architects of change.

8

Mary Kay Ash—A Confident Charismatic

Successful innovation is a feat, not of intellect, but of will.
—Joseph Schumpeter

I happen to believe there is one cardinal sin and that is mediocrity.
—Martha Graham

Mary Kay Ash is a charismatic whose confidence is contagious. Her iron will gave her the temerity to start a company out of vindication for her own personal mistreatment in two large, male-dominated organizations. Her retribution was to create her own firm to provide job opportunities for working mothers who had to cope with earning a living while running a household. Ash's vision was to allow a working mother to determine her own level of advancement and compensation, be her own boss, and create her own work schedule around the children's schooling. The result became Mary Kay Cosmetics, a multilevel marketing firm that so successfully realized the above objectives that its revenues in 1993 were $1 billion. Ash had created the idyllic company to meet the needs of the working female, and in the realization of her life-long dream created a gigantic business beyond her wildest fantasies. Her primary objective was not the traditional strategy of optimizing stockholders' profits. In fact, seventeen years after Mary Kay Cosmetics became a public company (1968) she bought all of the stock back and made it into a private company again because a stockholder had the audacity to question her pink Cadillac promotions, the very backbone of her promotional marketing strategy. This is a Horatio Alger rags-to-riches story of gigantic proportions. The Mary Kay Ash story demonstrates that anyone can pursue their dreams without following the ritualistic guidelines outlined by business experts.

Ash's success is ensconced in her personality. She mesmerizes her female consultants during the motivational pageants given each year in Dallas. These

171

consultants now number 250,000 and meeting or touching Mary Kay is the crowning achievement of their trip to Dallas. Ash is able to create an electric atmosphere in these meetings through her charismatic behavior, and brings the house down when she tells them "I created this company for you." (She means it because "their jobs" were the real objective for the genesis of Mary Kay Cosmetics.)

Ash, like many great success stories, started Mary Kay Cosmetics accidentally. Her main objective had been to write a book about working females and male chauvinism in the workplace. She had retired from twenty-five years selling products on straight commission with two different firms and decided to write her book on the mistreatment of women by male-dominated corporations. When she sat down at her kitchen table to outline the book she had two lists. One list outlined her negative experiences in male-oriented firms and how *not* to run a company. The other list outlined qualities needed in the ideal company, especially relative to career women with families and children. She suddenly realized that she had laid out the blueprint for an idyllic firm that would be sympathetic to the concerns of working women. Ash discarded the book at the moment of her "Eureka" flash and embarked on starting her ideal company. She later told the press, "In that instant, Mary Kay Cosmetics was born," and added:

> I wanted to create a company that would make it possible for a woman, even a woman with young children, to control how she runs her business. There would be no quotas and few rules, and consultants are free to set their own hours. That structure leaves a woman free to put her family first, which is essential. For where women are concerned they cannot function if they have problems at home. (*Savvy,* June 1985)

Ash's resilient self-esteem and confidence were essential ingredients in her new venture. Friends, relatives, her accountant, and her lawyer, all told her to give up the idea because it would fail. Ash ignored their advice and followed her plan, which was to realize her dream. Ash's unique products and her army of housewives and female consultants ultimately made Mary Kay Cosmetics very successful. However, the overriding factor has been Ash's confident charisma. She has that unique ability to motivate people to super achievement. One reason is the empathy she has for these women. She had once been in their shoes and could identify with all of the needs of the working mother. This innate knowledge comes across when she speaks to them.

Attending the Mary Kay Pageant Night in Dallas is akin to attending a Las Vegas revue or a revival meeting. The event begins with motivational company songs interspersed with speeches acknowledging field success stories. The whole event has an evangelical feel and builds to a crescendo when Ash herself appears on stage to award the pink Cadillacs, mink coats, exotic trips, and diamond-studded bumblebees. A fifty-piece band plays and women sob their approval. Ash gushes, "This company is not about profit and loss, but people and love." Later she says hello to the maid in the rest room and says, "How are you? "Fine," says the maid. "No," Ash responds, "You're great! Fake it till you make it."

This charismatic woman is now a great-grandmother but still preaches the great American dream to anyone who will listen. She is a marketing marvel and motivational mastermind. The Horatio Alger Award was given to her in 1978 for her "rags to riches" success story; Ash is now a member of the award's selection committee. The princess of pink has been on virtually every talk show including "Donahue" and "Oprah." She is the recipient of "Entrepreneur of the Year," "Distinguished Woman," and "Super Achievers" awards by various organizations. She was even given the "Outstanding Woman of the Year" award by a French magazine, *Les Femmes du Monde*. Ash is introduced at the pageant as the "Queen of Queens." This is in reference to her top performers, who are referred to as "queens," as in queen bees.

Ash's favorite inspirational hero and metaphorical mascot for the firm is the bumblebee. She has elevated the bumblebee to primal importance as the corporate symbol of success: "Because of its tiny wings and heavy body, aerodynamically the bumblebee shouldn't be able to fly. But the bumblebee doesn't know that, so it flies anyway" (*The Entrepreneurs,* 1986).

Gold and diamond bumblebee pins, each with twenty-one diamonds and costing about $4,000, are awarded to the "Queens of Sales" at the end of each fiscal year. It is the ultimate badge of success for a Mary Kay consultant. Ash says of the bee, "It's just like our women, who didn't know they could fly to the top, but they did." And it is just like Ash, who didn't know how to run a business but is now chairman emeritus of one of the largest cosmetics firms in the United States. She is a creative genius who would deny the title, but her results speak for themselves.

Personal Life History

Ash was born Mary Kay Wagner in Hot Wells, Texas, near Houston, around the end of World War I. She refuses to divulge her true age, always responding to the query, "A woman who will tell you her age will tell anything." Mary Kay was the youngest of four children, but eleven years separated her from her next youngest sibling. Therefore, she was effectively raised as an only child and was treated as an adult, which appears pervasive among all these women. Mary Kay's mother was a nurse turned entrepreneur who ran a restaurant during the formative years of Mary Kay's youth. Her mother was the financial provider for the family, working two jobs during Mary Kay's early life and instilling that work ethic in her daughter. Mary Kay's older brothers and sisters were much older and her father had been stricken with tuberculosis when she was just two. He was in the hospital for five years, so she never had the luxury of a normal childhood. Her father returned home, permanently bedridden, when Mary Kay was just seven years old. Her mother worked as a nurse and restauranteur, ultimately owning her own restaurant. Mary Kay soon became the cook and nurse for her incapacitated father. She describes this period as "having the telephone serve as an umbilical cord" to her absent mother. Imagine this seven-year-old standing on a box to reach the stove in order to help feed her invalid father. Ash says of her absent mother, "For many years I was asleep when she left and asleep when she came home." Mary Kay became an adult while still a child, which built a self-sufficiency still seen in her today. Her mother would call her throughout the day with the admonition, "Honey, you can do it." And Mary Kay would accomplish tasks normally reserved for much older children.

Mary Kay became the classic overachiever in school with straight A's. She was very competitive in everything she did. She wanted to be a nurse like her mother, or a doctor. In fact, she enrolled in medical school for one semester after she was married, only to drop out to go to work when her husband ran away with another woman. After graduating from high school her mother could not afford to send her to college on the meager earnings of their small restaurant, so the ever-ambitious Mary Kay did the next best thing at the time. She met and married a radio singer by the name of Ben Rogers, a man she describes as "the Elvis Presley of Houston." At age seventeen she started working in her mother's restaurant as a waitress, waiting for Ben to hit the big time. She had three children during her eight years of marriage to Ben but when he deserted her she had no alternative but to find some kind of work that fit her family needs and her talents. It turned out to be selling on commission so she could be home when the children got out of school.

A child psychology book saleswoman called on Ash at home to sell her a set of encyclopedias for the children. Ash could not afford such a luxury but wanted them badly enough that she inquired about how to get them in some other way. The woman, Ida Blake, told Ash she would give her a free set of encyclopedias if she could find her buyers for ten additional sets. Not knowing what a difficult task this was, Ash sold ten sets in a day and a half. This was a three-month quota for the company's accomplished sales personnel. Ash didn't have a car at the time and had to accomplish this herculean task on foot and by phone. She had achieved the impossible based on her own drive and verbal skills. Blake recognized her innate talents and offered her a job immediately. Blake became her first boss and business mentor. Ash was on the road to a successful career in direct sales, where buyer motivation is of paramount importance, and confidence and a work ethic are necessary for success.

Professional Background

Ash graduated from encyclopedias sales to Stanley Home Products. It was one of the few jobs that a mother of three could have without totally disrupting her family life. The job allowed her some flexibility with her schedule because she was a straight commission salesperson. The year was 1938 and Ash was grooming herself without knowing it for her role in building one of the world's great sales organizations some thirty years later. She had taken a job selling on commission during the Great Depression—an early indication of her gutsy demeanor. She had no formal education, no prior sales experience, and high disposable incomes were rare during the Depression.

Ash was an extremely successful salesperson due to her competitive nature. She says, "I was a compulsive competitor who entered every sales contest. When I won my first, I was crushed to learn that the first prize was a flounder light—as in a light to go jig fish by. I made up my mind right then that if I ever ran a company, one thing I would never do was give someone a fish light." Ash's first husband was a country-western singer for a group called the Hawaiian Strummers. He ran off with another woman during the war and left her with the three children. Ash says the children were under the age of eight and, "I was the sole support of those kids, and that was in the days before day care."

Ash was suddenly forced to make Stanley Home Products her career. Necessity pushed her to became a top sales producer. She won many sales awards and worked her way up the organizational ladder. On the trip up through the ranks she found herself passed over many times by men with less talent and knowledge. She never forgot the experience. It irked her when she was told that the men "had families to support." "It seemed that a woman's brains were only worth fifty cents on the dollar in a male-run corporation." Ash's negative experiences with equal treatment for equal contribution would never be forgotten and would one day become instrumental in the creation of her own firm.

One night, while attending a home party in a poor section of Dallas, Ash met the woman whose product would one day launch her into a business of her own. This woman was a cosmetologist who had the most terrific skin she had ever seen. Ash assumed the woman, being a cosmetologist, had some secret skin formula but was surprised to learn that the skin product the woman was using came from her father. Her father had been a hide tanner. He noticed that his hands looked much younger than his face. He started using the tanning product on his face while supplying his daughter with the product. The results were amazing. In 1953 Ash became an instant convert and guinea pig herself to this awful-smelling but revolutionary product. After her first facial, her ten-year-old son Richard came home from school, kissed her, and said, "Gee, Mom, you feel smooth." She was hooked and used the product for ten years prior to deciding to sell it herself. Ash converted her mother: "My mother . . . died at age eighty-seven, the nursing people couldn't believe her age. She looked like she was in her sixties."

Ash left Stanley Products shortly after meeting the hide tanner lady and went to work for the World Gift Company, a Dallas home accessories firm that was also in the direct sales industry. She helped build a dynamic sales organization throughout forty-three states over a ten-year period. Once again Ash was eminently successful, receiving numerous promotions and awards. Finally she was elevated to national sales director. Even this was a demeaning promotion. Ash says that that the owner of the firm thought only a man could be a sales manager: "So he called me a 'national training director' and paid me half as much." It was 1960; Mary Kay was earning $25,000 a year and becoming an experienced direct sales guru. She taught men sales functions and they would then be promoted to a position with higher pay than hers. Gender was the only difference that was to become a terrible irritant to the competitive Mary Kay Ash.

Ash's path to the executive suite was blocked by sexual discrimination and unconscious prejudices of the male executives in charge. Ash sums up this period of her life: "We've been 'token' this and 'token' that for so doggone long, that's where we are. When you get tokened out, you start your own business." An efficiency expert was brought in to analyze the organization. He recommended that Ash's power be curtailed. By this time, her youngest child, Richard Rogers, was twenty, and she had married a vitamin executive. For the first time in her life Ash had the luxury of financial security and was not required to take the chauvinistic flack. She immediately resigned from the company and reflected on her experiences and talents to move forward in a positive fashion.

Implementation of a Dream

Ash decided not to work, but to stay at home and write a book about her trials and tribulations in the male-oriented corporate world. Sitting at her kitchen table, much like Lillian Vernon, she outlined the various problems encountered by women in a male-dominated corporate environment. She made two lists. One was about her foibles in corporate America, the other list about those methodologies that should be incorporated in an ideal firm where such inequities could be avoided. She was determined to expound on how working women, especially working mothers, could be considered in the philosophical hierarchy of a corporate structure. Her "dream company" would treat everyone equally; promotions would be made on the basis of merit, and the products would be considered for their sales performance and "marketability," not "profitability." It suddenly occurred to Ash that she was describing the type of company she would like to start. She immediately shelved the book idea and Beauty by Mary Kay was born in the summer of 1963.

Ash's first problem was finding a product. She remembered the wonderful hide-tanning product that smelled like a skunk. It was an obnoxious smelling product but she had been using it for years and felt the foul odor could be eliminated. The woman who had been her supplier had died, so she contacted the woman's daughter and acquired the rights to the product. It still smelled horrendous but that would be corrected along with the necessary packaging. Ash used her $5,000 life savings to buy the rights to this unknown product, to rent a five-hundred-square-foot store front located in a large Dallas office complex, and to form Beauty by Mary Kay. Her only product was this single skin-care item to be supplemented by others as sales and profits would allow. Ash's husband was her advisor and administrative manager because Ash knew she was incapable of handling the administrative aspects of a new business venture.

One month before her dream store was scheduled to open in September 1963, Ash's husband had a heart attack and died. This was the third major crisis for this resilient woman. After the funeral Ash's attorney advised her, "Mary Kay, liquidate the business right now and recoup whatever cash you can. If you don't, you'll end up penniless." Ash's accountant gave her equally encouraging advice, saying, "You can't possibly do it." But Ash received encouragement from her children, decided to listen to her own inner voice. She opened the store in spite of everyone and the fates. The store opened on Friday the 13th in September of 1963). Ash had one sparse shelf of inventory and nine friends serving as beauty consultants.

Ash recruited her twenty-year-old son Richard to handle the administrative aspects of the business that her husband had planned to run. Ash's first decision was to take the tanning formulas to a Dallas cosmetics manufacturer in order to have them professionally prepared and packaged. The owner of this manufacturer thought so little of what she was doing that he turned her over to his young son and said, "Here, make this batch of stuff for this woman." Three years later she exacted her own sweet revenge; she bought the man's company and began her own manufacturing operation.

When a reporter asked Ash about her growth strategy she said, "I never dreamed we'd get out of Dallas." She continued, "I didn't consciously try to go anywhere; it just happened. Pretty soon we were in Texas, then Oklahoma,

Louisiana, and New Mexico. It didn't take long before we were in every state." Ash did what every great entrepreneur does; she executed her dream to perfection and ignored all expert advice. Many believed in her dream.

Ash has been associated with pink for so many years it appears to have been a planned marketing ploy. This is not the case. In fact, pink is not Ash's favorite color. She initially selected pink as the color for her skin-care containers because the color was compatible with the traditional white bathroom tiles. It has become her signature color and its more recent association with psychological calming makes Ash look more of a genius than she already is. She has capitulated, however, by painting her famous Dallas mansion all pink.

Ash's first year in business was tough but she managed sales revenues of $38,000. Second-year sales skyrocketed to a phenomenal $650,000. The company exceeded the magic million dollar mark in its fourth year. Direct sales consultants became the backbone of the company. They made her company a success. Her consultants are a reflection of the company philosophy on how wives and mothers should be treated in the workplace. According to Ash, "You can make $30,000 a year and still be home when the kids get off the school bus." Anne Mathews, a Miami-based consultant who joined the firm after her divorce, says, "It is the only place I know where management actively tries to prethink the problems a woman could run into."

Ash's unique brand of motivation helped grow the company into an overnight success. She preaches the gospel like an evangelist on a mission. Her favorite maxims are:

"I created this company for you."

"God first, family second, career third."

"We fail forward to success."

"God didn't have time to make a nobody. As a result, you can have, or be, anything you want."

"If you think you can, you can. If you think you can't, you can't."

"Fake it till you make it."

These quotes can sound corny but in the inspirational atmosphere of Mary Kay Cosmetics, and coming from the charismatic woman herself, they become spellbinding aphorisms to be followed at any cost. The message has become magic and Mary Kay Cosmetics ended its first decade in 1972 with sales revenues of $18 million. By 1968 the company was large enough to go public to raise needed capital for expansion. The stock was listed on the New York Stock exchange in 1976 and by 1978 the firm had 45,000 independent beauty consultants with sales of $54 million and net income of $4.8 million. By 1983 the firm celebrated its second decade in business with sales of $324 million and over 200,000 consultants selling the products. The firm broke the billion-dollar mark in the early nineties with over 250,000 sales consultants, many of whom drive the trademark Mary Kay "trophy on wheels," a pink Cadillac. When asked if she didn't think the pink Cadillacs were a tad gaudy, she responded, "What color car did your company give you last year?" Her consultants qualify for the pink Cadillac after they become a director for six months and meet certain sales criteria (fifteen recruits plus $600 a month worth of wholesale orders for six straight months).

Ash is a genius at marketing and motivation. Her marketing concept is simple. She observed that women were embarrassed to have facials in department stores where their naked faces were on display for the whole world to see. Ash's marketing innovation was to teach the consultant to give the facial in the privacy of a woman's home where she could teach her the nuances of skin care without an audience. "When was the last time someone from Estée Lauder called to ask how you liked what you purchased? Never! When you buy from Mary Kay, your consultant becomes your consultant for life."

Ash's personal and business operating philosophy is to live by the "Golden Rule." Networking is critical to all multilevel marketing sales organizations, and Mary Kay Cosmetics is no exception. A consultant earns 50 percent commission on every sale and if she can recruit twenty-four other women, she can earn $1000 a month. The average woman spends over $200 a year on cosmetics, so it is simple arithmetic to find the number needed to earn a living when you receive 50 percent of the sales price. Enough women bought into the program and by 1981 Ash had been responsible for fifteen women becoming millionaires through the sales of skin-care products. This was unprecedented in the field.

Ash took the company private by buying back all of the stock in 1985. She is the classic entrepreneur who is not inclined to have shareholders tell her how to run her company. One week prior to the buy-back a woman wrote a letter with this recommendation: "Now that we are a mature organization, don't you think it's foolish to give away those frivolous pink cars?" Those pink cars were the backbone of her motivational scheme and had become a national symbol for the company. Mary Kay decided that she did not need public money enough to jeopardize the very foundation of her concept. Two years later she elevated her son Richard to chairman of the board and she became chairman emeritus, with no further active responsibility other than her motivational speaking engagements.

By 1993, Mary Kay Cosmetics had become the largest direct seller of skin-care products in the United States, with more than 250,000 independent beauty consultants in nineteen countries worldwide. The firm is the second-largest direct sales cosmetics firm in the country, second only to the much older Avon. It is the third largest cosmetics company overall and it is Ash's wish to see her firm become number one in her lifetime. She is an inspirational leader who has revolutionized the way beauty products are sold and has provided more women with higher earnings than any other firm. According to the *Wall Street Journal,* Mary Kay Cosmetics has more women earning over $50,000 in annual commissions than any other company in the United States. Ash claims to have more African-Americans and Hispanics earning over $50,000 than any other corporation in the world. Earnings in excess of $100,000 are not uncommon and the ubiquitous pink Cadillacs are a testimony to her success and her motivational genius.

Temperament: Intuitive-Feeler

Ash is such a confident charismatic that it is difficult to imagine her in any negative light. She says about her Mary Kay venture, "I just never even thought about the fact it could fail. That was not a possibility." This is a classic personality trait found in all great creative geniuses. They believe to such a degree that they overcome virtually every potential problem. She fervently subscribes to this philosophy: "I believe that if you had the choice of two gifts for your child, $1 million on one side of the scale and the ability to think positively on the other, the greater gift would be the gift of confidence." Ash is expounding on a subject in which she is an expert, just as she is the consummate self-confident individual who reached the very top through the sheer power of positive thinking.

Ash is an ebullient and zealous speaker who has the ability to mesmerize her audience. Her consultants would follow her to hell if that were her destination. She is an extroverted personality type for whom "personal feeling" is more important than the "impersonal thinking." Her genuinely friendly demeanor is infectious and her philosophy of the "Golden Rule" attracts followers like a magnet. She admits to being a high-energy workaholic and says, "I've always functioned at a pace and with a God-given energy that would qualify me as a workaholic." Ash's enthusiasm is contagious and she lives her life with a Gandhian style attitude of, "Go—give before you receive." This is her philosophy for success.

Ash's unconscious drive and energy made her a creative visionary. Her unconscious inner energy was seen in every job she attempted. She was feminine but in a competitive and subtly aggressive manner. Feminists saw her as an ideal candidate to further their causes, especially since she defied male chauvinism and started her own company. Her response was direct and acrimonious:

I was never part of it, because they stood for a lot of things I don't believe in. They were putting on low heeled shoes, and cutting their hair like men, and taking off their makeup, and burning their bras. . . . I think God intended for us to be feminine and women and we should stay that way. (Jennings, 1987)

This is a strong statement from a woman who was once the subject of repeated discrimination in the workforce.

Ash has strong intuitive powers, always searching for the opportunities in life. She is the consummate optimist who looks for reasons to do something, not why not to. She is enamored with the possibilities, a typical right-brain-driven mentality. Her personality type is extroverted-intuitive-feeling-judging on the Myers-Briggs scale. Her high energy and charismatic appeal are coupled with a confidence that is off the scale. These traits make her a classic creative visionary with a unique sensitivity for her employees, her friends, and her associates.

Family versus Career

Ash waited until her children were raised before embarking on an entrepreneurial career. Her considerable experience juggling a family and job for over twenty years certainly cannot be discounted in her trek to the top. She learned the necessities of the working single mother the hard way. Her first husband deserted her during the war, and at the age of twenty-seven she found herself with three children under eight, forcing her to work on straight commission. She could have taken a salaried position but elected to work on commission in order to have the flexibility to serve as mother and father to her children. These dual roles eminently prepared her to start a company with a philosophy designed around a working mother. The Mary Kay Cosmetics business philosophy was created to assure women the freedom to work while maintaining the household. This philosophy has been instrumental in the company's enormous success. It is another reason why many thousands of women would go to war for Mary Kay if she asked them to.

Ash believes it is very difficult, if not impossible, to simultaneously be a successful wife, mother, and entrepreneur. "I don't think there is time in the day to have it all at once. How can you be a mother to three children, have all those cares and worries of a large corporation, and a husband and all the other things at once? I don't think you can!" (*Self-Made Women*, 1987).

Mary Kay married Mel Ash long after she had started Mary Kay Cosmetics. She cites her marriage to Ash as an example of the above difficulty in juggling the personal and professional. She was already established in Mary Kay

Cosmetics and did not have the added burdens of motherhood, but "I had to make some drastic adjustments in order to be the person he wanted as a wife. He did not want a chairman of the board for a wife. He did not want me telling him what to do in any way, shape or form. When I came home, he wanted me to be his wife, period."

Ash designed her recruiting brochure with the working mother in mind. It outlines the income variances for a woman working at Mary Kay versus her earnings in a nine-to-five job: "If you earn $200 for a 40-hour workweek, after taxes, Social Security, gas, parking, lunches, and child care are taken out, you'll clear $57. Twelve hours of Mary Kay work yields an average of $200 with little or no expense to you." This is another example that everything Ash stands for is in support of the working mother. She has total empathy for these women, and can identify with them because she was one of them for many years. Those twenty-five years as a working mother proved to be invaluable experience. Ash's children were grown before she started Mary Kay Cosmetics, enabling her to concentrate on her career only. However, her entrepreneurial success would not have been possible had she not spent those dreadful twenty-five years as a working mother selling on commission only. Ash admits to paying a terrible price during that period of attempting to juggle career and family simultaneously. Her children were often alone and she had to tolerate male chauvinism without an alternative solution. This made her very sensitive to the plight of working mothers. Consequently, Ash gave these working mothers the opportunity to control their own career destinies without having to forfeit a family life.

Life Crisis

Ash had a number of crises in her life, starting with her father's tuberculosis. "I took care of my father, and my mother had a very hard time just keeping everything paid." The telephone as Mary Kay's safety net. "I guess I called her twenty times a day. . . . How do you do this? How do you do that? How do you make tomato soup?" Ash's mother would patiently tell her how to perform the tasks and then add, "Now honey, Mother knows you can do it." Ash credits her mother for constantly building her self-confidence. "Mother constantly reinforced my self-image. She told me I could do anything in this world I wanted to do, if I wanted to do it badly enough, and I was willing to pay the price." Mary Kay paid the price and the result was an unbelievably self-confident individual who is the world's greatest optimist.

Ash's second traumatic experience occurred at age twenty-seven when her husband abandoned her. She was left alone with no real job or financial support. Ash persevered and learned to cope and become self-sufficient. At the time it was a disaster, but in retrospect it was a great training ground for her later experience as an entrepreneur. In fact, the experience became the philosophical basis of Mary Kay Cosmetics and is fundamental to the total concept. Without her intimate knowledge of what it took to manage a family and career, she could not have had the intuitive insight to create what is the premise and very essence of Mary Kay Cosmetics.

Ash's third crisis occurred on the eve of her planned launch of Beauty by Mary Kay, with the death of her second husband. "He just fell into his plate, and his face turned purple." That is when the experts advised her to drop her plans of becoming an entrepreneur. She admits to having had terrible fears since she had relied on her husband to handle all of the administrative aspects of her new business. But she ignored the experts, called her son to her side, and proceeded to open her store. The rest is history.

Ash is resilient in the face of most adversarial situations because she faced three major crises in her life and overcame all of them. Any one of the above crises would have been debilitating to most people. However, the strong-willed Mary Kay Ash became even stronger for her experiences. Nobel Prize winner Ilya Prigogine has shown that individuals who survive the "bifurcation point" (the critical stage in a crisis or in chaos) tend to become stronger for the experience. This certainly has been the case with Mary Kay Ash.

Confidence, Charisma, and Creativity

At an advanced age Ash can still bring a house full of women to tears and cheers with her mesmerizing personality. It is this effervescence that has captivated women and encouraged them to follow the Mary Kay dream. She adroitly uses the pink Cadillacs, mink coats, and diamond baubles as icons of success. They are her motivational monuments to Mary Kay's success. Women overachieve every month because of this inspirational mentor, Mary Kay Ash. She created the company to provide a better economic opportunity for women, and her consultants have bought into her dream and perpetuated it.

Ash said of her entrepreneurial venture, "Experts predicted my doom. Many well-intentioned people, including my attorney, assured me that my company would fail. . . . My attorney even went so far as to send to Washington, D.C., for a pamphlet detailing how many cosmetics companies were going broke each year." Her accountant told her to "liquidate the business right now" when her husband died unexpectedly. Ash believed in the dream and listened to her inner voice where the bumble bee metaphor was always present. She knew she would succeed and went on to build her empire, ignoring the experts on her way to the top.

Ash is the queen bee urging her female sales force to emulate her bumble bee metaphor. She constantly challenges them with, "God didn't have time to make a nobody, only a somebody." She stimulates their feminine spirit with her inspirational folk yarns like, "When God made man, he was only practicing. He looked down and said, 'That's pretty good, but I think I could do better.' So He created woman." Then she quotes from her favorite book, *Rhinoceros Success* by Scott Alexander, "We have all this capacity for greatness. Don't sit back and be a cow, be a 6,000-pound rhino. Charge!" Ash's motivational powers are contagious making her the Moses of direct selling. She leads her chosen to the promised land of wealth and happiness.

Ash's charisma and power of persuasion are clear. In the eighties one of her saleswomen said that just touching Ash gave her cold chills. When her friend Helen McVoy, a top earner with $375,000 in commissions in 1983, told her, "You know Mary Kay, I've touched you and I've never gotten chills," Ash retorted, "Well, what's wrong with you?" Now that is the power of positive thinking. One of Ash's favorite sayings gives credence to the valued role of women in the world of direct sales. She says, "There are three ways to get the word out fast: telephone, telegraph, and tell a woman." She laughs when telling this story, "I can't explain it, but something can start in New England and by nightfall be in California. It's the fastest network of communications in the world." Ash insists that this is the basis for her success: "Men don't understand our system, but it works! Everyone helps everyone else!" This mentality has given the Mary Kay operation an image of a vast sorority of women interested in beauty and money. She has built a business empire based on interpersonal relations, charisma, and confidence.

Summary

This confident charismatic is an inspiration for women everywhere. She is the ultimate role model for those needing to turn crisis into success and adversity into possibility. Her infectious optimism helped her to overcome many hardships and brought her to the seat of power and independence. Her story is an inspiration to all who feel they need a pedigree, Ivy League degree, or financial backing to make it big. An internally empowered belief system is all that Ash needed to realize her dream. Ash's story, like many others in this book, is an indication that "adversity with a positive perspective" can be more of an inspiration in life than the traditional factors of formal education, influential friends, and money. Having little else but a dream appears to have an edge over the above because it arms the person with the innate knowledge that they must try harder and never allow "any outside influence" to screw up their dream.

Since winning the Horatio Alger Award in 1978, Ash has been the recipient of many other awards from various associations. She is an inspirational speaker who still can motivate salespeople like no other person. She is a true creative genius. When she failed to break through that elusive glass ceiling in two different corporations, she quit both jobs. She then started her own company with the philosophy that there would be no glass ceilings or even rules or quotas. Whenever she had an innovative or intuitive idea she was told, "Mary Kay, you're thinking just like a woman." She vowed, "In my company thinking like a woman was going to be an asset, not a liability."

This grand matron of the skin-care industry never accepted defeat at the hands of the chauvinistic individuals in her life. Ash created her own non-chauvinistic environment, the one in which Mary Kay Cosmetics operates. This organization has become a model for direct sales firms everywhere. Its dynamic power and strength is a testimony to Ash's belief in the working female parent. Other large multilevel marketing firms have emulated her system. In Shakespeare's words, "Imitation is the sincerest form of flattery," which makes Ash's innovation one of the most flattered in the United States. Ash can feel confident that she has created the consummate work environment for the female working parent.

Ash's third husband, Mel, died of cancer in 1980, and Mary Kay now lives with friends in her Dallas home. Ash's home is her castle both literally and figuratively. She moved into this thirty-room pink mansion in a Dallas suburb in 1985. This palace is a paragon of power and success for the queen of direct sales. It features acres of carpeted floors and a nine-foot grand player piano with a constant flow of Liberace tunes gracing the halls. This $4-million home is ostentatious with its pink decor, which makes it an ideal showcase to entertain new recruits and illustrate the power of success. Yet Ash is still a product of her upbringing: she clips coupons—a holdover from her days of impoverishment. She is still more impressed with a good chili dog than with the latest Davinci gown.

Ash ignored her left-brain-driven lawyer, who said, "Mary Kay, you are dreaming." Her dream has turned into reality and she has moved into the castle. On the way to her palace she just happened to revolutionize direct sales in America. She continually turned tragedy into success. Her charismatic form of optimism has made her a fortune, but more than that it has created a unique work environment for women like her who want to have it all. Ash's business gospel is "How can I help each woman develop a more positive self-image?" This she has done better than anyone else in the world. For this she is to be recognized as a true creative genius.

Mary Kay Wagner Ash
Mary Kay Cosmetics
b. May 12, 1917?, Hot Wells, Texas

Dominant trait: Confident Charismatic

Religion: Devout Baptist

Mottos: "Praise people to success"; "God didn't have time to make a nobody. As a result, you can have, or be, anything you want"; "If you think you can, you can. If you think you can't, you can't." The bumblebee is the corporate motto and insignia

Philosophy: "God first, family second, career third." "Go—Give." "We fail forward to success."

Nicknames: Queen of Queens; The Pink Lady

Creation/innovation: Founded Beauty by Mary Kay, Friday September 13, 1963, with $5,000 from savings

Products/contributions: Unique skin creams and multilevel direct sales organization

Success: Company sales $1 billion with 250,000 sales consultants (1992). Became millionaire on public offering in 1968.

Self-description: "I was a compulsive competitor." "I didn't consciously try to go anywhere [expansion], it just happened."

Birth order: Fourth child. Eleven years between her and next youngest sibling. Raised as only child with an adult orientation.

Childhood transience: No travel. Left alone to care for invalid father from age 7.

Father's occupation: Invalid during Mary Kay's formative years. Mother was nurse and restauranteur.

Mentors: Mother was inspirational support and role model; Ida Blake was first boss and mentor

Childhood upbringing: Mother: "Anything anyone else can do, you can do better!"; "Honey, you can do it!"

Formal education: High school only—straight A student. Wanted to be nurse, then a doctor.

Life crises: Father incapacitated when she was 2. Ben Rogers deserted her with 3 children at age twenty-seven. Husband had heart attack 30 days prior to opening of first store.

Marriages/liaisons: Ben Rogers, vitamin executive, Mel Ash. One divorce, two died. Children: Marilyn, Ben, and Richard.

Risk-taking: "I didn't see it as a risk. I saw it as an opportunity." "I just never even thought about the fact it would fail. That was not a possibility."

Temperament: Extrovert-intuitive-feeler-judger

Behavior: Confident charismatic with ebullient optimism, competitive overachiever.

Career vs. family: Believes it to be very difficult indeed. Delayed venture until children were raised but created Mary Kay for career-oriented females with families.

Self-esteem: An awesome self-confidence and enthusiasm developed in childhood and nurtured by successful perseverance.

Hobbies: Public speaking, playing female mentor, and church

Heroes: God and the bumblebee

Honors: Member of the board of directors for the Horatio Alger Association, Horatio Alger Award winner, 1978, plus numerous awards as "Entrepreneur of Year" and "Career Woman of Year."

9

Maria Callas—Perpetual Perfectionist

Mad passion or passionate madness is the reason why psychopathic personalities are often creators and why their productions are perfectly sane.
　　　　　　　　—Jacques Barzun, *The Paradoxes of Creativity*

The greatest opera diva and prima donna of the twentieth century was a driven woman who defied the critics, opera impresarios, and the public in her rebellious march to the top of the music world. On her death in 1977, Pierre-Jean Remy, a Paris opera critic, said of her, "After Callas, opera will never be the same again." Lord Harewood, a London critic, described her as "the greatest performer of our time." Even Callas's detractors proclaimed her genius and impact on the operatic world. Callas and Rudolph Bing of the New York Metropolitan Opera were adversaries throughout her professional career (he actually fired her), but he said on her passing, "We will not see her likes again." This passionate artist was loved, idolized, hated, revered, and despised, but never ignored in her profession. Without a doubt, she influenced the world of opera more than any other person during the twentieth century, if not for all time. She dominated her profession for twelve years and was a prominent performer for twenty. Callas was an innovator and creator like no other person before or since due to her frenetic work ethic, obsessive perfectionism, and incomparable manic-depressive, driven energy. These characteristics were the byproducts of childhood dreams and crises that drove Callas to become a compulsive overachiever for much of her adult life.

This tragic heroine constantly played make-believe roles on the stage and, ironically, her life emulated the very tragic roles she performed in the theater. Callas's most famous role was playing *Medea,* a made-to-order part for this sensitive and emotionally unstable female portraying the tragedy of sacrifice and betrayal. Medea sacrificed everything including her father, her brother, and her children for the pledge of eternal love from Jason and the redemption of the Golden Fleece. After such devotion and sacrifice, Medea was betrayed by Jason, just as Callas was betrayed by her shipping magnate lover, Aristotle Onassis, after she had sacrificed her career, her husband, and her creativity. Onassis reneged on his promise of marriage and children after he had lured her into his lair, not unlike the fate that befell the fictional Medea. Callas's passionate portrayal of the sorceress was strikingly similar to her own tragedy. She played this part with such realistic passion that it would become her signature role on stage and finally as a movie. In fact, Callas's last major performance was playing in the artistically acclaimed movie *Medea* by Paolo Pasolini.

Callas was passionate artistry on stage with an incomparable presence as an actress. This gained her worldwide acclaim as a one-of-a-kind performer. Her volatile personality earned her the nickname "Tigress" and "Cyclone Callas" by an adoring and sometimes bewildered public. Callas understood the deep psychological significance of *Medea* as her alter ego, which comes out in this quote just prior to her final performance in 1961: "The way I saw Medea was the way I feel it: fiery, apparently calm, but very intense. The happy time with Jason is past; now she is devoured by misery and fury" (Stancioff, 1987).

Maria Callas, like other great artists, was a brilliant actress; she had an ability to totally empathize with the stage character. Shockingly, her real life was a continual reproduction of many of her on-stage characterizations. Medea used her sorcery to find Jason and sacrificed everything to secure his true love and eternal happiness. Callas used her talent for the redemption of her childhood dreams of artistic perfection and sacrificed everything for her Greek God Onassis. This tragic heroine was the consummate prima donna. She so identified with her parts that she became them. Or did she become a tragic character who sought out parts she could identify with both literally and emotionally? In any case, Callas *was* the "tragic" Medea even though she claimed, "I like the role but I do not like Medea." She *was* a "vestal custodian of art" as Norma, the rebuked heroine who chanced death rather than hurt her true love even though he had betrayed her. This was Callas's favorite role. She *was* a "mad" Lucia, forced to marry a man she does not love. She *was* "deserted" in *La Traviata*, where she played the attacked, insulted, and spurned heroine. She *was* a "passionate lover" in *Tosca*, where she resorted to killing for her true love. She *was* the "victim" in *Iphigenia*.

While reading Callas's story it becomes quite evident this child-woman was a victim before she ever played any part. This immensely talented diva became tragically entwined in the parts she performed on stage and in real life. The resemblance goes beyond theater. Most people get what they "really" want and become what they perceive themselves to be. Maria Callas is the personification of this prophecy. This emotionally wired woman searched for the things she wanted out of life and created her own reality. Pathetically, her destiny was tragedy in both life and the theater. Callas's manic depression knew no bounds, and it is what made her an incomparable talent on stage and the archetypal tragedy in real life. Callas's biographer, David Lowe (1986), describes her personal and professional tragedies: "Maria Callas was a soprano who drove audiences to a frenzy of adulation. Her vocal and personal ups and downs were as dramatic and extravagant as the fates of the operatic heroines she portrayed."

Life History

Cecilia Sophia Anna Maria Kalogeropoulos was born in New York City on December 2, 1923. Her name was later shortened to Maria Callas in deference to her new American homeland. An older sister, Jackie, had been born in Greece in 1917, and a boy named Vassilios was born three years later. Basil had been the mother's favorite but contracted typhoid fever at the age of three and died unexpectedly. This tragedy devastated the family, especially Maria's mother, Evangelia. The father decided impulsively to sell his thriving Greek pharmacy and move away from the area. Callas was conceived in Athens and born in New York City four months later. Her father, Georges, was an ambitious fortune hunter and entrepreneur who told his wife they were leaving for America the day before the journey. Her mother longed for another boy and refused to look at or touch her new-born daughter for four days. Maria's sister Cynthia was six years older and became her mother's favorite, to Maria's constant chagrin.

Maria's father opened the Splendid Pharmacy in Manhattan in 1927. It ultimately became a casualty of the Great Depression. Maria was baptized Greek Orthodox at age two and raised in the Hell's Kitchen section of Manhattan. The family moved nine times in eight years due to continued declining fortunes. Callas was considered a child prodigy. She began listening to classical records at the age of three. She went to the library weekly but often chose classical music over books. She wanted to be a dentist as a young child and then devoted her whole existence to singing. Classical records were her toys. She was a child prodigy who started piano lessons at age five and singing lessons at age eight. By age nine she was the star of recitals at Public School 164. A former schoolmate said, "We were spellbound by her voice." Maria knew *Carmen* at age ten and was able to detect errors in the Metropolitan Opera performances aired on the radio. Her mother was obsessed with realizing her own failed life through the talented Maria and pushed her to become a compulsive perfectionist. She signed her on a network radio show—"Major Bowes Amateur Hour"—at age thirteen and Maria traveled to Chicago, taking second place in a children's TV show.

At the age of six, Maria was struck by a car on a Manhattan street and dragged for a block. She was in a coma for twelve days and in the hospital for twenty-two days. She was not expected to live. This early trauma appeared to have instilled in her a passionate resolve to overcome all future hurdles in life and to compulsively overachieve in virtually everything she attempted. She recovered with no visible scars from this early crisis.

Callas later said of her childhood, "Only when I was singing did I feel loved." As an eleven-year-old she was listening to Lily Pons, the New York Metropolitan Opera diva, and prophesied, "One day I'm going to be a star myself, a bigger star than she." And she was. One of the reasons for such resolve was her maniacal desire to assuage a damaged self-esteem. Her older sister, Jackie, was always her mother's favorite. In Callas's words, "Jackie was beautiful, intelligent, and extroverted." Maria thought of herself as fat, ugly, myopic, clumsy, and introverted. These feelings of inferiority and insecurity made her into a classic overachiever in an effort to compensate. According to Callas's husband, Batista, Maria believed that her mother robbed her of her childhood. Callas told a reporter, "My mother . . . as soon as she became aware of my vocal gifts decided to make of me a child prodigy as quickly as possible." And "I had to rehearse again and again, to the point of exhaustion." Maria never forgot her negative childhood of intense practice and work; she told an Italian magazine in 1957, "I had to study, I couldn't waste time with nonsense. . . . I was deprived entirely of the joy of adolescence."

Maria ate to satiate her lack of affection from a distant but demanding mother and to assuage her insecurities. By the time she was a teenager she was five feet, eight inches tall and weighed two hundred pounds. Callas was to remain insecure her whole life, and in 1970 told a reporter, "I am never certain of myself, and I am frequently tortured by doubts and fears."

Maria's formal education ended at the age of thirteen when she graduated from the eighth grade in Manhattan. Her mother then split with her father, packed up the two girls, and headed for Athens. Maria's mother used family connections to gain for her a scholarship to the prestigious Royal Conservatory of Music. They accepted only sixteen-year-olds, so Maria lied about her age since she was just fourteen, though her height made it an easy ruse. Maria studied at the conservatory under the tutelage of the famous Spanish diva Elvira de Hidalgo. Callas would later say, "I owe all my preparation and my artistic formation as an actress and musician to Elvira de Hidalgo." By age sixteen she had won first prize in a conservatory production and started earning money with her voice. She sang at the Athens Lyric Theater throughout World War II, often supporting the family during this frenetic period. In 1941, at age nineteen, Maria sang her first opera, *Tosca,* for the kingly sum of sixty-five dollars.

Maria idolized her absent father and hated her mother. One of her voice school friends described Maria's mother as having delusions of grandeur, a woman who "pushed and pushed and pushed Maria." Maria's godfather, Leonidas Lontzounis, recalled the relationship between Maria and her mother following the latter's death: "She [Litza] was an ambitious, neurotic woman who never had a friend. . . . She exploited Maria. She even made Maria Callas dolls. She was a real money digger. . . . Maria sent checks every month to her sister, mother, and father . . . but her mother wanted more and more." Callas said, "I adored my father" and blamed her disappointments in life and love on her mother. She bought her mother a fur coat after a Mexican tour in 1950 and said goodbye to her forever. She never saw her again after the age of thirty.

Professional Background

Callas returned to New York City from Athens in the summer of 1945 to pursue her career as a diva. She was fearless despite her personal insecurities and said on leaving her family and friends for America, "At twenty-one, alone and without a cent, I boarded a ship at Athens headed for New York. . . . I was not afraid." She reunited with her beloved father only to find him living with a woman she could not tolerate. As testimony to the life-long frequency of her fits of volatility, Callas broke a platter over his mistress's head after she complained about her singing. Callas spent the next two years auditioning in Chicago, San Francisco and New York. Edward Johnson of the New York Metropolitan Opera offered her leading roles in both *Madame Butterfly* and *Fidelio*. Of the *Butterfly* offer, Callas said her intuitive "voices" advised her against accepting the roles. In a moment of introspection she admitted, "I was then too fat—210 pounds. Besides it was not my best role." Maria, never one to hesitate in giving an honest opinion, rationalized her decision as "Opera in English is so silly. Nobody takes it seriously" (*Life,* October 31, 1955).

While in New York Callas signed an agreement to appear in Verona, Italy, for an August 1947 debut in the title role of *La Gioconda.* While performing in Verona she was admired by Maestro Tullio Serafin, who became her musical mentor for the next two years. He booked her for roles in Venice, Florence, and Turin. The fates intervened to give Callas her first big break when a lead singer for Bellini's *I Puritani* became ill. Serendipity played the role of agent and she was offered the part of the taxing coloratura in the opera. Callas always had an extraordinary memory and shocked the music world by mastering the role in just five days.

Callas's career was on its way. The Italian opera community accepted her and she decided to make Italy her home, a place where she was finally wanted and desired. During this period Callas had been admired by an Italian industrialist who happened to be an opera fanatic—Italian millionaire Giovanni

Batista Meneghini. He was a bachelor and twenty-seven years her senior. The ever-impetuous Callas married Batista within a year of their introduction—April 21, 1949—and he became her manager, mentor, and companion for the next ten years.

Callas had already agreed to engagements in Buenos Aires, Argentina, during 1949 and left her new husband the day after their marriage to complete the three-month commitment to perform at the Teatro Colon. She then opened in *Norma* in Mexico City in 1950. Callas was forlorn in this third-world country, where she lacked any meaningful relationships or acquaintances. Her loneliness and insecurity reached its zenith at this time and she ate her way into psychological contentment. By the early fifties Callas had become very large, and her weight started becoming a detriment to her stage career. Her hypochondria knew no bounds. Her letters were filled with assertions of loneliness and fright. She was constantly sick, and wrote to her husband daily saying, "I must confess, I've been very ill in this damned Mexico from the moment I arrived. I haven't managed to be well one single day." And later, "I've broken my own record—8:30 in the morning and I've yet to fall asleep. I believe that I will go mad here in Mexico."

Callas was irritable, moody and constantly ill in virtually every city she sang. She was always her own worst critic, demanding perfection, which led her to fight with every opera director and most of the actors with whom she worked. Callas made her debut at La Scala singing *Aida* in 1950. It was here that she was finally recognized as an undeniable talent. Callas was notorious for ignoring the traditional steps up the ladder of success. She unconsciously assumed she was the best and should start at the top, which was irritating to the women who had struggled for years for their chance, only to be passed over in favor of a young upstart. Callas's attitude was, "Either you've got the voice or you haven't, and if you've got it, you begin singing the lead parts right away." She was made an official member of La Scala by opening the 1951 season in that great institution. This prompted *Life* magazine to give her the greatest praise that could be given an opera star: "Her special greatness has been achieved in the long-forgotten museum pieces which were taken out of mothballs only because at long last there was a soprano who could sing them." And Howard Taubman of the *New York Times* credited her with "having restored the ancient luster to the title of 'prima donna.' "

By 1952, Callas had reached the peak of her vocal genius. She sang *Norma* at the Royal Opera Covent Garden in London. It was at this time the press started deriding her about her enormous size and weight. A critic wrote that her legs were the size of the elephants. She was devastated and immediately went on a crash diet and lost a hundred pounds within eighteen months. Her husband intimated she used a tapeworm to induce the weight loss. It worked. Rudolph Bing signed her for three performances of *La Traviata* for the 1952/

53 season of the Metropolitan Opera. She canceled because her husband didn't have a visa. This incensed Bing and it started a ten-year adversarial relationship with someone Callas hardly needed to have as an enemy. This confrontation caused her debut in America to be delayed until her Chicago performance in *Norma* on November 1, 1954. Callas was an instant sensation. Bing capitulated on working with this volatile star and immediately began negotiations with her to perform at the Met.

Callas first sang *Medea* at La Scala in 1953, and her vibrant performance made this relatively obscure opera a huge success. Leonard Bernstein was the conductor and admired her talent. He said of her performance, "The place was out of its mind. Callas? She was pure electricity." Bernstein was to become a life-long friend and supporter. Bing then signed Maria for her New York debut to open the 1956–57 season in *Norma.* Callas was brilliant, but it was not so much her voice or acting as her style. Bernstein said of her, "She was not a great actress, but a magnificent personality." Callas's dramatic flair and effervescent stage presence made her different and helped her change the world of opera. Her recording studio manager, James Hinton, confirms her stage vitality: "Those who have heard her only on recordings . . . cannot imagine the total theatrical vitality of her personality. As a singer she is very individual, and the voice is so unusual in quality that it is easy to understand why some ears do not take to it" (*Current Biography*, 1956).

Callas often said, "I have an obsession with perfection" and "I do not like the middle way"—all or nothing was her way. Callas was a life-long work-aholic who was wont to say, "I work, therefore I am." Her bouts with depression were amplified by exhaustion and fatigue brought on by nervous anxiety and her compulsive work ethic. She continually sought help for her illness and fatigue. Dr. Coppa told her, "You are healthy. You do not have any disorder and therefore do not need curing. If you are sick, it is in your head."

Callas's continual bouts with ill health forced her to cancel numerous performances. Her idolizing but fickle public rebuked her for the cancellations. The British press denounced her for "another Callas walkout" in the mid-fifties when she was duped by La Scala into saying she was sick when she was instead trying to help out a scheduling error by the production company. Then she became embroiled in a La Scala scandal, when she left the stage after the first act due to illness, with the president of Italy in the audience. This led to numerous lawsuits and blackballing from the Italian stage. Callas was exonerated years later, but her reputation had been shattered.

Callas became embittered over the constant turmoil and legal actions. She was really a very sensitive child-woman emotionally, which was at the seat of many of her professional problems. It was during these business crises that she decided to put her personal life before her art for the first time in her life. She canceled a performance at the San Francisco Opera on September

17, 1958, due to ill health. The director, Kurt Adler, was furious and filed a complaint with the American Guild of Musical Artists, who later reprimanded her at a court hearing. These constant battles only added to her reputation as a turbulent entertainer who, like Norma, was into constant conflicts between her holy oaths and her passionate desire for love and adulation. Callas said:

> We pay for these evenings. I can ignore it. But my subconscious can't. . . . I confess there are times when part of me is flattered by the high emotional climate, but generally I don't like any moment of it. You start to feel condemned. . . . The more fame you have, the more responsibility is yours and the smaller and more defenseless you feel. (Lowe, 1986)

After a 1958 Rome performance of *Norma,* Maria was introduced to shipping magnate Aristotle Onassis by Elsa Maxwell, the famous American newspaper syndicated columnist and party giver. Callas and her husband were invited on Aristotle's infamous yacht, the *Christina,* and from that moment on her career was secondary to her enormous need for love and affection. This vulnerable woman was easy pickings for the worldly and womanizing Onassis. Like Medea, Callas did not hesitate to sacrifice everything to satiate her romantic needs. After her affair with Aristotle, Callas made only seven operatic performances in two cities during 1960 and only five performances during 1961. She sang her last opera, *Norma,* in 1965 in Paris, where she lived after having been jilted by Onassis. After Aristotle's marriage to Jacqueline Kennedy, Callas agreed to make *Medea* into a movie for Pier Pasolini in 1970. It turned out to be a great work of art but a commercial failure. The irony is that her last performance was to be in a role acting out a mirror image of her inner agony and torment. Callas was the spurned female and Pasolini's selection of her to play such a part was prophetic during a period when her tormentor, Onassis, was dying: "Here is a woman, in one sense the most modern of women, but there lives in her an ancient woman—strange, mysterious, magical, with terrible inner conflicts" (Pasolini, in Stancioff, 1987).

Temperament: Intuitive-Feeler

This passionately driven woman was an introverted intuitive who expressed her emotions in a feeling way. She approached life emotionally and personally. Her passionate approach to living was an asset while on stage and performing, especially in highly charged scenes. It was a detriment for the insecure manic-depressive who desperately needed acceptance and affection. Callas approached every relationship in the same way, and this inability to separate make-believe from real-life caused her a great deal of heartache throughout her life. Emotional outbursts and fever-pitch drama can work on stage but are often lost in real-life, professional relationships. Callas was destined to live and die by her emotions.

While married to Batista, Callas was very disciplined. Batista said she was as compulsive in the home as she was on stage. He wrote in his biography, "She was disciplined and meticulous in her musical preparation, so it was with her domestic habits." This obsession with perfection and order caused her to have panic attacks before each performance and severe anxiety. Afterwards she had violent headaches and insomnia. She was as intransigent as Thatcher and Meir, although in her mind she was not. Actually it was her impatience and intolerance of criticism that set her apart. She would never back down when she felt she was right on any issue and would say, "They say I'm stubborn. No! I'm not stubborn; I'm right!"

Callas, an introverted child-woman, was insecure and unstable. She lived her life in an obsessive drive to exorcise her childhood ghosts of inadequacy. "I am impatient and impulsive, and I have an obsession for perfection." This was put in perspective by a statement to the press about her perpetual discontent: "I'm never satisfied. I am personally incapable of enjoying what I have done well because I see so magnified the things I could have done better." Callas's compulsion to be perfect knew no bounds, nor did her worship of passion, "I am a passionate artist and a passionate human being." In many respects she was oddly prophetic, as illustrated by this philosophic comment about her life and work from her memoirs in the Italian magazine *Oggi* (1957):

> I am a simplifier. Some people were born complicated, born to complicate. I was born simple, born to simplify. I like to reduce a problem to its elements, so I can see clearly what I have to do. Simplifying your problem is halfway to solving it. . . . Some people complicate in order to veil. If you're going to simplify, you must have courage.

This is a profound statement for anyone with an eighth-grade education. Simplifying the complex is the essence of all great creativity, innovation, and problem resolution. It is the principle used by Edison and Einstein to resolve their great mysteries of the universe. Callas had great insight into her own intuitive strengths and weaknesses. Her intuitive powers led her to a belief in the occult and when a Turkish gypsy told her, "You are going to die young, madame. But you will not suffer," she believed her. She in fact fulfilled the gypsy's prophecy by dying young and without any suffering in her Parisian bedroom at the age of fifty-four.

Callas was myopic most of her life. She wore glasses from the age of seven, and could hardly see by the age of eighteen. In the fashion of most creative geniuses, Maria turned her lemons into lemonade. She resorted to memorizing every note of every score because she could not see the conductor's baton. In this way she became a totally autonomous performer who could move about the stage performing and acting rather than responding to the conductor. She gained complete freedom, which other performers not afflicted with an eyesight problem didn't have. This introverted, intuitive, feeling, and orderly woman became an enormous success, often in spite of her temperament, not because of it.

Family versus Career

Callas's sister Jackie wrote in a biography, "I gave my life to my family, Maria gave her life to her career." What Callas actually did was give her life to the redemption of her childhood fears of inadequacy and insecurity. She searched for happiness and found it by realizing her childhood dream of singing. She said, "I wanted to be a great singer" and gave insight into her emotional dysfunction when she said she only felt loved when she was singing. This emotionally driven woman married a man many years her senior to assuage her Electra complex (symbolic adulation of father), but more so to give her stability and acceptance as an artist. She never took Meneghini's last name but instead used her own name throughout the marriage, similar to many of the women in this work (Margaret Mead, Ayn Rand, Jane Fonda, Liz Claiborne, Madonna, and Linda Wachner). She would always be known as Callas, even though Giovanni Batista Meneghini was her surrogate father, manager, mentor, lover, and therapist-in-waiting.

Meneghini was a wealthy Italian industrialist who loved opera and Maria. He fought violently with his family over what they perceived to be a mercenary young American girl who was after his money. He gave up his firm of twenty-seven factories, saying, "Take everything, I'm staying with Maria." He was a faithful husband who nurtured her career and attempted to protect her from her detractors. She married him on an impulse. They were wed in the Catholic Church in 1949 even though she was a devoted Greek Orthodox. This turned out to be her Achilles heel eleven years later, when the church refused to grant her a divorce to marry Onassis.

During the early period of her marriage to Batista, Callas often talked of having a baby and thought it would solve many of her physical ills. It appears that she never seriously considered starting a family with a man so much older than herself. Batista was well into his sixties when she was in her thirties, the time when she was finally ready to sacrifice her professional life for a better personal life. She had affairs but was attracted to men of the theater such as director Luchino Visconti and Leonard Bernstein, both of whom were gay (Lowe, 1986). After she met Aristotle Onassis, nothing else mattered, including Batista. She said, "When I met Aristo, so full of life, I became a different woman."

Callas first met Onassis at a Venice ball in September 1957, when Elsa Maxwell adroitly played matchmaker and introduced them. Elsa was bisexual and had unsuccessfully coveted Maria and decided to vent her subtle revenge after numerous rejections by encouraging these two volatile Greeks (Stanicoff, 1987). In 1959 when her doctor prescribed sea air for Maria, she and Batista accepted Aristotle's invitation for a cruise on the notorious Onassis yacht, *Christina*. Their infamous voyage, which began with Winston Churchill, Gary Cooper, the Duchess of Kent, and other notables, marked the end of Callas's marriage. These two Greeks became embroiled in a tempestuous affair on board that ended both their marriages. The ever-childlike Callas, when approached by Batista over her flagrant affair, said, "When you saw that I was going to be swept off my feet, why didn't you do something?" As recently as a year before meeting Onassis, she had told reporters, "I could not sing without him [her husband] present. If I am the voice, he is the soul." Such was the attraction of Onassis.

According to Batista, "Maria seemed more voracious than I had ever seen her. She danced continuously, always with Onassis. She told me the sea was splendid when it was squally. She and Onassis were in love and danced all night every night and made love." Onassis was only nine years younger than Batista. Even though her husband was a millionaire industrialist, he was bland next to the cosmopolitan Onassis. Batista spoke Italian and broken English, while Onassis spoke fluent Greek, Italian, French, and English. He had billions whereas Batista had millions, and Onassis spent it frivolously, while Batista was frugal. Onassis threw Callas a party at the famous Dorchester Hotel in London and filled the hotel with red roses. This was not the style of her conservative husband. Callas was literally swept away by the international womanizer.

After the ill-fated voyage, Callas moved into a Paris apartment to be near Onassis. He divorced his wife, agreeing to marry Callas and allow her to have a family. She was ecstatic for the first time in her life and was like a teenager in love at age thirty-six. She virtually stopped singing and dedicated her life to her true love. However, Callas's Catholic Italian marriage to Batista interfered with her marital plans and she was unable to obtain a divorce until many years later. Batista used his influence with the church to delay the divorce until after Onassis had already met and married Jacqueline Kennedy (Menichini, 1982; Stanicoff, 1987).

Callas had sacrificed career and marriage for Onassis and was repaid with nothing more than a cheap affair for many years before and after his marriage to Jackie. She became pregnant by him in 1966, when she was forty-three. Onassis' response was, "Abortion!" It was an order (Stanicoff, 1987). At first she didn't believe he was serious until he told her, "I don't want a baby by you. What would I do with another child? I already have two." Callas was devastated. "It took me four months to make up my mind. Think how fulfilled my life would be if I'd stood up to him and kept the baby." Callas's friend and biographer, Nadia Stanicoff (1987), asked her why she did it. "I was afraid of losing Aristo." The irony is that when Onassis' butler called with word of his wedding to Jacqueline Kennedy, Maria told him prophetically, "Mark my words, the gods will get even. There is justice." She was right. Onassis' only son died in a tragic plane accident shortly after Callas's abortion, and his daughter, Christina, died shortly after Onassis' death in 1975.

Maria told *Women's Wear Daily* on Onassis and Jackie's wedding day, "First I lost my weight, then I lost my voice, and now I have lost Onassis." Callas even attempted suicide in a Parisian hotel. She was continually courted by Onassis after his sensational marriage to Jackie. He had the audacity to tell her he was divorcing Jackie to marry her and she was needy enough to believe him. When Onassis died in March 1975, she said, "Nothing matters anymore because nothing will ever be the same again . . . without him." This talented woman had sacrificed both career and marriage—just like Medea— for her Greek lover. Like Medea, Callas lost both. Her own personal needs for family and a mate were never met. She would end her days in a Paris apartment with two poodles, her surrogate children.

Callas told the London *Observer* on February 8, 1970, that the important things in life were not her music, although this comment was made after her career was over. She said, "No, music is not the most important thing in life. Communication is the most important thing in life. It is what makes the human predicament bearable. And art is the most profound way in which one person can communicate with another. . . .Love is more important than any artistic triumph."

It is strange that we worship that which is fleeting and unavailable and discount what is easy and available. Maria had conquered the operatic world and found it no longer important, and had been vanquished by love and romance but worshipped that elusive element in her life. She never valued family or romance on her hectic road to the top as an internationally acclaimed opera star. And when she decided that these were valuable commodities in life, they were unavailable to her. She had sacrificed everything for her professional life and negated her personal life, then she sacrificed her profession for Onassis only to end up wanting in both areas.

Life Crisis

This precocious child prodigy was destined for trouble from the day of her conception in Athens, Greece. Her parents had lost a beloved son, Vassilios, to typhoid fever just one year before Maria's conception. The family was still in mourning when the mother learned she was pregnant. Evangelia became preoccupied with having another boy. When Maria was born in New York City, nine months later, her mother refused to look at her or touch her for four days because she was a girl and not a replacement for her beloved lost son. This is not the ideal beginning for anyone. Maria would never forget this early rejection and repaid it when in 1950 she said goodbye to her mother and never spoke to her again.

At the age of six, Maria was involved in a catastrophic traffic accident in New York City. The doctors expected her to die. The newspapers referred to her as "Lucky Maria." It was shortly after her recovery that Maria became obsessed with music. Such obsessions shortly after a near-tragedy is a familiar finding in great creative genius. They are attempting to give meaning to a life that has been threatened. States of trauma create a fertile ground to imprint unconscious images on the psyche. This appears to have happened to the ever-vulnerable Maria. She survived this near-tragedy and became preoccupied with perfection. Her compulsion for overachievement evidently had some of its genesis during this traumatic period of her life.

Maria's next bout with crisis occurred when her father lost his business during the Great Depression and because of the family's financial troubles her mother attempted suicide. Evangelia ended up in Bellevue Hospital for a period while her father cared for the children. Callas's godfather, Dr. Lontzounis, said of her mother, "She probably was crazy." This trauma occurred when Maria was in the formative years of her development, ages seven to eleven.

Another major crisis occurred after Maria and the family had moved to Athens. She was living and singing in Athens when the Nazis invaded Greece in 1940 at the start of World War II. Maria was just a teenager at the time and the family faced starvation on numerous occasions during the occupation. "Maria literally ate out of garbage cans during the war," according to Nadia Stanicoff, her biographer (1987). "Maria considered it a sacrilege to throw away a piece of bread even when she was wealthy, due to her wartime experiences." Her eating binges just after the war appear to have been a function of her near starvation. Toward the end of the war, in 1944, Maria told of running directly across the path of a barrage of gunfire. She attributed her survival to "divine intervention." Callas was very spiritual throughout her life and had an occult side that defied logic.

Callas satisfied her emotions and appetites with food after the war and became very heavy. Her weight varied between 200 and 240 pounds during the period when she was making her initial artistic debut. Her wartime starvation was transformed into an eating binge that lasted seven years. In an attempt to control her ballooning weight she would eat only vegetables, salads, and rare steak, but finally resorted to a tapeworm to lose the weight in 1953. She lost nearly 100 pounds in a year and a half, becoming a svelte 135 pounds on a five-foot, eight-inch frame. She went through a psychological metamorphosis of a type analyzed in Maxwell Maltz's *Psycho-Cybernetics*. Her personality changed as her body changed. Batista said, "Her physique had undergone a drastic change, which in turn influenced her entire way of life. She seemed to be another woman with a different personality." Callas was suddenly more famous during this period for her dramatic weight loss than for her voice.

Dominant Trait and Success

Callas's insecurities were the driving force in her success. Alfred Adler preached that all humans strive for perfection and superiority in order to stave off feelings of insecurity and inadequacy. Maria Callas could have been the prototype for Adler's theory. She was the consummate perfectionist and workaholic in an attempt to overcome her deep-seated insecurities. She overcompensated in the Freudian sense of sublimation and utilized her weaknesses to make herself into the greatest diva in the twentieth century. How? She used her obsessive perfectionism and impatience to change the way the opera was sung. She created her own stage persona, one that set her apart from everyone else who had ever sung the arias. She was not afraid of being different and used her intuitive powers to know what was appropriate at any given moment. As Yves St. Laurent said, "She was the diva of divas, empress, queen, goddess, sorceress, hardworking magician, in short, divine."

In opera, Maria Callas had no parallel in history. Enrico Caruso comes the closest, as a male performer who mesmerized the general public in the early twentieth century. However, the last half of the century belonged to Callas. David Hamilton wrote in the *Encyclopedia of Metropolitan Opera* (1987), "Everything Callas did she made new, by a combination of imaginative resource and sheer hard work." He said, "No voice was ever shot through with so much theatrical character." Mary Hamilton described Callas as "having every attribute of the opera singer—a voice of enormous range (up to a high E flat), extraordinary stage presence, a colorful personal life." Nonopera buffs were just as overwhelmed by her performances. Elsa Maxwell said of her, "When I looked into her amazing eyes, which are brilliant, beautiful, and hypnotic, I realized she is an extraordinary person."

Callas always sought the solution to her problems outside of herself (external) even though the actual solutions were always inside (internal). The very qualities that launched her as an eminently successful diva and prima donna were the qualities, if used properly, that could have solved her personal problems. She never recognized this and continued to live her life as a perpetual perfectionist. Her impulsive, impatient, and obsessive drive for perfection elevated her to the top of her profession. Her inviolate work ethic created a creature who pursued only excellence. But these traits also made her sick and ultimately were responsible for the loss of her many friends and acquaintances. She was an authority in everything she did and captured the imagination of audiences in almost every language. Her mastery of English, Greek, Italian, Spanish, and French made her an unusual artist. She was mesmerizing on the stage, captivating in person, and she owed it all to her compulsion to be the best. Was the prize worth the price? Callas thought so.

Summary

Enrico Caruso was the quintessential male opera star of the early twentieth century and Maria Callas inherited his power fifty years later, becoming the most idolized diva of the theater. This prima donna with the tempestuous temperament was known by her press names of "Cyclone Callas," "Hurricane Callas," the "Tigress," and the "Diabolical Diva." Her nicknames tell the story of this controversial and immensely talented artist. Fortunately, Maria Callas is preserved on tape and in video for posterity. She underwent a revival in 1994 due to her depiction in the movie *Philadelphia*. Her record sales were still $1 million annually maintaining her role as martyr and tragic heroine. She is a creative visionary because she changed her profession more than any other female in history. Her accomplishments have earned her a place in posterity as one of the most innovative and creative individuals to grace the professional stage. Maria started with nothing but an eighth-grade education and a will to be the best and ended by dominating her profession worldwide for a period of fifteen years. She was considered the best of her era and some felt the best ever.

The tragedy of this woman is that she was always beset with problems emanating from her basic insecurities. She was introspective enough to see this in herself and said so: "It has always been like that, at every important turn in my career. . . . I have always had to pay for all my triumphs immediately without fail, personally, with a sorrow or a physical ailment" (Memoirs from *Oggi,* 1957).

Callas felt strongly that she had been snakebit by destiny and the irony of this statement is found even in her death. She died suddenly and mysteriously in her Paris apartment at the relatively young age of fifty-four. Her will could not be found, leading to speculation as to the cause of death Ironically, her two mortal enemies in the world inherited her $12-million estate. Either she had not left a will or it was confiscated by some motivated individual as some have suggested, and the courts awarded her estate to her ex-husband Batista and her mother Evangelia. Both were in their mid-eighties and outlived Maria to inherit her fortune.

This consummate perfectionist had reached the very top of the operatic world because of an intransigent drive for excellence in everything she did. She changed the world of opera and did so with flair and elegance. While she started with nothing, she converted a weakness—her volcanic personality—into a positive force that lit up the stage like no other women in history. Her particular contribution to creative genius and innovation was her intuitive sensitivity to excellence. Unfortunately for the world of opera the artist died before the woman. On September 16, 1977, when the woman died, the networks announced, "The voice of the century is silenced forever." She had turned opera into theater and, by dying theatrically, played the dramatic artist to the very end.

Cecilia Sophia Anna Maria Meneghini (Kalogeropolous) Callas
Opera singer and recording artist
b. December 4, 1923, New York City; d. September 16, 1977, Paris

Dominant trait: A perpetual perfectionist
Religion: Greek Orthodox, very spiritual
Motto: "I do not like the middle way. All or nothing."
Philosophy: "I work, therefore I am."
Nicknames: Tigress, Diabolical Diva, Hurricane Callas, Cyclone Callas, Prima Donna with the Tempestuous Temperament
Creation/innovation: Arguably the greatest operatic diva of the twentieth century. Memorized every note of every opera due to poor vision. This technique changed the profession.
Contribution: Dramatic theatrics and enthusiasm for the operatic art
Success: La Scala, Metropolitan Opera, Rome, Dallas, Chicago, London, and Paris opera houses
Self-description: "I am impatient and impulsive, and I have an obsession for perfection."

Birth order: Third-born child; sister, Jackie, was six years her senior
Childhood transience: Conceived in Greece, born and raised in New York City. Moved 9 times in first 8 years in New York during Depression.
Father's occupation: Owned a pharmacy in Athens and later one in midtown Manhattan
Mentors: Elvira de Hidalgo (Spanish diva), her teacher at the Athens Conservatory; Tullio Serafin; Batista Meneghini, friend, manager, and husband; Giusseppi di Stefano, opera co-star and lover.
Childhood upbringing: "My father . . . I adored. My father and I had a good relationship. . . . I always sided with my father. I was his favorite when I was a child . . . or maybe always."
Formal education: Ended formal school at 13 after graduating from 8th grade. Entered Athens Conservatory at 13 by mother, who lied about her age saying she was 16.
Life crises: Brother Basil died of typhoid fever just prior to her conception. Hit by Manhattan car at age 5, in coma 12 days, hospital 22. Mother attempted suicide when she was 7 and committed to Bellevue Hospital. Athens invaded and occupied by Nazis in 1940 when she was 17.
Marriages/liaisons: Married Giovanni Meneghini, a Verona industrialist (27 years older), at age 26 on April 21, 1949. Left husband for Aristotle Onassis. The affair lasted from 1959 to 1972.

Risk-taking: Traveled alone and rebelled against tradition
Temperament: Introvert-Intuitive-Feeler-Judger; Electra complex
Behavior: "Type A," impulsive, impatient, perfectionist, hypochondriac
Career vs. family: Career superseded any thought of family until her late thirties when she wanted a child by Onassis. He forced her to abort a pregnancy at age 43.
Self-esteem: Ego based on sublimated drive to excel
Hobbies: Watching TV and work
Heroes: Father, historical opera stars, and Aristotle Onassis
Honors: Lord Harewood of London: "The greatest musical performer of our time"; Rudolph Bing (N.Y. Met): "We will not see her like again." Pierre-Jean Remy: "After Callas, opera will never be the same again."

10

Liz Claiborne—Persevering Pioneer

Intuition is the gift of the gods; logic is its faithful servant.

—Albert Einstein

Ask a career woman, or any woman who shops, what "Liz" conjures up in their heads, and you receive an instant explanation deserving of a Madison Avenue market researcher. The names "Lizsport" and "Lizwear" gained national recognition faster than any other brand in the history of the garment industry. The first products were shipped in 1976 and by 1986 they were an institution for American women desiring professional, practical, and affordable clothing. "Liz" evokes an instant recognition of upscale but professional-looking, off-the-rack women's wear with a sporty flair aimed at working women everywhere. It has a universal appeal, a simple but functional style, and mix and match compatibility never before found in competitive clothing lines. "Fashionable, functional, and affordable" is the Liz trademark. What is amazing is that the "Liz" identity was created in less than a decade, an unprecedented feat in the dog-eat-dog "rag" business. As is so often the case, the sales and success curves tracked an identical upward spiral to the Liz brand-name recognition.

No other firm has experienced such dizzying growth as Liz Claiborne and not one of the eminently successful women in this book made as much money as quickly as she did (approximately $200 million in under ten years). The reason? Her timing was exquisite. She filled a need (stylish clothes) for an emerging market (professional females) at the right price (slightly above average) with built-in variety and multiplicity (mixing and matching for multiple outfits) in practical fits, styles, colors, and materials. The Claiborne designs were created for ordinary women, not models with impossibly thin torsos. She solved a problem that demanded resolution, and she executed it with elegance, style, and simplicity.

Claiborne changed the way professional working women dress. She gave them an opportunity to look chic and professional with off-the-rack ready wear. Her magic was in listening to her gut in designing clothes that she wanted to wear as a career business woman. And her gut did not mislead her, as the pundits had predicted. This pioneering spirit ignored the industry experts, who would never have agreed to her strategy. She believed in her own vision to "clothe the working American woman" and was willing to bet her family's savings ($50,000) on her dream. Her intuitive feel for what women like her wanted in clothing was right on line with what was happening in the world. As a working woman, Claiborne understood what the garment gurus didn't. She told *Fortune* (1987): "I was working myself, I wanted to look good, and I didn't think you should have to spend a fortune to do it. Only a couple of companies were catering to that emerging woman—both in traditional, suited ways. I felt we could do better."

Claiborne proceeded to implement her life-long dream of producing her own line of fashion women's wear. Her insight and vision have been instrumental in revolutionizing the women's wear industry and the marketing of working women's clothing. Liz Claiborne has dominated this segment of women's clothing like no other firm in history. *Women's Wear Daily* (1991) characterized Liz Claiborne as "a $2 billion phenomenon." *Fortune* magazine said of the firm, "Liz Claiborne has been a great pathfinder," and in 1992 ranked it fourth on its list of the "300 Most Admired Companies" in America. It was ranked second behind Levi Strauss in the apparel group. *Working Woman* (1992) gushed, "Today Liz Claiborne is not just one of America's most successful clothing companies—it is one of America's most successful companies, period."

This business phenomenon is one of only two firms founded by a female to have reached the *Fortune* 500, and it was the fastest to have made that prestigious list. It took just ten years of operation to cross the threshold into the sacred land of the *Fortune* 500 elite. Based on the "return on equity" barometer of success, *Fortune* in 1988 ranked Liz Claiborne first among all companies on their list for the years 1979-1988. Unbelievably, the firm had averaged a 40 percent return every year for ten years. This was incomprehensible for a firm that did not even exist until 1976. This caused *Fortune* to declare, "Liz Claiborne is America's most successful female entrepreneur." How did Claiborne attain this eminent stature? She had sensed a need in the market and then listened to her "gut" in satisfying and fulfilling that need. She told Elsa Klensch of *Vogue* in 1986: "My original concept was to dress the women who didn't have to wear suits—the teachers, the doctors, the women working in Southern California or Florida, the women in the fashion industry itself. They didn't need or necessarily want to wear suits."

Claiborne was willing to bet all of the family's savings on this vision of the future. She placed her bet on the come-line of female dress habits and came up with a win emblematic of breaking the bank in Las Vegas. The Liz

Claiborne company went on to become a $2-billion enterprise in 1991 and the darling of Wall Street. By the early nineties the firm so dominated the women's apparel business that it accounted for an estimated 5 to 10 percent of all department store sales in the United States. Claiborne's perseverance had paid off.

Personal History

Elizabeth Claiborne was born in Brussels, Belgium, on March 31, 1929, to American parents from New Orleans. She was the second-born child but the first-born female. Her older brother, Omer Claiborne, is the owner of an art gallery in Santa Fe, New Mexico. Her mother, Louise Fenner Claiborne, was a housewife and seamstress with a practical nature. Her father, Omer Claiborne, was an expatriate banker for Morgan Guaranty Trust Company who was to become a positive influence on her despite his old-fashioned, stodgy attitudes about life and women's place in it. He was a direct descendant of the famous William C. C. Claiborne who governed Louisiana during the War of 1812.

Claiborne spoke French before English, having grown up in Brussels. She describes her father as a "very old-fashioned" banker who loved art and history. He "dragged her around to museums and cathedrals" all over Western Europe giving her a cultural education so important in the world of creative design. She acquired a love of paintings and aesthetics from this early experience, which she felt was an enormous asset in her later work as a fashion designer. She says that this taught her to appreciate aesthetics, that "the look of things is as important as their function."

When Liz was ten the family fled the invading Nazis and relocated to New Orleans in 1939. Liz's mother taught her to sew at a very early age and her strict rules about clothing and appearance left their mark on the girl. "I was taught to 'look' at things. You don't just buy a chair, you buy a pretty chair." She was trained as to what to wear, when, and in what colors. This conditioning was intermixed with her father's instruction on art and aesthetics, which combined to instill in her the fundamentals of artistic design in clothing. Liz's formal schooling consisted of convent-like parochial schools in accordance with her Roman Catholic background. Her old-fashioned father did not think formal education was essential for a female (shades of Meir and Callas) and enrolled her in art school in Europe in lieu of finishing high school.

Claiborne attended art schools in Brussels, Belgium (1947), and in Nice, France (1948), and spent time at the Academie de Beaux Arts in Paris. Her father wanted Claiborne to become an artist and insisted that she study French Impressionist painting. Liz realized very early that she would never become a great painter and told the *Washington Post*'s Nina Hyde, "I went along, and I'm glad I had that training because it taught me to see; it taught me color, proportion, and many other things that I don't think I would have learned in design school." She says, "I then crammed and took pattern-making courses at night. . . . When you like to draw and love to sew—well, what else do you do but become a designer?" (This type of holistic education appears to be far superior to traditional educational training based on the findings on these women.)

Claiborne says that her Roman Catholic family was "dead-set" against her working in the fashion industry. She told Adam Smith of *Esquire* (January 1986), "It was—well, too New York, too rough." So the ever-adventurous Liz entered and won a national design contest sponsored by *Harper's Bazaar* at age nineteen while on summer vacation from art school. Her winning sketch was of a woman's high-collared coat with a "military feeling." This award gave her the confidence, moxie, and professional pedigree necessary to open doors to the New York garment industry. Using her newly won prize as an entree to the Seventh Avenue garment district, Claiborne defied her father, walked away from an art career, and left for New York City to make her fortune. Omer gave her fifty dollars and said a solemn goodbye feeling "a woman's place is in the home" and not in the sweatshop environment of New York's infamous garment district. She lived temporarily with an aunt and began looking for work. Claiborne had taken the first iconoclastic step in her drive to the top of fashion design. It took awhile, but she has more than lived up to the Cinderella story of "girl makes good" in spite of her father's nonsupport.

Professional Background

Claiborne's early art training was her admission ticket to the garment district. Her first job was with Tina Lesser, a maverick designer who could not draw. Claiborne's artistic skills got her this first job as a design assistant, but she was shocked to learn that she had been hired to model as well. This experience was excellent training for her later career, since she received great mentoring from the unorthodox Lesser. Claiborne described Lesser to the *Washington Post* as "a person with so much imagination and so unconventional in the clothing business. She had very definite ideas about how you constructed clothes and ruled with an iron fist, but she recognized talent and was fun to work with."

Claiborne was twenty-one in 1950 when she began her fashion career. She married a Time-Life Books designer, Ben Schultz, at the same time she started her career. Their only child, Alexander Schultz, was born in 1952 and Claiborne, unlike most women of the time, continued working. She was one of the rare working mothers in the 1950s and describes the period: "I was very career oriented, I worked to the last day of my pregnancy and came back to the office two weeks later. In retrospect it's not such a smart thing to do."

Claiborne got started in the era of the dress, the fifties. She always preferred pants to dresses but earned a reputation as a great dress designer very early in her career. She says, "It's almost like being an actress. You get channeled into a certain area," and that becomes your niche. Claiborne moved on to work for designer Ben Rieg, and then as a designer for Omar Kiam's assistant at his Seventh Avenue design house. She then spent two years designing for Junior Rite Company and one year at the Rhea Manufacturing Company of Milwaukee, where she met dress company executive Arthur Ortenberg. Just as the career path is sometimes a function of fate so also are personal relationships. Ortenberg would ultimately become her second husband after each ended their first marriages. They both took jobs in New York in 1957.

Claiborne had risen to the top of the design field after being named chief designer for Jonathan Logan, a division of Youth Guild. She stayed in that position for sixteen years, not out of loyalty or desire, but because she had a son in school and her new husband was "always experimenting and changing jobs. He had his own company and then that went out of business and he'd try this and that." Her response to his vagabond work habits was, "I had to be the Rock of Gibraltar." Claiborne told the *New York Times* in 1980, "I always knew I wanted to go into the fashion designing business." It was during the period at Jonathan Logan when she recognized the gap in the market for moderately priced career clothing for women. She was unable to convince the people at Jonathan Logan that mix-and-match coordinated sportswear for the emerging female workforce was a viable product innovation. Her frustration with the noninnovative fashion industry drove her to consider launching her own firm when her son and two stepchildren finished college in 1975. She left Youth Guild in December 1975 at age forty-six to fulfill her lifetime dream of creating fashion clothing for working women.

ENTREPRENEURIAL DREAM

Claiborne's vision of stylish, sporty, and affordable clothing for working women became a reality in early 1976. She and Arthur invested their $50,000 life savings, convinced friends Jerome Chazen (Arthur's college roommate) to handle the marketing, and Leonard Boxer to handle the production. They raised another $200,000 from Boxer and Chazen as well as other friends and acquaintances to form Liz Claiborne, Inc. Their total starting investment was $250,000. Liz displayed some thirty-five design pieces in her first group of clothes in the fall of 1976. Her casual camel jacket with matching color pants, knickers, pleated skirts, tattersall shirts, cowlneck sweaters, ponchos, shirt jackets, and hunting jackets were all styled in components that could be mixed and matched in combinations. They made a statement that was "outdoorsy" and "sporty." They were designed to meet the needs of the "new working woman" or the "yuppies" of the time. She empathized with the customer and used a pragmatic pricing scheme, asking herself, "If I were going to wear this to my job, how much would I pay for it?" and that became the price. Claiborne ignored traditional pricing schemes.

Claiborne's best seller was a velour peasant blouse and a crepe de Chine version for 1978. She sold 15,000 of these even though she only expected to sell 4,000. Even with this success the partners would have lost their total investment had they not turned a profit that first year. Her husband said, "By the time we were ready to ship the first collection, we were committed to producing $350,000 in goods. . . . We were personally impoverished." But Claiborne's market analysis had been right on target. The Liz Lady look was on its way to becoming ubiquitous in the department stores of America. By 1978 she had designed full skirts, loose tunics, and vests in rust and plum to meet the new layering look then in fashion. These met the needs of both office work and leisure. Claiborne coupled practicality with affordability by using polyester crepe de Chine in blouses because it was fifteen dollars cheaper than silk and stated, "It doesn't wrinkle and it is more practical—plus it looks like silk." The strategy and designs were correct and the firm was an immediate success, earning a profit in its first year on sales of $2.5 million. By 1978 sales had climbed to $23 million. The firm's success was based on Claiborne's intuitive feel for the needs of working women:

> I'm a great believer in fit, in comfort, in color, and I listen to the customer. I went on the selling floor as a saleswoman, went into the fitting room, heard what they liked and didn't like. Not that you do exactly what they want. What you do is digest the information and then give them what you think they ought to have. (*Fortune,* 1990)

Claiborne had complete empathy with the working woman. She described the idyllic Liz Lady to the *New York Times* in 1980: "My customer is the working woman. . . . She has no choice—clothes are not a variable for her. She needs a wardrobe, and she's more financially independent." Claiborne was constantly focused on consumer image and perception of value. She said, "I think women today have a great deal more self-confidence and want clothes that can help show it." She adds, "I'd rather appeal to a woman's idealistic version of herself. She's active, whatever her age. It's the same feeling we try to give in the clothes." She insisted on the same personal touch in the operation of the business. Former corporate marketing director Ken Wyse said, "The company runs like a Japanese company. People feel part of it." Claiborne added, "We decided from the start that we were going to be a very familial company." One example is that everyone is on a first-name basis in the company and even the company directory list, its 400 employees alphabetically by first name. Wyse adds, "She expects the best. The extra competition brings out the best in people."

The firm soon went through its initial investment and operating profits because of its fast growth and was having difficulty growing by 1980. The company decided on a public offering to raise additional capital in 1981. The firm's sales revenues had grown to $117 million by then. The offering was issued at $19 a share and raised $6.1 million in working capital. (An investment of $1000 in 1981 was worth about $30,000 by 1992.) By 1986, the firm crossed the threshold into the mystical land of the *Fortune* 500, and by 1987, sales passed the magic billion dollar mark. Retailers started saying, "Liz Claiborne knows what its customers want." And other apparel manufacturers started prophetically saying, "We are the next Liz Claiborne."

Claiborne and her husband were pragmatic in their approach to expanding the business. They refused to fall into the age-old ego trap of owning the manufacturing factories. Claiborne created the designs then farmed out the production to various factories in such obscure places as India, China, Taiwan, Hong Kong, Korea, and the Philippines. She told *Esquire* about the company strategy in 1986: "We don't do a design and then add the cost of producing and selling. We do a sample, and then we think—I think—if I was going to wear this to my job, how much would I pay for it? Then we try to keep the cost to that." This strategy forced the market to determine the prices instead of the manufacturing operations setting prices. The bidding to offshore firms forced costs to meet the market need, which is a very Eastern approach to pricing, in contrast to American logic.

Claiborne's vision was so accurate that the company became the fastest-growing and most profitable apparel company during the entire decade of the eighties. Some of her magic cannot be appreciated without looking at the numbers. Liz Lady clothes generate $400 to $500 per square foot of retail space. That is three times the average for all other clothing firms. By 1990, Liz Claiborne's sales were double those of the second largest women's wear vendor, the Leslie Fay Companies. Liz Claiborne, Inc., had become the role model for all competitors to emulate. Why? Because it had read the pulse of the working female better than any other firm. It was so close to the consumer that it had the ability to sense the needs of the changing consumer almost before the styles changed.

Claiborne refers to her customers as "Liz Ladies." The company's research methods included a unique customer sampling operation used to project the retailers' needs in the coming months. The company employed teams of people responsible for identifying the customers' needs and wants—unprecedented in the garment industry. The resultant profile of the customer—the Liz Lady—could have been a demographic portrait of most of the women in this book:

> She is real. She is complex. She wants to look appropriate. Fashion is a part of her life, but it isn't her whole life. Quantitatively her median age is 41.6, her median income is over $50,000, and she is likely to be employed in a white-collar job. She likes to be tasteful—but not to stop traffic. (*Working Woman,* April 1992)

Liz Claiborne violated tradition by supplying new selections six times a year instead of the conventional four. It created a clothing line that was between "classic" and "avant garde" designed for smart-looking, young female executives. But the company's primary talent was in executing its plan. The firm was operated more like a service than a product company. It implemented a unique "Claiboard" marketing program to all retailers who stocked the Claiborne product line. According to Irene Daria of *Women's Wear Daily,* "Claiboards are a trademarked concept using sketches, photos, and printed explanations showing how merchandise should be displayed in groups." This subtle but simple marketing ploy was instrumental in the company's initial success. It had a unique apparel line of mix-and-match sets and most retailers had never displayed such a complex product line. Today retailers understand the Claiborne concept of marketing, and in fact, it has become an industry standard. Only a visionary designer with incomparable confidence in her product would have dared such a unique approach. She was telling the retailer, "Here's how to properly service your customer so she continues to come back." It worked and the retailers appreciated the professional assistance and gave floor space from other manufacturers to Claiborne. The Lizwear line now has the highest penetration of retail space of any firm in the industry. In 1985 the company expanded into men's wear lines with the same enormous success. By 1988 the company was generating $125 million in sales in this new market niche. In 1988, *Fortune* named Liz Claiborne one of its "300 Most Admired Companies" in the United States.

Retailers began to realize that a company that benefits customers as well as Liz Claiborne should be listened to and given a disproportionate share of retail space in their stores. This obviously translated into higher sales. Maison Blanche of Baton Rouge, Louisiana, told *Women's Wear Daily* (1991), "We have increased their space in most stores by 25 percent over the past year." Macy's California dedicated 50 percent of the space for women's fine sportswear to Liz Claiborne clothing. Gottschalks in California dedicated 60 percent. This dominant space allocation translated into the highest sales per location of any garment manufacturer.

Camille Lavington, an international communications consultant, says,

"Women today want clothes to be dignified, beautiful, and luxurious—and comfortable, packable, and cleanable. All that and well-priced too. Liz Claiborne has figured out the formula like nobody else." Claiborne accomplished this with an intuitive feel for what the working women of the world wanted to wear. She persevered until she had it right and then continued trying harder. Her determination made Liz Claiborne the dominant supplier in virtually every category it entered. One interesting ploy was in marketing to the petite departments of fine department stores. One buyer said, "Her cut is a little bigger. But she puts a smaller size on it so psychologically women feel like they're buying the next smallest size. It gives them a lift about themselves." In addition the firm has 150 specialists with only one charter—to find out what customers want. Twenty-one consultants do nothing but insure that the clothes are arranged in the stores according to the "Lizmap" diagram—an optimum clothing display layout. Claiborne responds to inquiries, "We've been doing it since the day we started."

By 1990 the Claiborne clothing line and "Lizmap" diagram translated into the highest women's wear sales of any firm in the world, and approximately between 5 and 10 percent of all department store sales in the United States. One competitor remarked, "Claiborne is a role model for all sportswear companies, both in its merchandising concepts and its retail presentations." Another competitor, Leonard Rabinowitz, of Carole Little, Inc., said, "Liz Claiborne makes you realize that if you're going to be around, you have to be excellent at what you do. They set very good goals for us." Claiborne had sales of $1.2 billion in 1988 with profits exceeding $100 million for the first time. Having realized their wildest expectations for the firm Claiborne and her husband announced their retirement from day-to-day operations in June 1988. The company continued on its growth path by opening fifty-five outlet stores and expanding into fragrance and other cosmetic items for both men and women by 1990. Sales in 1992 were $2.2 billion, with over $200 million in profits. Not bad for a high school dropout with an intuitive flair for customer's needs.

Temperament: Intuitive-Thinking

Claiborne is introspective and introverted. Her intuition was the defining ingredient for her "Liz Ladies" fashion designs. Her self-confidence allowed her to follow her gut in spite of expert industry opinion to the contrary. Her intuitive approach to evaluating new products was similar to Lillian Vernon's. They both relied on their "gut" feel for what was right and were never deterred from that course of action. Claiborne was impatient and intolerant, common traits found in most perfectionist and creative personalities. In business she was shy and left all administrative and operating decisions to Arthur while she managed the creative effort. However, she was a control freak—as were most of these women—on all design and retail merchandising functions. She disliked media attention and left the badgering Wall Street analysts to her husband. However, when a customer or retailer called, she was available for hours to discuss the vagaries of the women's fashion business.

Claiborne was guilty of one of the weaknesses ascribed to most entrepreneurs. Innovators typically dislike the mundane business aspects of commercializing their concepts. The business details are looked upon as a necessary evil to realize their creative ambitions. Many women are too nice to function in the cold, hard world of Main Street, as their sensitivities are tested repeatedly. Claiborne had this quality. She constantly shied away from controversy and in an attempt at being "nice" was labeled weak by the media. They characterized her as not being tough because of her inability to embarrass people or scream at them, as is the standard operating procedure on Seventh Avenue. Often when Claiborne was confronted with designs she did not like she had the habit of saying nothing rather than embarrassing the person. This was often mistaken by male executives as weakness. But she was only being nice. She was firm when it came time to make an irrevocable decision on a new design. Excellence was her forte and if a design or product did not meet her expectations it never reached the market.

In a May 14, 1986, piece in the *New York Times,* Lisa Belkin wrote a profile of Claiborne's management style, saying, "She isn't tough enough." The article characterized Claiborne as running a "gee-gosh" enterprise "with a touch of Judy Garland and Mickey Rooney." Belkin wrote, "If you show her two designs, she'll say one is very nice and the other is O.K., which means she hates it, but she doesn't want to hurt any feelings." Sensitivity and introversion usually couple to create this type of behavior, and Claiborne was a highly sensitive woman and quite introverted. Nonassertive females are not often found in top executive positions in the boom-or-bust, dog-eat-dog garment industry. The self-preservation mentality of quarterly earnings performance usually dictates the behavior of most executives in the industry. Nice they are not! Claiborne was eminently successful, with a personality temperament not conducive to her environment which is further testimony to the awesome innovative contribution she made to the industry.

Claiborne is an unassuming woman. Once when asked the size of her net worth by a *Fortune* reporter, she responded, "A few million." He promptly informed her that it was closer to $100 million. Her housewife mother had raised her to value simple elegant solutions to complex problems. Her father exposed her to the arts and aesthetics, instilling the desire for functional elegance, style, grace, and form. Her upbringing conditioned her in the holistic (whole brain) style of Margaret Mead. It is this holistic mentality which gives these women the macro-vision required to succeed in the world of creativity and innovation. They are able avoid the clutter and see the big picture opportunities.

Intensity was seen in Claiborne's day-to-day business operations (a common entrepreneurial trait). These individuals learn to survive in stressful start-up environments and find it hard to change even after the firm is well established. This behavior caused Liz to be viewed by her employees as a bit arrogant, with an obsession for perfection. However, her style was oriented around quiet resolution of problems, based on her confident but introverted nature. Her impatience was often misinterpreted as aloofness, especially since she refused to talk to groups or large audiences. Arthur interfaced with the press except on design and fashion. He was autocratic while she operated as the creative and innovative force within the company.

Family versus Career

Liz Claiborne was always a working mother. At twenty-two, she returned to work two weeks after her son, Alexander, was born. That is not an uncommon event in the nineties but virtually made her a revolutionary woman in the fifties. Claiborne said of that time, "I was very career oriented." Even so, Claiborne refused to sacrifice everything for her entrepreneurial dream. She dreamed for years of creating her own women's clothing line, but refused to quit her job at Jonathan Logan and "go for it," until her son Alexander was an adult. She didn't want to jeopardize his security or, in her words, "have him destroyed" if the family went broke. Claiborne's role as a mother was instrumental in postponing her career dream until after her son graduated from college. In fact, she remained in a job she didn't like for sixteen years for the stability and security it provided her family. When Alexander was twenty-one, she resigned from Youth Guild and started Liz Claiborne, Inc.

Claiborne paid the price every working woman pays. She married Ben Schultz at age twenty-one in 1950 and also began her career. Her son was born shortly thereafter and she embarked on a life as a working mother. Liz was ahead of her time in juggling a career with family and her son paid the price of an often-absent mother. The marriage to Ben was the first casualty of this dual life. It lasted just seven years. She and Arthur Ortenberg had met in business and fallen in love. They divorced their respective spouses and married on July 5, 1957. They resided in New York City, where Claiborne worked as a designer for Jonathan Logan and he worked in the garment industry for himself and others. Arthur was more risk-oriented than Liz and gained a great deal of experience in entrepreneurial ventures during the next decade. Liz was the financial stability in the marriage through these years, Arthur job-hopped and floundered. She finally had enough of the risk-averse corporate world, where her revolutionary ideas fell on deaf ears, and resigned from Youth Guild in 1975. She and Arthur invested their life savings and started Liz Claiborne on January 19, 1976. Claiborne's son, Alexander, was twenty-one. Liz said, "If we were going to lose everything I wanted him to be old enough to handle it." Her son has never been interested in the business and is a Los Angeles jazz guitarist.

On paper Claiborne had taken the serial approach to entrepreneurial success by fulfilling her family responsibilities prior to her career venture. In fact, she could never have been so successful if she had not paid the price of twenty-five years as a fashion designer prior to embarking on her entrepreneurial venture. She, like Mary Kay Ash, worked during the day and was a wife and mother at night. Both of these women honed their skills and expertise at other firms before starting their own and consequently avoided many mistakes they might have made if they hadn't worked. They were independent spirits who chose to be working mothers when that was not in vogue.

Claiborne wouldn't have had the insight into the clothing void for the emerging professional woman had she not been in the workforce during the explosion of the working parent. Therefore, serendipity played a role in her success. Her shrewd analysis of the need for mix-and-match, affordable yet chic career clothes for the working woman was based on her own needs as a New York City fashion designer on a limited budget. She paid the price for such experience in time lost in making her start as an entrepreneur, but when she started she was well armed for the battle.

Claiborne is only one of two women in this book who started a family prior to entering the entrepreneurial arena. She was an adequate mother and an eminent entrepreneur. Her creative genius was realized only after her son was grown, so she was unobstructed when faced with starting Liz Claiborne, Inc. She was able to dedicate an inordinate amount of time and energy to the new enterprise, something often not possible for women with children waiting at home for dinner. It is quite apparent from this research that any and all distractions are detrimental to the creative process. Claiborne had few distractions in creating her dream and it became a monumental success because of her unencumbered focus. According to Liz and Arthur, "Our model of a successful entrepreneur is . . . the man or woman who has a successful business and a successful marriage." They have had both. Arthur was always the administrative and chief operating officer of the company, while Liz saw to the designs. A former marketing director for the firm refers to Arthur as "the wizard of Oz," because "He's the man behind the door—intellectual and godlike, introspecitve but dogmatic. He makes pronouncements." Arthur is outgoing while Liz is shy. She is serious, he jokes a lot. She watches the details, he watches for the big problems. She manages by doing, he by teaching. They were a great team.

Life Crisis

Claiborne's major life crisis occurred during her childhood in Europe, when her family was forced to flee the Nazi war machine in 1939 and return to the United States. Such moves are usually viewed as more traumatic for the children than the adults. However, the research on creative genius indicates that the children are less stressed than the parents, who experience far more dislocation than the children. The children learn to cope with the new and unknown, which appears to be very positive training for future innovators and creators. Both crisis and transience in the early lives of children appear to be positive forces in building characters in the area of self-esteem, self-sufficiency, and coping with the unknown.

Claiborne's traumatic experience confirms other research showing such dislocations as positive factors in later creative success. Claiborne spoke French before English and experienced a different culture in Europe as a child. She was at the impressionable age of ten, when forced to move to the United States. Such a transition demands learning to cope with a new culture, meeting new friends, functioning in different school systems, and interacting with different ethnic groups. Claiborne was raised in Brussels, Belgium, a cosmopolitan and sophisticated European city. She was suddenly transplanted to prewar New Orleans, where Caucasians were in the minority (just 45 percent of the population). Claiborne found herself in slow-paced southern city where the social system, including the schools, was still segregated. The city was unbearably hot, mosquito infested, and resistent to change. It was dramatically different from Brussels, and difference appears to be a critical breeding ground for creative genius. It teaches the young how to cope with novel situations and instills self-sufficiency. Claiborne learned to cope with the new, unknown environment, and then was sent back to Europe as a teenager—after the war—to continue her art education. There she studied art in three different European cities. This early transience appears to have been a causal factor in molding her personality to accept the new and untried.

Persevering Pioneer and Creative Success

Claiborne persevered through many years working for others on products she detested in order to get to the stage where she could do her own thing. And when she finally did it, she did it right. This woman is a classic creative genius because she is a pioneering perfectionist with a persevering spirit. She intuitively knew there was a void in the clothing products available to the working women in the mid-seventies. She had the focus, vision, and temerity to fill that market, which was devoid of elegance, style, and affordability.

Claiborne said, "I get more of a kick out of seeing women on the street wearing my clothes . . . than [when the clothes are] on the cover of fashion magazines." She was one of the first to demonstrate that fashion is not art, but based on pragmatic merchandising to the needs of the mass consumer. She knew that women did not identify with clothing designed for six-foot, hundred-pound, gaunt models. The emerging female workforce wanted clothes designed for them that were classy but practical. In hindsight, this is not a complex hypothesis, but in the mid seventies it was totally lost on tradition-bound clothing designers. Claiborne saw the need very clearly but was unable to convince her bosses. She quit her job, followed her "gut," and designed clothes for the "new" woman. And women everywhere responded with what economists label "dollar votes," making Liz Claiborne look like a genius by buying her fashions by the millions. Claiborne appealed to the masses, not the classes, and her simple solution to a complex problem made her enormously successful.

Claiborne was obsessed with high-quality clothes marketed via a precise but comprehensive retailing presentation. These traits emanated from her childhood conditioning, where her father insisted on class, elegance, and style in everything while her more practical mother insisted on sensible execution. The combination has made Claiborne an innovative genius who changed the world of fashion as much as anyone in history. Brenda Gall, senior industry specialist at Merrill Lynch summed up her success best: "Liz Claiborne is one of the all-time greats, not just in the apparel industry but in the history of the stock market" (*Vogue*, 1986).

Summary

Liz Claiborne, Inc., reached the zenith of all corporate expectations and dreams in 1990 when it was named the *Fortune* 500's most profitable firm. It had achieved this lofty stature after only fifteen years of operation. The firm in the early nineties was generating four times the sales level of the nearest top three competitors combined in the competitive women's clothing industry. Liz Claiborne is the third largest clothing manufacturer in the United States, shipping from 150 plants throughout the world to 3,500 retail outlets. It absolutely dominates its market segment, controlling 33 percent of the better women's sportswear business in the United States. The company is now penetrating the international markets with sales in Canada, Europe, the Pacific Rim nations, Latin America, and the Caribbean. Sales reached $102 million in foreign markets by 1992. All of this was made possible because an intuitive and persevering woman wanted to offer clothes she herself desired to wear. Her dreams encompassed high-style, practical clothing for the fast-paced career woman. The experts refused to consider her vision, so she found some partners, invested the family savings, and did it herself.

It is nothing short of amazing that within fifteen years this firm would dominate its industry like no other firm in history. Liz Claiborne is an anomaly in that it grew faster than any other such firm in the history of the industry while maintaining tight control over its merchandising techniques. This phenomenon left its competitors in its wake. The company owns the baby boomers. A 1992 *Forbes* article on the fashion design industry summarized the market by saying, "It is no longer a contest if you throw in Liz Claiborne." *Forbes* called Liz Claiborne "a phenomenon" after the firm generated over $1.2 billion in women's apparel business and another billion in men's wear and fragrance revenues in 1992. No other manufacturer of women's clothing does even $1 billion, yet Liz Claiborne does well over $2 billion. Her firm dwarfs the others, and Claiborne and her husband have reaped the spoils of their success. Their personal net worth, based on stock holdings, reached an unbelievable $200 million within their first ten years of operation. The great American Dream was still intact.

The successful couple resigned from the company board in August 1990 to spend more time on Tranquility Ranch in Montana (they can visit the Turners), a retreat on St. Bart's in the Virgin Islands, and an unpretentious oceanfront house and guest cottage in the village of Saltaire on Fire Island. Arthur said of their parting, "The sooner the company gets out from under our mythic infallibility, the better off it's going to be." They spend their time on environmental causes and philanthropic enterprises. They said on leaving the company, "We always intended to leave before we became irrelevant." How could a creative visionary who took a childhood dream of art and fashion and combined it with the needs of the emerging working woman to revolutionize the world of women's wear ever be irrelevant? She first listened to her gut and then to her customers, giving them what they wanted at an affordable price. This combination turned out to be one of the great success stories in the history of American business. Liz Claiborne, the persevering pioneer, is a creative genius who would have made her father proud.

Elizabeth "Liz" Claiborne
Fashion designer
b. March 31, 1929, Brussels, Belgium

Dominant trait: Persevering Pioneer
Religion: Roman Catholic
Mottos: "Listen to the customer." "I like to appeal to a woman's idealistic version of herself."
Philosophy: "Clothe the working American woman." "Listen to the customer."
Nicknames: Reluctant Revolutionary, Wizard of Working Women's Wardrobe, Liz Lady
Creation/innovation: Spotting a need in the market and intuitively pursuing it. "Lizsport" and "Lizwear" lines dominate the working women's sportswear market in the United States.
Products/contributions: Mix-and-match affordable but elegant clothing for the working woman. In 1993 Liz Claiborne, Inc., accounted for as much as 10% of department store sales in women's wear.
Successes: Revolutionized professional women's clothing. First woman in fashion named Entrepreneurial Woman of the Year (1980). Earned $100 million faster than any other woman in this book. First firm (1986) founded by woman to join *Fortune* 500 list.
Self-description: "I'm the 'Liz Lady,' an average American woman."

Birth order: First-born female with one older brother, Omer
Childhood transience: Moved to New Orleans at age 10, then Baltimore. Traveled Europe as a child and again as a teenager attending art classes in three cities.
Father's occupation: Expatriate banker descendant of Louisiana's Gov. Claiborne (1812).
Mentors/role models: Learned aesthetic appreciation from her father—that "form is as important as function"—and simple solutions from her mother.
Childhood upbringing: Conservative father taught her art and history. Her mother's influence was in sewing, color, and image.
Formal education: Parochial schools in Belgium. Learned French before English. High school dropout due to old-fashioned father who felt she should not go to school.
Life crisis: Escaped Nazi juggernaut in 1939 and moved to New Orleans.
Marriages/liaisons: Married twice: Ben Schultz (1950) with whom she had a son, Alexander. She divorced Schultz to marry Arthur Ortenberg in 1957.

Risk-taking: Bet her life savings on Liz Claiborne in January 1976 at age 47. Would have been broke if company had not been an immediate success.
Temperament: Introvert-intuitive-thinker-judger
Behavior: Quiet, aloof, impatient, and an intense perfectionist
Career vs. family: "Our model of a successful entrepreneur is . . . the man or woman who has a successful business and a successful marriage"
Self-esteem: Built in childhood by father
Hobbies: Runs and swims daily. Still loves art and photography.
Heroes: American Indians
Honors: "Entrepreneurial Woman of the Year" (1980), first woman so honored; *Fortune*: "America's most successful female entrepreneur" (1987); honorary doctorate from Rhode Island School of Design (1991); National Sales Hall of Fame (1991).

11

Jane Fonda—Renegade Innovator

I have long been in revolt from all things, from the authority of others, from the instruction of others, from the knowledge of others; I would not accept anything as truth until I found the truth myself; I never opposed the ideas of others but I would not accept their authority, their theory of life.
—J. Krishnamurti

Man's opinion of "self" and the world influences all his psychological processes.
—Alfred Adler

She was known as "Lady Jane," "Hanoi Jane," and "Citizen Jane," all of which conjure up positive and negative emotions in virtually everyone. Many men hate her for her political activism and most women admire her because she was strong enough to stand up for her beliefs and never backed down from the establishment regardless of the heat. No matter what your feelings, this woman was a resilient talent who revolutionized the videotape industry, influenced the world of fitness, set new standards for actresses to emulate, and led with her heart in social activism.

Jane Fonda is an enigma who utilized an innovative and rebellious attitude to achieve her goals. She achieved in widely diverse areas, yet the magnitude of her accomplishments in numerous fields are what most people just dream about. She had a habit of ignoring the experts and tradition in the inimitable style of the classic entrepreneur, invariably following her heart in the pursuit of her dreams. Fonda never allowed the so-called experts to interfere with her sense of the truth, and she took enormous flack on the road to the top. Even so, she remained a dynamic personality, willing and able to change with the dictates of the situation.

Fonda is the ultimate paradox. She grew up in virtual anonymity relative to her leading man father, Henry Fonda. Yet she has surpassed him in every

225

field or medium she attempted with the possible exception of the stage. Fonda excelled not because of superior talent or beauty but because she was obsessed with being the very best she could be. After her first stage performance at the age of twenty-one, she promised herself "to do nothing else in life but become the greatest stage actress there ever was." This vow came just after her first role in *There Was a Little Girl,* which launched her into a life of show business. Fonda became the best, or close to it, in everything she attempted. She also created a public image as one of the most complex and controversial personalities of our time. She was a sex symbol extraordinaire in her twenties, a virulent revolutionary in her thirties, a fitness guru in her forties, and an exceptional entrepreneur and CEO of her own chain of fitness centers in her fifties. Fonda accomplished all of these things coincident with functioning as a world-class actress and part-time producer. She was energy incarnate, and she has had more reincarnations than any other public woman in history, with the possible exception of Madonna. Fonda's paradoxes are nonpareil in her myriad roles and domains:

Sex symbol, Barbarella, who ended up espousing the feminist movement.

Miss Army Recruiting of 1962 who founded the Fuck the Army organization in 1971 and earned the nickname "Hanoi Jane."

A chain-smoking marijuana junkie and pill-popping anorexic/bulimic who became the guru of the health and fitness industry.

Severe critic of cosmetic enhancement surgery who had eye lifts and breast implants.

Virulent anticapitalist who became a bottom-line-obsessed capitalist worth close to $100 million.

New Left advocate of socialistic causes who financed radical husband Tom Hayden, only to divorce him to marry Ted Turner, a conservative.

If nothing else, Jane Fonda is her own woman. She has never kow-towed to any group or organization. She has an intransigent spirit and her strong will has earned her the respect of women everywhere. Her tenacity won her the title of America's Most Admired Woman (Roper Poll, 1985), and she has been near the top in various Gallup polls of most-admired women. In 1984 Fonda was ranked just behind Mother Teresa, Margaret Thatcher, and Nancy Reagan. Her universal admiration comes from her resilient nature and spunk, which repeatedly defied the establishment. Fonda accomplished what most woman only dream of and did it with style. Her internally generated empowerment makes her an role model for most compliant housewives of the world.

She never allowed the power elite to dominate her and that quality intrigues and excites those who have been man-handled by the top dogs.

Paradoxically, Fonda has been the submissive wife to three charismatic men. She found a sexual mentor in Roger Vadim, an ideological and political mentor in Tom Hayden, and a power mentor in Ted Turner. She was the acquiescent housewife and mother to her first two husbands although she was always the top wage earner in the family and the most visible and powerful person. With Ted Turner, Fonda has a man who is a self-made billionaire, and even more visible and powerful than she is. This love match will prove very interesting indeed.

Fonda has made forty movies which have brought her seven Oscar nominations. She won academy award as best actress for *Klute* (1971) and *Coming Home* (1978). She personally produced *Coming Home,* along with four other movies, including the much acclaimed *On Golden Pond* (1981), which starred her father and her childhood role model Katharine Hepburn. Fonda has been a hard-driving perfectionist with a will of her own. This renegade innovator turned fifty on December 21, 1987, with three exercise videos on *Billboard* magazine's "Top 20." This hardly seemed the venue for anyone at the half-century mark. Her adoring public has spent an unprecedented $500 million on her exercise products.

Fonda's very first workout tape, released on April 25, 1982, hit the top of the charts at a sixty-dollar price tag and stayed there for three years. Before Fonda *no one* bought tapes; they only rented them. Her first video fitness recording became the very top videotape seller in history. Jim Meigs, editor of *Video Review,* said, "Jane Fonda is the biggest selling success factor for the entire video business." When she released her *Workout Book* in 1982 it sold 1.8 million copies, the largest-selling nonfiction book, except the Bible, at the time. Everything Fonda has done has been spectacular or excellent. She has been a consummate actress, a producer, a videotape star, and an author. Even her flirtation with political activism was accomplished with flair and drama. As "Hanoi Jane" she was the most notable and memorable protestor of the Vietnam War. Regardless of what anyone may think of her politics, no one can ignore her gutsy and fearless demeanor in communicating her beliefs. Her success has been recognized by industry leaders in every medium she has touched and she is deserving of the accolades of a true creative genius who changed the world for the better.

Personal Life History

Little "Lady Jane" Fonda was born in Doctors Hospital in New York City on December 21, 1937. She was the first-born child of actor Henry Fonda, who was fast becoming an institution on the stage and in the movies. He was a perfectionist who had writing and artistic ambitions before bowing to the call of the theater. Jane was destined to inherit his perfectionism and theatrical talent. Her mother, Frances Seymour, was Henry's second wife. Actress Margaret Sullivan, Fonda's first wife, committed suicide. Frances was a widowed socialite turned recluse. She was an emotionally disturbed wife and mother whose bizarre behavior was incited by the tyrannical and womanizing Henry. Frances had another daughter, Frances de Villars Brokaw (nicknamed Pan), by her previous marriage to alcoholic financier George Brokaw. Jane's mother desperately wanted a son so as not to obfuscate her first daughter's position within the family.

Jane was born in New York while Henry was starring in a Broadway play. Frances was dismayed about having a daughter instead of a son and froze Jane out emotionally. She immediately gave Jane over to a governess and refused her any affection, much like Maria Callas's mother, who also had wanted a son. Fonda would later say, "I didn't like her to touch me because I knew she really didn't love me." Bonding never took place and it would haunt them both for many years.

Jane was a bicoastal child and moved back to Hollywood shortly after her birth in a trip she would make repeatedly over the years. She was hyperactive and a tomboy in an obsessive attempt to win her father's love. She told *Ms.* magazine, "My only major influence was my father. He had power. Everything was done around his presence, even when he wasn't there. . . . I became my father's son, a tomboy. I was going to be brave, to make him love me, to be tough and strong." She was to say in the eighties, "I always had a deep-rooted psychological need to be a boy."

Fonda was chubby with a trim mother who constantly criticized her weight. This psychological conditioning ultimately led to Fonda's twenty-year bout with anorexia and bulimia. Fonda admits to her love-starved childhood saying, "As a young girl most of my dreams evolved from the basic need of being loved and being frustrated in fulfilling that need." One reason for her lack of affection was Henry's perpetual absence. Josh Logan, Jane's godfather and Henry's best friend, characterized Henry as a very cold, noncaring father. Brook Howard, Jane's childhood friend, said, "Hank terrified everyone" and was never around. Logan added, "Henry always seemed to be someplace else—even when he was right in the room. He didn't know how to show love toward his family or maybe he just didn't want to." Jane would say, "I was in awe of my father. As a girl I would do naughty things just to gain his attention." Jane so disliked her mother, she said she always wished Katharine Hepburn was her mother.

Jane spent her first years in California, where she was in the constant care of a governess who discouraged holding or kissing. The governess said affection would make Jane too emotionally dependent. This was the identical conditioning Ted Turner received from a father desiring to make him feel insecure. Jane's early sensory and emotional deprivation turned out to be counterproductive to the intention, as it molded her into an emotionally dependent adult. Jane attended a series of boarding schools and private academies starting with Brentwood Town and Country Day School in California. Her mother was becoming more and more insecure and neurotic. During the war, Frances turned to other men for affection and to medication for relief of depressive states (not unlike Gloria Steinem's mother). Jane turned to horses, athletics, and books for escape. Her friend and neighbor Brooke Howard was her outlet for affection and companionship. Brooke's mother had been Henry's first wife and the two families maintained a strangely intimate relationship for many years until Brooke's mother took her own life. Brooke says of this period, "We were all sort of in awe of Jane. Nothing seemed to faze her. She was athletic, very self-reliant, very tough. Like tempered steel." Jane internalized her feelings of abandonment and confusion. When Henry took the title role in *Mr. Roberts* on Broadway in 1948, Jane was eleven. The family relocated to Greenwich, Connecticut, where Jane attended Greenwich Academy. Her best friend Brooke Howard soon followed with her family.

Jane's mother became a recluse in Connecticut. She virtually never left her bedroom and became a domestic tyrant. Jane was faced with creating her own entertainment and became extremely self-reliant. Her father was absent and her mother was emotionally ill. Neither was emotionally attached to her, so Jane became her own woman as she entered her teenage years. Then Henry precipitated disaster by asking Frances for a divorce in order to marry twenty-one-year-old Susan Blanchard, the stepdaughter of Oscar Hammerstein. Frances became so distraught that she had a nervous breakdown and was committed to Austen Riggs Sanitarium for the mentally disturbed. On April 14, 1950, Fonda's mother committed suicide by using one of Henry's razor blades to slash her throat from ear to ear. Jane was twelve and her brother, Peter, was ten at the time. The children were told she had had a heart attack, only to find out the horrible truth later from friends.

Henry married Susan Blanchard nine months after Frances's suicide and Jane finally had a role model whom she adored; Susan was just ten years her senior and loved her dearly. Peter Fonda had always been his mother's favorite and was distraught over her death. He shot himself while his father and Susan were on their honeymoon, and teetered between life and death for four days. During the next few years Jane's life became even more frenetic with traveling, moving, and family dysfunction. She attended Emma Willard Boarding School in upstate New York, where she became known as independent and a renegade. One classmate said, "Jane was a leader and she was not afraid of the spotlight." She challenged the strict authority of the school. One of the rules was that all students had to wear high heels and pearls to dinner.

Jane showed up wearing her high heels and pearls, and nothing else, according to a number of the students. Her years of self-reliance had taught her defiance and rebellion and she was not afraid to display it.

Fonda matriculated at Vassar College, and after four years in an all-girl high school, she went wild on discovering attentive and virile males. Her friend Brooke had enrolled in Vassar with her and in a stroke of understatement said, "Jane was not a great student. She spent her entire freshman year out of the classroom." Fonda herself later conceded, "I went wild." She lived a libertine existence at Vassar. One of her school alumnae said discretely, "She was socially promiscuous—so easy it was almost a joke." She missed curfews and disappeared for days at a time. Her father married Countess Afdera Franchetti during Fonda's freshman year, his fourth marriage, only adding to Fonda's emotional confusion. Jane pleaded with her father to let her drop out of Vassar and go to Paris to study art at the Sorbonne. Fonda was a master of psychology, knowing her father to be a frustrated artist who would not deny her his first love. Henry gave his consent and enrolled her in the Beaux Arts school in Paris. She later admitted to living a life of debauchery in Paris on the Left Bank, saying, "I went to Paris to be a painter, but I lived there six months and never even opened my paints." Little "Lady Jane" was well on her way to becoming "Provocative Jane" of the early sixties.

Professional Background

Fonda began her show business career in New York studying acting under Lee Strasberg at the famous Actors Studio. She was introduced to Strasberg by his daughter, her good friend Susan. Strasberg immediately seduced her both emotionally and intellectually. This older mentor made her feel wanted, in her words, "He was complimenting me and said he saw a tremendous amount of talent, which absolutely changed my life. Nobody had ever told me that I was ever good at anything." She was overwhelmed by his attention, and said, "I was a different person. I went to bed and woke up loving what I was doing. It was as if the roof had come off my life!" Fonda attended Eileen Ford's modeling agency to earn money to pay for her acting lessons and was signed on the spot for the cover of *Vogue*'s July 1959 issue and several other name magazines. It was one of the few times she had to rely on the Fonda name to get by. She modeled to support her real ambition much as Gloria Steinem, who was also modeling in Manhattan at the time with the same objectives: to finance her true avocation. Ironically, they both followed remarkably identical paths and ended up marching with militants like Cesar Chavez ten years later.

The Actors Studio was to change Fonda's life. It was a method acting school designed to draw the "inner self" out into the role being played. And Fonda had an abundance of untapped unconscious energy for the taking. One of the directors was Andreas Voutsinas who, according to Henry Fonda, was a Svengali-like influence on the young, impressionable Jane. She moved in with him and remained under his influence for several years, to her father's chagrin. Fonda made her broadway debut in *There Was a Little Girl* (1959–60), and her film debut as a cheerleader pursuing a college athlete (Tony Perkins) in *Tall Story* (1960). She had by now decided to become the greatest actress in the world and was beginning to show promise. She received "most promising new actress of the year award" by the New York Drama Critics. Her first movie role of any significance was as an adolescent prostitute in *A Walk on the Wild Side* (1962). She was miscast as a frigid young housewife in *The Chapman Report* (1962) and paid the price of her choice. The *Harvard Lampoon* named her the "Worst Actress of the Year" for her performance. However, critic Stanley Kauffmann said, "A new talent is rising—Jane Fonda." He went on to say, "In all her films she gives performances that are . . . conceived without acting cliché and executed with skill." Fonda's first role as a comedienne came in the movie *Period of Adjustment* (1962). By this time she was being touted as the next queen of Hollywood, motivating the chauvinistic Jack Warner to comment, "She's got a good future if you dye her hair blonde, break her jaw and reshape it, and get her some silicone shots or falsies" (Anderson, 1990, p. 83).

During this period Fonda was named "Miss Army Recruiting of 1962" and, draped in red, white, and blue, she gave an impassioned acceptance speech to new recruits. She praised the armed services in their fight against the communist regimes. Less than ten years later the Pentagon wanted to bury her in red, white, and blue and rued the day it ever graced her with such accolades.

By 1963, Fonda became less than enchanted with her career progress and left the tutelage and bed of Andreas Voutsinas. She accepted an English-speaking role in *Les Felins* (1964) in Paris. The French press immediately dubbed her "La BB Americaine" an allusion to the French sex symbol Brigitte Bardot, whose husband, Roger Vadim, had made her a star. Fonda met Vadim on the set when he became her director for her first French-speaking role, in *La Ronde/Circle of Love* (1964). Fonda's halting French accent gave her a unique screen persona, which charmed the French. She soon became enchanted with the idea of making Paris and Roger Vadim a part of her future. Vadim was known as a sexual Machiavelli for his shrewd manipulation of women and the media. Ironically it was she, not he, who was the instigator in their passionate relationship. Fonda became the aggressor in their first sexual encounter, which so intimidated the satyr Vadim that he was unable to perform—to his horror. The actress and director finally consummated their relationship in a torrid marathon of sexual bliss. They began living together in a passionate relationship that led to a Las Vegas marriage in 1965.

Vadim directed her in the role of a young bride to an aging billionaire in *The Game Is Over* (1965). Vadim's biggest international hit, *Barbarella* (1968), starred Jane as a kinky erotic space maiden. It was a science-fiction burlesque movie that was destined to leave Fonda with a sex-kitten image which would last for some years. Fonda's image was an important factor in Vadim's voracious need for fantasy and a provocative lifestyle. During this period Vadim would bring home women for ménage-à-trois and various perversities in order to satisfy his enormous sexual appetite. *Barbarella* and this period were a blatant model for what Vadim called their new period of sexual freedom, and what Fonda would later characterize as her sexual exploitation (Anderson, 1990).

Fonda commuted to the United States during many of Vadim's indiscretions and made films. She played a gun-toting frontier school teacher in *Cat Ballou* (1965). Another box office success at the time was her Neil Simon movie with Robert Redford, *Barefoot in the Park* (1967). She followed this with a series of movies: *The Chase* (1966), *Hurry Sundown* (1967), and *Any Wednesday* (1967). Fonda got pregnant during a ski trip in the Alps in early 1968 and had her daughter, Vanessa, in Paris on September 28, 1968. Pregnancy changed not only her body but her emotional being. It would alter her life and was the beginning of the end of her marriage to Vadim. She evolved into a different woman while pregnant. Fonda later reflected on the time, saying that the pregnancy changed her: "My fears, my hang-ups . . . they just vanished." She said, "I finally understood that we don't give life to a human being only to have it killed by B-52 bombs, or to have it jailed by fascists, or to have it destroyed by social injustice. When she [Vanessa] was born—my baby—it was as if the sun had opened up for me. I felt whole. I became free." Fonda came to the United States to film *They Shoot Horses Don't They* (1969) and declared, "I'm a revolutionary woman." Not many understood the magnitude of that statement, not even Fonda herself.

Fonda was pro-American in her arguments with her European friends over the Vietnam War. When her friend Sharon Tate was mutilated and murdered during the filming of *They Shoot Horses,* Fonda went through a metamorphosis. Not long after, Fonda joined a friend on a trip to Calcutta and was aghast at the starving children and the huge disparity between rich and poor. When she stepped off the plane in New York on New Year's Eve 1969 and was told she had won the New York Film Critics Award as best actress for *They Shoot Horses,* she said the film was "a very forceful condemnation of the capitalist system." Fonda had gone over the edge and had become a full-fledged political activist.

Fonda told Vadim on Valentine's Day 1970 that she was leaving him. She left Vanessa in his care and immediately joined New Left activists, supporting the Black Panthers and the militant American Indians in their various causes. Fonda financed her own whirlwind national junket protesting for every cause that reeked of abuse. She said later, "I took off on that trip a liberal, and I ended up a radical." She was soon actively campaigning against the war in Vietnam and proclaimed, "Because of my success in films, I have more power—and I intend to use it." And use it she did. Fonda actually went through a few million dollars including her own earnings and her mother's inheritance. She would spend the next five years as a political and social activist and the next twenty years financing Tom Hayden's progressive Democratic ventures to the tune of millions of dollars.

Jane Fonda was one of the people found on Nixon's infamous "enemies list" and was labeled an "anarchist" and an arch enemy of the United States by the FBI. Six undercover agents were assigned to her daughter's kindergarten class and she was harassed and badgered by the FBI everywhere she went. She received constant death threats. Cleveland, Ohio, customs agents actually threw her in jail on a return trip from Canada based on a trumped-up drug charge, saying her tranquilizers and vitamins were LSD capsules. The constant harassment finally drove her to file suit against their tyranny for violations of the First, Fourth, Fifth, and Ninth amendments. She said, "It was part of an organized systematic attempt to discredit me . . . to make those of us who opposed the Nixon administration appear irresponsible, dangerous, and foul-mouthed" (Anderson, 1990, p. 298).

In 1971 Fonda took time off from her social causes to make a film that would launch her back into the limelight and Hollywood superstardom. *Klute* was a picture about a prostitute threatened by a homicidal maniac with Fonda playing the part of Bree Daniel. She won the best actress award for her emotionally inspired portrayal of Bree. Pauline Kael of the *New Yorker* wrote, "She has somehow got to a plane of acting at which even the closest closeup never reveals a false thought." Jane made one more movie with Donald Sutherland, *Steelyard Blues* (1973), prior to a political activism period that would precipitate a four-year hiatus from Hollywood. It is interesting to note here that Fonda's most provocative and heartrending work came at a time when she was emotionally charged over the Vietnam War. Both *They Shoot Horses* and *Klute* were filmed during this period.

In July 1972 Fonda earned the nickname "Hanoi Jane" by visiting North Vietnam, where she made several radio broadcasts over Radio Hanoi. She urged American airmen to stop bombing the North, conjuring up images of Tokyo Rose during World War II. She brought on herself the wrath of the hawks in the United States Congress, and was censured in the Maryland and Colorado legislatures. Several members of Congress attempted to have her tried for treason. A Manchester *Union Leader* editorial advocated that she be shot if convicted. During this radical period Jane met Tom Hayden and married him in an emotional and physical surrender to his democratic socialism.

By 1976, Fonda felt the social climate had changed because of Watergate and she returned to filmmaking with the movie *Fun with Dick and Jane*, starring George Segal. She then made *Julia* (1977). She was back on a roll in Hollywood and formed her own production company in 1977. Her first two pictures were huge successes, *Coming Home* (1978) and *The China Syndrome* (1979). Then *Nine to Five* (1980) with Lily Tomlin and Dolly Parton became a huge box office winner. Her production of *On Golden Pond* (1981) was also a success and what she calls her "deepest professional experience." It starred her father, who was dying at the time. Henry died four months after he won his first and only Oscar for his film portrayal. This was Fonda's second picture to gross over $100 million and ironically it was the catalyst for her father's grand exit from show business.

THE MOVE TO FITNESS

Fonda embarked on a whole new field—health and fitness—after the Vietnam debacle. It was a diversion into entrepreneurship and a 180-degree change from her past life. However, she was well prepared since she had always been obsessive about her personal fitness and decided to write on the subject, open a chain of studios, and make videotapes. Although this excusion into the world of business appears to be a bizarre departure from her antibusiness stance, it is understandable in the context of her compulsive need to create and innovate. What better avenue than an area where she had inordinate expertise. It is a telling tale that she entered this business when she turned forty. A woman who made her way on her looks and figure was unconsciously determined to show the world that fitness is not necessarily a function of age. And that subtlety is what made her an overnight success.

Fonda opened her first workout studio in Beverly Hills in 1979, to be followed by four more clubs in other West Coast cities. She taught exercise classes in some of them. She then produced a pictorial book in 1981, *Jane Fonda's Workout Book,* which would sell two million copies by 1986. It earned an astonishing $20 million in the first year for Simon and Schuster. Fonda produced more books, but her big entrepreneurial success came with the release of her now famous fitness videotapes. Fonda revolutionized the video industry by selling fitness via home instructional video. Prior to Fonda's fitness videos, a movie video was only rented and never considered saleable. Jane proceeded to sell more tapes than anyone in the history of the videotape industry. When asked about her success as a fitness entrepreneur she responded, "There wasn't much about business I did understand. It came to me like a bolt of lightning, the way my best ideas usually do [she is intuitive], that the only thing I really know about is being healthy, being fit. I knew I had credibility in that area, so it made sense to make it my business." Her credibility was based on her spectacular physical condition in her forties, and when she turned fifty she had three exercise videos on *Billboard*'s top 20. Fonda went on to confirm her knowledge of the fitness business: "I'm enough like other women to be able to give them what they and I want. For twenty-five years I went to dance classes. I saw so many women like me who took the rigorous training not because they wanted to become professional dancers, but because they wanted to reshape their bodies."

Fonda earned $20 million in her first two years in the fitness business. Stressing a "go for the burn" routine resulted in 1.8 million copies of the *Workout* book being sold in the first year. She was convinced that Tom Hayden was destined for the White House and contributed all of the revenues and profits from her exercise empire to his Campaign for Economic Democracy. This is a real tribute to her willingness to put all of her inner convictions on the line no matter the cost to her, emotionally or financially. Fonda's video and fitness business started netting a cool $35 million annually by the end of the eighties. When Jane and Tom finally broke up in 1989, She gave him an additional settlement estimated at $10 million. This was only a pittance compared to the millions she had donated to his cause during the eighties. Fonda kept approximately $60 million in the divorce, but considering she had earned it all, the $10 million was a magnanimous offer on her part.

Temperament: Intuitive-Thinker

Fonda is a perfectionist who is obsessive about being the very best she can be whether it is acting, loving, or playing revolutionary or entrepreneur. Her 132 IQ makes her bright but not brilliant. Fonda more than anything else is an independent and self-sufficient woman who is never afraid to go where others fear to tread. She is an iconoclast with a renegade mentality who never fears departing from consensus, and has always been comfortable with ambiguity. However, it is her innovative spirit that has made her unique and successful. Fonda has always been attracted to strong men, which appears to be an unconscious attempt to gain the love never offered by her strong but cold father. When Fonda managed to attract strong men, she found that she was the strong one in the relationship, not them, prompting her retort, "If you're a strong, famous woman, it's not easy to find a man who isn't threatened." She has found one in the flamboyant and powerful Ted Turner.

Jane Fonda is an extroverted-intuitive-thinking-judger on the Myers-Briggs personality scale. She is the classic Promethean spirit who sees the big picture and possibilities in life and deals with things in a rational, structured manner. Her energy comes from the external world of people and events. Not surprisingly, she is often preoccupied with social issues. Fonda is almost hyper when presented with a new project. She has enormous powers of focus and concentration and a compulsion for perfection. In other words, her creativity is spawned from an inner well of energy that knows no bounds when she becomes dedicated to a concept. She is a creative visionary in the strictest sense of *Webster's* definition of having a "strong aptitude for bringing new concepts into existence."

Fonda has had numerous role models and mentors on her drive to the top starting with her father when she was young. Henry Fonda was the central focus of the family and she was mesmerized by his every word. Fonda says, "I was in awe of my father." Katharine Hepburn was her early female role model. As a teenager she was enthralled with her stepmother Susan Blanchard, Henry's third wife. For a brief period after college Lee Strasberg became her mentor and lover, soon followed by Andreas Voutsinas. The latter liaison lasted three years. Fonda's three husbands were all mentors and fantasy father figures: Vadim was her sexual mentor, Hayden her ideological mentor, and Turner her power mentor. Fonda has recently decided to emulate Katharine Hepburn as her role model for her mature stage. She told Janice Kaplan of *Vogue* (February 1984), "Hepburn is an extremely important role model as I get older."

Family versus Career

On paper Fonda had it all—both family and career. However, her attempt to juggle family, career, and social activism was fraught with casualties. The first was her daughter, Vanessa, who she left with Vadim while she embarked on a whirlwind campaign to fight for sociopolitical causes. The second casualty was her marriage, when she filed for divorce from Vadim on returning from her social consciousness trip across the United States. Fonda met with about the same degree of success as most women do who are torn between their nurturing instincts and their professions. But she made her life even more complex by adding two more dimensions: political activism and an entrepreneurial interest.

The Vietnam War proved to be a major obstacle in Fonda's personal life. She became politically active in her cause against the war at the time of her first pregnancy. This distraction continued through her new relationship with Tom Hayden, which spawned a boy whom she named after an Irish rebel Troy O'Donovan Garrity. Jane placed both children in the care of others and in boarding schools while she traveled with Tom Hayden to pursue his sociopolitical battles. Making movies was also a distraction but not to the same degree as international trips and fighting the system.

When her children were still preteens Fonda embarked on a whole new career as a fitness-club entrepreneur, fitness author, and exercise video impresario. And amazingly, at almost the same time, she began a movie production company, IPC, to make her own movies. Fonda's flirtation with multidimensional activities was mind-boggling. In other words, she was making movies, producing movies, campaigning for her husband in a race for the California Senate, and launching a fitness empire while attempting to play mother and wife. With this kind of scenario something has to give, and in Fonda's case she was not able to spend quality time with her children as many noncareer moms do. It is amazing that she had time for anything with such a hectic schedule. She certainly paid the price: significant stress on the marriage and her family. She and Tom Hayden finally split up in 1989, once the children were old enough to be away at school.

Fonda was rebellious before rebellion was chic. She told columnist Hedda Hopper in 1961 that marriage was "passe," and continued, "I think marriage is going to go out, become obsolete. I don't think it's natural for two people to swear to be together for the rest of their lives." She then implemented her philosophy by entering into an alternative lifestyle relationship with Roger Vadim in Paris. Only when she became pregnant did her value judgments become less iconoclastic. Fonda left Vadim in 1970, when she heard the calling of social activism. In 1971 she met Hayden, one of the famous Chicago Seven and cofounder of Students for a Democratic Society. On July 4, 1973, they had a love child Troy O'Donovan Garrity, named in honor of an Irish hero, who was also a hero to the Viet Cong. Troy was in high school when they divorced and Jane made him a commitment that she would not remarry until he graduated. She kept her promise and refused to marry Ted Turner, of Turner Broadcasting fame, until after Troy's graduation ceremony, a testimony to her guilt feelings over her less-than-indulgent role as mother.

After Hayden, Fonda entered into a short-lived liaison with a young Italian actor. Then she was courted by Turner. These two are an interesting if not bizarre couple, combining a unique blend of similar family histories with a diametrically opposite philosophical view of the world. Their political leanings and philosophies are so different it is nothing short of a miracle that they were ever able to get together with any sensible dialogue. Their saving grace is an identical temperament, a strong social consciousness, and entrepreneurial genius.

Fonda married the younger and more powerful Ted Turner in 1991 on her fifty-fourth birthday. She immediately retired from show business, saying, "Ted Turner is not a man that you leave to go on location. He needs you there all the time." She has settled down with a man whose lifestyle and persona have some interesting parallels to her own. Their backgrounds and personality traits are so similar it is almost surreal. Both are rebellious innovators who defy the establishment at every turn. Both had parents who killed themselves in a ghastly way. Both were educated in single-sex schools, had transient childhoods, and were the first-born child in a family of two. They had self-employed fathers, and each was on drugs or medication much of their lives (he a manic-depressive on lithium and she an anorexic and bulimic on sixty to a hundred vitamins a day plus tranquilizers) (Anderson, 1990; Davidson, 1990). Both are interested in ecology, love the outdoors, and owned ranches before they met. And they have identical temperaments. Truth is truly stranger than fiction.

Opposites attract according to psychotherapists Jung and Adler. I am convinced that opposites seldom stay together because of the very things that attract them—their differences. The strength of these two entrepreneurial geniuses is their identical Promethean temperaments. They are compatible personality types—intuitive-thinking-judgers—on the Myers-Briggs personality scale. Each was a product of parents who made them feel very insecure. Both are renegade innovators. And they both love horses and the outdoors, which feeds into their social consciousness.

Fonda is more malleable and dynamic than Turner. She seems to be able to mold her persona into whatever setting is correct for her at the time and has done so repeatedly over the years, changing philosophies every decade. A series of paradoxes haunt their relationship, conjuring up Jung's synchronicity* theory. Jane and Ted were both children of privilege having spent many years alone in boarding schools during their formative years. Jane escaped an unhappy childhood through horses, Ted with sailboats. Both had domineering fathers who nurtured a love/hate relationship, conditioning both of them with a passionate need for overachievment. Bizarre as it seems, each of them had a parent who died from violent suicide, unable to cope with depression over dysfunctional personal lives. Both Fonda and Turner are virulent rebels who dropped out of their respective fashionable New England colleges. Fonda at Vassar College and Turner at Brown University led promiscuous lifestyles. Both admit to having spent their college days in a passionate effort to seduce as many of the opposite sex as possible in a desperate search for sexual fulfillment. Both have been addicts to prescription drugs and pills. Jane was a twenty-three-year bulimic and Ted is a manic-depressive. She is obsessive. He is compulsive. They are both energy incarnate, driven by an unconscious need to overachieve (Landrum, 1993; Anderson, 1990).

On paper Fonda has had a respectable personal life while maintaining a multifaceted professional life. It is not clear how successful she was in her personal life even though she has been eminently successful professionally. She admitted to *Vogue* in 1984, "I have to be honest about it. There's no way I could do everything I do if I didn't have money. I can afford to have someone help me with my children, pick them up from school when I can't be there,

---

*Synchronicity is Carl Jung's theory that there are no coincidences; we create our own self-fulfilling prophecies either consciously or unconsciously.

and make dinner at night." Fonda is suggesting that it is possible to have both but you better be successful enough to afford it. She has changed since meeting Ted Turner. Fonda told Nancy Collins on "Prime Time Live" in September 1993, "I can't imagine any movie that I ever made or could make in the future that would be worth giving up the three months of being with Ted. . . . Careers in the entertainment business are very difficult on marriages. . . . And Ted said to me in the beginning, cut what you're doing in half. And I did. And then he said about six months later try cutting it in half again. And I did."

Life Crisis

Fonda spent her early life in bicoastal transience, which taught her how to cope with new and foreign environments. She was schooled in numerous all-girl schools that offered her plenty of opportunities for female role models while she was young. Living in boarding schools in California, Connecticut, and New York taught her self-sufficiency and independence. She constantly fought for the love and affection of a father who was emotionally absent, and a mother who was emotionally disturbed for much of her childhood. Even so little Lady Jane was treated as a queen and doted on by friends and relatives, which unknowingly built her self-esteem. This is a repeated finding in most great creative visionaries. Fonda has admitted to not liking her mother since she "really didn't love me." Because of her father's coolness and her mother's lack of love, Jane was tormented with an obsessive need to overachieve.

Fonda was just eleven when her mother had a nervous breakdown and was committed to a mental health hospital, where she ultimately killed herself. This crisis molded Fonda's character. It instilled in her a terrible feeling of guilt plus an insatiable drive for perfection and need to overachieve. A most heartrending episode caused Jane's twenty-year bout with bulimia. Her mother had come home from the mental hospital for an obviously planned last visit with Jane and Peter. Jane decided to play a horrible trick on her emotionally disturbed mother. She took on the role of ringleader prompting Peter to hide out with her for an hour while her desperate mother called out in vain for them. When her mother's nurses said they must leave, Frances said, "Not yet. I must talk to her." After an hour her mother cried out Jane's name and then left the house despondent, never to return. Two days later, on April 14, 1949, Frances Fonda slit her own throat. Jane took the news of her mother's death without emotion while Peter sobbed uncontrollably. Jane kept her feelings to herself but felt the internal guilt over the ill-treatment of her mother. This apparently instigated Fonda's long-term bout with bulimia. This event triggered many years of nightmares according to Fonda's friend Brooke Howard. She said Fonda's "wild screaming went on for hours" every night throughout her teen years.

As previously discussed, not long after his mother's death Peter Fonda nearly killed himself and languished near death for four days after shooting himself supposedly accidentally with a shotgun on the first day of his father's honeymoon with Susan Blanchard. Fonda feared for Peter's life but, unlike Peter, was very happy about her father's new marriage. Jane and Peter were close but they had materially different relationships with their parents. Peter would later say, "She was demanding our father's attention in every way she could get it, running away from Vassar and doing far-out freaky numbers in Paris, where she was supposed to be going to art school but was running around with the top playboys of the jet set world." Fonda never quite recovered from the guilt over her mother's death and it drove her to become an obsessive perfectionist. It appears that her early crises were the mother of much of her later creativity and instilled in her an obsession to be the very best.

Renegade Innovator and Success

This rebel looking for a cause found it in the Vietnam War. But she was also active in attempting to correct the gross social inequities with respect to American Indians, black issues, feminist causes, and union discrimination. Fonda approached her political activism with the same zeal she had used to attack the movie industry. She used her media clout and personal financial resources in the pursuit of equality and freedom. She was the only political activist with her own press agent, whom she used to help spread propaganda for her causes.

Fonda the radical agreed to make the film *They Shoot Horses Don't They?* primarily because it was considered the first American existential novel, according to no less an authority than Albert Camus. This is a testimony to her vision and her rebellious nature. Fonda's greatest conquests in both business and the arts were in areas where she had an emotional commitment and an innate knowledge. Her greatest movies were the ones she personally produced and helped finance: *Coming Home, The China Syndrome, Nine to Five, On Golden Pond,* and *The Dollmaker.* Fonda then opted for the fitness business, which she also knew on a very personal and emotional level and in which she was eminently successful, even though the experts predicted her early demise. Both enterprises turned out to be sensational moneymakers and artistic successes.

Fonda paid a terrible price for her renegade behavior. She describes the cost:

I was followed. I was threatened. My bank account was taken illegally by the FBI without a subpoena. My home was broken into, my phone tapped. The FBI later apologized. My basic rights were being violated. . . . It was a time when they called me strident. It was a strident time, and one used the tactics considered appropriate to the time. (*Vogue,* 1984)

In an attempt to assuage her guilt and justify her Hanoi broadcast, Fonda agreed to a "20/20" interview with Barbara Walters on June 17, 1988. She told Barbara, "I was trying to end the killing, end the war, but there were times when I was thoughtless and careless about it and I'm very sorry that I hurt them [GIs in Vietnam]. And I want to apologize to them and to their families." Jane went on to tell Barbara Walters, "I took off a liberal, and ended up a radical," which she insists was never her intention. Even so, her renegade nature has been instrumental in making Fonda a creative genius. She would never have achieved at the level she has without her obsessive defiance of the system.

Fonda approached acting, movies, social reform, and most other things in her life in a defiant manner. Her nonconformist approach to business is shown by her unusual selection of a partner for her IPC production company. She hand-picked Bruce Gilbert to head the day-to-day operations of this multimillion dollar enterprise. His pedigree includes experience as one of the daycare attendants at Vanessa's school. It was this ability to *not* "know" too much that makes Jane unique in much the same way that it paves the way for success in most creative and entrepreneurial geniuses.

Summary

Jane Fonda was a love-starved child who used her insecurities to achieve enormous accomplishments in the fields of acting, publishing, fitness, and movie production. She is an Academy Award–winning actress with two Oscars on her mantle after seven nominations. Fonda evolved from radical to mogul in one short decade. Her selection of mates is even more paradoxical. She divorced the left-wing radical Tom Hayden, one of the original Chicago Seven, and married Ted Turner, a very conservative capitalist. She started out in life as delicate little "Lady Jane," evolved into "Provocative Sex-Kitten Jane" in her twenties, and became the hated "Hanoi Jane" in her thirties. In mid-life she became "Capitalist Jane," and now appears content in her fifties as "Citizen Jane."

Jane Fonda has been a renaissance woman. She fashioned a magnificent theatrical career and talent into a world-class entrepreneurial ability. Her multiple dimensions defy reason, especially when this complex woman was eager to take on none other than the United States government, the FBI, President

Nixon, and Congress. She sued this prestigious group in 1973 for $2.8 million over physical and psychological harassment, and won an out-of-court settlement in May 1979. What moxie. Fonda is a fearless competitor, a perfectionist, and a Promethean spirit who changed the world because of her innate ability to see the opportunities and possibilities in life. She never hesitated to put her emotions or her money on the line and her courage has made her the consummate innovative visionary.

Fonda's influence spanned four decades. Her timing has been impeccable. Her particular genius was the ability to reincarnate herself from a youthful "sex kitten" image in the fifties to the free-spirited actress of the sixties and the rebellious political activist of the seventies. Fonda then reincarnated herself again to revolutionize the fitness industry during the eighties. It appears she is now poised to play a significant role in saving the world with her ecologically minded husband, Ted Turner. Global warming and preservation of the species are their causes. No doubt she will prove up to the challenge and as capable as she has been in the past with this worthwhile new program. No matter the outcome, Jane Fonda has piqued our interest. Her genius can be found in her unique ability to be the most admired and hated of women at the same time; to be the most idyllic and most reviled actress; and to be a successful business entrepreneur while criticizing capitalism. She is certainly a maverick innovator of major proportions which has qualified her to be one of the creative geniuses of this era.

Jane Seymour Fonda
Actress and fitness entrepreneur
b. December 21, 1937, New York City

Dominant trait: Renegade innovator
Religion: None, Spiritual
Motto: "Be healthy, be fit."
Philosophy: Social consciousness
Nicknames: "Lady Jane" as a child; "Hanoi Jane" as an adult
Creation/innovation: Two Academy Awards as best actress in *Klute* (1971) and *Coming Home* (1978); best-selling hardcover book *Jane Fonda's Workout Book* (1.4 million sales); best-selling videotape in history (5 million sales). Sued U.S. government, the president, and Congress—and won.
Success: Two Academy Awards from seven Best Actress nominations; best-selling book; best-selling videotapes of all time
Self-description: "I'm a revolutionary woman." Competitive drive, search for truth, and tireless seeker of perfection due to unrequited childhood love

---

Birth order: First-born child. Younger brother, Peter (actor)
Childhood transience: Bicoastal with constant travel
Father's occupation: Self-employed actor, mother was a housewife
Mentors: Father rejected her needs for affection but was her role model. Lee Strasberg and Andreas Voutsinas were surrogate fathers; Roger Vadim; Tom Hayden. "My only major influence was my father. He had power. Everything was done around his presence. . . . I became my father's son, a tomboy."
Childhood upbringing: Mother (Frances) was preoccupied with health and beauty. Her suicide deeply affected Jane.
Formal education: Brentwood Town and Country, Greenwich Academy, Emma Willard Preparatory School (all-girl boarding schools). Dropped out of Vassar College in her second year to study art (Paris) and acting (Actors Studio)
Life crises: Mother committed to sanitarium when Jane was 12; Fonda blamed her mothers' eventual suicide on herself.
Marriages/liaisons: Three marriages (Roger Vadim, Tom Hayden, Ted Turner) and two children Vanessa Vadim (1968) and Troy O'Donovan Garrity (1973)

Risk-taking: Fearless when following her emotional feelings of right and wrong.
Temperament: Extroverted-intuitive-feeling-judger
Behavior: Rebellious overachiever (perfectionism led to bulimia)
Career vs. family: Family always sacrificed for career or causes
Self-esteem: Modeled after father and virtually every man in her life
Hobbies: Exercise
Heroes: Henry Fonda, her "monument" father, and Lee Strasberg, her teacher
Honors: Numerous acting awards. 1984 Gallup poll of "Most Admired Women" ranked her just behind Mother Teresa, Margaret Thatcher, and Nancy Reagan. The 1985 Roper poll ranked her the the most admired woman.

12

Estée Lauder—Impatient Overachiever

Probable impossibilities are to be preferred to improbable possibilities.

—Aristotle

Estée Lauder created a cosmetics empire with nothing more than a dream. She had no money, no merchandising experience, no technical expertise in the chemistry of skin care or beauty, and no business experience. Yet she was able to create a beauty empire beyond compare. She is the uncrowned queen of the multibillion dollar cosmetics industry who socializes with royalty. She created products found on the dressing tables of women and men around the world: Estée, Youth Dew, Clinique, Aramis, Prescriptives, JHL, White Linen, and Night Repair.

Lauder was an indefatigable workaholic who had boundless energy. Her spirit, inspiration, and insight made it happen. How? She was a master of "image." She molded her own image as meticulously as she did her products and accomplished both with elegance and duplicity. She scrupulously modified her Jewish immigrant persona into one she had conjured up as a child. She decided to look, act, and function like a genteel and debonair socialite and refute all vestiges of the girl raised over a hardware store in Queens. And she succeeded. She became the reincarnation of her image, and successfully accomplished the same with her products and company image, making them into sophisticated products appealing to a "carriage trade" market. Image for her products was as important as the image she was creating for herself. Lauder refused to acknowledge anything less than the finest image in either pursuit. Perfection was Lauder's forte. And she accomplished these dual objectives with elegance, style, and aplomb. During the past thirty years it has been difficult, if not impossible, to differentiate between what is real and what is fantasy in the Estée Lauder story. She made a meteoric rise from the streets of Queens to become a philanthropic social leader and scion of the largest privately held cosmetics firm in the world. Nothing is left of the poor immigrant girl.

245

Lauder has socialized with First Lady Nancy Reagan, the Duke and Duchess of Windsor, Princess Grace, Begum Aga Khan, movie stars, and media moguls. And Lauder made it happen through the sheer force of her will. She meticulously molded her own image, earning her the title "Queen of Cosmetics." Estée Lauder is the confirmation of "thinking makes it so." Psychology gurus tell us to dress the "role" or "image" of the job desired and the job will be ours simply because we fit the image or "identity" of that role. Estée Lauder is living proof of this theory at work. She not only created her personal image out of her fantasies, she was able to create the Estée Lauder Cosmetics empire out of her vision.

Estée Lauder started with little more than a dream at age thirty-nine and proceeded to build the largest privately held cosmetics company in the world. Now Estée Lauder sales revenues in the early nineties exceed $2 billion annually; only Avon and Revlon boast higher sales. Lauder is a creative visionary who relied upon extraordinary ambition, flair, high energy, impeccable taste, perseverance, innovative merchandising, and hard work to achieve her goals. An impatient overachiever, she defied improbable odds to get to the top of an intensely competitive industry. Perfection and image were her forte.

Lauder's cosmetics empire has made her one of the richest women in the world, with a net worth of $5.2 billion, according to *Fortune* magazine ("The Billionaires," 1991). Lauder was the only self-made woman on this list of billionaires. This impatient visionary built her empire in the Horatio Alger tradition. She had a dream, worked hard, and found serendipity in her corner. Her rags-to-riches story is even more grand because of her misleading stories about her own heritage as a countess with a genteel European background. She misled the media into believing her less-than-accurate stories for many years. Only when Lee Israel researched her unauthorized biography, *Estée Lauder: Beyond the Magic* in 1985 (Israel), did the truth surface of her real childhood in the squalor of Queens. Lauder's dreams became realities, allowing Cinderella Estée to inherit the magic kingdom. She credited her own unique reality and her dreams have become more "real" than she ever imagined, making Lauder an excellent role model for young women everywhere.

Lauder, the once struggling huckster of skin cremes, now lives out her fantasies in real life as the proud owner of a Manhattan townhouse, a villa in St. Jean-Cap-Ferrat, a London flat, and an oceanfront retreat in Palm Beach. Not bad for a young woman who started with no money, no formal education, and no technical expertise. Young Esty, as she was called as a child, did possess one critical ingredient required of all great achievers—a dream. And she pursued that dream with impatience and aggression, which led her through that seemingly impenetrable glass ceiling of female ascendancy. She is similar to the other women in this book in that she created her own ceilings instead of relying on the ceilings of others. This allowed her to navigate to the top without encountering the normal barriers. Her story is an inspiration that gives credence to the sheer power of mind over matter. But the implementation was not so simple. Lauder paid a terrible price, as she poignantly describes in her book *Estée* (1985): "The most insidious myth of all is the one that promises magic formulas and instant success. I cried more than I ate. There was constant work, constant attention to detail, lost hours of sleep, worries, heartaches."

Lauder rose to the occasion and, in her mind, the price was well worth the reward. This queen of cosmetics is a gifted visionary who deserves accolades for her role in changing the world of cosmetics.

Personal Life History

Estée Lauder was born Josephine Esther Mentzer on July 1, 1908, in the Corona (the Italian immigrant) section of Queens, New York. Esty was the youngest of nine children, only one of whom was a full sister. Her mother had had seven children from a previous marriage and two had died. Esty's Hungarian Jewish father was a self-employed owner of a hardware store in Queens; her Czechoslovakian Catholic mother cared for a huge brood of immigrant children. Lauder admits to having been ashamed of her immigrant "old country ways" and her parents' heavily accented English. "I desperately desired to be 100 percent American," she says, not unlike the views held by the young Lillian Vernon, Maria Callas, and Golda Meir. Lauder worked in her father's retail store. Golda Meir, Margaret Thatcher, and Oprah Winfrey had also worked for their parents. But she dreamed "of being an actress—name in lights, flowers, handsome men." Working in the store instilled retailing and entrepreneurship at a young age. Lauder describes her father as her major influence and "early mentor and support" during those years in Queens.

Lauder was six at the outbreak of World War I when her uncle John Schotz came to visit and became an extension of the family. He was a chemist who specialized in his own secret-formula skin creams. Uncle John became young Esty's "magician, role model, and mentor." "He captured my imagination and interest as no one else ever had." She saw him as her everything, saying "Uncle John loved me; I loved him, and my future was being written in a jar of snow cream." Uncle John's arrival occurred when Lauder was at a very impressionable age, and he proceeded to mold her future more than either of them would have suspected at the time: "I recognized in my uncle John my true path. . . . I watched and learned, hypnotized." Esty became "obsessed with clear glowing skin" during her whole youth and actually hawked her uncle's skin creams from age sixteen through her twenties. She said in her biography, "I didn't have a single friend [at Newtown High School] who wasn't slathered in our creams." She was in awe of Manhattan and vowed she would one day live in that "extraordinary place." She lived to become a female power broker in this city of omnipotent potentates.

Lauder believes she inherited her sense of "beauty" from her attractive mother and her sense of "character" from her father. Lauder's entrepreneurial father gave her an innate knowledge of self-sufficiency in life. Uncle John was her first real mentor. She describes him in her autobiography with adulation: "I was smitten with Uncle John. He understood me. What's more, he produced miracles." There were not a lot of miracles in the squalor of Queens during this era, so in Lauder's mind Uncle John was the one individual responsible for her escaping from reality into fantasy.

Esty's sister Grace was two years older, leaving Esty, the baby of the family, to be idolized and doted upon. She attended Public School 14 in Corona until the eighth grade. There is no record of her graduation from high school, according to Israel, which was not unusual in those days. As a teenager, Esty had a "remarkable complexion," which helped to create her self-esteem and image. The positive feedback on her magnificent skin attracted her to the world of beauty and Uncle John's magic skin cream. She learned the techniques of marketing and merchandising early, saying, "To sell a cream, you sold a dream in the early days."

Lauder spent a number of summers in Milwaukee, Wisconsin, which she came to know and love. Lauder considered moving there at one time. Not long after leaving school she was courted by Joe Lauter (he later changed his name to Lauder), who nicknamed her "Blondie" during their courting period. They courted and were married on January 15, 1930, in a formal Jewish ceremony. Lauder was twenty-two and ecstatic. In Lauder's inimitable words, "The bride's skin was glowing. . . . Estée Lauder was about to be born." They would have their first child, Leonard, in 1933, with Estée selling skin creams to supplement Joe's income as an accountant. In that same year the New York phone directory showed a listing for Lauter Chemists, an indication of their first entry into the beauty business.

Professional Background

Lauder became queen of the United States cosmetics industry in the age-old tradition of all great entrepreneurs—she started at the bottom, where all great creative effort begins. It is in the bowels of entrepreneurial stewardship where the ego must be subjugated to the necessities of survival. She began by selling her skin creams in beauty salons in uptown Manhattan during the Depression. She created a market for her unknown skin-care products through the sheer power of salesmanship. Lauder would stop people on the street to demonstrate the benefits of her "Super-Rich Creme." She preached the power of beauty to anyone who would listen. Lauder always established her own ground rules; she is cynical of those who say she has been lucky. Her rule is classic among entrepreneurs who believe as she does: "People do make their own luck by daring to follow their instincts and taking risks." But beauty was Lauder's deity, bringing her to say "I was irrevocably bewitched by the power to create beauty," and "Never underestimate *any* woman's desire for beauty."

Beauty and skin creams became Lauder's passion even after she became a wife and mother. Indefatigable, she would give free demonstrations at salons, hotels, private homes, the subway, or wherever the opportunity presented itself. She operated out of a midtown beauty salon but never missed a chance to perform her magic anywhere, anytime. It was during this period that she learned one of the merchandising innovations that would later make her a billionaire. During those early days in Manhattan she created the "free gift with purchase" promotion now so popular in department stores. She had an almost Gandhi-like belief that "whatever we give away, God will give back to us." She would give free lipsticks to the Depression era women who purchased her skin cream beauty treatment. Free gifts would become her signature over the years, to the annoyance of her competitors.

A testimony to Lauder's perseverance and energy was her approach to creating a market for this virtually unknown product: "One summer after another, I pushed myself, lauding creams, making up women, selling beauty. In the winters I'd visit these eager ladies at their homes, where, with a bridge game as a backdrop, I'd make up their friends and sell more creams" (*Estée*, 1985).

Lauder used this approach for entry into the social registers of New York. She would arrange to have herself introduced to New York's most influential hostesses in order to get invited to their parties and sell her products. Social contacts were important for the beauty business, therefore she decided to realize her childhood dreams and become an elegant lady of class and distinction. She started resorting to fabrications and embellished the truth in the pursuit of sales and a new heritage. She called her product the "Super-Rich All Purpose Cream." It was only second to her "image" in the promotion of her products and career.

Lauder emulated the rich and famous and mimicked society women. She had decided "image" was the most successful factor in building a beauty business. She dressed like her elite customers and imitated their behavior. Lauder soon found that "confidence breeds beauty." She could have added the word "success." Lauder made herself into a sophisticated and debonair lady of beauty and her role became indistinguishable from the reality. She had a single-minded focus on beauty in a jar that subjugated everything and everybody else to second place, including her husband, Joe. Their marriage in trouble, Estée obtained a divorce from Joe on April 11, 1939. She used mental cruelty as a basis. She and six-year-old Leonard relocated to Miami Beach, where the ever-ambitious Estée set up a concession at the swank Roney Plaza Hotel on Collins Avenue. This was the golden era of Miami Beach and Lauder was looking for the gold. Her fantasy "Image is Everything" was her driving force.

Lauder spent the next three years promoting her skin creams to affluent vacationers and retirees in Miami Beach. From most accounts she was seeking upward mobility as a master plan in her march to the top. She had decided that a more direct route might be through existing money and heritage. She dated a Dr. John Myers, an English philanthropist, for a time and then Arnold Lewis, a Dutch-born president and chairman of International Flavors and Fragrances. Lauder learned the fragrance business from Lewis during this time. Lauder also became very enamored of Charles Moskowitz, an executive of Metro-Goldwyn-Mayer, but this relationship never materialized into something permanent. Her Miami Beach years were spent, accoring to Israel, in search of a rich prince who would help realize her dreams. It was not to be. After four years of searching for her own Golden Fleece, Lauder became tired of the chase. Then Leonard became ill, which reunited her and Joe as caring father and mother. A new spark ignited and they were remarried on December 7, 1942, with a mutual agreement to make a go of the cosmetics business together. They agreed that Estée would be in charge of all marketing and product responsibilities as president, and Joe would be in charge of finance, manufacturing, and administration. This became the unofficial launch of the Estée Lauder cosmetics empire.

Lauder opened her first store in New York City in 1944. Her cosmetics empire was interrupted briefly in December 1944 when she gave birth to their second son, Ronald. She returned to work almost immediately and Estée Lauder, Inc., was formed in 1946. The products of this new firm were "Creme Pack" for blemished skin, cleansing oil, "Super-Rich All Purpose Creme," nourishing lotion, face powder, eye shadow, and clear red lipstick. Lauder selected "Lauder Blue" as an "image" package to give a pedigree trademark for all Estée Lauder products. It became their signature color. In need of manufacturing and storage facilities, the Lauders converted a Manhattan restaurant into a factory, using the stoves to cook the creams and oils for their skin care products. Lauder would sell during the day and cook up the products on the stoves at night.

Lauder decided that carriage trade stores with the distinctive image of Saks Fifth Avenue would be their exclusive domain. This fit her overall scheme of things, and she proved a genius in her selection. She worked diligently and finally convinced Saks Fifth Avenue to place a large $800 order for Estée Lauder skin creams. Receiving this initial order from a major store with the prestige she envisioned necessary for the company's success made her ecstatic. She said later, "It was the single most exciting moment I have ever known." It should have been, as it was destined to launch Estée Lauder into the mainstream of the cosmetics industry.

Lauder had decided that her products demanded prestigious customers doing business in high-traffic, impulse locations. Such retailers turned out to be high-end department stores able to carry customer credit. Saks Fifth Avenue met all these objectives. Lauder was right on target with her market assessment and Saks sold out its entire initial order within two days. The success at Saks catapulted the fledgling cosmetics company, with a staff of two (Estée and Joe), into a national cosmetics company. It gave them the impetus to compete with the likes of Revlon, Charles of the Ritz, Helena Rubinstein, and Elizabeth Arden. Estée was always the dominant executive in product and marketing decisions. Joe was the submissive one in the executive hierarchy. It was her dream, and her company, but they did it together as family.

Lauder's marketing genius was in aiming her products at upscale outlets like Saks, Bloomingdales, and Macy's. It created the company's image as a prestigious firm with the quality demanded by the very best. Estée personally became a persuasive traveling salesperson dedicated to the penetration of every fine department store in the United States. Joe managed the factory and administration. She was an inveterate overachiever who would not allow any store to sell the product if it was not the most prestigious store in that city. All of the sales girls were personally trained by Lauder. They had to be the best to sell the Estée line. She demanded that they be pretty, elegant, confident, and totally committed to the Estée beauty approach. For several years Estée paid the price of frugality. She took buses and trains to her locations and ate in the company cafeterias. It paid off. It would not be long before she could buy her own bus line and chain of restaurants.

Lauder's ambitious drive to dominate the prestigious department stores began to pay off by the early 1950s. The Estée Lauder line could be found in I. Magnin's, Marshall Field's, Nieman-Marcus, and Bonwit Teller. A testimony to this woman's tenacity and mental toughness is how she broke the Nieman-Marcus account. Stanley Marcus told the *New Yorker*: "Estée Lauder came in without an introduction. . . . Barged her way in. She was a cyclone on the selling front. She could outsell me any day." One department store executive said, "She was a tyrant, but a creative one." A Neiman-Marcus executive recalled, "She'd come into the stores and almost *shove* Charles of the Ritz on the floor and go *storming* upstairs if she found that she had lost one inch of real estate [shelf space]." Lauder's competitive zeal was without equal and one of the major factors of her success. She considered Revlon, Rubinstein, and Charles of the Ritz her mortal enemies and fought them as if they were in a war. Her family operation expanded in 1958 when her oldest son, Leonard, left the Navy and joined the firm at the age of twenty-four. He was being groomed to become heir to the throne.

In 1965, Estée Lauder was still a $14 million business and *Women's Wear Daily* reported that Revlon in 1969 was in 15,000 stores to Estée Lauder's 1,200. She and Charles Revson engaged in a heated battle of love/hate. They were both children of Jewish immigrants, self-educated, both entrepreneurs armed with little but genius and an obsession with business. Lauder accused Revlon of copying her products and said to the media, "50 percent of Revlon's R & D [research and development] is done here [at Estée Lauder]." When Leonard came up with the idea of competing head-on with Revlon in nails, Estée commented: "Right now Charles Revson is my friend. He doesn't take me seriously. . . . He thinks I'm a cute blond lady. . . . The moment I put something on the market that competes with him, he's going to get upset. He's going to get difficult. And we're not big enough to fight him (Lauder, 1985).

But Lauder would be big enough and would fight him. She always found a way. She became frustrated in those early days in the '50s and '60s with snobbish ad agencies who refused to give her the time of day because of the small size of her account. During those growth days, she made every marketing decision in the company. She was perturbed at the traditional ways of advertising cosmetics and in an impulsive rebellion against the experts, shifted all of the firm's available funds for advertising ($50,000) to gift promotions. Her "free gift with purchase" was spawned at this time. Lauder had taken "lemon" and turned it into "lemonade" and her innovation ultimately revolutionized the way department stores promoted and sold cosmetics. Lauder's implementation of the now famous "free gift with purchase" for anyone buying Estée Lauder products has become an industry standard promotion. During the 1980s, when Lauder was well into her seventies, she could still be found at the Saks Fifth Avenue store in New York City spraying her latest scent on the ladies' wrists. It is this focus and determination that has taken her company to the pinnacle of the cosmetics world.

Lauder introduced her first fragrance, called "Youth Dew," in 1953. It was a combination of bath oil and perfume, which was not perceived a luxury, as were cosmetics during the time. Priced at $8.50, it was affordable for the majority of women and sales took off. This fragrance product proved to be the turning point for Estée Lauder. It launched the company, making it a multimillion dollar enterprise. Saks Fifth Avenue once again launched her new product and the store was astounded to find that 80 percent of its beauty sales were in this new category. By 1984, Youth Dew alone accounted for $150 million in revenues for the Estée Lauder company.

By 1960, the ever-aggressive Lauder had launched an international program and personally broke the prestigious Harrod's account in London. She was forced to resort to some sales creativity to break the prestigious Galleries Lafayette account in Paris. When she could not get the manager to agree to stock her products, Lauder "accidentally" spilled her Youth Dew on the floor during a demonstration in the middle of a crowd. The appealing scent was pervasive and aroused customer interest and comments. The manager capitulated and gave her an initial order. The ploy was just one of the many inventive methods used by Lauder to expand her business. She always sold the "sizzle" not the "steak." She said in her biography, business was "pure theater—in the end that's what it was. Pure theater for me." To Lauder it was all an act. She was the actress and she played her part in Oscar-winning fashion.

Lauder was always focused. In her words, "I was single-minded in the pursuit of my dream" and that energized focus is what helped launch Estée Lauder as a major force in the world of cosmetics. By the mid 1970s Lauder products were sold in more than seventy countries throughout the world. In 1973, Lauder promoted her son Leonard to the presidency of the company. She remained his boss as CEO, with Joe elevated to the position of chairman.

The company entered the men's fragrance business in 1964 with the introduction of Aramis. Then in 1968 the enormously successful Clinique line was introduced as a unique hypoallergenic skin care line. Another of Lauder's many innovations came with this product. She decided to outfit the women at the counters in lab coats in order to convey the serious medical nature of this new product. Then she went out and hired the editor of *Vogue*, Carole Phillips, as the head of the Clinique division. It turned out to be a brilliant move as Carole was identified with beauty and health and knew how to communicate with groups of all ages who were desirous of both beauty and health. The product line has been enormously successful over a wide age group. By 1985, Clinique had reached $200 million in annual revenues and become one of Estée Lauder's major products.

Department stores were Lauder's passion and, by the end of the 1980s, Estée Lauder products accounted for more than one-third of all beauty aids sold and one-quarter of all men's cosmetics sold through this distribution channel. The company prospered and entered the 1990s as the third largest cosmetics company in America, with ten thousand employees and sales in excess of $2 billion. Only two much older firms, Avon and Revlon, remain ahead of Estée Lauder, but they are both public firms. Lauder is now retired with an estimated net worth from her innovation—beauty in a jar—of $5 billion, according to *Fortune* magazine. Not bad for a woman who started by hawking her wares door to door. This impatient overachiever describes her success simply: "I was a woman with a mission." When asked about her impatience, she says, "I started late. I didn't have the time for waiting, nor the disposition." Lauder continues to be the firm's creative genius, even though her son Leonard and her grandchildren now occupy the executive suites. Lauder follows her axioms, which are endemic of all entrepreneurial success: "Trust your instincts" and "Create don't copy." She always preached the importance of the "intuitive" or "gut" approach to successful achievement. She was not afraid to go where others feared to tread—the hallmark of all great creative visionaries.

Temperament: Intuitive-Thinker

Estée Lauder is an extroverted-intuitive personality. In business she had a long-range vision and was always aware of the possibilities and opportunities. She was energy incarnate, running from city to city, to build her empire from the ground up. Lauder is a classic right-brain-driven visionary who sees the forest, not the trees when evaluating business opportunities. She intuitively knew her strength was qualitative not quantitative, and delegated all number-crunching to Joe. Lauder assumed the responsibility for sales and marketing and the creation of new product concepts. She was Ms. "Outside" and Joe was Mr. "Inside" in the building of Estée Lauder. Estée personifies the right-brain intuitive mentality or "gut"-type decision making of all great entrepreneurs. She said, "I act on instinct, quickly, without pondering possible disaster and without indulging in deep introspection." This trait made her into an eminent creative genius.

Lauder was always more inclined to opt for quality than quantity in products, markets, and life. She was a rational decision maker who operated in a very structured way, made decisions hastily, and moved on to the next opportunity. Her impatience made her intolerant of procrastination in others. Lauder's decisions were always final. She operated "differently," with an eye on her objectives regardless of any established policy or procedures. Her aphorism "People do make their luck by daring to follow their instincts, taking risks" is a testimony to her belief in the entrepreneurial approach to business. Lauder summarized her success formula in her biography saying, "Risk-taking is the cornerstone of empires." This formula is the entrepreneurial creed and by following it Lauder lived to see the enormous rewards of her gambling spirit.

Lauder proved to be an inveterate, impatient overachiever. She worked tirelessly to perfect every nuance of her business and couldn't understand why others did not have her same energy level and enthusiasm. Estée exuded style, persistence, panache, and a unique flair for the dramatic. She was driven and never lost the focus of creating "beauty in a jar." She never faltered even when her lawyer and accountant told her, "Don't do it. The mortality rate in the cosmetics business is high and you'll rue the day you invested your savings and your time into this impossible business." (Mary Kay Ash had received the same advice from her lawyer and accountant. She, too, ignored their advice.) Estée Lauder was a workaholic, never considering the time of day or the personal sacrifice required to achieve her objectives. She never forgot her childhood dreams, and lived her life fulfilling those dreams through hard work and sacrifice.

Family versus Career

When Estée married Joe Lauder at age twenty-two, she was already focused on a career in beauty. She never lost sight of that goal even after the birth of their son Leonard in 1933. Lauder was more determined to pursue her career in cosmetics than in preserving her family during the thirties. She was fanatically ambitious and left Joe during this period to seek her fortune with the big spenders of Miami Beach and Hollywood. While there, Lauder was wooed by an international fragrance executive, an English philanthropist, and an MGM mogul. None of these power brokers offered to take her off into the sunset or made a major commitment.

Lauder relocated to Miami Beach with Leonard, intent on finding her niche in the world of beauty and cosmetics. It was not to be, but Lauder had already indicated a willingness to sacrifice almost anything for the redemption of her dream. When no white knight showed up, she was courted by Joe in 1942 and remarried him within the year. Lauder's nurturing nature was involved in the decision. Leonard had become seriously ill and both met at his bedside concerned over his health. The relationship was reignited by this crisis. They remarried and agreed to live in New York City and become mutually involved in the cosmetics business. They had another child, Ronald, in 1944. It turned out that the birth of their first store and last child occurred almost simultaneously.

Lauder had never stopped promoting her skin creams throughout Leonard's youth. And Ronald's birth in 1944 did not stop her from opening their first retail store in New York. Because of their parents' entrepreneurial bent, both boys spent a great deal of time in boarding schools during their formative years. Their ambitious mother was traveling the country penetrating fine department stores with Estée Lauder products. The children saw their father more than their mother because of her interminable travel schedule. From all accounts Lauder was a good mother, but it is very difficult to have two masters, and beauty had been her master since her teens. Though more absent than not, when she was at home Lauder was a doting mother. This appears a typical trait of most great female entrepreneurs.

Life Crises

Lauder's older sister, Renee, contracted polio when Estée was very young. Estée, her sister, and her mother relocated to Milwaukee for a year in an attempt to avoid catching this incurable disease. This event was traumatic enough to be mentioned in Lauder's biography, which carefully avoided discussing virtually all of her early childhood. Estée was eight when the First World War broke out and Uncle John Schotz moved in with the family in Queens. He became an enormous influence on the impressionable Estée, who had been enamored of beauty since she was a young child. She would soon become obsessed with "beauty in a jar," which he called his magic "Creme Pak." Lauder said, "I was irrevocably bewitched by the power to create beauty." Uncle John's magic elixir fulfilled her childhood dreams of beauty and elegance during a time when the world was engaged in the conflagration known as the "war to end all wars."

Lauder's major life crisis was being raised in a ghetto area known as Corona in Queens. Lauder's passion for beauty was inconsistent with this upbringing, and she spent much of her life denying this reality. She denied her heritage to everyone and it appears she may have even deluded herself into believing she had a European heritage, spawned in a Hapsburg castle. The truth finds her as the byproduct of an immigrant jungle. She never admitted to this truth and spent her life changing reality into her fantasy, at times refuting the truth. She fantasized—actually lied to the press—for years in an overt attempt to erase her early life from existence (Israel, 1987). Lauder's hyperactive imagination kept her in a dream world until middle age, when she became her fantasy. Lauder's first purchase after becoming a millionaire was a Palm Beach estate, to be followed by homes in southern France and London, all in addition to the family's New York home.

In her biography, Lauder described her father as a genteel European gentleman who never worked. Her fantasy had him traveling to various spas in Europe and living an aristocratic life tending to his horses while his wife lounged in the salons in Baden Baden. Lauder said he disdained the bourgeois world of the working class. The reality was that Lauder's immigrant father ran a grain and hardware store in a New York immigrant ghetto. Lauder's mother was a seamstress attempting to keep food on the table for her brood of seven children. The palace was an apartment over the hardware store housing seven children. A final testimony to Lauder's terrible hang-up over her heritage was her refusal to acknowledge her parents' death, according to Lee Israel in her biography *Estée Lauder*. One of the ways young Esty dealt with her circumstances was to change her name from the inelegant Josephine Esther Metzer to one with more class, Estée.

Lauder experienced one great business crisis during the growth stage of her company. All products and packaging had been completed in 1968 for the launch of the Clinique "hypoallergenic" line of products. The packages were well into production when it was discovered that the name "Clinique" was already taken by another firm. Panic ensued. Estée and Joe negotiated with the owner of the name, Edward Downe of Downe Communications. They offered $5,000, what they considered an exorbitant amount, for the rights to the name. Downe laughed at them. The ultimate ransom agreed on was $100,000, a veritable fortune for the still-fledgling firm. Lauder capitulated. The crisis of her business life was over, but never forgotten. Clinique took off to un-precedented heights and the company grew faster than ever.

Impatient, Overachieving Success

"Business is a magnificent obsession" says the effervescent Estée Lauder. This opinionated and autocratic empress reigns over an industry she has dominated for almost thirty years. Impatience and perfection are the tools Lauder used to build her company and to penetrate the department store counters where she now reigns supreme. Lauder recognizes the power of her unconscious or inner voice in her drive to the top. She says, "An executive comes to know the special vagaries and unique sensibilities of her business and her own inner voice that tells the truth—if she listens hard enough." Lauder is saying that she uses her feminine intuition—her "gut" feelings—to make decisions. She adds, "I have never yet met anyone who learned her business from a book or a school." This admonition is consistent among all our visionary women.

Lauder resorted to flamboyance in her dealings and had a unique flair driven by an awesome self-esteem. One only has to read Lauder's autobiography to come away with a feeling that this lady was a success because she believed. She believed even when her lawyers and accountants disbelieved. She said, "I set my own ground rules" in describing her success in business. An executive of Charles of the Ritz thought she was mad. Describing her "free gift" promotional schemes, the executive said, "She'll never get ahead. She's giving away the whole business." Charles of the Ritz is now out of business and the "mad" queen of cosmetics is still growing. Estée Lauder still gives away gifts and generates over $2 billion in sales annually. Lauder's impatient and at times impertinent overachieving was her strength. She claims a number of "Lauderisms" as the ticket to success, saying "Create your own style" and do not be afraid of the "trial and error" approach:

Estée's Rules of Success in Business

1. Find the proper location.
2. When you're angry, never put it in writing.
3. You get more bees with honey.
4. Keep your own image straight in your mind.
5. Keep an eye on the competition.
6. Divide and rule.
7. Learn to say no.
8. Trust your instincts.
9. Act tough.
10. Acknowledge your mistakes.
11. Write things down.
12. Hire the best people.
13. Break down barriers.

14. Give credit where credit is due.
15. Train the best sales force. (Lauder, 1985)

Summary

Lauder became the queen of the cosmetics industry by being different. She changed the way beauty is purveyed and purchased. She is responsible for products that have become household names: Estée Lauder, Youth Dew, Clinique, Prescriptives, Aramis, Devon, JHL, White Linen, and Cinnabar. Lauder's company is the dominant firm in cosmetics, perfumes, and men's toiletries in department stores throughout the world. In addition, Estée Lauder is the largest privately held cosmetics company in the world. In 1988 the firm had 33 percent of the United States market in prestige cosmetics and was building a strong international base. By 1992 they had increased their international revenues to $700 million out of a total $1.9 billion.

Lauder has counted as friends such notables as Princess Grace, the Duchess of Windsor, Begum Aga Khan, and Rose Kennedy. She has dined with presidents and royalty. Bob Hope, Lauren Bacall, Frank Sinatra, and Walter Cronkite are on her guest list. When Princess Diana and Prince Charles came to America, Princess Diana requested just three guests: Robert Redford, Bruce Springsteen, and Estée Lauder. *Harper's Bazaar* named Lauder as one of 1967's "100 American Women of Accomplishment." She is the recipient of hundreds of awards for career achievement, and in 1968 was awarded the "Spirit of Achievement Award" by the Albert Einstein College of Medicine for her "unique skills and imagination . . . and for her lasting gifts of beauty that have delighted women everywhere." Lauder was honored as one of the "Outstanding Women in Business" in 1970 by *Forbes*. She received the French Legion of Honore by the French government in 1978 for helping restore the palace at Versailles with a personal contribution and fund-raising soirees.

Estée Lauder is a true creative genius. She is a classic entrepreneur and innovator who refused to listen to experts. Her overachievement was accomplished with a mix of impatience and perfection. She never accepted anything but the best from her products, employees, or retailers. Her unique flamboyant style differentiated her from the pack and made her products ubiquitous in a world tuned into beauty. Lauder was a catalyst in making that happen. She said, "Never underestimate any woman's desire for beauty" and spent her life fulfilling that need. Lauder's insight was second only to her gambling nature: "Risk-taking is the cornerstone of empires." Her risk-taking mentality and impatience helped her change the world of cosmetics distribution and for that she is a creative visionary deserving of the spoils of her many victories.

Estée Lauder (Josephine Esther Mentzer)
Estée Lauder, Inc.

b. July 1, 1908, New York City

Dominant trait: An impatient overachiever

Religion: Jewish

Mottos: "Never underestimate any woman's desire for beauty"; "Whatever we give away, God will give back to us!"; her own epitaph: "Here lies Estée Lauder—Who made it and spent it!"

Philosophy: "Create, don't copy"; "Trust your instincts"; "When you're angry, never put it in writing"; "Business is a magnificent 'obsession.' "

Nicknames: Goldie, Estée, Queen of Cosmetics

Creation/innovation: Built the largest cosmetics firm in the United States from scratch, which currently generates $2 billion in annual revenues.

Products/contributions: Cosmetics, perfumes, and men's toiletries: Estée Lauder, Youth Dew, Clinique, Prescriptives, Aramis, White Linen, Devon, JHL, Azuree, Cinnabar

Success: Built a giant corporation without education, money, or technical expertise. *Fortune* estimate of net worth in 1991: $5.2 billion

Self-description: "I act on instinct, quickly, without pondering possible disaster and without indulging in deep introspection. . . . I was quicksilver and driven. . . . I was single-minded in the pursuit of my dream."

Birth order: Last-born daughter of nine children, only one of whom was her blood sister

Childhood transience: Parents immigrants. Traveled extensively with mother as a child, according to her biography. Lived in Milwaukee and New York City

Father's occupation: Hardware store merchant in Queens

Mentors: Mother's beauty and Uncle John Schotz's "Super Rich All Purpose Creme." "I believe today, that in my Uncle John was my true path."

Childhood upbringing: Raised in Corona—an Italian and Jewish settlement in Queens; English was the least-spoken tongue. She does not acknowledge the era.

Formal education: Newtown High School (dropout)

Life crises: Her sister had polio as a child. "Clinique" name already in use. Had to pay large sum in exclusive use.

Marriages/liaisons: Married Joe Lauder 1930, divorced 1939, remarried 1943

Risk-taking: "Risk-taking is the cornerstone of empires."

Temperament: Extroverted-intuitive-thinking-judger: Promethean temperament

Behavior: Flair, perfectionist, driven, massive ego, workaholic, persistent

Career vs. family: Sacrificed husband and family in early years for her dreams of beauty business

Self-esteem: Built in childhood through an identity with beauty and ideal complexion. Her rallying call to escape from an unacceptable lifestyle.

Hobbies: Partying and entertaining the rich and famous. No sports.

Heroes: Duchess of Windsor, Princess Grace, Begum Aga Khan, Rose Kennedy

Honors: French Legion of Honore (1978); "Top 10 Outstanding Women in Business" (1970); *Harper's Bazaar* 1967 "100 Top American Women of Accomplishment"

13

Madonna—Psychosexually Driven

Sex and power are inextricably intertwined.
—Michael Hutchison, *Sex and Power*

"Our Lady of Perpetual Promotion" reached the pinnacle of success as the decade of the eighties came to an end. Her genius was based on her unique ability to violate all traditional approaches to a business segment—records, videos, concerts, dress and jewelry, books—and to change that market/product to fit her idea of reality. Madonna repeatedly entered a market with an aberrant stance only to become the trendsetter of a new vision. In other words, she never followed, but led through an iconoclastic approach to the medium. Her style was copied. Her clothes and jewelry, although bizarre, were mimicked. Her videos were imitated. *Webster* defines genius as the ability to influence others for good or bad. Madonna did just that and an equal number of people have felt it was either good or bad.

Madonna entered 1990 with twenty-one consecutive number-one hit records, surpassing The Beatles' all-time record of number one hit singles. That same year she gained financial independence, becoming the highest-paid female entertainer in show business with a cool $39 million in earnings. In 1990, *Us* magazine ranked her number one in the top 100 "Most Powerful People in Entertainment." She has surpassed her wildest fantasies by being ranked ahead of Michael Jackson, Bruce Springsteen, and Prince. Madonna's business acumen and entrepreneurial talent were becoming legend when such bastions of male capitalism as *Forbes* (October 1990) named her "America's Smartest Business Woman." Forbes concluded she had a "brain for sin and a bod for business." In the past ten years Madonna's likeness has graced the covers of every national magazine, with the possible exception of the *Christian Science Monitor*. Her success has made her the most visible show business personality of the era, and arguably of the century. Marilyn Monroe's notoriety pales by comparison.

261

Perversity reigns supreme in all that Madonna touches. She has a self-proclaimed commitment to change the social mores of a doubting society. She desecrates all dogma whether in the form of Catholic doctrine or society's taboos against incest, bisexuality, and bestiality. Madonna's rebellion knows no bounds, and she flaunts all traditional values of the establishment. Parents do not understand the allegiance of their idolizing teenagers. It is simple. Madonna is the ideal spokeswoman for their adolescent defiance against societal edicts. She is the unlikely role model for groups of ever-faithful teenage disciples who worship free spirit. Madonna is their consummate heroine due to songs like "Material Girl," "Papa Don't Preach," "Like a Virgin," and "Express Yourself." These counterestablishment songs and videos appeal to both defiant teenagers and alternative lifestyle groups, who comprise the vast majority of her following. Madonna acts, dresses, and preaches freedom, independence, and autonomy—the gospel for all teenagers storming through their adolescent rebellion stage of development. She is a "Material Girl" living on the edge of social acceptance. Her innate ability to reinvent her image every few years is amazing. She doesn't seem to be able to defile her image beyond her miraculous powers to remake it. Madonna's ever-faithful apostles keep standing in line, waiting for her next unusual or perverse move. That particular talent has made her a creative visionary of extraordinary genius.

Personal Life History

Madonna was born Madonna Louise Veronica Ciccone on August 16, 1958, in Bay City, Michigan. Her father, Tony Ciccone, is a first-generation Italian-American, and her mother, also named Madonna, was of French Canadian ancestry. She has two older brothers, Anthony and Martin; two younger half-sisters, Paula and Melanie; and a half-brother, Christopher, who works for her. Christopher is the one seen in the *Truth or Dare* documentary. Madonna, as her mother's namesake and first-born female in the family, was always very close to her father. He was the most influential person in her life as a young girl. Madonna idolized her mother, who died when she was just five and a half. In Madonna's mind her mother was a saint, but as we know saints and idols only become such after they are deceased. Her mother has been raised to a deity in Madonna's eyes. She told MTV in 1992, "My mother is like a fantasy to me. She is the perfect picture of a human being, like Jesus Christ." After her mother's death, Madonna feared her father would die and leave her alone, which drove her to even more dependence on his love and affection. Her father became everything to her, including her role model, from the moment her mother died. She says, "My father was very strong."

Madonna was raised in a permissive family environment where both parents had a laissez-faire attitude toward their children. Tony preached "always challenge your mind and body." Madonna later said that this encouragement "definitely shaped my adult life." Such positive reinforcement when young has been found to be a pervasive influence in the lives of creative and entrepreneurial women. Nuns became her most influential role models after her mother died. Lonely, she identified with the nuns as her surrogate mothers since they were virtuous authority figures (teachers) in the parochial schools she attended. They had such influence that she admits, " 'The Flying Nun' was my favorite show. They were all-powerful and perfect and I was obsessed with being a nun."

After her mother's death Madonna was forced to play mom to the younger children and asked to change diapers and babysit when she wanted to be out with her friends. (Gloria Steinem had similar childhood experiences, which affected her as an adult.) Her father finally married one of the babysitters. His marriage to Joan Gustafson when Madonna was eight devastated her. She said, "My father made me call her mom. I couldn't, wouldn't say it." Other major influences included Nancy Sinatra, her teenage idol. The female Sinatra's "These Boots Were Made for Walking" record inspired Madonna to pursue a dancing career. She became a high school cheerleader. Classmate and cheerleader friend Karen Craven says, "She was always out to shock." According to Karen, Madonna "was absolutely fearless and would flip to the top of a human pyramid without panties, causing sheer havoc among the male members." This renegade mentality, where shock attracted attention and garnered male approval, had been learned by her success in a talent show at age nine. Madonna came on stage at St. Francis's talent show in a skin-colored bikini which elicited horror from her conservative father. The audience gave her a rousing ovation and she won the contest, which imprinted titillation in Madonna's repertoire of behavior.

Madonna was intelligent, scoring 140 on a high school IQ test. She was a good student who got straight As at Rochester Adams High School, where she graduated in the top 2 percent of her class. But education wasn't her thing. At fourteen she met Christopher Flynn when she enrolled in his dance class. Flynn, who was gay, became her male mentor, role model, confidant, and soul mate. When they met he told her, "God, you're really beautiful. You have a face like an ancient Roman statue." Madonna was hooked, saying, "No one had ever said that to me before. My whole life changed." Later, Madonna said of Flynn, "He was my mentor, my father, my imaginative lover, my brother, everything, because he understood me." Flynn would be the major influence on Madonna's life for the rest of her high school years. Because of his influence she became addicted to dancing, and followed Flynn everywhere, including to sexual liaisons with his male friends.

Madonna had a cynical attitude about virginity, saying, "I saw losing my virginity as a career move." At sixteen she finally seduced Flynn to show her love for him. It was a one-time romance as he had no interest in any female. Flynn and a high school counselor were instrumental in getting Madonna a scholarship to the University of Michigan School of Music in 1977. Flynn died of AIDS on October 27, 1990. Madonna paid all his medical bills and eulogized him at the funeral. It is because of Flynn (and her homosexual brother, Christopher) that Madonna has been such a supporter of AIDS benefits throughout her career (Shelton, 1993). Madonna spent one year studying dance at the University of Michigan in Ann Arbor before deciding her destiny was in the Big Apple.

Professional Background

Madonna arrived in New York City in July 1978 at the age of twenty with thirty-seven dollars in cash, dance slippers, and a dream. She was lonely, hungry, and often emaciated during those early years attempting to break into show biz in the toughest market in the world. Reminiscing about that time she said, "I'd write in my journal, pray to have even one friend. . . . But never once did it occur to me to go back home. Never!" After some Broadway dancing auditions, most of which failed, she resorted to posing nude in an art studio to earn money for food. (The pictures ultimately ended up in *Playboy* and *Penthouse* just one month prior to her wedding to Sean Penn in 1985.) She even made an underground soft-core film for no pay to gain needed exposure within the industry. She auditioned for musicals and films with no success. During this period Madonna lived by her wits, often rummaging through Manhattan's garbage cans for survival. Eating refuse is a tough existence for a dedicated vegetarian attempting to stay healthy for her rigorous dance auditions and rehearsals.

Madonna took up with some graffiti artists and moved in with one by the name of Norris Burroughs. He threw a party attended by Dan Gilroy, a musician, songwriter, and comedian. She then moved in with Gilroy in a converted Queens synagogue resplendent with Judaic symbols and artifacts. (Such impulsive careeer moves would become her signature operating style through the years.) During that first night in the synagogue Gilroy strapped a guitar on Madonna and taught her a chord. She recalled, "That moment really clicked off something in my brain." Maybe music, not dance, was her ticket to stardom.

Madonna's relationship with Gilroy was but two weeks old when the ever-ambitious woman met Patrick Hernandez. In May 1979 Patrick Hernandez, a minor disco star, had a hit called, "Born to Be Alive," which grossed $25 million. His producers were auditioning for fresh young faces to back him up. Watching Madonna perform, they were so impressed with her passionate delivery, they offered to bring her to Paris and mold her into a star. She was tired of eating out of garbage cans and accepted immediately. This turned out to be a three-month debacle and Madonna slept her way through the Left Bank in an ephemeral pursuit of a show biz career. Pellerin, one of the producers' wives, recalled Madonna's Paris excursion: "She was very beautiful and dated a lot of French boys. . . . But she thought they were very old fashioned, and she was very free. Very free. Very liberal. She wanted a lot of boys" (Anderson, 1991; Bego, 1992). Madonna's memory of the experience was succinct, "I'm attracted to bums." She had little knowledge of French and left in a huff with the admonition to Hernandez, "Success is yours today, but it will be mine tomorrow."

Madonna came home to New York City and moved back in with Dan Gilroy, her struggling young musician friend and lover. He became her mentor and taught her the drums and guitar and she idled away the days playing and writing songs. By 1981 she had written fourteen songs, many of which became her repertoire over the next few years. She then linked up with Steve Bray, a college boyfriend who played the drums and wrote songs. With him as support, she formed her own band, alternately known as the Millionaires, Modern Dance, Emmy, and Madonna. During this period Madonna met Camille Barbone, an agent who would become her manager-mentor-lover. Barbone gave her important introductions and cleaned up her act. Barbone introduced her to Mark Kamins, who signed her for Sire Records, a Warner Records label for new artists. Seymour Stein, the president of Sire, told *People* magazine, "When she walked into the room, she filled it with her exuberance and determination. It hit me right away. I could tell she had the drive to match her talent." Mark Kamins gave testimony to her charismatic style when he told *Time,* "She had this incredible sense of style. She had an aura."

Madonna was signed to her first album by Warner. *Madonna* was released in July 1983 with songs mostly written by her over the past few years, such as "Holiday," "Lucky Star," and "Borderline." The last crept up the charts and reached number one by the spring of 1984. *Rolling Stone* magazine named her the number two "Best New Artist" for 1984 behind Cyndi Lauper. In 1985, *Rolling Stone* named her number two behind Tina Turner in a number of categories: best female singer, sexiest female, and best-dressed female.

Madonna's second album, *Like a Virgin* (1984), and the music video of the same name, catapulted her into the spotlight and made her an overnight pop icon. Her hit songs "Like a Virgin," "Touched," and "Material Girl" dominated the record charts and airwaves in late 1984 and early 1985. Her "Material Girl" video spoofed a song from *Gentlemen Prefer Blondes* called "Diamonds Are a Girl's Best Friend." This was her first direct identification with her role model/heroine, Marilyn Monroe. This music video and record gave her national recognition as a blonde bimbo with balls. Feminists decried her celebration of gold-digging in the video, claiming she was flaunting her unabashed sexuality for economic profit.

During this period Madonna gained a reputation for using and discarding managers, producers, friends, and whoever could help advance her career. Most of these people have a less-than-strong feeling for Madonna as a person. Madonna, however, has the resilient demeanor found in most entrepreneurially oriented visionaries. Her response to these charges is, "All those men I stepped all over to get to the top—every one of them would take me back because they still love me and I still love them." What confidence and positive perspective she has about a negative part of her career building.

Madonna's role in the "Punk Alice in Wonderland" movie titled *Desperately Seeking Susan* in April 1985 gave her instant universal recognition as a multi-faceted artist. She launched her first national concert tour only weeks after the release of the hit movie. Her wannabe fans flocked to the "Virgin" concerts dressed in her bohemian movie punk fashion attire. Madonna's look became a pervasive fashion statement with teenagers everywhere. She suddenly became a fashion guru of sorts. Everything she wore for the next few years became an instant hit with her teenage fans. America's teenagers emulated her rebellious style in both action and dress. The Madonna mystique was underway. Madonna became an overnight role model for millions of teenagers, who idolized this maverick "Express Yourself" female. She was the model identity for teeny-boppers bent on escaping the tyrannical grasp of all authority figures, including family and school. Madonna's marriage in 1985 to "Brat Pack" teen idol Sean Penn (five years her junior) only crystallized and reinforced her idolatry with the teen set.

Madonna's third album, *True Blue,* became an internationally acclaimed megasuccess. Songs from the album "Live to Tell," "Papa Don't Preach," and "True Blue" became huge hits. With this album Madonna was named *Rolling Stone*'s 1986 "Female Artist of the Year," "Best Female Singer," "Sexiest Female," and second "Best Dressed Female." She made the movie *Shanghai Surprise* with Sean Penn in 1986 which proved to be a disaster. It was produced by George Harrison of Beatles fame. She was to make numerous movies but never reached the success of *Desperately Seeking Susan.* Only in *Dick Tracy,* as the femme fatale Breathless Mahoney, did Madonna achieve any semblance of acclaim as an actress. Her personally produced documentary, *Truth or Dare,* was filmed during 1990's "Blonde Ambition" tour, but it was considered a cult film not for general release. Nonetheless, it became the highest-grossing theatrically produced documentary of all time. Madonna violated industry tradition and financed it herself to the tune of $4 million. Her advisors were upset with such a terrible business move and were blown away when it grossed $15 million in the first few months.

The "Material Girl" reached the zenith of controversy in 1992 when she released her much maligned *Sex* book, published by Warner. It hit the newsstands with unbelievable fanfare and derision due to its explicit sexual content, complete with scenes of bisexuality, bestiality, masturbation, multiracial sex, and matching dialogue. The *London Times* called it "the desperate confection of an aging scandal addict." The book generated $50 million worth of revenue during the first month at $49.95 a copy. Profit on the first printing was $20 million. A typical quote found in newspapers around the country: "She's the most sick, twisted psycho that ever existed. I will buy the book when I get paid Friday. It turns me on." Madonna told MTV interviewer Jonathan Ross, "The book is more 'fiction' than 'fact.' " Her intent was to shock the public into a more liberal interpretation of sexually acceptable material. She said the book is legitimate entertainment since "reading and watching are the safest kind of sex anyway."

Madonna's persona in "Express Yourself," "Like a Virgin," "Material Girl," and as Breathless Mahoney were merely symbolic fantasies of Jean Harlow, Marlene Dietrich, Marilyn Monroe, and Carole Lombard. This "Bimbo of Babylon" lives life as an illusion with the world as her audience. She has reached the top of the entertainment world by mimicking famous women of the past using contemporary props and icons to make them currently acceptable. She proselytized images of Monroe, Harlow and Dietrich—concepts that were proven entities—and gave them a Madonna look. Nostalgia works and Madonna understood how to modify an old but proven commodity, into a modern profitable venture.

One of Madonna's ingenious promotional coups was in creating a one-name image for herself. The name "Madonna" is memorable, inspiring, and powerful. In some respects it explains her compulsion for narcissistic individuality. Marilyn Monroe never would have made it as just Marilyn. Even Michael Jackson cannot command attention using the name "Jackson" only. Madonna has become an icon with a name to match and she has very adroitly pulled off one of the truly great marketing promotions in history. She is controversial at best, but she is part of this research effort because she made it to the very top of her profession and did it on her own. She not only made it to the top, she has demonstrated remarkable staying power for over a ten-year period.

Temperament: Intuitive-Thinker

Madonna is an extroverted-intuitive, that type Carl Jung characterizes as the tycoons, innovators and entrepreneurs of the world. She is also a dedicated "Type A" workaholic who drives herself to achieve. Her self-esteem is a function of her latest success, as she needs to win at all costs. "I have the same goal

I've had since I was a little girl. I want to rule the world" and "I'm a control freak" (MTV interview, 1992). To her, success is in the score, not in playing the game. She runs her operations intuitively. Madonna is CEO of Boy Toy, Inc., in addition to a number of other corporations, and manages them with an entrepreneurial flair. This woman, who is the embodiment of self-indulgence, has had only three vacations in ten years, saying, "I never take time off if I can help it." She told *Working Woman* (1991): "I run this company based on instinct. I'm an instinct player and instinct actor, and I use it to guide me in business. I think one of the things that makes me a good employer is that I was an employee for such a long time."

Madonna is very organized, spending each morning detailing the day's goals and objectives for her staff and herself. Her employees call her a "sequential thinker," someone who can put a great many details in order very quickly. Her publicist, Liz Rosenberg, says, "She isn't big on wasting time." Rosenberg adds that Madonna is frugal and often does her own laundry when on the road. Intensity is a Madonna trademark. Backup singer Donna Delory says, "She works very hard." According to an industry manager, "She's very smart and she maintains control, but she treats people badly. . . . I believe she pays her people well in order to abuse them" (Bego, 1992).

Madonna is a right-brain-driven person who sees the forest rather than the trees in everything she does. She is an enigma in that she is an artist who is also an accomplished entrepreneur, highly sensitive to personal issues, yet hard as nails, a flamboyant creator of the new and innovative, yet a control freak by her own admission. She opts for the opportunities in life and sees the possibilities of any venture regardless of its risk potential. Emotional factors seldom bias her business decisions, as she is incisive and rational and in total control of her life and business.

Madonna the entrepreneur is just the opposite of her "sex kitten" media image. She is a hard-driving taskmaster and an obsessive workaholic. Her agent, Freddie Demann (Michael Jackson's ex agent), says, "I don't believe Madonna's taken a full week off in nine years. She's willing to defer a relationship, throw having children aside—perhaps forever—in the elusive search to be a celebrity." In the words of her own egoistic self-analysis, "I am ambitious, but if I weren't as talented as I am ambitious, I would be a gross monstrosity." Demann says, "She has the most unbelievable physicality I've ever seen in any human." She maintains that through rigorous conditioning and exercise, which rank high on Madonna's list of priorities. She has her own personal trainer, Rob Parr, who puts her through a demanding daily workout including a six-mile run, followed by an aerobics workout, laps in the pool, and two hours of lifting, stretching, and abdominal exercises. It is not the regimen for the weak of body or spirit.

Madonna says, "I'm a really disciplined person." She owes her business and artistic success to this discipline. Her regimen is to program every aspect of her life. "I sleep a certain number of hours every night, then I like to get up and get on with it. I set aside three hours . . . to make phone calls and do business. Then I set aside the hours I have to exercise. Then I set aside the hours for creativity." She is an absolute "control freak" in her words, which is a telling part of her personality.

Power is an important facet of Madonna's being. "It's a great feeling to be powerful. I've been striving for it all my life. I think that's just the quest of every human being: Power." This drive manifests itself in her enormous competitiveness. "I'm not interested in anyone I can't compete with. There's got to be that fight." Madonna's lack of formal education is made up in street smarts, according to a Los Angeles lawyer who sued her in one of her Sean Penn fiascos. He says, "I would take her street-smart business sense over someone with a Harvard MBA any day."

This "Lady of the Immaculate Perception" operates her business with a rationality not found in most females, especially those competing in the entertainment jungle. She is aggressive and self-sufficient, traits also found in every woman in this work. Her outrageousness, creativity, and strong will work together to make her a unique entertainment commodity. But it is Madonna's self-confidence and energy that truly set her apart from the pack. *Time* magazine said that her "personality is an outrageous blend of Little Orphan Annie, Margaret Thatcher, and Mae West."

Madonna's renegade demeanor demands that others agree with her or they cannot be her friend. Her "my way or the highway" mentality is the classic autocratic approach of many creative visionaries. She loves fine art and at times leans to the arcane or bizarre in her tastes. One of Madonna's more outlandish paintings is *My Birth* by Frieda Kahlo, hung inside the entrance of her home to test visitors' compatibility with the mistress of the house. This bloody painting shows the artist's head protruding from between the mother's widespread legs. Madonna says, "If somebody doesn't like this painting, then I know they can't be my friend." Madonna is the maverick who violates tradition and only wants to associate with others who have a similar rebellious nature. One-time friend Sandra Bernhard, gays, alternative-lifestyle individuals, and other iconoclasts have become her soul mates.

Family versus Career

Madonna married Sean Penn on her birthday, August 16, 1985, in Malibu, California, accompanied by huge fanfare. He was five years younger, dark complected, and very slight of build. Supposedly, he reminded her of her father in his youth, adding to the Electra-complex mystique of Madonna's life (Bego,

1992). This combination of youth, build, and dark complexion have been the types that appeal to Madonna's sexual appetites. Many of her soul mates have been gay and most of her male companions have the above physical characteristics. The marriage was a disaster from the start with scandal after scandal marring their relationship. They became known as the "poison Penns." Reporters avoided them in fear of Penn's mercurial temper and threats with guns and knives. Penn had a compulsion to beat up reporters, her, and anyone else who happened to disagree with him. He was extremely volatile and once tied her up and threatened her life for hours according to her biographers Anderson and Bego. The marriage lasted only three years, mostly spent apart while either Penn was in prison for attacking the press or Madonna was on location or on tour. Scandal was the highlight of their stormy marriage. He was maniacal and when faced with her extramarital affairs would become violent. He once threw her fully clothed into the pool and once stuck her head in a gas oven. Penn reached the peak of his maniacal behavior in 1989, breaking into her Malibu house, beating her for two hours, and tying her up in a nine-hour ordeal. Madonna was bruised and battered when she filed for divorce the next week. She gave him the $4-million Malibu house and has remained single since (Anderson, 1991; Bego, 1992).

During her twenties Madonna had one marriage, two abortions, numerous affairs with both sexes, and maintained a provocative lifestyle befitting her image. According to her biographers, she continues to maintain that she wants a family with or without a man. But her career always seems to take precedence. During one of her reconciliations with Penn she promised to bear him a child if he recanted on his drinking and hostile behavior. She reneged on her promise when Warren Beatty offered her the Breathless Mahoney part in *Dick Tracy.*

Madonna's agent in the early eighties, Camille Barbone, says, "She loves sex. There's a strong maleness in Madonna. She seduces men the way men seduce women. . . . She's a sexual human being. She can only communicate in that way. It's all she knows. It's got her everything. At the same time, sex means nothing to Madonna. It's a means to an end. She thinks of sex in the same way as some men—very promiscuous men" (Anderson, 1991). And Erica Bell, a black dancer and close friend in the early days, says, "Madonna's not afraid of anything. We'd get all dressed up and drive in her limousine to [Manhattan's] Avenue D. When she spotted some good-looking Puerto Rican boy, she'd order the driver to stop the car, then roll down the window and call out, 'Hey, cutie, want a ride?' " Bell described parties in Madonna's apartment where "Madonna slept with three or four guys at once." They even played an elevator game of seducing unsuspecting young men between floors. Barbone once estimated that Madonna had slept with at least one hundred different men between 1979 and 1983. That is some kind of libidinal drive, reminiscent of the sexual proclivities found in many males. Madonna certainly could be labeled a "man-izer." Her period of nymphomania (early '80s according to her biographers) made the casting easy in *A League of Their Own,* where she played the role of "All the way, May." She fit the image well.

But maternal she was not. One of Madonna's closest advisors has said, "Madonna doesn't have a maternal bone in her body." Madonna disagrees with this assessment, telling *USA Today* in 1992:

> Sean and I wanted to have a child. And we talked about it all the time—Warren and I. Um, it just wasn't the right time. . . . I think about having children all the time. There is one part of me that says, "Oh God, I wish I was madly in love with someone and it was something viable." . . . It's important to have a father around, so when you think about that, you have to think, "Is this person the right person?"

In 1993 she told the newspaper, "I'll probably never get married again." But she added that she intends to become a mother at some time in the near future. Madonna certainly has sacrificed family for career thus far in her young life. She is approaching her biological limits and will have to decide whether or not to pursue a family in the near future. It appears that Madonna's unconscious driven nature to succeed will get in the way of any attempt to share her time with a husband and a baby. Only time will tell. Madonna has opted for the professional over the personal in the march to the top of her profession, which appears to be a necessary concomitant of success for career women. Madonna is certainly introspective, summing up herself and marriage: "I'm a workaholic. I have insomnia. And I'm a control freak. That's why I'm not married. Who could stand me?" (Anderson, 1991).

Life Crises

Madonna lost her mother to cancer at the age of five and a half. This was so traumatic it left an indelible mark on her psyche that has much to do with the personality we see today on MTV and elsewhere. Her obsessive need to dominate, control, and "rule the world" are found in her early trauma over her mother's untimely death. Chapter 6, on the crisis in the lives of these women, described how "superlearning" occurs in traumatic states. The trauma puts the person in a theta or trancelike state of shock. The theta state is already particularly strong in children and when coupled with a crisis it is compounded. This is what evidently happened with Madonna, where her next few years of interrelationship with her father, nuns, and religious icons were magnified and imprinted into her (unconscious) psyche. She had no control over this traumatic event and therefore is obsessed with controlling everything in her life as an adult. Madonna uses father and mother images and religious icons as unconventional stage props in an attempt at controlling those things she could not control in her childhood. Madonna told *Vanity Fair* in 1992 that her need to dominate stemmed from "losing my mother and then being very attached to my father and losing my father to my stepmother and going through my childhood thinking the things I loved and was sure about were being pulled away." Madonna is convinced she is well-adjusted, although she is in therapy for perfectionism and an obsessive need for achievement (*Vanity Fair*, 1992):

> I didn't have a mother, like maybe a female role model, and I was left on my own a lot, and I think that probably gave me courage to do things. . . . I think when you go through something really traumatic in your childhood you choose one of two things—you either overcompensate and pull yourself up and make yourself stand tall, and become a real attention getter, or you become terribly introverted and you have real personality problems. (*Vanity Fair*, October 1992)

A very insightful self-assessment. Madonna was imprinted and conditioned at that early age with an irrepressible need to excel and to seek love and adulation from anyone and everyone. She has become a self-fulfilling prophesy of her childhood needs, a repeated pattern found in female visionaries. They tend to realize their childhood fantasies for greatness in their adult lives. In Madonna's case she was also acting out (literally and figuratively) a need for fatherly affection and security. Her rebellion is little more than a cry for help as she was abandoned as a child (by her father) and has determined as an adult to decry the need for anyone who will ever hurt her again. She admits:

> I have not resolved my Electra complex. The end of the "Oh Father" video, where I'm dancing on my mother's grave, is an attempt to embrace and accept my mother's death. I had to deal with the loss of my mother and then I had to deal with the guilt of her being gone and then I had to deal with the loss of my father when he married my stepmother. So I was just one angry, abandoned little girl. I'm still angry. (*Vanity Fair*, April 1990)

The framed snapshot Madonna keeps on the table by her bed is of a dark-haired, innocent-looking, teenage femme fatale. When asked if that was her mother, Madonna said, "Yes. She was sixteen. I could never look like that in a picture." Madonna's early trauma and crisis have made her a woman who needs to seduce all males but can never allow them to own her emotionally. She said, "Like all young girls I was in love with my father. . . . I kept saying, if you die, I'm going to get buried in the casket with you." A testimony to her Electra complex was the line in *Truth or Dare* when she said, "I fell right to sleep [with my father] after he fucked me. Just kidding" (Anderson 1992).

This kind of dialogue gives credence to Madonna's desperate need for fatherly love, and her attempt to quell her needs for paternal love and affection. The early life crisis has been a critical part of that need and instrumental in creating one of the most libidinally driven females of the twentieth century.

Libidinally Driven Success

The launch of Madonna's book, *Sex* (1992), was the most extensive international introduction of a book in history. Over 750,000 copies went on sale simultaneously in Japan, Great Britain, France, Germany, and the United States. The estimated profits on this initial printing alone were $20 million, an unprecedented entrepreneurial coup. This, coupled with her tour and record successes, has made her an entertainment superstar. Only Madonna's inability to conquer movies has kept her from being acknowledged as the greatest entertainment phenomenon ever. *Sex* has been the low point in her career artistically and the high point in demonstrating her need to exorcise past ghosts. Madonna rebels against all those things that were once held dear to her and the ultimate rebellion is to castigate those sacred icons held in reverence by traditional institutions.

Madonna's persona has been inordinately influenced by her early parochial education. Her early role models were very religious: her mother, her father, Madonna, Christ, Catholic nuns, and Christopher Flynn. Without a mother, Madonna idolized her mother's memory and other authority figures, in addition to the Catholic idioms and images she would one day desecrate on stage. Madonna's need to rebel against this early dogma was based on forced discipline during her traumatic period. Madonna's unconscious rebellion against dogma that she never bought into led her to use the religious icons (crucifixes, rosaries, Bibles) as perverse props in her erotic performances. She has frequently used her mother's grave as a scene in her pop videos.

Madonna's perverse identity with the name Madonna has driven her to sublimate an internal need for affection into a paradoxical form of imagery. This mother figure (the Madonna)—who epitomizes virginity and purity—is on stage portraying every sexual perversity possible. Madonna blasphemes virginity through exhibitionism, defiles the Church by masturbating with its symbols, and reviles the establishment through her bizarre costumes and raiments. Madonna's irreverent acts almost seem to be those of a defiant child rebelling against a society that denied her the love of her mother.

Madonna is the classical example of Freud's "sublimated libidinal energy." Freud said that virtually all creativity is a function of redirected sexual energy, and that no great achievement takes place in anyone who is psychosexually satisfied. In other words, people who are totally sexually satisfied will never achieve anything, according to Freud, because they have no drive left for other achievements. Napoleon Hill, in researching the great creators of the Industrial Revolution (Rockefeller, Ford, Carnegie, Edison) found that "sex energy is the creative energy of all geniuses. There never has been and never will be a great leader, builder, or artist lacking in this driving force of sex." Madonna meets Freud's and Hill's criteria for creative success. She summed up her libidinal nature by telling *Vanity Fair* in 1992, "I love my pussy. I think it's the complete summation of my life." Most people might think such a thing, or maybe consider such a provocative statement to a friend, but to tell the press? When asked about the nature of her music video "Express Yourself," she responded, "Pussy rules the world" (*Vanity Fair,* October 1992).

When Madonna exploded onto the entertainment scene in 1984 with "Like a Virgin," she discovered that the entertainment business was much like her childhood upbringing in Catholicism. The Roman Catholic Church is infamous for instilling "fear" in its following with "love" of Jesus as the reward. This is its way of controlling the minds and emotions of the constituency. Madonna has attempted to use this love/fear dichotomy or love/hate dichotomy to control the entertainment industry. The one thing Madonna hated was apathy, so she decided to go down the path of aggressive refutation of all traditional values in the interest of furthering a career that had mediocrity painted all over it. She got immediate confirmation from her adolescent and gay audiences, who also admire renegade behavior. These groups live their lives on the edge as they are fighting the establishment at every turn. Madonna is their mentor, role model, and heroine as she defies all tradition and flaunts all convention.

Madonna reached the peak of perversity in 1992 when she released the book *Sex.* Japan banned the book. In the United States a national television poll asked viewers if Madonna had gone too far; Madonna's fans supported her attempt to effect a change in the mores of society with 79 percent in favor to only 21 percent in opposition. Madonna told a reporter who asked for her definition of "S&M" that to her it meant "sex and money," a classic tongue-in-cheek response to the public furor over her nonconformist sex-ploitation. Madonna expressed her attitude on the subject of sex best when she said, "The best way to seduce someone is by making yourself unavailable." She is recommending that if you go where others are not, you will achieve what you want—the axiom for all great creative genius. Madonna's philosophy of life was described best in her comment to MTV on October 21, 1992: "I would like to offset the sexual mores of society and my behavior, videos, book are all aimed at changing those behaviors. . . . Our society is beset by an evangelic scrutiny of what's right and wrong and I am determined to 'change' it if I can."

Madonna has demonstrated an almost messianic desire to rebuke the Catholic Church. She somehow blames the church for much of society's problems and, consciously or unconsciously, her own. She appears to blame Mother

Church for her own internal value judgments and guilt orientation, saying, "I grew up with two images of a woman: the virgin and the whore." It is this dichotomy that she continues to confuse in her life and art. Madonna has evidently been blessed or cursed with an abnormal level of testosterone, the hormone that determines competitiveness, sex drive, risk-taking, and creative bent.

Madonna's personal and professional lives have been aligned around sexual perversity since she was very young. On stage at the school talent show at age nine she horrified her father by coming on stage almost nude. "I was practically naked, but the talent show was my one night of the year to show them who I really was and what I could really be." Madonna won the talent show as the audience was captivated by her performance. This positive experience reinforced her need to titillate audiences, and she would use the ploy the rest of her career. She had been conditioned to use shock to achieve success at age nine, and this positive imprinting became her model for achieving her goals. Madonna is not unique as a similar approach has been used by most great creative geniuses. Early imprints of success via devious means become imprinted on their young psyches only to be reincarnated in their adulthood. This conditioning and learning is especially strong when the event is during a crisis or traumatic period. It is my opinion that Madonna's experience at age nine was instrumental in creating a woman who believes that "Pussy rules the world."

One of Madonna's characteristics must be admired. If nothing else, she is honest in her perversity. She is out front in her bizarre and irreverent use of religious icons in her shows and videos. She may be offensive to the Church and appear sacrilegious to most people, but she is more honest than many women seen walking the streets of the world with crucifixes dangling precariously and blatantly between amply exposed cleavage. These women are declaring their faith and simultaneously using the religious icon as a tantalizing attraction to their bodies. They are simultaneously saying, "I have faith," but "I am a sexually seductive female," bringing attention to the sensual via the spiritual. Such delusion has never been Madonna's approach or intent. Women who use their crucifixes to attract attention to their bodies are not being honest with themselves or their religion. Madonna uses her icons as props and has never denied the intent. She never flaunts them in any way other than as an entertainment medium. She has never attempted to aggrandize her own sexuality other than for the commercial success of her act. Madonna has been overzealous and indiscrete in the use of the Church's icons, but she has at least been honest with herself in their use. Many women should be so honest, especially those who put her down for what they use dishonestly.

Much of Madonna's sexual perversity is obviously unconscious—concocted to exorcise her childhood needs for affection and approval. Unfortunately, it has become the focal point for her whole career. Madonna's excessive libidinal energy, perversity, and sexuality have become the major attraction for the media. This has given her an enormous amount of free exposure, since the press pursues and demands sensationalism. Madonna has superb insight into the motivations of the press and constantly feeds their needs by blaspheming the Church and ridiculing what she terms "America's sexual repression." The press has in turn made Madonna the most visible, photographed, and debated female in modern times. The controversial Madonna has been able to impact her industry as much as any woman in history and her libidinal energy appears to have been highly instrumental in that achievement. It has made her a true creative visionary.

Summary

You may love her or hate her, idolize her or despise her, but you cannot ignore Madonna. Mark Bego, one of Madonna's many biographers, sums up her image as "saint, savior, sinner, siren, slut." Madonna is destined to be remembered as the most conspicuous star of the twentieth century and one of its truly memorable celebrities. She started with nothing, attained the pinnacle of stardom, and stayed there for a long time with little talent other than drive and ambition. Madonna truly epitomizes the female who has taken a passionate childhood dream and made it into an adult reality. Madonna is a female who knows who she is, where she is going, and never allows anyone to get in the way. Focus and determination are the weapons she has used to realize her childhood dreams. Once the door opened and she tasted success she never allowed the door to close. She became master of her destiny and left many bodies on the roadside in her inexorable drive to the top.

The "Material Girl" is an enigma. She is a rare combination of artist and entrepreneur who is emotional yet rational. A Promethean spirit with a desire to "rule the world." Her "Type A" workaholic nature is accented by an enormous libidinal drive. Madonna is a perfectionist, but wants it done now. Maternal she isn't, but her ability to titillate and motivate both teenagers and counter-culture groups has kept her number one in the entertainment world for a long time. Madonna has been a sensitive supporter of the fight against AIDS, describing it as the worst thing to happen to the world since Hitler. At the same time she has a bitter vendetta against the Catholic Church. In her inimitable words, "It sucks the big one. I think it's disgusting. I think it's hypocritical. And it's unloving. It's not what God and Christianity are all about." These expressions are fears and anxieties of a lonely young child forced to adhere to the dogma of Mother Church during a period when she was in deep trauma.

Her fall 1993 New York City bus ads showing her alongside the real Madonna caused outrage among Catholic groups. Her 1993 Girlie Show Tour prompted British novelist Julie Burchill to comment, "She looks like a whore and thinks like a pimp . . . the very best sort of modern girl."

Madonna is frugal and frivolous, often at the same time. She watches the pennies on every bill passing over her desk as CEO of her many corporations, yet will squander millions for a bauble that fits her fancy. She offered an exorbitant $4.9 million for a Miami Beach Italian Renaissance mansion, which had a value of $2.15 million. The owners didn't want to sell and she wanted it so much she offered them a price they couldn't refuse. Madonna's net worth, estimated at over $100 million by *People* magazine in 1993, allows her to gratify her wildest dreams. Madonna's contract with Warner in 1992, purportedly worth $60 million, also helps keep her in vegetarian meals.

Her mercenary dog-eat-dog style has turned close friends into bitter enemies. Sandra Bernhard told *Laugh Factory* (March 1994), "I feel sorry for her because she doesn't know who she is. She tries to steal other people's identities." What Sandra doesn't understand is that particular style is the essence of all great achievement. One must fantasize the impossible and Madonna is the consummate expert at such emulation.

Madonna rebels against all dogma and it is this rebellion that is at the core of what drives her. She is living testimony that childhood dreams and desires can be achieved through tenacity and temerity. She has mediocre talent, but has packaged it with a stage presence that has sensual appeal so that talent became a secondary issue. This master of self-promotion uses her macro-vision of what the world really wants in entertainment and gives it to them uncensored. Madonna's unconscious childhood dreams of grandeur were actualized into success via a perverse sense of the world's entertainment needs. Madonna's story qualifies as one of the great Horatio Alger rags-to-riches adventures. She reached the top without the help of superior talent, education, contacts, or money. Only hard work, a keen intuitive sense, perfectionism, and perseverance carried her to the top of her field, not unlike most great creative visionaries. In her case, an enormous libidinal drive gave additional impetus to her success. Being voted the worst actress for 1993 in the film *Body of Evidence* never deterred her.

Madonna Louise Veronica Ciccone
Entertainer, actress, recording star, CEO

b. August 16, 1958, Bay City, Michigan

Dominant trait: Libidinally driven

Religion: Raised Catholic but nonreligious

Mottos: "I have the same goal I've had since I was a little girl: I want to rule the world!"; "I like the challenge of merging art and commerce"; "Pussy rules the world"; "I love my pussy, I think it's a complete summation of my life."

Philosophy: "I think that's just the quest of every human being: Power"; "My behavior, videos, book [*Sex*], are all aimed at changing the mores of society."

Nicknames: "Nonnie" as child, Material Girl, Herself, Snatch Batch, Boy Toy, All the Way Mae, Bimbo of Babylon

Creation/innovation: A self-promoting corporate powerhouse, CEO of Boy Toy, Inc., Siren Films, and Slutco to enhance an image of "Our Lady of Perpetual Promotion"

Products/contributions: Broke Beatles' record with 16 successive top singles. By the end of 1993, she had made 20 music videos, 11 movies, 7 albums, 2 Broadway shows, 27 singles, 3 MTV performances, and 5 international tours.

Successes: *Forbes,* "America's smartest business woman . . . and wealthiest woman in show business" (1990). With 1991 earnings of $65 million and over 100 million records sold by 1994, estimated at $500 million in Warner revenues, she is arguably "the most famous woman in the world" at age 35.

Self-description: "I'm a workaholic. I have insomnia. And I'm a control freak. That's why I'm not married. Who could stand me?"

Birth order: Oldest daughter with two older brothers, two younger half sisters, and a younger half brother. Closest to gay brother, Christopher.

Childhood transience: Moved from Bay City to Rochester, Michigan, at age 8

Father's occupation: Automotive and defense contractor engineer

Mentors/role models: Christ and nuns as child, then father, and later Marilyn Monroe. Chris Flynn mentor in teen years. "My father was very strong. He was my role model."

Childhood upbringing: Permissive parents allowed freedom to err. Hated stepmother, Joan; was changing diapers and babysitting by age 9. Became an iconoclast at 9 and said, "I don't need anybody."

Formal education: Parochial grade school, a 1976 graduate of Rochester Adams H.S. where she was a straight A student with IQ over 140—top 2% of class. One year on dance scholarship at the University of Michigan School of Music. Dropped out to pursue career in New York City.

Life crisis: Mother died December 1, 1963, when Madonna was five and a half. Her "everything" father betrayed her by remarrying three years later.

Marriages/liaisons: 100 lovers in three years in New York. Married 3 years to actor Sean Penn. Hundreds of liaisons of both sexes; two abortions.

Risk-taking: Former manager Camille Barbonne: "Madonna lived on the edge always and was not afraid of anything."

Temperament: Extroverted-intuitive-thinking-judger: Promethean temperament

Behavior: Perfectionist, workaholic, ambitious, and sexually driven

Career vs. family: Sacrifices everything for career. Maternal instinct lacking

Self-esteem: Developed in childhood through talent, beauty, and father's love.

Hobbies: Reading, performing, and exercising (runs 5 miles daily and works out); collects fine art: Picasso, Tamara da Lempicka, Leger, Haring

Heroes: Marilyn Monroe, Carole Lombard, and Jean Harlow, all flashy blondes

Honors: 1989 music awards ceremony "Artist of the Decade"; *Musician* magazine "Woman of the Year," 1990

14

Golda Meir—Intransigent Confidence

They can because they think they can.

—Virgil

One person with a belief is equal to a force of ninety-nine who have only interests.

—John Stuart Mill

The independent state of Israel would not have happened had it not been for Golda Meir. She was a focused and driven woman who sacrificed her life daily for her dream—a free, independent Jewish nation. She was a dreamer who never allowed daily crises to crack her self-confidence, unabated enthusiasm, or intransigent desire for a free Zionist state. Meir was an enigma in that she owned but two dresses, yet was described as enchanting and captivating by both friends and adversaries, including the wife of a long-term lover. She could be near starvation and yet be the enthusiastic life of the party. Death knocked at her door daily for many years yet she remained the consummate optimist. She was always willing to sacrifice anything for the redemption of her childhood dream—Zionism. Her years of hardship and living in constant fear of annihilation formed an omnipotent and intransigent will that constantly guided her on the long road to the top.

Golda Meir finally realized her dream on May 14, 1948, when the United Nations voted for the independent partition of Palestine. Knowledgeable politicians said, "If Ben-Gurion is the father, Golda is the mother of the Israeli State." She had won her life-long battle and sobbed uncontrollably during the ceremony. Little did she realize that her battle would result in twenty-five more years of fighting in order to keep the Arabs from pushing her people into the Mediterranean Sea. Meir would have been shocked if someone had told her that just twenty years later, on March 27, 1968, she, Golda Meir, would be unanimously voted the fourth prime minister for her beloved nation and the only female head of state in the world.

This Russian immigrant with just a year of college education was raised in a Milwaukee ghetto and became the only woman signer of the Israeli Declaration of Independence, its first ambassador to Russia, its first minister of labor and insurance, its first female foreign minister, and finally its first and only female prime minister. Meir's spirit, tenacity, and confidence helped her create the state of Israel and ultimately led to her becoming its first female leader. Meir was a pioneer role model for subsequent female leaders such as Margaret Thatcher and Indira Gandhi and an inspirational role model for every female who aspires to the role of international power broker.

Personal Life History

Meir was born Goldie Mabovitz on May 3, 1898, in Kiev, Russia (Ukraine), as the seventh child of Moshe and Bluma. Her parents were very nonconventional, as they were married without the traditional matchmaker. (Having nontraditional parentage appears to be highly correlated to creative genius. Edison, Einstein, Catherine the Great, and Margaret Mead all were from long lines of independent renegades.) The cruel Russian environment ended the lives of her five brothers during the nine years between her sister Shana's birth and her own. Shana was so much older that she acted as a surrogate mother for most of Goldie's early life. Shana taught her to read and write since she never had the luxury of a formal school until she arrived in Milwaukee as an eight-year-old.

Clara, Meir's baby sister, was four years her junior. Life was very difficult in Russia where Goldie spent the first eight years of her life. She reminisced in her autobiography, "There never was enough of anything, not food, nor warm clothing, not heat at home." She never forgot this unhappy period of her life and the horrifying experiences of the Russian pogroms, which were forever imprinted on her psyche. Goldie first heard the words "Christ Killers" from screaming attackers who killed innocent people because of their faith and ethnic background. Golda said at age seventy, "I remember how scared I was, and how angry."

Goldie's father left for the "Golden Medina"—the United States—when she was five. He found employment in Milwaukee and sent for the family. Her mother then used her moxie to bribe officials, forge papers, and have Goldie pose as a five-year-old when she was actually eight. The passport was for another five-year-old as they left illegally. Her seventeen-year-old sister, Shana, posed as a twelve-year-old. All of their baggage and clothes were stolen, and only the irrepressible Goldie did not get violently ill on the month-long voyage. Moshe had settled in a Milwaukee ghetto, working alternately as a carpenter and for the railroad. Goldie's mother opened a grocery store beneath their two-bedroom apartment after just two weeks in Milwaukee. She couldn't even speak English. What an inspirational role model for the young Goldie, who became a store clerk at age nine.

Shana was the greatest influence on Goldie's life. She was her heroine, revolutionary spirit, and teacher during their early years in Russia and those early days in Milwaukee. Goldie idolized Shana as her idyllic role model, saying, "For me, Shana was perhaps the greatest influence on my life . . . a shining example, my dearest friend and my mentor." Her mother was a role model of a different kind, as she single-handedly ran a dairy store and grocery despite lacking knowledge of retailing, English, buying strategy, or the product.

Goldie read and read as a young girl. She discovered Dostoyevsky, Tolstoy, Chekhov, and Dickens. She didn't start her formal schooling until age eight, in Milwaukee, yet she graduated as valedictorian of the Milwaukee Elementary School (Mead and Steinem had similar delayed schooling). Goldie spoke Yiddish and Russian at home and English at school and with her friends. The Milwaukee ghetto clapboard houses looked like palaces to Goldie. She was so entranced by books and school that she longed to become a school teacher in Milwaukee, saying in her autobiography, "I wanted to be a teacher ever since I was eight." Goldie was very attractive as girl, according to her school friend Regina, who said, "Four out of five boys fell in love with her. . . . She was so vibrant and attractive."

Goldie's sister Shana had married and moved to Denver for tuberculosis treatment and the two communicated regularly by mail. Goldie's parents decided girls did not need formal education and arranged a marriage for Goldie at age fourteen with a thirty-year-old insurance salesman. Goldie, the intransigent child and self-confident teenager, ran away to Denver to live with her sister in order to complete her high school education. She lived in Denver for two years with her rebellious sister, who still held weekly Zionist meetings in her home. These meetings fascinated the impressionable Goldie and molded her into a quasi-revolutionary. One of the males attending Shana's meetings was Morris Meyerson, whom Goldie would ultimately marry. Goldie became enraptured with the Poale Zion movement and became an immediate zealot. Independence and an iron will were already deeply ingrained in her. She and Shana had a falling out and Goldie returned to Milwaukee to finish her schooling. She graduated from North Division High School as vice president of her class in 1916, but she was already deeply indoctrinated into Zionism.

Goldie joined the Poale Zion organization at age seventeen and began speaking at rallies while attending high school and teaching English at night to immigrants. She and her Zionist friends earned the label "Zionuts" due to their enthusiastic passion for the movement. She enrolled in Milwaukee

Teachers Training College for one semester and taught Yiddish at the Jewish Center when not attending class. She was a very passionate woman in everything she attempted, and was becoming an inspirational speaker in English, Yiddish, and Russian. During the winter of 1918, at age nineteen she was the youngest and prettiest delegate selected to the Jewish Congress being held in Philadelphia. This was the beginning of a life of such events.

Goldie married Morris Meyerson at age nineteen but had already decided by this time that her destiny was to live on an Israeli kibbutz. She told Morris of her plan and invited him to join her. Meir's biographer, Martin (1988), said, "In her imagination, Goldie had already left America. In her own inner being, she was already working the land in some Palestine desert." She told Morris he could follow or stay, but she was committed. As an example of her commitment and tenacity, two weeks after her marriage, she accepted an assignment to the West Coast of the United States to raise money by speaking on Zionism. Her father was furious: "Who leaves a new husband and goes on the road?" Meir was obsessive about the Zionist cause and said, "I was prepared to travel anywhere" and "Whatever I was asked to do, I did. The party said I should go, so I went." Meir's biographer said, "Morris was a mild nothing compared to Goldie's life force." Once she had accepted the fact that there was no other solution for the Jewish problem but a national homeland, she said, "I decided to go there." When asked if she would have gone without her new husband, she said, "I would have gone alone but heartbroken."

Goldie was recognized as a leader of the movement. She had applied for the right to go to a kibbutz at age eighteen but was refused due to her age, though she had already mentally committed to Palestine. This young "Zionut" traveled the United States for two years raising funds for fare on the *Pocahontas,* a chartered ship destined for Tel Aviv. She had been recruited to raise funds for the trip since "I could speak both English and Yiddish fluently, and I was prepared to travel anywhere" to get on that ship. This was to be her history for the next fifty years. Meir talked Shana into joining her in making Palestine their new homeland and the future home for the "wandering Jew." Shana left her husband in the United States, joined Goldie, and boarded the *Pocahontas* with her two children.

The *Pocahontas* was bound for Tel Aviv as the *aliyah* or third wave of immigration. It was a disaster waiting to happen. Goldie said, "It was a miracle we lived through the journey." The ship left on May 23, 1921, with Goldie (age twenty-three), her husband, Morris, her sister and two kids, and twenty-three enthusiastic Zionists. The voyage was a disaster from the beginning: there were mutinies, death, near starvation, and an assassinated captain. Finally, the captain's brother went mad. The group arrived in Tel Aviv on July 14, 1921, half-starved and with no luggage. Their Shangri-La was to be Tel Aviv, which was in fact a twelve-year-old desert town with no vegetation or natural resources. It resembled "another planet." It was so primitive and barren that everyone in the party cried and wanted to leave, including Shana. Only an ebullient Goldie was ecstatic, saying, "I was profoundly happy." The others were devastated. In fact, one-third of the group ultimately returned to the United States. On landing, Goldie officially changed her name to Golda to start her life anew.

Professional Background

Meir and her husband found themselves in Palestine, a 240-mile-long strip of desolate land only one-fourth as wide as it was long. This desert was the realization of Meir's childhood dreams of a Jewish homeland and she loved it from day one. Meir often said, "Jewish people had the right to one spot on earth where they could live as a free, independent people." She was committed to making this stark strip of desert their permanent home. The Meyerson's were assigned to the EMEK kibbutz in Merhavia, a communal village, more collective than any communist would ever dare create. These villages shared everything: clothes, food, children, and mates. Most of the inhabitants had malaria, there were no toilets, the water was contaminated, and the food was often inedible and usually spoiled. And the ever-optimistic Meir was "absolutely fulfilled." She loved the kibbutz life and was immediately elected to the steering committee at age twenty-three. She was the delegate to the Zionist convention and met many of the future leaders of the nation: Ben-Gurion, Berl Katznelson, Zalmon Shazar, and David Remez (all were future lovers) (Martin, 1988).

Meir's sister and soul mate, Shana, admonished her, saying, "Goldie didn't want to be what she was, but what she ought to be." Shades of Ayn Rand and Aristotle!—their exact definition of innovative and creative behavior. But Meir's innovative contribution was to be a long enduring struggle against a world mentality of religious discrimination. She began her creative struggle by picking almonds, raising chickens, caring for children, and teaching English while she was learning Arabic and Hebrew. The kibbutz life proved too tough for Morris. He hated it and the couple moved back to Tel Aviv to start their family. Sarah was born in 1923, and Menachem in 1926. Meir worked in Jerusalem as secretary to the Women's Labor Council and took in laundry for extra income. She was made treasurer in 1924, allowing her to travel to various international conferences. In 1928–29 she was a delegate to the American Zionist party and returned to the United States for the first time since she had left. In 1929 she was elected a delegate of the World Zionist Congress. It was there she became involved with her mentor/lover Shazar Zalman, who was instrumental in her assignment as secretary of Pioneer Women in the United States in 1932, where she organized American chapters. Meir relocated to New York City and traveled the country for two years. Her fluency in English, Russian, Yiddish, Hebrew, and some Arabic was instrumental in not only this job but most of her future posts. Meir said in her autobiography, "I did not choose a career. I did not choose a profession. It all just happened." Actually, Meir did choose something—a dream, which she followed until her death.

A male associate said of Meir during this period, "Goldie was a prime mover, doing a variety of jobs, outstanding at whatever she did." Biographer Martin (1988) says, "She was striking, very good looking and had a certain air of mystery about her." He added, "Her eyes were magnificent." She had become a revolutionary *femme fatale* in spite of the fact that she never owned more than two dresses at a time or wore makeup for over thirty years. She was a private person, although never a loner, who maintained a constant stream of confidential romantic liaisons.

During the thirties Meir became a world traveler on behalf of the World Zionist Organization and the Jewish Agency for Palestine. She held many posts, including the chairman of the board for Kupat Holim, the firm providing medical services for almost half of Palestine's Jewish population. During this period she was known as the "Golden Girl" of the Zionist movement while living a spartan life. She seldom had electricity, gas, or a personal phone and slept on a day couch the majority of her life. The giants of Israel were her friends, associates, and lovers. They loved her, according to Martin because "she was strong enough to show her weaknesses." She would cry when there was no food but thought nothing of confronting men holding machine guns with cold-blooded composure.

When the Arabs joined Hitler's Axis powers prior to World War II, Meir went on a speaking tour urging her young countrymen to join the British. She was instrumental in the enlistment of 33,000 Zionists into the British military effort. During the war she was named head of the Zionist Political Department and served on the British War Economic Advisory Council. In 1943 Meir went to trial with the British over their management of the Palestine state. She gained national notoriety by refusing to back down in the face of the intimidating British judge. She told him, "You should not address me in that manner" when he was speaking down to her. The people loved her temerity.

In the postwar struggle to establish a permanent Jewish state, Golda sided with Ben-Gurion's group, who were arrested and in jail during one of the most critical times in the history of the Zionist state. The leaders appointed Meir the titular head of government. During this period the ship *Exodus,* bearing 4,700 displaced Jews from northern Europe including four hundred pregnant women, was attempting to reach Palestine. The political machinations with the Arabs and British came into play in an international incident when British destroyers blocked the ship's path to Palestine. Meir made the ship her private mission and went on board in defiance of the British forces and declared, "All of you will yet come to us." After the *Exodus* incident Albert Spencer, secretary of the British War Council, said, "Golda was the most capable woman I ever met. . . . Like Mr. Churchill, she was the simple solution to any problem."

The United Nations finally voted for partition of Palestine and the independence of Israel in 1946 causing U.S. Secretary of State James Forrestal to say, "The 45 million Arabs are going to push the 350,000 Jews right into the ocean." It was at this moment that the Jews finally stopped fighting for independence and started fighting for their lives. And the fight was a daily one. During the first two weeks of the U.N. resolution, 93 Arabs, 84 Jews, and 7 British soldiers were killed. Meir was put in charge of Jerusalem, where the fighting was fiercest. She persevered and lived through a virtual nightmare of death and devastation. She slept four hours a night for months and told the inquiring media how she pulled it off: "We intend to remain alive. Our neighbors want to see us dead. This is not a question that leaves much room for compromise." David Ginsberg, speaking at the Jewish Congress in 1946, said, "Dynamic was a good name for her. . . . This was not a style or pattern, not something she developed or learned. This was simply the way she was, the way she had been all her life, the way she would always be." Always an eloquent speaker and ready with an incisive and elegant description of the complex, Meir defined their survival, "We had a secret weapon, no alternative."

Two enormous events preceded Israel's independence. The country had no money, and the king of Jordan had promised that fifty million Arabs would be willing to sacrifice ten million of their numbers to annihilate half a million Jews in Palestine. This was a staggering threat. The Arabs were willing to sacrifice 25 percent of their people for a 240-mile strip of barren real estate that the Jews had actually purchased* from their predecessors. Meir proved providential in both battles. On the eve of independence she was chosen to meet with King Abdullah of Jordan to forestall an imminent war. When warned by friends that she would die, Meir responded, "I would walk to hell if there was a chance of saving one Jewish soldier's life by my action."

Meir masqueraded as an Arab wife and crossed the border to meet with Abdullah, who purportedly was more afraid of her than she was of him. The Arab driver was "so terrified he made us get out some distance before we reached our destination." The king asked why she was so impatient to have an independent state. In her inimitable fashion, Meir said, "I didn't think 2,000 years should be described as 'being in a hurry.' " She told Abdullah there would be war and Israel would win. Writing her autobiography, Meir said, "That was the sheerest audacity on my part, but I knew we had to win."

---

*Most of the real estate had actually been purchased for exorbitant prices during the 1920s and '30s from the Arabs.

Meir's second mission in creating the new nation was to raise monies necessary to protect it from instant annihilation by the ten million Arabs surrounding them on all fronts. The Arabs were just waiting to attack, and an Israeli on the front lines called Meir pleading for the right to give up the territory because the tanks he would need to fight cost $10 million. She responded with "O.K. You stay and I'll get you the $10 million for your tanks." She later said, "I had a lot of *chutzpah*. Where was I going to get $10 million?" She immediately left for America and started passionately pleading for money, starting with her political role model and heroine, Eleanor Roosevelt.

Henry Mentor was head of the American Zionist movement. He was a hard-boiled chauvinist and not a believer in spending so much for so few people in a desert on the other side of the world. Mentor, like many men before him, was blown away by Meir's charisma. He told the press, "Golda's fire was a furnace. This woman was magnificent." He then began introducing her as the "most powerful Jewish woman in the world today," which she was. She pulled off the greatest miracle in the history of Israel's long fight for independence. She used her charisma, her magnetism, and her inexhaustible energy to raise $50 million in three months. The magnitude of that feat is obvious when you consider that $50 million was equal to three times the entire oil revenue of Saudia Arabia in 1947. Ben-Gurion said on her return, "Someday, when history will be written, it will be said that there was a Jewish woman who got the money which made the State possible."

On her return, on April 13, 1948, the indefatigable Meir had a heart attack. Exhaustion and stress had taken their toll. Her nonstop worldwide effort to raise money to stave off an Arab war had been successful, but she was forced to take a three-week rest. Meir was once again on her feet when Palestine was, declared the state of Israel on May 14, 1948. The motto of the "Golden Girl" was "If you will it, it is no dream," and sure enough her intransigent will had made her dream a reality. The fifty-year-old Meir was the only female of the twenty-four signers of the Israeli Declaration of Independence. The new nation was born with Meir sobbing uncontrollably as a band played "Hatikvah," the Jewish national anthem. This document ended 1,887 years of Jews wandering without a country. Meir was once again assigned a post in Jerusalem, where it was expected the greatest fighting and unrest would occur. Men were dying at her side daily and there was shooting everywhere. Meir would carry hand grenades in her underwear and bra for those on the front lines (Martin, 1988).

In September 1948 Meir was named Israel's first ambassador to the Soviet Union. She was assigned this position, not out of political favoritism found in most governments, but because she was the most eminently qualified individual for this post. She spoke fluent Russian, and having been born in Kiev she knew the culture, and besides, she was the most astute diplomat in the government. Meir took her daughter, Sarah, with her to Moscow, but returned in April 1949 to assume a new cabinet post as minister of labor and social insurance under Premier David Ben-Gurion. In this position, Meir became the architect of the nation's national insurance plan. She spent the next seven years in this gratifying and rewarding assignment. Meir was appointed foreign minister in June 1956, becoming the Israeli delegate to the United Nations. She spent ten years as a globe-hopping diplomat with enormous success playing Joan of Arc to the newly emerging African nations. She had an almost evangelic personal mission to help the now struggling nations of South Africa. She made their survival her personal vendetta.

At the age of sixty-eight she resigned the cabinet post to take a less-taxing position as the secretary to the governing Mapai party.

Meir resigned this position in July 1968 because of poor health and advancing age. Only months later she was jolted back into public life with the sudden death of Prime Minister Levi Eshkol. On March 17, 1969, Golda Meir was unanimously elected Israel's fourth premier. On taking office she said, "Our fate cannot, and will not be determined by others." This tenacious woman had finally headed the nation she spent a lifetime creating. She was not about to be an easy adversary for the Arabs.

Peace and contentment as head of state of her beloved country was Meir's goal. A ceasefire was negotiated but the borders were in frequent conflict. Meir's leadership was beset by frequent controversy and she was with Israel's Arab enemies "at seventy . . . working longer hours than I had ever worked before and traveling more." Meir's response to her critics who said she should be more concerned with Israel's image, was, "If we have a choice between being dead and pitied and being alive with a bad image, we'd rather be alive and have the bad image." Peace was to be short lived. Imminent danger was always at hand but the ceasefire gave false security to some in her cabinet. Meir had an intuitive sense that war was imminent and advised her cabinet and advisors about her feelings, especially after an Israeli fighter shot down a Libyan Boeing 727 in March 1973, killing 106 people. The plane had inadvertently ventured into Israel's air space and the event was accidental. Meir immediately flew to Washington to meet with President Richard Nixon.

Yom Kippur is the Day of Atonement and the most solemn of Jewish religious holidays. Many of Meir's cabinet members were off on holiday in 1973, but Meir's female intuition sensed something wrong. There were reports of Russians moving out of Arab territories and other signs that made her wary of Arab intentions. Her advisors and cabinet members said, "Don't worry. There won't be a war." Her intuition told her otherwise. Israeli intelligence advised her of Russian families fleeing Syria. She called an emergency meeting at noon on October 5, the day before Yom Kippur, and with very few prominent members in attendance declared, "Look, I have a terrible feeling that this has all happened before. It reminds me of 1967. . . . I think it all means something." Meir's chief of staff, minister of defense, chief of intelligence, and chief of commerce all agreed: "No problem existed." Meir later said, "I should have listened to my heart and ordered a callup. I knew that I should have done so, and I shall live with that terrible knowledge the rest of my life." Meir's intuition proved right on target, with a tragic loss of 2,500 Israeli lives, many of whom would have been saved if Meir's cabinet would have believed in her intuitive powers.

Meir was always courageous and believed strength was important in countries and people. If this woman had not been strong the nation would not have survived. And without her inner strength she would never have had any power with which to operate. Meir was in her mid-seventies during the Yom Kippur War, but never left her office for more than an hour. She slept barely four hours a night, catnapping at her desk in a constant vigil over her beloved nation and its young soldiers. On the fifth day of the war, with annihilation at hand, she called U.S. Secretary of State Henry Kissinger in the middle of the night. His adjutant said it was the middle of the night, wait until morning. Meir said, "I don't care what time it is. We need help today, because tomorrow it may be too late. I will personally fly incognito to meet with Nixon. I want to go as soon as possible."* Meir's strength and confidence worked and an American airlift arrived in time to save the battle and the nation. This resilient seventy-five-year-old woman had once again used her intransigent spirit to save her nation by refusing to accept no as an alternative to action.

Meir resigned on April 10, 1974, after five turbulent years as prime minister. She was about to turn seventy-six: "It is beyond my strength to continue carrying this burden," she said. There were eighty thousand Jews in Palestine when she arrived in 1921, and three million when she left office in 1974. This ever-confident woman was a pillar of strength her whole life. Her final statement as a government official gave credence to her hawkish and powerful approach to survival: "If Israel is not strong, there will be no peace." She may well have said, "If woman is not strong and confident, she will have no power," which is the essence of this powerful woman.

Temperament: Intuitive-Thinking

"Golda had an unerring instinct and intuition . . . both logical and intuitive at the same time," said biographer Ralph Martin (1988). Martin was describing Meir as a Promethean spirit, a union of intuition and rationality that is the personality combination most often found in creative visionaries. Meir had additional qualities that helped her become one of the world's great states-women. She was a confident charismatic with a flair for inspirational speak-

---

*Kissinger capitulated and invited her to Washington.

ing. Her motivational speeches were her most noted talent, a trait shared with Oprah Winfrey and Mary Kay Ash. David Ben-Gurion heard Meir's speech to the British Parliament and commented, "I trembled at her daring words. Her speech shook the convention. She spoke with genius, assertively, bitterly, with hurt, sensible." U.S. Supreme Court Justice Arthur Goldberg called her a "firebrand." Meir had always been the "Golden Girl," which was sometimes lost on those who knew her only as a seventy-year-old matronly woman.

Meir's self-confidence was legend. She went to the Vatican in 1973, the first such visit by any Israeli official. The pope was taken aback when she took an offensive, not defensive position in their discussions. She told him, "We are through forever with being at the mercy of others." Meir's visit represented the first official recognition of the Jewish State by the Vatican, a testimony to her intransigent confidence in Zionism. She admitted in her autobiography, "I had more than my share of self-confidence" during this time.

Meir was blessed with strength and determination along with an extroverted and vibrant personality. She never equivocated over any decision. Biographer Peggy Mann spent time with her in Tel Aviv in 1970 and said, "When she makes a decision, it's made." Mann said Meir's cabinet was jokingly referred to as "Golda's Kitchen Cabinet," with "decisions cooked up in Golda's kitchen." Simcha Dinitz, Meir's political advisor, said, "She has the best qualities of a woman—intuition, insight, sensitivity, compassion—plus the qualities of a man—strength, determination, practicality, purposefulness." Meir's intuitive powers give credence to the potential for future female leaders. Meir's intuition during the 1973 Yom Kippur War was a demonstration of the female as leader using her intuition to sense danger. Meir's keen sense was ignored by the male members of her cabinet, which cost many Israeli lives.

Family versus Career

Meir married Morris Meyerson, an introverted classical musician on December 27, 1917. She was nineteen and already a passionate Zionist who made Morris promise that Palestine would be in their future. He promised, but didn't know the urgency of this driven woman. The party called on her to travel to the West Coast to raise money for Zionism just weeks after their marriage and she left saying, "The party said I should go, so I went." Not long after that trip Meir decided that Palestine was to be the couple's Elysian Fields, and she went. Morris did not want to go but capitulated to the much stronger Golda. Morris was miserable living in the kibbutz in Palestine and convinced his wife to leave for Tel Aviv to have their children. This scenario would continue as Meir was always willing to sacrifice everything for the realization of her dreams. She and Morris went their separate ways shortly after she met Shazar

Zalman in 1928, although they never divorced. Meir had always been willing to sacrifice herself, her family, and her husband for Israel.

Meir had intimate relationships with some of the greatest minds in Israeli history. She had an affair with the scintillating and womanizing Zalman Shazar. He was a "wild man with an encyclopedic mind" who became her mentor and lover. Ironically, this mesmerizing and hypnotic orator was to become the future president of Israel who swore her in as prime minister in 1968. This may be the only instance in history where a president had sworn in a prime minister who had been his former lover (Martin, 1988). These two traveled the world together during the thirties. Shazar promised to get a divorce and marry Meir, but he never did. Even so, this dynamic leader was without doubt the most influential man in her life. The affair was to be the beginning of numerous such liaisons which caused her detractors to label her "Meir the Mattress."

Meir had intimate relationships with many of the great men in the Zionist world. David Ben-Gurion, David Remez, Bert Katznelson, Zalman Aranne, and Henry Montor were the most noteworthy giants with whom she worked and played during the formative stages of her career. They were all instrumental in her drive to the top. Remez's love lasted a lifetime and he gave her many assignments within the party. Meir said, "He was my real compass" and her mentor for a long time. She often admitted, "I loved him very much." Katznelson, known as the Socrates of Israel, appointed Meir to her first executive position as head of the Department of Mutual Aid during the thirties. Meir remarked that Arrane brought fantasy into her life. Montor was a dynamic American fund raiser. He became her confidante and lover when she was seeking funds in America during the thirties.

Meir's actions were without malice. She was just a passionate woman who lived life as she saw and felt it. She was so driven that she never stopped to worry about who was left at the gate. Remez was a life-long lover and even his wife was enamored of Meir's charisma. Mrs. Remez described Meir as having "enormous personal magic." Meir admitted placing her career ahead her family: "I know that my children, when they were small, suffered a lot on my account." This dedicated workaholic would have sacrificed her very being for Zioniss—it was synonymous with her career; it was her family.

Life Crises

Meir's life was one continual crisis from her birth in poverty-stricken rural Russia to her days during the twenties in Jerusalem when she nearly died of starvation. Meir was born in the middle of the pogroms in Russia in a peasant environment, and she never really got over the trauma of those early years. "At age four I remember how scared I was, and how angry. . . . If there is any logical explanation . . . for the direction my life has taken . . . it is the desire and determination to save Jewish children from a similar experience." She added, "I have a pogrom complex." The killing of Jews was what Meir remembered as a child. When her mentor and role model sister Shana became an ardent revolutionary, she was destined to a life in support of Zionism.

If the pogroms were not bad enough, Meir came into the world after five siblings had died from the dastardly conditions in rural Russia. She and her sisters lived with their grandparents during the time her father was locating their new home in America. It was an unhappy period for Meir. She never forgot those terrible years and while in her seventies she reminisced about the tragedy of children facing an early life like hers: "All men, women, and children, everywhere . . . are entitled to spend their lives productively and free of humiliation." Zionism and a free Israel was her answer, based on her own early experience with crises. Meir dedicated her whole life to the eradication of those elements that tormented her childhood. Such horrors as "Christ killers" flung as epithets would not be possible in an independent Jewish state.

Transience is an important factor in fostering independence and creative vigor in potential creative geniuses. Moving to new cultures enhances self-sufficiency and coping with the unknown. Meir had such experiences beyond the norm, which appear to have contributed to the development of her creative vision. She moved from Kiev to Pinsk at age five, was smuggled out of Russia at age eight, arrived in Milwaukee without ever having attended school (her sister Shana taught her to read and write), ran away to Denver at age fourteen, came back to Milwaukee at age sixteen and landed in Palestine at age twenty-two. Meir had also traveled America preaching the gospel according to Zionism. Meir then became an international vagabond for the next thirty years, traveling from continent to continent while actually living in Israel, the United States, and Russia. No other female in this book, with the possible exception of Jane Fonda, had the same amount of transience in her life. And none faced death constantly as Meir did. Her intransigence and resilience were definitely a function of the trauma and crises in her life.

Meir's optimism allowed her to succeed. She had so much confidence that nothing ever deterred her from her goals. It is nothing short of amazing that anyone could have a positive attitude in a life constantly beset by death, starvation, and catastrophe. Meir's life was lived in constant crisis and only optimism and an awesome self-confidence allowed Meir to succeed and become a creative visionary.

Intransigent Confidence

Golda Meir was an optimistic woman who was confident to a fault. Her iron will was similar to that of Margaret Thatcher, who acceded to the head of the British political system just one decade after Meir rose to the highest office in Israel. Meir was certain in the face of ridicule and derision. She was fearless with death lurking around each corner. Her will was indomitable when there was no reason for such conviction. In other words, Meir's confidence was a function of her internal self-esteem and image. Even so, she maintained great humility throughout her life. She said, "I have never forgotten that I came from a poor family or ever fooled myself into thinking I was honored anywhere for my beauty, wisdom, or erudition." An indication of her strength of character occurred during the Yom Kippur conflict, when she said, "Intransigence became my middle name; I had decided there was not to be a repetition of Hitler's Final Solution." Meir resolved to stay in Israel until death and convinced her countrymen to do the same. She had fought to build the nation of Israel and was not about to see it taken away without the greatest fight the world had ever seen.

One irony of Meir's accomplishments is her nonreligious orientation. She became head of a state highly identified with religious orthodoxy. It would seem that anyone so driven would have been devout. Not so with Meir. When she was married in Milwaukee in 1917 she and Morris decided not to get married in the temple by a rabbi—an unheard of request in her community. Meir's mother was beside herself. Golda said, "We were sociologists, tolerant of tradition, but in no way bound by ritual. We neither wanted nor needed a religious ceremony." Meir's mother persevered and the couple was married by a rabbi.

Meir realized her youthful dreams because of her dedicated focus and confidence. She was a living example of the aphorism "If you will it, it is not a dream." Meir's teenage nickname, "Zionut," was prophetic, as that was her mental state throughout most of her life. Meir passionately believed and it was that belief that drove her to eminence in her chosen profession. She was fearless and rebellious and never equivocated on any decision. Meir was virtually ego-less in that she accepted her fate and never attempted to use her friends and lovers to attain power. They bestowed power on her because she deserved it. Meir helped create a nation through her mesmerizing and tenacious dialogue, the subtlety of which was lost on many. She launched an international public relations campaign for "share of mind on Judaism." She raised the money that saved the country in 1948, and then helped save it through her spellbinding diplomacy. Without Meir's intransigent will and awesome self-confidence the state of Israel would probably not have come into being.

Summary

Golda Meir was a strong but simple woman. On election to the top position in her nation she said, "I was dazed. I had never planned to be Prime Minister. . . . I had never planned any position. . . . I had planned to come to Palestine, to go to Mehravia, to be active in the labor movement." Meir accepted her destiny with the utmost humility and then became so diligent in fulfilling her responsibilities that she never left her office for days at a time. How many men would have done that? The Israeli press wrote: "It is difficult for a people whose religion assigns women a place of honor in the home to accept the idea of a woman at the head of a political department. With all due respect to women of good sense and diligence a woman should not be placed at the helm of one of our central political bodies." (Martin, 1988)

Were they wrong! Meir had only one God and that was the world of Zionism where the Jewish people could call some nation home. Helping create that was her genius and her only agenda in life. Meir confirmed this saying, "I have no ambition to become somebody." Her lack of clothes, makeup, and the other symbols of success are testimony to her simple needs. All Meir needed was the realization of her dream. To this end Meir was a dedicated disciple of her nation; fearless, she never shied away from any responsibility. Confirmation of her fearlessness is her statement, "I can honestly say that I was never deflected from doing something because I thought I might fail."

Golda Meir is one of the world's great women. She helped change the world for the better because she—like Martin Luther King, Jr.—had a dream. She never allowed her personal needs or wants to detour her from the path to that dream. She focused on creating a Zionist state and when it came to fruition she focused on keeping it safe. When the nation asked Meir to become its leader, she left the solitude of her home, books, and music and led her nation through a war of survival. Her daughter, Sarah, is married and living in Israel. Her son, Menachem, is a concert cellist who studied under Pablo Casals. She is in every respect the creative female visionary who reached the top because of her emotional and mental commitment to what she believed. Golda Meir bought into a childhood dream and spent her life chasing it. She left the world better than she found it and did so with nothing other than her personal integrity and self-confidence.

Golda (Mabovitz) Meyerson (Meir)
Israeli politician
b. May 3, 1898, Kiev; d. December 8, 1978, Tel Aviv

Dominant trait: Intransigent confidence

Religion: Jewish, not devout

Motto: "Never be excited. Always be calm and act coolly. Be brave."

Philosophy: Herzl's "If you will it, it is no dream"; "If you believe in something you should go try to accomplish it." "Teaching girls various trades are more important than women's rights."

Nicknames: "Golden Girl" (from young girl to mid-life), "Zionut" (as a teenager), "Meir the Mattress" (by political enemies), "Intransigent" (by politicians)

Creation/innovation: Instrumental in the creation of the state of Israel: first female prime minister, 1969 to 1974.

Products/contributions: Zionist leader, consummate money raiser, brilliant diplomat

Successes: Inspirational and mesmerizing speaker. Prime minister of Israel for five years

Self-description: "I had more than my fair share of self-confidence."

Birth order: Second-born daughter; sister Shana 9 years older; sister Clara 4 years younger. Four boys and a girl died between Shana and Golda's birth, due to peasant conditions.

Childhood transience: Moved within Russia at age 4 and to Milwaukee, Wisconsin, at age 8; to Denver, Colorado, at age 14; and to Israel at age 23.

Father's occupation: Moshe, a carpenter; mother, Bluma, operated grocery store

Mentors: Sister Shana, Eleanor Roosevelt, Shazar Zalman, David Remez, Bert Katznelson, Zalman Aranne, and Henry Montor (the latter five being political giants and lovers)

Childhood upbringing: Pogroms in Russia imprinted fear of oppression; Shana's influence as revolutionary Zionist inevitably led her to Zionism

Formal education: Sister taught her until age 8. Graduated Milwaukee H.S. with honors; one year at Milwaukee Normal Teachers College. Left to join Paole Zion.

Life crises: Pogroms in Russia at age 4, near starvation in 1920s kibbutz, and in Jerusalem; she faced death every day from Arabs in Israel

Marriages/liaisons: Married Morris Meyerson at 19 in 1917, in Milwaukee. They separated in 1928. Had two children, Sarah and Menachem. Had numerous liaisons from age twenty-five on; six of her relationships were with giants of Zionism

---

Risk-taking: "*No* fear of failure, I can honestly say that I was never deflected from doing something because I thought I might fail." Carried hand grenades in her bra and dressed like Moslem wife to meet King Abdullah of Jordan.

Temperament: Extroverted-intuitive-thinking-judger: Promethean temperament

Behavior: Fearless "firebrand," rebellious, self-confident, strong-willed

Career vs. family: Constantly sacrificed family, husband, and children for Zionism.

Self-esteem: Built in childhood through survival in ghastly conditions

Hobbies: Singing, reading, and speaking on independent states including Africa

Heroes: Sister Shana, Theodore Herzl, Eleanor Roosevelt, David Ben-Gurion, Zalman Shazar, David Remez

Honors: In 1969 she ranked fourth among America's most-admired women. Honorary degrees from University of Wisconsin, and Reform Jewish Hebrew College

15

Ayn Rand—Macro-oriented Intuitor

The man who produces an idea in any field of rational endeavor—the man who discovers new knowledge—is the permanent benefactor of humanity.

Every man is free to rise as far as he's able or willing, but it's only the degree to which he *thinks* that determines the degree to which he'll *rise*.

An inventor is a man who asks, Why? of the universe and let's nothing stand between the answer and his mind.

I swear by my life and my love of it—that I will never live for the sake of another man, nor ask another man to live for mine.
　　　　　　　　　　　　　　　　　　　　—John Galt, *Atlas Shrugged*

Ayn Rand, Russian immigrant, epitomizes the capitalist credo and entrepreneurial spirit embodied in the female success stories in this book. This woman stepped off a boat at Ellis Island at the age of twenty-one, speaking little English, with fifty dollars in her pocket and a dream to change the world via the written word. She proceeded to change the way the world thinks about sociopolitical economics and has had an enormous impact on the world of entrepreneurship, government, and economic philosophy. Her name is synonymous with the visionary Promethean temperament to such a degree that she is listed as the prototype for the classic intuitive-thinking personality in most psychological journals.

Ayn Rand's adulation of egoism and laissez-faire individualism made her the surrogate mother of both objectivism (a morality of rational self-interest) and the Libertarian Party (an antigovernment political party). A lasting tribute to her image and philosophy of life was enacted at her 1982 funeral in New York City, where the only flowers were in the form of a giant dollar sign venerating her idolization of the capitalist way of life. Even in death Rand defiantly insisted that "enlightened self-interest" was the only correct metaphysical and epistemological system worth pursuing. She was a creative genius of the first order and a tremendous influence on the American political system, educators, philosophers, and entrepreneurial spirits everywhere, including most of the women in this book. Her influence emerged from her dedicated writings and constant lecturing, with her two best-selling novels establishing man as "Ideal Man" and man as "Rational Being."

Rand's personal philosophy was based on "man as a heroic being, with his own happiness as the moral purpose of his life, with productive achievement as his noblest activity, and reason as his only guide." This quote could have been imprinted on the psyches of every one of the thirteen contemporary visionaries in this volume, each of whom has emulated this philosophy in one sense or another. This ideology also epitomizes the life and drive of Rand's personal role model, Catherine the Great, along with other great historical female visionaries such as Margaret Mead, Madame Curie, Rachel Carson, and Mother Teresa.

Personal Life History

Ayn Rand was born in the shadow of Catherine the Great in St. Petersburg, Russia, on February 2, 1905. She was raised in the artistic splendor and iconoclastic heritage of her role model Catherine. She was the first child of a self-made Jewish merchant, Fronz, whom she adored, and a housewife gadfly mother, Anna, whom she hated. Named Allisa Rosenbaum, Rand was the first of three daughters. She was a precocious child who taught herself to read and write at age four at a time when Trotsky, Lenin, and Stalin were in the process of revolutionizing her native country. She was a byproduct of that system although diametrically opposed to its philosophy. She was an introverted child who used books as her escape and fell in love with French novels before the age of ten. Victor Hugo became her favorite author. She decided to become a writer by age nine, and said in the classic Promethean style, "I will write about how people could be, not as they are." Rand's favorite novel was *Les Miserables,* and her favorite early hero was Cyrus, a sacrificial French hero of adventure novels.

Rand says it was at this early age that she began to think in macro larger-than-life terms with "principles" being an important part of her thinking. She said, "I began to ask myself the why? of ideas." She said, "I don't remember the genesis of my stories—they would come to me as a 'whole.' " Rand described herself in her childhood as a "hero worshipper." She said, "I would have been extremely indignant at any touch of the idea that women's place was in the home or young ladies should be young ladies." She said, "I was always in favor of . . . intellectual equality, but women as such didn't interest me."

The outbreak of World War I was devastating to the nine-year-old Rand as St. Petersburg was under siege and the family was almost killed. The Russian Revolution occurred when she was twelve and her father lost everything. He became just another laborer struggling to put food on the table and save the family from the hated Reds. This left an indelible imprint on Rand. When she first heard the Communist doctrine of "you must live for the state," as a teenager, it was about as disgusting a concept as she had ever heard. Thereafter she dedicated her life to proving it wrong. She said that at age thirteen Victor Hugo influenced her more than anyone because he was so far above everyone else. His work drove her to believe in the power of the written word as a means to great achievement. Rand said, "Victor Hugo is the greatest novelist in world literature. . . . One does not settle for any lesser values, neither in books nor in life."

This set the stage for Rand's emotional commitment to write stories of an epic scale based on heroic accomplishment. At age seventeen she told a shocked college philosophy professor, "My philosophical views are not part of the history of philosophy yet. But they will be." He gave her an "A" for her tenacity and confidence. While in college her cousin had read Nietzsche, whom Rand had never heard of, and gave her one of his books with the prophetic comment, "Here is someone that you should read, because he beat you to all your ideas." Rand entered the University of Leningrad at age sixteen and graduated in 1924 at age nineteen with a degree in history. She worked briefly as a tourist museum guide before leaving for Chicago at age twenty-one for a two-week visit. She bid her family farewell, never intending to return. She said, "I saw America then as the freest country in the world, the country of the individual."

Rand landed in New York speaking no English and armed with nothing but a typewriter and some clothes raised from her mother's sale of her jewelry. Ironically, the ever-inventive Russian immigrant selected the name Ayn as a shortened version of her given name Alissa (or Alice) and exercised her creativity by selecting her surname from the logo of her Remington Rand typewriter. After a few months in Chicago, Rand moved on to Hollywood intent on a career in acting and/or writing for the movie industry. She met a gorgeous young actor named Frank O'Connor, whom she married in 1929. Part of O'Connor's romantic allure was based on her expiring visa. Her marriage placated the immigration officials, who granted her U.S. citizenship in 1931. They would be married for fifty years and he would become her friend, confidant, and editor, but she never took his name. She always intended to become an eminent writer and decided to keep her own name as a testimony to her future, even though its lineage was a used typewriter.

Rand began writing and finished her first play, *Penthouse Legend,* in 1933.

It was produced in 1934 on Broadway for a short run. This gave Rand the incentive to write her first novel, *We the Living,* published by Macmillan in 1936. It was her first work decrying the totalitarian state and those who would sacrifice their "self" for the "state." Rand then embarked on her first great novel, *The Fountainhead,* which took her four years to complete. At times the workaholic would spend thirty straight hours at the typewriter, without a break for food or sleep.

Howard Roark was the hero protagonist of *The Fountainhead* and became the vehicle for espousing Rand's philosophical doctrine. Roark would be her first hero, created as the "ideal man." The novel was a fight between good and evil: Roark was "good" and the bureaucratic establishment "evil." Rand's husband told a reporter after *The Fountainhead* became a sensational hit, "She has total honesty. . . . She never wondered if she was going to succeed. The only question was how long it would take." It didn't take long. In 1943, *The Fountainhead* was published to acclaim with many important critics hailing it as a remarkable effort. The *New York Times* book review of May 1943 called her "a writer of great power" with a "subtle and ingenious mind and the capacity of writing brilliantly, beautifully, bitterly." The book made the national bestseller list twenty-six times during 1945 and Rand was hired to write the screen version for Gary Cooper. She was on her way.

Professional History

Rand began writing *Anthem,* eventually published in 1938, while still a teenager in St. Petersburg, Russia, but knew she could never complete and publish a novel on the "defense of egoism" in Bolshevik Russia. She delayed finishing it until she arrived in the United States in 1926. Upon her arrival, Rand first worked as a movie extra and screenwriter for Cecil B. DeMille, later as a waitress during the Depression, and often as a secretary. She worked as a freelance writer to pay the bills while writing her two great novels based on her objectivist philosophy. Rand authored *We the Living* (1936), *Anthem* (1938), *The Fountainhead* (1943), *Atlas Shrugged* (1957), *For the New Intellectual* (1961), *The Virtue of Selfishness* (1964), and *Philosophy—Who Needs It?* (1982). These seven books have sold close to thirty million copies during the past forty years. Literary critic Lorine Purette, after the publication of *The Fountainhead,* wrote, "Good novels of ideas are rare at any time. This is the only novel of ideas written by an American woman that I can recall." Later, in 1964, *Playboy* wrote, "Ayn Rand . . . is among the most outspoken and important intellectual voices in America today."

Rand's two major works are now considered classics even though the experts of the publishing industry initially refused to publish them. *The Fountainhead* and *Atlas Shrugged* were said to be "too intellectual" and had "no mass market" by the publishers, twelve of whom turned down *The Fountainhead.* They said the book was too controversial, with an improbable story line. Bobbs Merrill finally published it despite thinking it would never sell. *The Fountainhead* sold four million copies in the next ten years and became a classic cult book. Hollywood made it into a 1949 movie starring Gary Cooper as Howard Roark— the "Ideal Man" who became the fictional character defending individualism and egoism. Rand was convinced that the world was being ruled by the laws of the tribe, which were destined to make man into a mediocre animal motivated by altruism and hedonism. This first major work was aimed at exposing Communism as the mortal enemy of creative and innovative man. In Roark's words, "We are approaching a world in which I cannot permit myself to live." Roark perseveres in the book to become triumphant as an iconoclastic symbol for the ideal man who in many ways exemplifies the thirteen superachievers in this book.

Rand wrote the first line of *Atlas Shrugged* in 1946 with the apocalyptical line "Who is John Galt?" and then spent the next twelve years attempting to answer the question in philosophically sound dialogue. John Galt's famous radio speech toward the end of the book took two years to write and was 500,000 words in length. (For those not familiar with the magnitude of that number, the book you're now reading is less than 175,000 words long.) In her inimitable style, Rand refused to allow Random House to cut one word of the dialogue. "Would you cut the Bible?" she asked. The hero of the book was really "man's mind," as seen through protagonist John Galt, who in actuality was Rand's alter ego. *Atlas Shrugged* aimed at "a moral defense of capitalism" and the pursuit of "reason." Rand was preaching the same gospel that has made the thirteen women in this book great: "Every man [woman] is free to rise as far as he is capable or willing, but it's only the degree to which he thinks that determines the degree to which he will rise."

Atlas Shrugged is more epic myth than novel and expounds on the philosophical errors of collective societies. John Galt epitomizes the entrepreneurial spirit in mankind, which was never more apparent than his famous line, "I will never live for the sake of another man, nor ask another man to live for mine." And Galt's closing action was to draw the almighty dollar sign in the sand with the admonition, "We are going back to the world." Rand despised altruism and hedonism and espoused Nietzsche's "Overman" or "Superman" concept with the aphorism, "The strong are destined to conquer and the weak to perish." She instilled in John Galt all of the traits of the consummate "Superman." He was annointed with "intransigent rationality," "inviolate self-esteem," and "implacable realism" incarnate. Speaking on capitalism Galt says, "There is no anonymous achievement. There is no collective creation. Every step in the development of a great discovery bears the name of its originator. . . . There was no collective achievement involved. There never has been. There never will be. There never can be. There is no collective brain." *Atlas Shrugged* has become a classic philosophical novel in the same sense that *Crime and Punishment* by Dostoyevsky has become a classic psychological novel. Since 1957 it has sold in excess of five million copies and still sells over a hundred thousand copies each year.

After her monumental achievement with *Atlas Shrugged,* Rand spent the rest of her career defending and preaching the gospel of objectivism. The *Ayn Rand Letter* was produced for many years preaching the merits of objectivism, and the *Objectivist Bulletin* is still in print. Philosophy classes now use Rand's books as texts for classes on metaphysics and epistemology. Rand has had an enormous impact on society and capitalism and probably had more to do with the demise of the Berlin Wall than all of the politicians and bureaucrats in the world put together. The Nathaniel Branden Institute in New York City became the center for the objectivist philosophy, and Alan Greenspan is one of the more famous of its twenty-five thousand graduates during the 1960s. Greenspan became the economic advisor to presidents Richard Nixon and Gerald Ford, and now serves as chairman of the Federal Reserve Board. Rand herself was a visiting lecturer espousing the objectivist philosophy during the 1960s and 1970s at many university campuses including Harvard, Yale, and Columbia.

Temperament: Intuitive-Thinking

Ayn Rand was an independent spirit and workaholic blessed with macro-vision. She was an introvert with an intuitive-thinking personality type as defined by the Myers-Briggs personality scale. Her Promethean temperament is often used to describe the creative and innovative personality type of behavior by psychologists testing personality. Rand was considered dogmatic in her beliefs and was even arrogant in her dealings with less gifted individuals. She was somewhat reclusive and impatient to a fault. She was a hit on three Johnny Carson shows during 1967 and 1968 and received the most mail in the history of NBC's late night shows. Mike Wallace was reluctant to interview Rand because of her reputation as a difficult subject. Rand would not appear on television talk shows unless she was guaranteed that she would be interviewed alone, would not be edited, and would not be confronted with quotes from her enemies. Wallace said she captivated his crew with her mesmerizing personality, and when he sent his staff for a pre-interview, "They all fell in love with her."

Rand never equivocated on anything. She was a true iconoclast who constantly berated liberals: "Intellectuals are the parasites of subsidized classrooms." She described her favorite contemporary author, Mickey Spillane, as "A true moralist. His characters are all black and white, never gray. Grays don't interest me." She felt the same about mankind, "Just as man's wealth is self-made, so is his soul self-made." Rand was quite reclusive and very serious on most subjects. Living alone after her husband died in the late 1970s she was still a workaholic who loved classical music and argued her philosophy with messianic fervor. Her favorite motto was "Check your premises and watch your implications," indicative of her precise and logical approach to life and philosophy. Rand's lawyer sums up her personality with this observation: "Dealing with Ayn Rand was like taking a post-doctoral course in mental functioning. . . . Her lucidity and brilliance was a light so strong I don't think anything will ever be able to put it out. *The Fountainhead* is Ayn Rand" (B. Branden, 1962).

Rand was a fan of Aristotle and adopted his aphorism that "Fiction is of greater philosophic importance than history, because history represents things only as they are, while fiction represents them 'as they might be and ought to be.' " Rand was a lifelong antifeminist who regarded man as superior, but she considered Dagny Taggert of *Atlas Shrugged* to be the "ideal woman." She felt that love was not a self-sacrifice but "the most profound assertion of your own needs and values. It is for your own happiness that you need the person you love, and that is the greatest compliment, the greatest tribute you can pay to that person." Rand decided that she was an atheist at the age of fourteen and wrote in her diary:

> First there are no reasons to believe in God, that there is no proof of the belief; and second, that the concept of God is insulting and degrading to man—it implies that the highest possible is not to be reached by man, that he is an inferior being who can only worship an ideal he will never achieve.

The personality temperament of Ayn Rand is identical to that found in Catherine the Great, Einstein, Edison, Picasso, and the majority of the female leaders in this volume. She personifies the Promethean spirit regardless of whether one agrees or disagrees with her beliefs. Her philosophy is what defines her and, in her words, she "is the concept of man as a heroic being, with his own happiness as the moral purpose of his life, with productive achievement as his noblest activity, and reason as his only absolute."

Family/Career Dichotomy

Ayn Rand married Frank O'Connor, a struggling actor, during the 1920s "because he is so beautiful." He was the personification of the unconscious hero image she so adored. She desired to be around heroes and O'Connor was a living, breathing Hollywood hero. He was six years her senior, and the marriage of convenience gave her a permanent visa and citizenship in 1931. She would say later that she had a shotgun wedding and Uncle Sam was holding the gun. O'Connor became her editor and companion throughout her life, even though she embarked on a thirteen-year affair with Nathaniel Branden in the mid-1950s.

Rand had become Branden's mentor after he was captivated by *The Fountainhead* as a young Canadian student at the University of California at Los Angeles. Branden idolized Rand and they became closer and closer. The mentor and disciple relationship evolved into an emotional and physical one in 1954. According to Nathaniel's wife Barbara Branden, Rand, the consummate rational thinking woman, called Branden's wife, together with her husband for a rational and intellectual resolution to this emotional crisis. Rand convinced them to accept the liaison in philosophical terms as an "intellectually agreeable sexual encounter" good for all parties. Branden was twenty-five years younger than Rand, worshiped her, and was a devoted disciple of her writing and philosophy. Rand viewed their affair as a sexual release for two kindred spirits, but more accurately, as a metaphorical scene from her about-to-be-completed work, *Atlas Shrugged*. Ayn was Dagny Taggert and Nathaniel was John Galt, and their fantasy was being acted out in real life in the heartland of capitalism—Manhattan. Barbara Branden, Nathaniel's wife said in her biography on Rand, "Ayn never lived or loved in reality. It was theater or fantasy in Ayn's dream world. Even sex with Branden."

Branden became Rand's lover, confidant, and heir to the throne of objectivism. He devoted his life to spreading its gospel. He created the Nathaniel Branden Institute, dedicated to the study of objectivism; he started the *Objectivist Newsletter,* to communicate the philosophy worldwide; and he published the *Ayn Rand Newsletter,* to espouse capitalism. Branden was the individual most responsible for spreading the objectivist philosophy, which was ultimately to become the credo of the Libertarian party. In 1958, Branden fell in love with a younger woman and attempted a rational split with Rand. She was now sixty-three, he was thirty-eight, and Rand saw his rejection as a denial of truth. Unconsciously she saw it for what it was—a rejection of her due to her age. Rand was destroyed. She never spoke to Branden again.

Rand's career took precedence over every aspect of her life. She never considered children; there was never time. She dedicated her childbearing years to the completion of her lifelong dream, writing *The Fountainhead.* Soon thereafter, in 1946, she wrote the line "Who is John Galt?"—she was forty-one at the time—and she was never deterred from finishing that challenge. Frank O'Connor was supportive, following her down the highway of life on her terms. Ayn Rand sacrificed everything for the realization of her childhood dreams: her Russian family, her husband, and her maternal nature. She would have said it was a small price to pay since she certainly achieved her childhood ambition of creating "Superman"-type heroes that will survive as classics for the literary and philosophical worlds to argue over for centuries to come.

Life Crises

Rand was devastated at the age of nine when her Russian family was almost killed by the invasion of German troops during World War I. Three years later, when she was just twelve, the chaos turned to total disaster with the Bolshevik Revolution, which took her father's business and caused the family to leave their home and possessions in St. Petersburg and flee to Odessa in the Crimea. During the trip they were almost killed by thieves who accosted them on the road. The family returned to St. Petersburg three years later and found that the Communists had seized control of all business and industry and ruled with an iron fist. The family lived in daily fear for their lives from the rampaging Bolsheviks. They lived off past savings and survived by their wits. The Communist slogan "Man must live for the state" became inculcated into the psyche of this precocious teenager and she vowed at this time to show the world that the "state should live for man," not vice versa. Rand never forgot this horrifying part of her life, in much the same way as the early days in Kiev shaped Golda Meir. Psychologists have recently learned that superlearning takes place in crisis-type environments, which puts people into a theta-type state of stupor or shock. It appears that these early crises, when Rand associated everything horrible with the Communists, spurred her to a lifetime dedicated to the destruction of anything associated with state control. She said later, "I began to understand that politics was a moral issue" and "I was opposed to the government or society or any authority's imposing anything on anyone."

Rand was "desperately alone as a teenager" and very unhappy with her life. She was always a serious child and valued daring and chivalry as her means of excitement. She did not like her mother, even though it was her mother who got her the visa to America. She idolized her father but was not close to him, because he was absent a lot, first because of business and later due to the Russian Revolution. Rand's introspective nature led her to seek out books as a haven for her imagination. Victor Hugo was her idol, with Dostoyevsky and Tolstoy close behind. These great writers supplied Rand with fantasy heroes who were her escape into a better reality. Rand finally did escape to America in 1926, and after stepping off the boat on Ellis Island and seeing the great metropolis with its skyscrapers, she said, "This is the symbol of everything I admire in life."

Macro-Vision and Intuitive Success

Rand's macro-vision and intuitive-thinking personality drove her to enormous accomplishments. She wrote the greatest philosophical epic novel in history in a language she could barely speak. Her achievements were attained because she never lost sight of her childhood objective of turning heroes into great philosophical spokesmen for society. Howard Roark became the personification of the consummate individualist and John Galt became synonymous with Reason. In Rand's words, *"Atlas Shrugged* is a mystery story, not about the murder of a man's body, but about the murder—and rebirth—of man's spirit." Rand felt that *The Fountainhead* was based on "the ideal man." Her temperament gave her the impetus to revere the possibilities and opportunities in life. It made her despise negativity in any form and specifically the mediocrity associated with altruism, hedonism, and collectivism. Rand's desire for heroes and larger-than-life characters was not only spawned early in her life, they were also consistent with her macro-vision of life. She always viewed the world in a holistic fashion, with the entrepreneur at the core of what was right. Risk-taking and innovation, her icons, have never been more succinctly and accurately described as in John Galt's treatise in *Atlas Shrugged*:

> The man who produces an idea in any field of rational endeavor—the man who discovers new knowledge—is the permanent benefactor of humanity. . . . In proportion to the mental energy he spent, the man who creates a new invention receives but a small percentage of his value in terms of material payment, no matter what fortune he makes, no matter what millions he earns.

This speech espouses a philosophy and personality type uniquely entrepreneurial, creative, and innovative. Rand's Promethean spirit was consistent with her philosophical dogma. Both are succinctly manifested in this quote: "I submit that any man who ascribes success to luck has never achieved anything and has no inkling of the relentless effort which achievement requires." These last two quotations are the essence of the intuitive-thinking personality, which views life in a macro right-brain way. This mentality is necessary for all great achievement and critical in all great achievers in life, be they men or women.

Summary

Ayn Rand conjures up feelings of derision and hatred from most liberals and intellectuals. She felt strongly that the world was "black and white not gray—Good vs. Evil—and there is no justification ever for choosing any part of what you know to be evil." Compromise was not in her vocabulary. Philosophers loved her or hated her, but for the most part never accepted her. The literary community never accepted her, but she outsold the very individuals who defiled her. Certainly no one ever spoke of Rand with indifference. This consummate champion of entrepreneurship was "challenging the cultural traditions of two and a half thousand years" and consequently was bound to upset most religions, political systems, and economic dogmas. Rand was dogmatic in her belief in the freedom of the individual to take risks, and was the champion of those who desired to risk changing the existing ways of things. That is what creative genius, entrepreneurship, and innovation are all about. Ayn Rand is the quintessential guru of the philosophy and temperament needed to compete in such a world.

Rand died on March 8, 1982, in her beloved New York City. The *New York Times* wrote, "Ayn Rand's body lay next to the symbol she adopted as her own—a six-foot U.S. dollar sign." Rand's enlightened self-interest would have been totally realized if she had lived just eight more years and had seen the crumbling of the hated Berlin Wall and the demise of the Communist Party in Russia. Ayn Rand is destined to go down in history as the philosophic spokesperson for the capitalist system, not unlike the role played by Karl Marx for Communism. Her *Atlas Shrugged* will find its place next to Marx's *Communist Manifesto* in universities and other intellectual habitats whenever political and economic systems are debated.

Ayn Rand was the consummate "creative genius" who emulated her hero, Catherine the Great. She said as a child, "I thought I was exactly like Catherine." And at age fifty-five she said, "You know, I am still waiting to this day" to achieve like Catherine. I believe that history will place Ayn Rand very near Catherine as one of the truly great Russian females who dared to change the world, and then had the temerity to go out and do it.

Alissa Rosenbaum (Ayn Rand)
Author and capitalist philosopher
b. February 2, 1905, St. Petersburg; d. March 6, 1982, New York City

Dominant trait: Macro-vision/Intuitive-thinker

Religion: Atheist (Jewish parents)

Mottos: "$"; "Man is a heroic being, with his own happiness as the moral purpose of his life, with productive achievement as his noblest activity, and reason as his only guide"; "Check your premises and watch your implications."

Philosophy: "Metaphysics = Objective Reality; Epistemology = Reason; Ethics = Self-Interest; Politics = Capitalism." Enlightened self-interest for man

Nickname: "The Fountainhead"

Creation/innovation: Objectivism philosophy and Libertarian party principles

Products/contributions: Eight books, most notably *The Fountainhead* and *Atlas Shrugged*

Success: First philosophical novel in epic form: *Atlas Shrugged*

Self-description: "I'm a hero worshipper"; "Dagny [heroine of *Atlas Shrugged*] is myself with any possible flaws eliminated." Dedicated atheist from age 14.

Birth order: First-born daughter with two younger sisters, Natana and Elena

Childhood transience: Family fled the Bolsheviks when Ayn was 9 and moved from St. Petersburg to Odessa, then back to St. Petersburg when she was 14. Traveled to Switzerland, France, and London. Moved alone to the United States at age 21.

Father's occupation: Self-made man, a Jewish merchant (chemist). Frustrated writer who discussed political philosophy with Ayn as teenager.

Mentors: Catherine the Great, and an autonomous/independent mother.

Childhood upbringing: Raised in individualistic and nonreligious family. Hated mother and idolized father. Defiantly independent. Precocious.

Formal education: Taught herself to read and write at 5. Hated school (knew more than teachers). Went to private school, then graduated from Leningrad University in 1924 at age 19.

Life crises: Lived through horror of WWI at 9, Bolshevik Revolution at 12, near starvation as teenager, and unemployment in U.S. Depression

Marriages/Liaisons: Married Frank O'Connor (1929); had affair with Nathaniel Branden in the 1950s.

Risk-taking: Risked her esteem and acceptance daily with an intransigent rebelliousness against government, the establishment, intellectuals

Temperament: Introverted-intuitive-thinking-judger: Promethean temperament

Behavior: Rebellious independence. Impatient, arrogant, dogmatic visionary

Career vs. family: Sacrificed family for ideology

Self-Esteem: Built in childhood through acceptance from adults due to bright, articulate, and precocious dialogue. Built esteem through rational thought.

Hobbies: Intellectual debate and dialogue on philosophy and politics

Heroes: Catherine the Great, Cyrus (hero from French novel), Aristotle, Nietzsche, Victor Hugo, Dostoyevsky, and Mickey Spillane

Honors: Honorary doctorate, Lewis and Clark College, 1963. Worshipped as goddess of laissez-faire individualism by Libertarian party and *Reason* magazine

16

Gloria Steinem—
Rebellious Social Conscience

And whoever wants to be a creator of good and evil, must first be an annihilator and break values. Thus, the highest evil, belongs to the greatest goodness; but this is being creative.

— Friedrich Nietzsche

Gloria Steinem is the feminist who comes to mind when any issue of consequence is discussed relative to women's rights. She is not only at the forefront of all female issues, both politically and socially, she is a chic multidimensional woman with class, dignity, and intelligence. She has become the confidante of the elite, benefactor to the weak, companion of the rich and famous, femme fatale of our social conscience, and the idyllic mentor for all liberated and thinking women of the world. She has functioned as the uncrowned leader of the women's movement in the United States since 1970. She made the term *radical* chic during the turbulent seventies by adding a dimension of class and sophistication to a movement aimed at changing society.

Steinem's articulate use of the written and spoken word as a means of rebellion was a change from the aggressive demonstrations so prevalent during the sixties. Her attractive, articulate, and educated demeanor was a welcome contrast to the "Women's Lib" stereotype. Most rebellious females had turned off the male power brokers who were in a position to grant concessions and offer legislative relief to the feminist movement. These hostile and sometimes eccentric women dissidents attempted to change the system via adversarial battles of the mind and body, and were not persuasive on terms understood by the male power elite. Not so with Steinem.

Most feminist leaders are angry and have become rebellious mavericks inclined to use defiance and anarchy in order to be heard and to bring about

313

change in an inequitable system. They are prepared to violate the sensibilities of the establishment and upset the norms of the status quo. Many feminists have been prepared to flaunt their lesbianism and alternative lifestyles in order to be heard. Steinem was smarter. She used her femininity to gain a hearing in the hallowed halls of the establishment. As Shakespeare so poignantly showed in *Julius Caesar,* it is easier to destroy from within than from without. Steinem was uniquely equipped to elicit change from the very men with whom she socialized and dated, to the disdain of many of her sisters.

Steinem was determined to change the inequities of the system but was equally determined to accomplish her objectives within the confines of that system; she was therefore an acceptable adversary to those in the influential hierarchy. Steinem's strength was in being overtly heterosexual, educated, middle class, and desirable to those influential individuals she was protesting against. Most feminists of the time were lacking in such an "acceptable persona": unable to identify with their oppressors, they chose to do battle as adversaries, not equals. It is always difficult to change what you do not understand or communicate with those with whom you do not have any empathy. Steinem understood both the problem and the individuals in the system because she was more like them than her defiant sisters. Her ultimate success was due to her ability to empathize with men. She argued for immediate parity and equality while her sisters simply demanded it. Change is usually evolutionary, not revolutionary, therefore Gloria Steinem will go down in history as a greater facilitator of change and social reform than most of her more virulent sisters.

Those in the male establishment identified with Steinem even when they did not agree with her. They had difficulty identifying with most of the homosexual and uneducated faction of the feminist leadership. Steinem's "normal" behavior granted her acceptance in those places where change was being born and therefore she was able to implement many positive changes for the cause of feminism. This talent and her identity with the so-called male establishment has caused Steinem continuing animosity from within the hard-core element of the feminist community. Her femme fatale nature would come back to haunt her during the mid-seventies. Her attractive and acceptable demeanor was a virulent turn-off to many of the renegades within the feminist leadership. They were never comfortable with her ability to operate within both arenas and would never grant her the leadership within the movement that she so wanted.

Steinem is a creative genius due to her contribution to social reform within the women's movement. She had a primary role to play in changing the world for the better relative to issues of female equality. In some respects she has been a renaissance woman: never really working within the corporate womb, Steinem has led a freelance life, worshipping her freedom, and decrying pressures to become part of any permanent organization. Steinem earned her livelihood in many ways, first as a freelance reporter for the *New York Times, Glamour,* and *Ladies Home Journal* among others. She was a model and a consummate interviewer of the rich and famous. She functioned as editor for *Esquire, New York* magazine, and later *Ms.,* in addition to having been the cofounder of *Ms.* magazine. Steinem was also cofounder of the "Women's Action Alliance" along with Bella Abzug, Betty Friedan, and Shirley Chisolm. She found time to author four books, march and lecture for various feminist and minority causes, and assist in various presidential political campaigns. She has been a veritable whirlwind of creative activity that could give her recognition as an innovative genius.

One testimony to Steinem's successful career came when she was named "Woman of the Year" by *McCall's* in 1972. In 1983 she was selected as one of the "Top Ten Most Influential Women in America." Steinem is a visionary of the first order and a woman who has pioneered for women's rights. If one woman was responsible for 1993 being called the "Year of the Woman" it was Gloria Steinem. She was the catalyst for Janet Reno, Hillary Clinton, and the unbelievable success for female candidates as U.S. congresspersons, governors, and senators during the nineties. She has helped change the way society thinks, votes, and functions and for this Steinem is an archetype of female creative genius.

Professional Background

Gloria Steinem's first job came after completing a fellowship in India as co-director of the Independent Research Service. This Boston-based operation turned out to be a front for the Central Intelligence Agency and a source of great controversy after Steinem gained national prominence in the seventies. From this first job Steinem moved to New York City in 1960, where she started her writing career. Her first article for *Esquire* was appropriately titled "The Moral Dilemma of Betty Coed." A prophetic last paragraph in this piece declared, "The real danger of the contraceptive revolution may be the acceleration of woman's role-change without any corresponding change of man's attitude toward her role." Steinem was still not a feminist but only a progressive-thinking female interviewer with a social conscience.

Steinem found her niche as a freelance writer in New York in the early sixties interviewing socialites, a role that would turn out to be great training for her ultimate role of confronting the power elite female issues. Steinem interviewed these people and wrote articles on them for *Esquire, Glamour, Vogue,* the *New York Times, Cosmopolitan, McCall's,* and many other publications. Her charm, charisma, intellectual precocity, and attractive persona helped her gain a foothold in the celebrity interviewing business in a big way.

She wrote articles about Barbra Streisand, James Baldwin, and John Lennon while becoming friends with many of the rich and famous people she interviewed. Regular luncheons were held with the likes of economist John Kenneth Galbraith and New York Mayor John Lindsay.

Steinem wrote an undercover story about the Playboy Club in the early sixties. It was to become her first real foray into the world of discrimination and feminist issues. Her story, "I Was a Playboy Bunny" was written for the now defunct *Show* magazine in 1963. It was an exposé of the sexist environment in which the Playboy bunny was compelled to work. Steinem made much of the fact that bunnies made their living scantily clad and exploited by both patrons and management. Steinem wrote her first book, *The Beach Book,* in 1963, a frivolous work describing the art of sun worshiping. She spent time as a script writer for NBC's "That Was the Week that Was" in 1964–65. In 1968 Steinem made the philosophical transition from the glitzy show business world to serious political issues. Clay Falker gave her a weekly column titled "The City Politic" to write for his new magazine, *New York.* This was to become the vehicle for Steinem's eventual move into political activism. Searching for an interesting story for her column rather than a radical cause, Steinem attended a meeting of the New York liberation group called the Redstockings, which planned to protest the abortion hearings of 1968 in Albany, New York. This case of human suffering would become her life-long rallying cry. She says this was her first realization that it was the "system" and not the "individual" who was at fault. She concluded, "I had thought that my personal problems and experiences were my own and not part of a larger political problem." Her sudden insight awakened her to the inequality and discriminatory practices that existed for blacks, Indians, females, and migrant workers.

Steinem's sudden intuition led her to couple advocacy journalism with political activism. She soon joined migrant worker organizer Cesar Chavez on his Poor People's March in California, served as treasurer for the Committee for the Legal Defense of political activist and Communist Angela Davis, supported U.S. Sen. Eugene McCarthy's insurgent campaign for the 1968 presidential nomination, and backed author Norman Mailer for the mayoralty of New York City. Steinem then wrote an article, "After Black Power, Women's Liberation" and made the transition from trendy camp and the "femme fatale of the intellectual cocktail set," to feminist leader with a vengeance. Steinem's new friends were to become congresspersons Bella Abzug and Shirley Chisolm along with women's activist and author Betty Friedan.

Steinem joined with Abzug, Chisolm, and Friedan in July 1971 to form the National Women's Political Caucus (NWPC), which encouraged women to run for political office. She then became a founder of the Women's Action Alliance, a tax-exempt organization for mobilizing nonwhite, non-middle-class women and men to combat social and economic forces of discrimination. Steinem's leadership role evolved quickly, due to her multifaceted and high-profile image, to writing, speaking, and campaigning on the issues. In 1971, *Newsweek* labeled Steinem, "A liberated woman despite Beauty, Chic, and Success." During a New York abortion hearing in the early seventies, one nun and fourteen men testified on the issue of whether a woman should be allowed to abort an unwanted pregnancy. Not one qualified woman was called on at the hearings to testify on what was clearly a "woman's problem." This violated Steinem's sensibilities on the subject, and she struck out to conduct her own personal hearings with women who wanted an abortion or who had had one. Steinem herself had had an abortion before her trip to India, after graduating from Smith College. She had never discussed this dark part of her life but her introspective social consciousness brought out her deepest darkest secret. The hearings prompted her to go public on her abortion for the first time. This launched Steinem emotionally and intellectually into the feminist movement in a big way.

Steinem formulated her fundamental views and beliefs on social values during her college days and especially during her sojourn in India, where she joined the "Radical Humanist" group during a period of social unrest. Steinem's basic values were of equality for everyone, making her an avid "integrationist" on civil rights issues during the sixties. Steinem's values never changed, but her causes would shift dramatically between 1960 and 1975. During the 1960s Steinem's causes, in rank order, were:

1. Civil rights for black people in America;
2. Ending the Vietnam War;
3. Helping the poor;
4. Women's rights.

Notice that women's rights were last during this, her "trendy period" in the turbulent sixties. Steinem had been very socially conscious during those early years. Women's issues were not number one on her list of priorities until the emerging issues of abortion and the Equal Rights Amendment of the seventies awakened her sensibilities to these female-only causes. These issues changed her priorities: Steinem's list during the seventies and eighties became primarily feminist in nature:

1. Reproductive freedom for women;
2. Honoring and balancing career with family by according more respect to traditional female jobs;
3. Making families more democratic with couples sharing the in-house duties;
4. Taking politics out of the culture to ensure that women's lives and problems are taken as seriously as men's.

Steinem's feminist activism began in earnest when she led the Women's Strike for Equality in 1970. She had only recently become the cofounder of the Women's Action Alliance and her aim was to assist Bella Abzug and Shirley Chisolm at the National Women's Caucus in 1971. Steinem wrote much of the philosophy for their political platforms during those early days of the movement. Her attractiveness and articulate insight made her an overnight sensation and a feminist superstar.

Steinem's overnight notoriety in turn gave her the impetus and backing to cofound *Ms.* magazine in 1972. This magazine became her platform for communicating the feminist philosophy in a worldwide distribution network. Her role changed from artsy spokeswoman to virulent but visible role model for the abused housewife and discriminated-against female worker. Steinem's work changed from freelance writer to lecturer, marcher, media personality, and political activist.

Steinem cofounded, edited, and wrote for *Ms.* magazine, launched in December 1971 with the assistance of Clay Felker, who financed the first issue as a women's supplement to his *New York* magazine. Warner Communications then invested $1 million in the venture. The January 1972 inaugural issue included a full-page petition for legal abortion signed by over fifty prominent women who had had abortions, including Steinem, while flaunting Wonder Woman on its cover. *Ms.* would remake Steinem into the titular head of the feminist movement. The first issue sold out 300,000 copies within eight days and became an overnight success with women everywhere. By the summer of 1972 the magazine was publishing articles such as "Down with Sexist Upbringing," "Why Women Fear Success," and "Can Women Love Women?" By the mid-seventies the magazine's readership rose to 500,000 per issue and it became the alter ego for the feminist movement.

The overnight success of *Ms.* launched Steinem into the national limelight and she became the "Godmother of the Feminist Movement." She had a way with words and was called on to write the principles and goals for many women's groups. She would write slogans for Shirley Chisolm and Bella Abzug during this period and coined some interesting slogans aimed at communicating the philosophy of the feminist cause:

"If men could get pregnant, abortion would be a sacrament";

"The point is not the choice we make, the point is the power to make a choice";

"Reproductive freedom for women";

"Women are prisoners of their clothes";

"Real wisdom only comes from life experience well digested";

"Free choice is essential to love";

"A woman cannot mate in captivity."

Ms. magazine was to bear the brunt of the problems caused by disputes between various factions of the feminist movement. The left wing and lesbian sect repudiated the magazine's identity with the Equal Rights Amendment, which had been passed in Congress during the seventies. The ERA was never ratified by the States, but the ideological strife caused by the controversial issue caused a break within the feminist movement. The radical sector vilified Steinem and her magazine as "a mouthpiece for backsliding bourgeois feminism," according to the *New York Times*. Steinem's leadership position was being questioned.

Steinem had created *Ms.* as a magazine "for women, by women, and about women." There were no fashions, recipes, or tips on makeup. She wrote articles on working women coping with the vagaries of balancing a career and family, women's sexual and medical problems, and female educational issues. *Ms.* would continue a turbulent life as a tax-exempt operation until 1987, when in its fifteenth year of operation John Fairfax, Ltd., a large Australian communications conglomerate, acquired the magazine for an estimated $15 million. Steinem was given a five-year consulting contract as contributing editor by the new owners to continue espousing the feminist cause. She has continued as contributing writer for the magazine, which in 1993 is being published quarterly.

Personal Life History

Gloria Steinem was born on March 25, 1934, in Toledo, Ohio, the second-born daughter of Ruth and Leo Steinem. Her sister, Susanne, was eight years older and as much a mentor/parent as a sibling. Gloria Steinem and Golda Meir had similar relationships with older sisters, and each ended up spending their last years of high school living with their sisters, in Gloria's case in Washington, D.C. Gloria's mother was a well-educated (Oberlin College) Protestant whose own mother, Pauline, had been a leading feminist just after the turn of the century in Toledo, Ohio. Gloria's Jewish father, Leo, owned and operated a summer resort by the name of "Ocean Beach Pier" in Toledo. The rest of the year he led a vagabond existence traveling between Michigan, Florida, and California buying and selling antiques. Gloria spent her formative years traveling the country with her dad in a house trailer, spending as little as two weeks at a time in any given school. Gloria's mother was emotionally ill during most of this time and stayed in Toledo on many of these trips. This was a happy time for Gloria as she and her father would go to movies and share milkshakes while living a free and frivolous lifestyle traveling the country.

Gloria's parents divorced when she was eleven which caused a radical change in her life. Her father was a free-spirited Willy Loman type who enjoyed saying that his office was his hat. His obsession with freedom seems to have had a permanent influence on Gloria, as she has spent her life avoiding permanent commitments in jobs, mates, and organizations. Her lifelong constant has been an adroit avoidance of committed employment or romance. She appears committed to remain free of any shackles that even hint of tradition or the establishment. She often said, "I wouldn't want to know how much money I'm going to earn next week, or that I'm going to have two weeks vacation next year."

This early transience with her itinerant father gave Gloria the experience of learning to cope in new environments, a critical factor in the early lives of innovative visionaries. At the age of eleven she and her mother spent one year living near Smith College, where Susanne was enrolled. During her years traveling with her father Gloria had never attended school like normal girls. She finally started attending regular school in the sixth grade when her father and mother split and she stayed in Toldeo and entered dance school. She then began dreaming about dancing her way out of Toledo. Gloria danced at the local Elks Club and won a local TV dance contest. She says, "I thought I was peculiar. Ideas mattered to me. I escaped into books, into fantasy. I lived inside my head." *Little Women* by Louisa May Alcott was one of her favorite books and Alcott became her role model. Gloria lost herself in fantasy in order to cope with an unhappy existence from caring for an incapacitated mother while her father relocated to California. She said she wished she had been adopted and that her real parents would come and take her away. She often dreamed of becoming a Rockette dancer in New York since her mother was incoherent and her father was unavailable (similar circumstances as Madonna's).

After Gloria's father and mother split she became the caretaker for her mother, Ruth, who became more and more incapacitated by her "anxiety-neurosis." This was to leave a lasting impression on Gloria. Later in life she would use her mother's forced nurturing as the reason for her own resistance to having children. She had been forced to spend her youth nursing and feeding her bedridden mother and she felt she had enough of that life. Steinem graduated from Western High School in Washington, D.C., in 1952. Her sister was instrumental in getting Gloria accepted at Smith College. Steinem was inducted into Phi Beta Kappa and graduated magna cum laude in political science from Smith in 1956.

After graduating, Steinem accepted a fellowship to India for two years in order to "run away" from her commitment to marry Blair, her college sweetheart. She was to repeat this scenario of running away from numerous commitments over the next twenty years. In India, Steinem studied at the universities of Calcutta and Delhi. She began her flirtation with radical causes by joining a group fighting for redistribution of the wealth. The poverty in India, which had so affected Mother Teresa years earlier and would motivate Jane Fonda even more so fifteen years later, had a mesmerizing effect on young Gloria. She marched with the "Radical Humanist" group and wrote freelance articles and an Indian guidebook titled *A Thousand Indias*. She said of her experience, "India has too many people, too many animals, too many customs, and too many gods—too much of everything."

It was in India that Steinem first caught fire politically when she noticed that the "classes" and "masses" were different. She came back to America saying, "I discovered that I'd been ghettoized as a white person—there were no black girls at Smith, for example—and in retrospect I was furious. I came home filled with this crusading zeal to make this country [the United States] aware of what was going on in Asia" (Henry and Taitz, 1987).

Temperament: Intuitive-Thinking

Gloria Steinem is an introvert with a Promethean spirit (intuitive-thinking) who perceives the world in a right-brain rational manner. She is a classic visionary who sees the forest through a thicket of trees. Steinem's focus is on the possibilities in life and she is intellectually inquisitive with a long-range view of life. Her macro-vision makes her excel at patterns and principles. Her personality type is insensitive to authority: competence is her only criteria for success. She epitomizes the behavior found in all great creators, entrepreneurs, and innovators.

Steinem has emulated her father as a free spirit and has resisted permanent ties in both her personal and professional life. She symbolizes her mother as a sensitive and androgynous woman who worships education and knowledge. Her defiant and maverick nature seems to have come from a permissive upbringing by educated parents who treated her as an adult during her formative years. In *Revolution from Within* (1993), her book on self-esteem, Steinem says, "My parents never believed in spanking, hitting, or abuse of any kind." This, she says, "helped me . . . become rebellious." This early training formed a character that was not afraid to defy authority. Steinem concedes that her temerity came from her early training:

> I think that's precisely what growing up is—steadily learning to take more and greater risks. While it's easy—and helpful—to see the facility for risk-taking grow in a child, it's important to remember that this process continues all our lives. (*Cosmopolitan*, 1989)

Steinem operates qualitatively, not quantitatively. She couples this with a preference for a rational or "thinking" approach to decision-making. This is in contrast to a "feeling" approach preferred by most females. This places Steinem in the minority (25 percent), as 75 percent of women in America tend to prefer a 'feeling' approach to problem resolution. She prefers to live her life in a structured rather than spontaneous way. That is, she would rather make a decision and move on than let the matter stand without resolution. Gloria's composite temperament of introverted-intuitive-thinking-judger represents only 1 percent of the U.S. population, which places her as a real minority on the Myers-Briggs scale of personality types.

Steinem's fearlessness and ability to take risks in the face of unknown adversaries makes her a renegade type. She has always been willing to risk her self-image, self-respect, and person in fighting for her causes. She demonstrated this during the riots in Harlem after Martin Luther King's murder and then again during the riots at the Chicago National Convention in 1968 when she ventured into risky terrain and controversy without regard to her own well being. Her most gutsy demonstration was in announcing her abortion to further the cause of her sisters and *Ms.* magazine's success. Steinem says it was at this time "I lost my sense that the police protect you." Her marches in defiance of the establishment with Cesar Chavez and the Women's Strike for Equality, and for the ERA hardened her to the realities of risk and reward. She concluded that we are in control of our destiny and told *Look,* "We have to learn to lead ourselves."

Family versus Career

Steinem has sacrificed family and children for a career her whole life. She went steady in high school, became engaged in college, and has had a string of serial relationships and engagements throughout her life. She had an abortion and ran off to India after graduating from Smith in order not to have to follow through with marriage (Henry and Taitz, 1987). She appears to have been torn between her urge for companionship and romance and a commitment she was not comfortable with. Two more engagements and a string of serial long-running romances were to be part of her balancing act between the romantic needs of her overt heterosexuality and her equally strong need for freedom. She is a desirable and vibrant female in body yet needs freedom from commitment. Her career was always first but did not interfere with her constant committed relationships. She just does not allow the relationships to become too permanent.

Steinem's life-long fear of a permanent commitment was psychologically based in her years of nurturing her incapacitated mother. She loved and cared for her mother through years when she would have preferred to be out playing with other kids. This left her with a conflict of values. She says of this period, "I attempted to be my [mother's] caretaker when I was too young to care for myself." This appears to have totally negated any desire for nurturing her own children or the willingness to commit to a lifetime with one man.

Steinem's romantic liaisons have included Hollywood producer Mike Nichols, playwright Herb Sargent, Olympic star Rafer Johnson, and politico Ted Sorenson. Friends in her little black book included John Kenneth Galbraith, who wrote the introduction to *The Beach Book* (1963); Ted and Bobby Kennedy; New York Mayor John Lindsay; and presidential candidates Eugene McCarthy and George McGovern. Steinem dated high-profile males who were often the very men being castigated by her sisters.

During the sixties period Steinem was engaged to Bob Benton who she had worked with at *Esquire*. *One Woman's Power* described how they even went so far as to buy wedding rings and get a license only to see the license expire as Steinem found reasons not to follow through. She referred to her serial relationships as "mini-marriages." These relationships included Paul Desmond, Dave Brubeck's stellar tenor sax man. He was followed by Tom Guinzburg, president of Viking Press, and boss-turned-lover Clay Falker. Falker had been her editor at *Esquire* and the owner of *New York* magazine and they became romantically involved during the time she worked for him. She describes her relationship with Sorensen as "a mistake." The Nichols affair was put more subtly: "I mistook his intellect for heart." Of Guinzburg she said, "I thought he liked books." And in the case of Herb Sargent, "We stopped growing together." Ex-boss Harvey Kurtzman describes Steinem romantically: "Sexually she has an extraordinary appeal," which gives credence to the long line of very eligible men who found her attractive. All of these men became her lifelong friends, even after the relationships came to an end.

Steinem became a bit more cynical during the seventies: "Marriage makes you legally half a person, and what man wants to live with half a person?" Although a friend, Jane O'Reilly, said, "I don't think she believes in everlasting love for one person; she concludes love affairs and then carries on the friendship." Stanley Pottinger, a lawyer heading the Justice Department's civil rights division during the mid-seventies became a friend, confidante, and lover during those frenetic years of fighting for the ERA. A number of romances with powerful and successful men followed over the years but none led to a permanent commitment to marriage or family. Liz Smith, the New York columnist and a friend of Steinem's says she was too philosophical about why a marriage and family could not effectively work. Her rationality became her nemesis. Smith describes Steinem's approach this way: "If I told her about a disastrous love affair, she told me about the cultural and social strains that had broken it up." It appears Steinem may have known too much about why a relationship could not work, which has been shown to be the cause of nonsuccess in any type of creative venture.

During the seventies and eighties Steinem had some serious male relationships, but she always had a new cause or political conquest that got in the way of the romance. David Susskind said during the seventies, "What Gloria needs is a man," in response to her constant evangelism and lack of commitment to a family life. Steinem rationalized and justified her selection of a career over family with articulate pontifications such as "self-discovery is the ultimate aim in life." In *Revolution from Within* (1993), Steinem gives credence to her introspection: "I think the truth is that finding ourselves brings more excitement and well-being than anything romance has to offer." That sounds like rationalizing her preference for the "professional" over the "personal." The professional is always safer than the personal, but not normally as gratifying. When younger, Steinem felt she had to get married to fulfill her mission in life and become whole, which was an admission of the need to survive as a woman. She recalls saying, "I'll definitely get married." Later she said, "I kept thinking, but not right now. There's one thing I want to do first." Then feminism came along and she was hooked into leading her sisters toward a better future. The sisterhood camaraderie became her surrogate family and the way she could avoid potentially fatal permanence of male/female relationships.

Many women have had both a career and a family but something always gets sacrificed in the process. Recent studies have shown that stress is the price even when women successfully pull off the dual roles. It appears the ever-intellectual Steinem probably thought her way into a career-only life. She came very close to marriage, many times, but her tremendous need for nurturing her fellow woman (her sisters) kept her from fulfilling her maternal desires. Steinem's first roommate, Barbara Nessim, a painter in New York, said, "I always talked about getting married. Gloria never did. Oh, she dated a lot, men were always falling in love with her. But I think Gloria loved humanity more than human beings. She was always more interested in world love than human love." Steinem's philosophy on career versus family was never more poignantly described than in this 1988 statement to the press, "I cannot mate in captivity." Having arrived at this sinister conclusion is very telling and not an attitude conducive to a harmonious relationship with a partner who has already been prelabeled.

Life Crisis

Steinem's mother, Ruth, had a number of nervous breakdowns prior to Gloria's birth. Steinem blames her mother's emotional dysfunction on mistreatment by male bosses. No one knows the true genesis but the affliction certainly became the reason for constant crisis in Steinem's early life. Her mother was bedridden during much of Steinem's childhood, and Gloria was forced to function as nurse, companion, and parent. The experience is still indelibly imprinted on her almost sixty years later, as she still discusses the subject in her books and articles. Steinem's mother's incapacity has left her with great resentment over having been forced to sacrifice her youth to become caretaker.

Steinem's travail turns out to have probably been the very thing that groomed her to be creative. Trauma has been shown to spawn great creativity in people who survive the experience. Linda Leonard, a Jungian psychologist, said, "Out of inner chaos and emotional upheaval can come creative, energizing visions that bring new life to the individual and the culture." This appears to have been a motivating influence in the case of Gloria Steinem, who has often admitted to an inner chaos during her formative years in Toledo, Ohio.

Unhappy childhoods have a similar influence on the personality of the creative and innovative. The "divine discontent" theory of psychiatrist Anthony Storr is a telling argument in the case of Steinem, who was so unhappy as a youth she would fantasize that she was adopted and would be rescued and taken to a 'normal' home environment by her real parents. This unhappy period in her life was probably instrumental to her great contributions to the world of writing, feminism, and humanitarianism. The traumatic early life probably caused her to fantasize and dream of a happy, make-believe world where she could be queen. These larger-than-life fantasies are what drives the creative to emulate a utopian existence and allows them to tap their unconscious for a life that they then go out and create.

Trauma and crises in the young tend to instill in them an ability to cope with worst-case scenarios without panicking. It grooms recipients in street smarts and makes them resilient to the machinations of those fighting to maintain the status quo. Steinem's renegade nature was certainly enhanced by her early bouts with crisis. Her statement "Do one outrageous thing in the cause of simple justice during the next twenty-four hours," from her book *Outrageous Acts and Everyday Rebellions* (1983), is just one example of Steinem's passion for bucking the system. Most people learn early on not to fight the system since it can bury you. Those like Steinem who survive great crisis learn that in reaching the bottom, nothing else can hurt them. They learn to move on without fear of the unknown since they have already dealt with the trauma of the unknown. They become comfortable operating in less than congenial environments.

Steinem fantasized through books and daydreaming to survive in East Toledo. She then decided to dance her way out. These classic tactics are often used by the creative and innovative to survive trauma in their lives. Steinem evidently programmed her unconscious to imagine visions of a utopian reality that then became her destiny. These traumatic experiences conditioned her to feel comfortable traveling through India, a foreign and hostile country, at the age of twenty-one. It also gave her moxie when interviewing the rich and famous in the Big Apple in her twenties. And it finally allowed Steinem to face the male power brokers in her fight for female rights during her thirties and forties. Steinem's resilient self-image and self-confidence emerged out of a traumatic youth.

Femme Fatale: A Rebellious Social Conscience

When Steinem spoke of women's problems and placed the blame on men, her voice was heard since she was the girl about town (Manhattan) who dated the same type of men she was castigating. Many other female leaders of the seventies were rightfully objecting to the inequities in the system and blaming establishment men, but often they were sleeping with other women. This approach to change is analogous to a priest giving birth-control instructions to unwed mothers. It might sound good coming from a concerned source but it lacked real credibility. Steinem had credibility and it helped launch her as the quintessential female leader of the last half of the twentieth century. Steinem even found time to grace the covers of *Glamour* and *Vogue* magazines and to write for the *New York Times, McCall's,* and numerous national publications. These dalliances in the world of culture and society helped her influence the very people with whom she was associating.

Steinem's "rebellious social conscience" helped her change a gender-based world into one less inclined to use the length of hair as a determinant of talent. Her impact on society led *McCall's* magazine to name her "Woman of the Year" in 1972, saying she had become "the women's movement's most effective spokeswoman and symbol." Steinem had already made the cover of *Newsweek* and years before had made the cover of *Glamour* as a chic model. She reached the pinnacle of her influence and power during the mid-seventies, when *Ms.* was in full swing and the abortion and ERA issues were in the limelight. Her social consciousness and rebellion have been her most striking behavioral traits. These have at times proved to be both her greatest strength and her greatest failing which is a common finding in all personality traits. The extrovert is always accused of being too loud and the intuitor of being too lacking in common sense.

Steinem's influence and success caused her to be selected as one of the ten most influential women in America by *Harper's Bazaar* in September 1983. This award was based on her work in what she refers to as "the pink collar ghetto." Steinem says, "While it's very important for there to be women in the boardroom, women astronauts, and women plumbers, it doesn't affect the lives of those who are in predominantly female jobs." Steinem has had the unique ability to function in diverse roles. She has been strong but not strident, intellectual while identifying with the working class, attractive but in a "normal," girl-next-door kind of way. Steinem's sense of humor is often disarming to an emotionally charged audience of both followers and dissenters. These combined traits have helped make her an enormous influence on females relative to political elections, constitutional law, and discrimination.

Steinem, the political activist has been instrumental in the recent rise of such feminine leaders as Diane Feinstein, Barbara Boxer, Pat Schroeder, Kim Campbell, Anne Richards, Kay Bailey Hutchison, Elizabeth Dole, and Janet Reno. She has always been controversial—the destiny of anyone with a cause— but she has never wilted in the face of controversy or power. This testifies to her Promethean spirit. Steinem is the consummate radical and rebellious personality who has used her own unique version of feminine guile and charisma coupled with a social conscience to reach her lofty objectives.

Summary

In *Megatrends for Women* (1992) Aburdeen and Naisbitt talk of the empowering of women in order to overcome the inequities of the system. They could have been describing Gloria Steinem when they said, "Metaphorically, the Goddess is awakened. . . . The spark of women's power, beauty, and creativity, long buried or forgotten, has never been reborn on such a mass level." They predict that women will transform every sector of contemporary life from the boardroom to political life. They predict a female U.S. President by the year 2004 and eventual female dominance in sports and science. If this is to happen, Gloria Steinem would have to be considered, at worst, a superlative catalyst who helped make it happen; at best, the leader most instrumental in its realization.

One feminist during the radical seventies described Steinem as epitomizing "the Eternal Feminine . . . the Sexual Object sought by all men, and by all women." She has been an anomaly to many of the radical left, who had a hard time identifying with a woman about town who was dating and socializing with the very power elite that the movement was regularly lambasting. Steinem's persona was out of place in the movement. Most people believed that one could not be a radical attempting to change the system and also be a fundamental part of the system. In other words, those who are being exploited cannot join those doing the exploiting. Some even wanted Steinem to be less of a sex symbol, less chic, since these roles were considered counterproductive to their cause of destroying the system that revered such things. Steinem's succinct and elegant response was, "I'm not going to walk around in Army boots and cut off my hair."

Steinem radiated a chic grace in mesmerizing the media and her faithful following during the seventies and eighties. She could have taken any number of career paths, but she chose the cause of feminine equality and thereby sacrificed family, money, and position. She accomplished a great deal and probably exorcised her past ghosts of childhood unhappiness and insecurity through an adulthood of servitude to the altar of feminine empowerment. Her personal power was intelligence, attractiveness, writing ability, and public speaking skills, which led her to the top of her field. Steinem's charismatic charm gave her access to the power elite in Washington and on Wall Street and prompted legislation that would not have occurred without her contribution. Many of the reforms in female pay, job advancement, and political representation— as governors, congresspeople, and senators—can be directly traced to the pioneering work of Gloria Steinem.

Gloria Steinem is a classic intuitive-thinking personality who used her insecurities to fight an inequitable system. She combined her vision and intellect to build a philosophy for the feminist movement that has provided the impetus for the progressive legislation being enacted in the nineties. If in fact a female president is elected by 2004, Gloria should be singled out for her part, as she was the voice and the vision behind the pulpit. The price she paid was the sacrifice of a lifetime mate or family.

Steinem's family has been her "sisters" and her "feminist supporters." If she has an identity and family, it is the ERA, equality for women in every venue of business and life, female congressional leadership on an equal basis with men, and empowerment of women in every walk of life. These things are Steinem's fulfillment, and due to her efforts it appears they will be close to realization during her lifetime.

Gloria Steinem
Feminist, author, political activist
b. March 25, 1934, Toledo, Ohio

Dominant trait: A rebellious social conscience
Religion: Father: Jewish, Mother: Protestant, Gloria: Nonreligious
Motto: "Do one outrageous thing in the cause of simple justice during the next twenty-four hours."
Philosophy: "The point is not the choice we make, the point is the power to make a choice."
Creation/innovation: Founder of Women's Action Alliance and *Ms.* Magazine
Products/contributions: Started *Ms.* and wrote *Outrageous Acts and Everyday Rebellions* (1983), *Marilyn* (1986), and *Revolution from Within: A Book of Self-Esteem* (1992).
Success: *Ms.* magazine and acknowledged leader of the feminist movement in U.S.
Self-description: "I guess it's a matter of being the right person in the right place at the right time. I'm an accident of history."

Birth order: Second-born daughter. Sue was eight years older and Gloria was raised as an only daughter.
Childhood transience: Traveled the U.S. in mobile home with father as a child. Left home in high school to live with sister and then to Switzerland for a year in college.
Father's occupation: Owner of beach club and vagabond antique trader throughout U.S.
Mentors: Louisa May Alcott; "Being with her father felt so much safer than being with her mother" (*One Woman's Power*). All-girl school provided many early role models.
Childhood upbringing: Father said, "My office is my hat." She had a transient childhood as a result. Father was the dominant influence. Mother's anxiety and emotional illness were constant problems—Gloria nursed her mother for years.
Formal education: Never attended any school for a full year until 6th grade. Smith Women's College, magna cum laude, Phi Beta Kappa, 1956, in political science
Life crises: Parents divorced at age 11. Mother's mental relapse at age 14.
Marriages/liaisons: Abortion on graduation from college. Many engagements and relationships to very strong men; never able to make permanent commitment.

Risk-taking: Fought the system at every turn. Never afraid.
Temperament: Introverted-intuitive-thinking-judger—Promethean temperament
Behavior: Rebellious and independent. Always shared father's desire for freedom from commitment and total independence.
Career versus family: Sacrificed family for career repeatedly; numerous engagements without permanent commitment. Abortion at 21.
Self-esteem: Built esteem through daydreaming and dancing.
Hobbies: Intellectual debate, writing, and dancing
Heroes: Louisa May Alcott and Charlotte Brontë
Honors: *McCall's* "Woman of the Year" (1972); *Harper's Bazaar* "Top 10 Most Influential Women in America" (1983)

17

Margaret Thatcher—
Indomitably Competitive

Every breakthrough, every leap forward in history has developed on right-brain insights, the ability of the holistic brain to detect anomalies, process novelty, and perceive relationships.
—Marilyn Ferguson, *The Aquarian Conspiracy*

Governments should be given *power* by people instead of people given power by governments.
—Lady Margaret Thatcher

The "Iron Lady" was the most powerful female in the world for a ten-year period during the 1980s, a period when she was a catalyst and facilitator of the relationship between Ronald Reagan and the Soviet Union's Mikhail Gorbachev. Margaret Thatcher was strong but honest, opinionated but empathic, competitive but cool. Thatcher reached the very top of a male-dominated power elite through dedicated perseverance and struggle. Her meticulous climb to the pinnacle of power started from the unlikely position of lower-middle-class England. She pulled off the impossible: a lowly shopkeeper's daughter, reared in a home with no indoor plumbing, had the temerity to invade the private reserve of male power and become the prime minister of Great Britain.

A perceptive vision and focus assisted Thatcher's rise to the leadership of England's Tory (Conservative) party, and her determination and competitiveness allowed her to remain in power longer than any other British leader of the twentieth century. As Britain's first female prime minister, Thatcher was expected to get little accomplished because of the roadblocks—imaginary and real—set against any female leader in a bastion of male power. But it turned out that Thatcher accomplished more via innovative legislation than her previous three predecessors combined. She turned around a sinking economic ship faster than any of her supporters or adversaries believed possible. She was able to do it because of her inviolable belief in what was right and the guts to see it through. Lady Thatcher (she was knighted in 1993) has left an indelible mark on her country and on British society, and has established an even greater heritage for aspiring young female leaders to follow.

Margaret Thatcher came to power with a conviction-based philosophy for government and a strong pragmatic attitude. These unique qualities were brought to bear on a stodgy and consensus-bound body politic. Most of the established bureaucrats hated her, but also feared her, and with good cause. The Iron Lady was not about to be pushed around and taken lightly. She dared to be different because her father instilled in her the belief that it was quite all right to be different. Her father, Alfred Roberts, entrepreneur turned preacher and local politician, preached to his daughter the doctrine of independence. He instilled in her the belief that "different" people lead and "parasites" follow. He told her "to never follow a crowd, lead it." Young Margaret followed her father's sage advice and became a leader the world will not soon forget. Thatcher is a superb "female leader" role model for young women everywhere. She broke ground that needed to be broken. This indomitable lady led with a sense of "purpose and direction" and now in every school room it can be said, "Yes, Virginia, you can aspire to the position of prime minister (or president), just like Margaret Thatcher did!"

Personal Life History

Margaret Roberts was born above a grocery store in Grantham, England, just north of London on October 13, 1925. Grantham was also the home of another famous Englishman, Sir Isaac Newton. The Roberts lived an austere life: no garden, no running water, and no inside toilet. Margaret was the second daughter of a religious father, Alfred, and a seamstress mother, Beatrice. As the baby, Margaret was doted on by her father who realized his own ambitions through his overachieving daughter. Margaret was much like her father, while her sister, Muriel (four years her senior), was more like her mother. Consequently, Alfred, the businessman, councilman, and part-time Methodist preacher, doted on Margaret, determined to mold her into his ideal. He let her know that she could aspire to anything she wanted and did not set limits on her because of her gender. Beatrice Roberts was a devoted housewife who had little impact on the molding of Margaret.

Alfred Roberts had little formal education, but delighted in the fact that Margaret listened to his every word. He was a voracious reader and was in constant search of knowledge, a trait he would pass on to his daughter. They would go to the library together and select two books a week to read. He was dedicated to molding her into the son he never had and into a woman who would "lead, not follow." He instilled in her the merits of a strong work ethic and Victorian integrity. Roberts never tolerated the words, "I can't," or "It's too difficult." Margaret adored him and remembered years later his admonition, "You make up your own mind. You do not do something because your friends are doing it. You do not follow the crowd because you're afraid of being different. . . . You lead the crowd, but you never just follow" (Murray, 1980).

Roberts instilled in his daughter that being "different" wasn't a liability but an asset. It was a positive trait to be admired. This early tutelage became a useful tool to Margaret as an adult, when she found herself operating in a male world where no female had ever been. She had to perform in a new and "different" environment, unknown territory for a woman fighting to survive in a man's world. She learned well, became an avid reader, and was very competitive in sports. Her headmistress at the all-girl school in Grantham said, "She was a very good speaker as a little girl." A former student said, "She was bright, studious, and serious even as a five-year-old."

Margaret started piano lessons at age five and won a poetry recital at age nine. After the win the headmistress congratulated her saying, "You were lucky, Margaret." Margaret tersely responded, "I was not lucky, I deserved it." Always an inveterate debater, Margaret was on her high school debating team. She was also the youngest hockey captain ever at her school. She was an excellent student according to Margaret Goodrich, a lifelong friend, who says, "She could use words correctly at a far earlier age than most of her school friends." Margaret always felt her father "knew" everything and followed him at age ten to council meetings, where she got a taste of the theatrics of political repartee. Roberts became mayor of Grantham while Margaret was in high school, which gave her early training in the nuances of political leadership.

Margaret was a serious and lonesome child. She never went to movies or dances, because these luxuries were not permitted in the Roberts' household due to her father's dogmatic religious convictions. Her job in the family store provided her with the fundamentals of business and entrepreneurship. An early example of her drive and tenacity came when she needed four years of Latin to qualify for a scholarship to Somerville College, the finest women's college at Oxford. She crammed four years into one and received a partial scholarship to Somerville. When she arrived at Oxford she had still never attended a dance, having lived an austere life of overachievement and meeting the demands of a doting father.

Thatcher's ambition became apparent at Somerville. A roommate friend remembers, "Her ambition was boundless. Up at 6:30 to study and home after dark." During her second year Thatcher fell in love with the son of an earl but was turned down by his mother for being the daughter of a grocer. Political debate was the only extracurricular activity in which she participated at college and she joined the Oxford University Conservative Association, which saw fit to elect her its first female president in 1946.

Thatcher graduated with a bachelor of science degree in chemistry in 1947 and took a job as a research chemist for Xylonite Plastics in Mannington, Essex. Her next move would be as a cake filling tester for J. P. Lyons in Hammerworth, London. She is the only prime minister in British history to have a formal education in the physical sciences. Her career as a chemist was short-lived, as her heart was in politics and the law. She changed jobs to Lyons ice cream in order to be closer to a potential political seat which was about to open in Dartford, Kent. The solid Labour district was an impossible challenge but the indefatigable Thatcher was not deterred. Thatcher spent just three years at these interim positions in industry, ultilizing her education in chemistry, her heart set on a law degree. Her marriage to Denis Thatcher in 1951 allowed her to enter law school. She received her law degree in 1953 and went to work as a barrister for five years during the fifties. An interesting factor in Thatcher's formal education is that she attended all-girl schools from kindergarten through Somerville College, never once having to compete for the attention of male students. The irony of this is that she then went on to wrest power from men and was never intimidated in facing them in Parliament or other positions in government. Evidently her female role models in school encouraged her to compete with males, not to seek their approval. It may also have had something to do with her image among the powerful politicians of the world of being "more male than female."

Thatcher would later characterize her mental processes as derived from her diverse education. She describes herself first as a scientist, where "you look at the facts and you deduce your conclusions." Then she became a lawyer, where "you learn your law, so you learn structures. . . . You judge the evidence, and then, when the laws are inadequate for present-day society, you create new laws." She became a tax specialist, quite unusual for a woman in her day. But Thatcher was not deterred by the biases in that male-dominated bastion of power. As Thatcher explained her choice of tax law: "I was keenly interested in the financial side of politics, so I went into the revenue side of the law." All of this was grooming her for politics as she was now familiar with business, law, taxes, and scientific processes.

Professional Background

Margaret Thatcher was a young college graduate working as a chemist when she decided to run for Parliament for the Conservative party in Dartford, Kent, in 1948. The Dartford chairman was asked, "Would you consider a woman?" "Oh no! Not a woman! Dartford is an industrial seat." Thatcher's competitive and indomitable spirit gave her the courage to be, at age twenty-three, the youngest candidate and the only woman to run for national office that year. She had no chance of winning: the Labour party had a majority of twenty thousand votes. This did not deter Thatcher from quitting her job with the plastics company and relocating to the Dartford area in order to be close to the seat she was pursuing with a passion. After campaigning and working twenty-hour days for a six-month period, she went down to defeat. The politicians commented, "She had a fantastic amount of energy." One night during the campaign a supporter had offered her a ride to the train station, and she accepted. The supporter was Denis Thatcher, a divorced industrialist; the innocent ride to the station began a two-year romance that culminated in their marriage. Although Thatcher lost the election for Dartford, she had made Conservative party members take notice, winning 36 percent of the vote in an election where she wasn't expected to get as much as 20 percent.

Thatcher took time out from her political aspirations for marriage, family, and a five-year period practicing at the bar. She gave birth to twins named Carol and Mark in 1953, and just four months later she passed the bar exam. Thatcher practiced patent and tax law until 1961. In 1959 Thatcher once again ran for a seat in Parliament in the wealthy suburb of London known as Finchley. She won this seat at age thirty-three and was on her way in a career well suited to her oratorical gifts. This ambitious woman had already spent years as a research chemist, patent lawyer, tax barrister, mother of twins, and wife to an industrialist.

In 1961, Prime Minister Harold Macmillan noticed Thatcher's diverse talents and appointed her joint parliamentary secretary to the Ministry of Pensions and National Insurance. Edward Heath was her mentor in 1967 (though he later became her bitter adversary). He selected her as a key cabinet member of his Conservative shadow government (the cabinet of the party out of power). Thatcher was then named the shadow minister of gas, electricity, and nuclear energy, and later minister for transportation, education, and science. Thatcher's educational credentials in chemistry and law held her in good stead for this selection, but her oratory, work ethic, and integrity made Heath notice her as a woman of great potential. When Heath was elected prime minister in 1970, Thatcher became his only female cabinet member when she was appointed Secretary for Education and Science.

Thatcher first gained national recognition when she decided to abolish the free milk program for children. She had decided to reform welfare waste by reallocating monies away from the school milk program to teachers. She always felt the welfare state was the major cause of societal problems and her entrepreneurial leanings got her in much trouble with left-wing politicians over this decision. The not-so-subtle opposition members shouted her down in Parliament with admonitions of "Thatcher the Milk Snatcher" and "Ditch the Bitch." The *London Sun Times* blasted her in headlines such as "The Most Unpopular Woman in Britain"; Thatcher became known as "that bloody woman" to the people on the street. Thatcher's decision to reform welfare waste was a nearly disastrous move for her. The welfare cut of £4 million looked as if it would destroy her career in politics. The ever-resolute and strong-willed lady vowed, "I'm not going to be beaten by this." This setback instilled an even stronger resolve in her as a politician of "conviction." She staunchly defended her decision and ignored the negative press which ultimately moved on to other easier foes.

Striking miners and the enormous union power held Britain's economy in a viselike grip during the early 1970s. Heath's government capitulated to the constant threat of strikes by the union and the demands of their striking miners. Confidence in the Conservative party and its leaders eroded, causing Heath to resign in March 1974, eventually ushering in a Labour government. Eleven months later Heath was removed as party leader. The party was in much disarray, with no apparent plan to resolve the crises in government. No male had the temerity to step forward, so Thatcher seized the initiative and declared her candidacy to become the first female in history to lead the party. In February 1975 Margaret Thatcher became the first woman to assume leadership of any party in Britain. She campaigned vigorously against the welfare state and vowed to correct the power struggle between labor and management. "Vote Right to keep what's Left" became one of her rallying cries. She told the National Union Executive in June 1975, "There are too few rich and too few profits" and in October, "The way to recovery is through profits." Finally, in a Thames TV speech in April 1979, Thatcher took a lethal shot at the unions which was to be a prelude to her future regime: "There are people in this country who are great destroyers; they wish to destroy the kind of free society we have. Many of these people are in unions."

During the four years following her ascension to power Thatcher was the leader of the minority party, while Harold Wilson and James Callaghan led the ruling Labour party. The Labour government became impotent while the unions become omnipotent. The 1979 "Winter of Discontent" became a strike-crazed nightmare as every imaginable union from garbage collectors and gravediggers to schoolteachers and hospital workers went out on strike. By March 1979, the British public had had it with traditional politicians and labor unions. England had witnessed a precipitous decline in economic and worldwide power since the beginning of the century. In 1900 England controlled 450 million subjects, which at the time amounted to 25 percent of the world's population.

By 1979 the country had lost its power base and was nearing economic collapse with no one ready, willing, or able to become the leader of a country in chaos. Thatcher was never one to retreat from any great challenge. If nothing else, she was fearless. Political commentator Paul Johnson said at the time, "Even her most venomous opponents will admit that she has bounteous reserves of truly Churchillian valor." Lord Pennel said in typical British chauvinistic fashion, "She was the only one *man* enough to stand for the leadership." In May 1979 Margaret Thatcher was elected prime minister of Great Britain for a five-year term with 43.9 percent of the vote. "Them or us" was her non-subtle approach to accepting new members into the party or her immediate power elite. She would ask, "Is he one of us?" and if not was rejected as a member of her team.

Thatcher had always been an indomitable optimist, believing that she knew the way. Her integrity was inspiring and refreshing to an electorate not used to such forthright honesty. One political biographer, who was not one of her most avid fans, wrote of her:

> Her style was built on domination. None of her colleagues had ever experienced a more assertive, even overbearing, leader. That had always been her way of doing business, and it became much more pronounced when, having defeated all her male rivals in 1975, she needed to establish a dependable ascendancy over them. With her command of facts and figures and her reluctance ever to lose an argument, she seemed so damnably sure of herself that nobody could suppose there lurked much uncertainty anywhere in her makeup. Certitude was her stock-in-trade. . . . There were supporters and opponents, and almost no one in between. (Young, 1989)

The woman said to be "hopelessly middle-class" by those within her party was finally prime minister at age fifty-three. This indomitable personality had survived many struggles in her trek to the top of her party. Thatcher was now positioned to lead her nation, and finally able to implement her plans for a better Great Britain. She was adamant about taking an almost libertarian approach to government which would have delighted Ayn Rand and other antigovernment types. Bureaucrats had been her lifelong nemesis and she now was about to become their greatest headache. Her leadership was kicked off in a speech to Parliament that gave them a hint of what was to come. She knew what was needed and was prepared to implement the dramatic changes with the certitude of an autocratic leader. She borrowed a quote from Abraham Lincoln to emphasize her position to Parliament in 1979: "You cannot strengthen the weak by weakening the strong. . . . You cannot help the poor by destroying the rich. . . . You cannot help men permanently by doing for them what they could and should do for themselves."

Thatcher kept her word. One month after taking office she slashed the top tax rate on earned income from 83 percent to 60 percent and reduced the highest tax rate on unearned income from 90 percent to 75 percent. She raised value-added taxes, removed restrictive foreign exchange controls, and did away with wage and price guidelines. Thatcher's biggest and most important contribution was to sell off government-owned enterprises and public housing to the people, a move designed to encourage ownership and increase entrepreneurship. Within a year most people thought that Thatcher would go down in history as England's worst prime minister. But she knew better. This determined and confident woman did not capitulate to the nay-sayers or bureaucrats, because she had the courage of her convictions. Everyone always knew where Thatcher stood on any issue and "Thatcherism," if nothing else, defined a platform that was completely understood by supporters and adversaries alike. Thatcher never waffled on controversial issues which is why she was ultimately elected to three full terms in office and will go down in history as one of England's great prime ministers.

Examples of Thatcher's forthrightness can be seen in every facet of her leadership. On her gender, she told the *Daily Mirror* (March 1980), "I don't notice that I'm a woman. I regard myself as the prime minister." On feminism, "The feminists have become far too strident and have done damage to the cause of women by making us out to be something we're not" (*Times,* May 1978). And in 1984 Thatcher told the *Times,* "People who go out prepared to take the lives of other people forfeit their own right to live." On her work ethic: "I've never had more than four or five hours sleep. Anyway, my life is my work. Some people work to live. I live to work" (*Daily Mail,* February 1985). In 1993 she told C-SPAN, "I actually only slept 1.5 hours at times but was willing to sacrifice a few hours of sleep to have my hair done."

A testimony to Thatcher's dedicated philosophy came in a speech to the Small Business Bureau, "I came to this office with one deliberate intent: to change Britain from a dependent to a self-reliant society; from a give-it-to-me to a do-it-yourself nation; a get-up-and-go instead of a sit-back-and-wait Britain." This statement could have been written by Mary Kay Ash or any of the other great women in this book. Thatcher understood very well the essence of free enterprise and what makes it go. And this "Iron Lady" would not be deterred from her objectives as she would tell the Conservative Party conference in October 1980, "We shall not be diverted from our course. To those waiting with bated breath for that favorite media catch-phrase, the U-turn, I have only one thing to say: you turn if you want; the Lady's not for turning." Thatcher never turned and never let up in a feverish effort to make Britain a great nation once again. Thatcher's political philosophy succeeded based on her oft-repeated chant "Chart your course and follow it with integrity and success follows."

Many key members of Thatcher's party would assert, "There is no one in politics I would sooner trust." Airey Neave, Thatcher's mentor said, "Personal courage, that is her great quality." Others were not so kind. The *Economist,* commenting on her ascension to leadership of the party in 1975 said, "Her victory could keep the Conservative Party in opposition for the next twenty years." The magazine was wrong as were many of Thatcher's adversaries over the years. French President Giscard D'Estaing said, "I do not like her. She is not like a man and not like a woman." Based on her success in turning around a faltering Great Britain, D'Estaing was correct in his assessment of this Iron Lady. She was better than most of the men who had preceded her and she was unlike any other woman in having achieved the highest position in Britain. She certainly is a creative genius of the first order based on her ability to take limited personal resources, use them to get to the top, and stay there for a prolonged period of time. She is the quintessential role model for women throughout the world who have aspirations of breaking through the proverbial glass ceiling.

Thatcher went out of office as she had come in, with great controversy. Her intransigent stand on controversial issues created a furor in 1990. Her community "poll tax" (a discriminatory tax against the working classes) was levied equally on all citizens—a very unpopular move. Then Thatcher created a rebellion within her own party by opposing Britain's full participation in the European monetary system (intended to create a common currency throughout Europe). Thatcher was forced to resign as party leader (and therefore as prime minister) in November 1990. She was succeeded by her chancellor of the exchequer, John Major. Margaret Thatcher had held office since May 1979 and become the longest-serving British prime minister of the twentieth century.

Temperament and Behavior Characteristics

Margaret Thatcher is an extroverted intuitive with a propensity for detail. She contrasts with most females in the world by using a "thinking" or "rational" solution to problems rather than a "feeling" or "emotional" response. Trained as a scientist, Thatcher used her education to further her career. She was always very systematic and never equivocated on any topic. She preferred to make a decision and live by the consequences instead of the more typical political approach of "wait and see." In other words, Thatcher preferred completion to procrastination or equivocation. She was very confident in her own ability to analyze a problem and select a solution, and never worried about dissenters. Thatcher told the *Daily Express* in 1987: "We don't change our tune to whoever we are talking," a testimony to her intransigence.

Thatcher was a nonconformist and indomitable spirit. She extolled the virtues she was raised with: freedom, hard work, thrift, personal responsibility, and a dislike for socialism. The Russians did her a monumental favor in bequeathing her the nickname "Iron Lady." It was too harsh in some respects, but turned out to be an advantage since it gave her the strong image she needed to lead and command an electorate not sure about having a woman at the helm. Most female leaders face an inherent image problem. They carry the unwarranted baggage of weakness in the face of any strong opposition. Women are not expected to fight an aggressive battle when faced with grave danger or intimidation. This is not necessarily warranted, but in Thatcher's case it was far from the reality. Thatcher loved a fight and was so competitive it irritated her adversaries, especially men who were not accustomed to such strength of resolve in women. Thatcher confused and intimidated men with her unshakeable stand on what she believed to be right. In her words:

> I am not hard. I'm frightfully soft. But I will not be hounded. I will not be driven anywhere against my will. . . . I am the leader of the pack. What's a leader for but to lead the pack? Of course they are behind me. If they were in front of me they would be the leaders. (1980 British TV broadcast)

Thatcher never equivocates or becomes submissive in battles of the mind. This personality trait has made her an indomitable figure who exudes strength of character and resolve, admirable and necessary traits for any great leader of either sex. This demeanor conjures up varying emotions in her constituency and violent dislike in her enemies. R. C. Longworth of the *Chicago Tribune* in 1989 described Thatcher as "perhaps the most admired, hated, fascinating, boring, radical and conservative leader in the Western World." The Queen Mother of England gave one of the more complimentary descriptions of this forthright woman: "Margaret Thatcher looks you right in the eye. Not many do that, especially when speaking to royalty."

An ex-employer said of Thatcher, "Her ambition was boundless." And Thatcher's most ardent admirers would constantly press her "to relax, lighten up." She was intense, strong, and fearless. Even her father said, "Margaret is 99.5 percent perfect. The other .5 percent is that she could be a little warmer." Thatcher's intensity is wrapped up in an energy that drives her beyond limits set by normal people. She is a workaholic who buries her adversaries by sheer force of zealous energy. Thatcher admitted as much to the *Sunday Daily Mail* in 1985 with this honest portrayal of her work ethic: "Some people work to live. I live to work."

An example of Thatcher's tenacity and fearlessness was demonstrated by her aggressive handling of the Argentine invasion of the Falklands Islands just two years into her leadership. This island was 8,000 miles from England and had but 1,800 British subjects along with 650,000 sheep and ten million penguins. It was not an asset base most leaders would dare risk their career and the lives of 250 soldiers over. Argentina had invaded the island betting on the fact that a new female prime minister, leading a troubled nation many miles away, was not about to risk everything over some remote island in the South Atlantic. Many in Thatcher's party thought her mad to risk so much for so little, which prompted the press to say, "Thatcher is crazy. She thinks she is wonder woman." Were they wrong! Thatcher donned her Wonder Woman cape and without hesitation launched ninety-eight ships carrying eight thousand men to the region. It was the principle that counted, and "aggression cannot be tolerated at any level." Her strength, competitive nature, and integrity rose to the fore and turned a potential disaster into an overwhelming victory.

When the press asked Thatcher about the potential for failure, she retorted, "Failure? The possibilities do not exist." Thatcher was correct and within weeks told the press, "We knew what we had to do and we went about it and did it." She then told *World This Weekend* "A bully has no respect for a weakling. The way to stop a bully is not to be weak." On the issue of law and order the Iron Lady said, "People who go out prepared to take the lives of other people forfeit their own right to live." These words sound very much like Ayn Rand. The Falklands success gave her a landslide victory in 1984 ensuring her another six years of British leadership.

Family versus Career

Marrying a divorced man ten years her senior allowed Thatcher to devote time to her law degree and then concentrate on a life in politics. Denis was the proprietor of his own well-entrenched paint business and financed her law school education. Thatcher became pregnant and gave birth to twins, Carol and Mark, in August 1953 and appeared to be well on her way to the life of an English housewife and mother. But this was not to be. Four months after the twins were born Thatcher decided to sit for the bar. Soon afterward, when the twins were just a year old, she started practicing law. When they were six she decided to run for a seat in Parliament. Thatcher won her government seat at the age of thirty-four and never left full-time political office after that time. Margaret ended her law practice in 1961, becoming a full-time politician and part-time wife and mother.

Thatcher wanted both family and career and was determined to have both. It took its toll on her, though: she was often exasperated at the dual responsibilities, and the children often spent more time with nannies than they did with their mother. A long-time close friend of the family said, "She is an unbelievably successful politician, but an unsuccessful mother, and she knows it."

Thatcher told the *Daily Telegraph* in 1968, "If we couldn't afford to have resident help in the home, I would give up my career tomorrow." She was fortunate to have the financial independence to subsidize outside help in balancing her career and family. She told *Cosmopolitan* in 1983, "I hope we shall see more and more women combining marriage and a career. Prejudice against this dual role is not confined to men. Far too often, I regret, it comes from our own sex. . . . It is possible to carry on working, taking a short leave of absence when families arrive and returning later." Thatcher was able to have both and did them concurrently. She paid the price, but she is a living example that a woman can get to the top and not have to sacrifice her maternal instincts for a career. The sacrifice is qualitative and as indicated by the women in this book, the career normally takes precedence, except in periods of crisis.

Life Crises

Thatcher was a teenager when the Battle of Britain was being waged in the skies over her country and city. Grantham was but a few miles from a major Royal Air Force (RAF) base and consequently had the distinction of being the most bombed city per capita in England. When Thatcher was fifteen a total of thirty thousand bombs hit the city of Grantham, aimed at its tank-manufacturing industry. This must have left some indelible marks on young Margaret, but she has never acknowledged them publicly. In any case her hatred of the atrocities committed by the Nazis and her adoration of British war hero and politician Airey Neave seem to give some credence to the influence of the terrible bombing during her teen years.

Crisis is a motivating force for great achievement, based on conclusions from recent research. In Thatcher's case she lived her life as a woman possessed and fleeing from one crisis to another. She stepped into the leadership of the Conservative party when it was in crisis and no one else had the temerity to step in to help. This type of pressure never seemed to bother Thatcher and she actually appears to have been inspired by the great challenges in her life. History has shown that great problems make great leaders and no one ever achieved anything worthwhile without taking enormous risk. Thatcher was a risk-taker who never backed down when the going got rough, and that is what made her great.

Indomitable Competitive Spirit and Success

Margaret Thatcher reached the top because of her indefatigable spirit and competitive drive to be the best. She had unbelievable energy. School friend Margaret Wickstead said, "I have never met anyone with Margaret's infinite capacity for work." She was the classic overachiever according to Chris Ogden, a biographer, who said her first address to Parliament "was given with such zeal the Congress was stunned into silence." In defense of her own competitiveness and capitalism she said, "Competition serves the people very much better than monopolies." Her indomitable spirit and fearlessness were best illustrated by her statement to biographer Patricia Murray (1980) when asked, "Do you have any particular fear?" In her inimitable honesty Thatcher said, "I can't think of one at all. . . . I'm not afraid of flying, hospitals . . . dying. . . . No, I really can't think of anything at all." She told an American television audience in December 1993, "You get used to sleeping four hours a night and can do it without ill effects. At times I only slept 1.5 hours." This woman was truly an Iron Lady with a will to match and it was this penetrating focus and strength of character that has made her one of the truly great creative visionaries of our time.

Summary

The Iron Lady started out in life in a home without running water and made it to Number 10 Downing Street with little more than determination and a gift for oratory. Thatcher was fond of Sophocles' quote, "Once a woman is made equal to man, she becomes his superior." She certainly is proof of that aphorism according to many political minds in the world. Thatcher turned around a government floundering and on the verge of collapse. "Thatcherism" is her heritage. It characterizes her regime and philosophical approach to "popular capitalism." She implemented her "Thatcherism" philosophy through a persistent but practical strategy. She sold off $30 billion worth of shares in British Telecom, British Airways, Rolls-Royce, and other nationalized businesses to the public. Then dedicated much energy to getting the government out of the business of "business," and put many of the working people back into their own homes. Her government was instrumental in selling over one million public housing units to the occupants during the mid-eighties, thereby raising the percentage of homeowners in England from 52 percent to 66 percent (only 63.9 percent of Americans owned their own home in 1988). Thatcher got inflation under control, reduced the unions' power dramatically, and improved the economic growth rate to a level higher than it had been in decades.

Thatcher became friends and an ally of both Mikhail Gorbachev and Ronald Reagan. She was an internationally renowned stateswoman who could hold her own with anyone. She left office in 1990 a proud woman and deservedly so. She had become the most powerful woman in the world with the help of a herculean work ethic, her inviolable integrity, a competitive spirit, and a magical gift for oratory. When asked about her success, she gave most of the credit to her father. On taking office in 1979 she said, "I owe almost everything to my father. . . . He taught me that you first sort out what you believe in.

You then apply it. You don't compromise on things that matter." Her father's tutelage, coupled with her role models during fifteen years of all-girl schooling, gave Thatcher a self-image that was set in concrete. She had never had to compete in school with males and was not socialized to believe that the approval of males was a necessary concomitant for success.

In her 1979 campaign pledge, Thatcher promised to reduce inflation, break union power, create new industry and trade, bring back prosperity, and radically shake up the social welfare system in Britain by dismantling the welfare state. She accomplished all of these goals with elegance and style. Britain is better for having bet the farm on this simple but strong-willed woman who had a dream and never allowed anything or anyone to interfere with its achievement. Margaret Thatcher has changed the world for the better by being a creative visionary.

Margaret Thatcher
British politician
b. October 13, 1925, Grantham, England

Dominant trait: Indomitable and competitive

Religion: Methodist and Anglican

Mottos: "You cannot strengthen the weak by weakening the strong"; "Vote Right to keep what's Left"; "I am not a consensus politician, I am a conviction politician."

Philosophy: "Without the strong, who would provide for the weak? When you hold back the successful you penalize those who need help."

Nickname: "Iron Lady"

Creation/innovation: First woman in British history to serve as prime minister, 20th century's longest-serving prime minister, most powerful woman in the world during the 1980s

Products/contributions: Denationalized British industry

Success: Turned around Britain's declining economy and made it competitive, curtailed union domination of industry. Ideal role model for young girls.

Self-description: "Some people work to live. I live to work. . . . I would like to pack each minute with sixty seconds of distance run."

Birth order: Second-born daughter; sister, Muriel. Margaret became the "son that her father never had." According to Thatcher he doted on her and taught her that being different was good.

Childhood transience: North of London primarily, with some trips

Father's occupation: Grocery store owner, part-time Methodist minister, and mayor of Grantham while Margaret was in high school

Mentors: Father, Alfred Roberts; Katie Kay at Oxford; Edward Heath in Tory party; Airey Neave

Childhood upbringing: Raised in puritanical and frugal environment with intense work ethic and groomed by father to be independent and self-sufficient

Formal education: Kesteven and Grantham all-girl schools; Oxford—Somerville College, chemistry, 1947; law school and bar, 1953.

Life crisis: "More bombs hit Grantham per capita during Battle of Britain than any other British city." There were 30,000 Britons killed in war. Thatcher was age 13 to 15 during this time.

Marriages/liaisons: Married Denis Thatcher December 1951; a Victorian virgin

---

Risk-taking: "Fearless" and "driven"—indomitable

Temperament: Extraverted-Sensor-Thinking-Judger—Epimethean temperament

Behavior: Determined, ambitious, workaholic, competitive, tough, intense, humorless, confident, messianic zeal, high energy, and personal courage

Career vs. family: Constantly juggled family for career successfully. Sat for bar when twins were 4 months old, practiced law when they were 1, stood for Parliament when they were 6

Self-esteem: Built in childhood by father and personal self-sufficiency built on success

Hobbies: Intellectual political debate. Writing *The Downing Street Years* (1993)

Heroes: Father, Edward Heath, and Airey Neave

Honors: Many including Lady Thatcher. For ten years the most powerful woman in the world

18

Lillian Vernon—
Internally Empowered Entrepreneur

Successful innovation is not a feat of intellect, but of will.

—Joseph Schumpeter

Lillian Vernon is a giant in the world of female entrepreneurship because of her intuitive sense of what people want to buy across a myriad of product types. She has labeled her talent "my Golden Gut." She avoids using traditional market research techniques or focus groups to arrive at new product decisions. Instead, she is content to rely on her "Golden Gut" approach to product selection. Vernon feels she has a unique ability to sense the "average woman's" buying motives, being an "average woman" herself. Even though her success indicates she is *not* an average woman, Vernon's strategy has worked for many years. She maintains that her intuitive powers have been an important variable setting her apart from the pack. Although a keen intuitive sense is found in all great entrepreneurial and innovative individuals, most are not aware of their unique ability. Vernon is aware of this important personality trait and has used it to make the Lillian Vernon Corporation a leader in a highly competitive industry.

Vernon is an empowered, independent woman who has launched merchandising promotions that would terrorize traditional managers. One example of her nontraditional approach to promotion is her 100 percent money back guarantee of ten years for any product purchased from her catalog which does not meet the customer's total satisfaction. Keep in mind that the products sold in Vernon's catalogs are personalized items with the owner's initials or name imprinted, thus eliminating the product from resale. Try and get approval of that marketing promotion in a *Fortune* 500 company. The pink slip would be imminent. Vernon's unique and often iconoclastic approach to marketing shows the absolute confidence she has in her products and in her own decisions.

347

Her moxie and confidence have obviously been communicated to her massive customer base. She places the customer and service as her number-one priority, which is why the Lillian Vernon Corporation has been such a huge success.

Vernon's visionary genius and "Golden Gut" helped her launch the business from her kitchen table in 1951. She has since fashioned it into an internationally known powerhouse that mails in excess of 140 million catalogs annually, generating over $170 million in revenues in 1993. About 4 million customers purchase personalized gifts annually from her catalogs, the most notable of which have been Hillary Clinton, Tipper Gore, Frank Sinatra, Steven Spielberg, Loretta Lynn, and Arnold Schwarzenegger. Vernon's success has caused industry leaders to dub her the "Queen of Catalogs."

Vernon is an internally empowered and independent woman who reached the top of her profession by utilizing *simple* principles for resolving intricate problems in a dynamic world—a classic approach in all creative endeavors. This simple approach has repeatedly produced elegant solutions to complex problems, making Vernon one of America's eminent entrepreneurs. Vernon's business philosophy lives and dies by her aphorism, "I never sell anything I won't have in my own home." Another of her mottos is "Make the most of every opportunity." Vernon's management success is based on an internal focus manifesting itself in an awesome self-confidence. Vernon says, "I never let my mistakes defeat or distract me, but I learn from them and move forward in a positive way." She adheres to the principle of focusing on the "possibilities in life," not the problems inevitably faced by all entrepreneurs. Quality, not quantity, is her driving force. This operating style has helped build Lillian Vernon Corporation into the dominant gift catalog firm in America.

The Lillian Vernon Corporation went public in 1987, becoming the largest business founded by a woman to be listed on the American Stock Exchange. In 1993 the company posted sales of $173 million, making it the preeminent firm in the gift catalog industry. Vernon herself is a charismatic speaker for many business schools, six of whom have awarded her honorary doctorates. She is a director for many nonprofit organizations such as New York University, Bryant College, Children's Museum of Art, and on and on. This successful entrepreneur is now a wealthy woman due to her many years of hard work dedicated to excellence in whatever she tried. Like almost all successful entrepreneurs, Vernon never did it just for money. She started the company to supplement the family's income and since then it has always been a labor of love. To Vernon it has never been work because it is her passion and her life. But when people work diligently and passionately to be the very best, they end up the victor. Vernon is now financially independent. Her membership in the Committee of 200 (a group of the nation's most influential businesswomen) and the Women's Forum has acknowledged her as one of America's preeminent leaders. These groups were founded as leadership role models for young women aspiring to break through that proverbial glass ceiling as pioneering entrepreneurs or female professionals.

Personal Life History

Lillian Menasche was born on March 18, 1928, in Leipzig, Germany, the first daughter of an upper-middle-class industrialist. She had an older brother, Fred, who died when she was a teenager. The family left anti-Semitic Germany for Holland when she was five years old. They were then forced to flee Holland for the United States in 1937, when Lillian was just ten. These moves were negative experiences at the time, but in retrospect appear to have been a strong character-building factor in Vernon's success as an entrepreneur. These abrupt moves to foreign environments gave her a unique ability to cope with the unknown and built a resilient self-assurance in her. She was forced to learn new cultures, languages, and friends. Dealing with these unknowns as a cultural pioneer is the identical challenge faced by all entrepreneurs.

Herman Menasche was a loving father and became Vernon's first role model in life. His persistence and tenacity became indelibly imprinted on Lillian's young mind. She was impressed that he was able to adapt to terrible inequities that were not of his making and to move on in a positive fashion. He was never defeated by the harsh realities that forced him to sell a successful manufacturing business in Germany because of his ethnic heritage. He then started over again in mid-life, first in Holland and then in the United States. Vernon says his tenacity gave her an excellent role model for her later pioneering role as a businesswoman: "I guess my father was my role model, and his adaptability made a lasting impression on me. It's a quality I admire in people today—the ability to turn on a dime and do what has to be done."

Vernon describes her father's perseverance as one of the guiding principles in her climb to the top. She confides, "I so admire the fact that if he couldn't sell zippers anymore, he found something else in short supply, and got into that." Young Lillian attended three different schools and was taught in German, Dutch, and English prior to the eighth grade. She started school in Germany, moved on to Holland, and spent most of her school time in New York City. Lillian was a voracious reader and was raised in a permissive family environment. She was given the freedom to err and explore, which was instrumental in her later success.

As a teenager Vernon's role models became the pin-up female movie stars of Hollywood's golden age, the thirties and forties. Vernon also became enamored of a female entrepreneur in New York City during her college days. Estée Lauder was just making her major move into retailing and Vernon selected her as a mentor and emulated many of her actions. Lauder was a glamorous

New York cosmetics entrepreneur who started and presided over her own firm with an iron fist. Vernon has done the same. Like Lauder, Vernon spent her teenage years fantasizing about being beautiful and popular, since she was hypersensitive about being an immigrant and was enamored of Hollywood movie queens. She desperately wanted to be Americanized, a trait she shared with Lauder and Ayn Rand. Ironically all three women were immigrants, ended up in New York City, and became creative geniuses.

Vernon inherited her father's European work ethic and started working as a teenager. She had various jobs, the first of which was working as an usherette in a movie theater at the age of fourteen for the worldly sum of ten cents an hour. She then worked at Baton's Candy Shop as a salesgirl and says the experience was enormously beneficial to her later life as an entrepreneur: "These jobs all involved working with the public, so I learned to deal with all kinds of people and to handle myself with all personality types. It also helped me overcome being shy. I had to be outgoing." Vernon graduated from Julia Richmond High School in 1946. She attended New York University, where she majored in psychology, but dropped out in her junior year to marry Sam Hochberg and settle in suburban Mount Vernon. Vernon's Mount Vernon kitchen table was then to became part of history.

Professional Background

When Vernon began her mail-order firm at her kitchen table in 1951, she was a twenty-three-year-old pregnant housewife attempting to earn extra money for a growing family. She used $2,000 received as wedding gifts to finance her initial inventory of purses and belts and to place a $495 advertisement in *Seventeen* magazine. Vernon was operating in the classical style of the Promethean spirit and was prepared to pioneer in new fields where others had never traveled. Can you imagine Sears offering to personalize belts with a full money-back guarantee? Yet Sears was the largest catalog retailer, and Vernon's major competitor. Or imagine any other public firm offering a new product to a new market with no track record of success. Only an entrepreneurial spirit could operate in such a foreign environment. Sears, Montgomery Ward, or Speigel would never consider such an audacious undertaking.

Vernon was brave enough and maybe naive enough to do what no one else was willing to do. But she intuitively knew that women like herself would buy her products, and that "gut" knowledge gave her the innate confidence to pursue her own path. Her strategy made eminent sense to her, so she was able to ignore what the rest of the world thought. Vernon's genius was in offering customers the unique products they desired. Her strategy was doing what the established competitors were afraid to do: offer personalized one-of-a-kind products that were not mass-market items. Vernon was willing to take risks that the big boys were afraid of, and it became her strength. She had discovered niche marketing even though she had never heard of the concept. "Go where others fear to tread" is the rallying cry of most great entrepreneurs, and Vernon did exactly that. She took advantage of the weaknesses of the giants of the catalog industry (the inability to offer small-run niche products) and turned them into her strengths. Her basic strategy became the protective barrier to entry for the firms that could have buried her during those formative years. Vernon's insight made her a virtual overnight success.

Vernon's first two products, a belt and purse, included free personalization. Her first mail-order ad produced $32,000 worth of orders during the first twelve weeks of operation. Vernon was ecstatic about the unexpected success and advertised a personalized bookmark to see if she was just lucky the first time around. Sales more than doubled with this new product, and Vernon was on her way in more ways than one. She was not only financially successful but gained confidence with each new product success. Her success ballooned with one creative offering after another in product areas she herself found appealing. Vernon's next round of products included tote bags and brass knockers, and then anything she could think of that was "unique and affordable" and could be personalized. Vernon specialized in items of high value to "women like myself." She admits that her all-time favorites are pencils, but they never matched the success of her hugely successful dominoes. One of Vernon's more imaginative products were shamrock-patterned pantyhose for women desiring to celebrate St. Patrick's Day in style.

Vernon's intuitive feel for a product has always been her ally and she used this vehicle when entering the highly competitive mail-order catalog industry. She was about to compete head-on with the big firms, when in 1954 she published her first sixteen-page, black-and-white catalog. She mailed it to 125,000 existing and prospective customers. This strategy raised her annual revenue to $150,000 by 1955, when the company was still known as Vernon Specialties (named after her home town in New York). Vernon still wore many hats in the operation. She was the copy writer, buyer, and mail-room manager by day, and chief financial officer at night. As with all great entrepreneurs, Vernon always "knew everything that was going on" in the corporation, and still does. By 1965 the firm was large enough to incorporate and she formed the Lillian Vernon Corporation. By 1970 the company had annual revenues of $1 million. This unprecedented growth was due to Lillian's hands-on operating style, which she ascribes to the following business philosophy:

1. Always be considerate of others.
2. Don't be afraid to get your hands dirty.
3. Make time to have fun.

4. Use common sense in all decisions.

5. Plan your hunches and use your head.

One of Vernon's pet peeves is committees. She describes a committee as a group that takes "minutes" and wastes "hours." She is also adamant about empathizing with the customer, which has resulted in the company motto: "Thou shalt know thy customer." Vernon still relies on her "Golden Gut" for most major decisions and says she is normally 90 percent correct in her decisions on new products. Vernon's philosophy is, "You don't need a weatherman to tell you which way the wind is blowing. You do need to gather the important information, act on your best judgment, acknowledge and correct any mistakes." One clear testimony to this ideology is Vernon's total reliance on her twelve million catalog customers to cast economic votes on whether a product is viable or not. Vernon adamantly insists it is cheaper to launch a product, even if it is a failure, rather than do classic market research prior to launch. Most entrepreneurs would agree, as their axiom is most often: "You cannot do market research on something that has never been done before," or "You cannot effectively predict the success of future products based on the performance of past products." Vernon believes in this simple "gut" approach to management, which she sums up as "I try to use common sense in all of my decisions—perhaps common sense is the core ingredient in the entrepreneur."

Vernon's first husband, Sam Hochberg, worked with her until their divorce in 1969, which she says was a toll of the business. Vernon has continued as the chief buyer of merchandise for the company and travels the world—approximately 100,000 miles per year—in pursuit of unique but practical gifts that women like her would want to buy. Vernon's genius was in expanding her firm into niche product personalization coincident with the emergence of the totally impersonal shopping malls and video purchasing distribution channels. Vernon intuitively recognized that she was competing for "share of mind" of a female audience that wanted service and quality at an affordable price. As the gigantic department stores became more and more "depersonalized" with less and less service, Vernon became more personal and more distinctive as a competitive strategy. And it works. Vernon personalized the most impersonal of shopping—direct mail. One of the ways she has accomplished this is by using her "gut" to appeal to the consumer who wants service, quality, and unique personal products. The coup de grâce of this "personal" strategy was naming the business and catalogs after herself and her home town. This gave her catalog and company a personal feel for customers tired of dealing with corporations and acronyms.

Vernon still reads every word of copy on each new catalog and retains final approval on every catalog layout. Her famous money-back guarantee has been supplemented with a nineties version of customer service offering to fill orders by phone, fax, or mail 24 hours a day, 7 days a week, 365 days a year. Lillian Vernon Corporation went public in 1987, with Lillian selling off 31 percent of the firm for $28 million. She used some of the money to open a state-of-the-art, 486,000-square-foot national distribution center in Virginia Beach, Virginia. In 1990, Lillian Vernon Corporation was named the "Catalog of the Year" by the Catalog Trade Association. In 1991 Vernon opened her first outlet store in a suburb of Washington, D.C., to sell off discontinued products. The success of this approach has been so good that she now has six such stores strategically located along the East Coast. By 1993 the firm was publishing eighteen catalog editions including a new entry, "Lilly's Kids," aimed at children. Personalization has been her forte from the very beginning, making her firm the dominant personalized merchandiser in the country. The firm shipped over three million units of personalized items in 1993, and a Gallup Poll shows Lillian Vernon as one of the most well-known catalog companies in the United States, with brand recognition in excess of thirty million adults.

Vernon still travels extensively for the company and launches over 1,100 new products each year. Between 1988 and 1993 the firm mailed over 472 million catalogs featuring 65 million products. A testimony to Lillian's unique product approach is the 65 million personalized Christmas ornaments sold since their introduction in 1968. This competitive female entrepreneur has been eminently successful operating in a field dominated by men. She will go down in history as one of the female leaders of mail order, ranking with the likes of Richard Sears and A. Montgomery Ward. This internally empowered entrepreneur started with a dream and ended with an empire. Her awesome success is a testimony to her female intuition working overtime in bringing unique products to customers wanting personalized service. The catalog industry has become pervasive, with new catalogs emerging monthly, but none have been able to dislodge Vernon from her dominant leadership position at the top of the industry.

Temperament and Behavior

Lillian Vernon is an independent Promethean spirit who is the archetype for the classic female entrepreneur. She is an internally empowered (driven) woman of strong convictions with an autonomous spirit. She uses her intuition to make all of the important decisions in her life. Lillian has adamantly used her "Golden Gut" to make the most important decisions in the firm from the very beginning, often to the chagrin of younger business school graduates whom she hired as middle managers. At first she was convinced that "luck" was a variable in her continuing success. Then she decided that statistical probability was not involved in her "good fortune," but rather the more intuitive and personal factors of expert product selection, purchasing acuity, and insightful promotional programs. She says her success is due to "relentless effort and achievement" (sounds like a quote from Ayn Rand). It was really based on her perceptive business sense and her demands for qualitative excellence. Vernon insists that her success is based on instinct, not market research. I would add self-confidence and a flair for entrepreneurial risk-taking as important variables in Vernon's success. Her admonition "I never sell anything I won't have in my own home" is a testimony to that self-confidence and self-esteem.

As a leader and boss, Vernon is tough but fair. She is an opinionated and vocal executive who always says what she feels. She is a great people person who uses an extroverted personality as an asset in talking to everyone who will listen about her product selections. Vernon's impatience and structure are attributes that assist her in the ever-dynamic catalog business. Vernon is the classical Promethean temperament known as an extroverted-intuitive-thinking-judger on the Myers-Briggs scale of personality. She fits these types, who pursue the opportunities in life and are highly imaginative risk-takers. These types are the architects of change in the world. Vernon uses her vision to see the forest, not the trees, with a constant focus on the possibilities, not the liabilities. She is a macro-vision woman who sees the positives and ignores the negatives. More than anything she is an internally empowered independent female who knows where she is going at all times and uses her own driven energy—not others'—to realize her dreams.

Family versus Career

Vernon married Sam Hochberg after dropping out of New York University in 1950. When she became pregnant she intended to be a full-time mother supplementing the family income with her home-operated business. "We did not have enough to live on . . . to have an apartment, have a child, have a car. I wanted household help, so there was not anything to do but go to work." Vernon expected to become a mail-order legend in her own time: "I woke up one day and said, I have a $130 million business." When queried about starting the business out of her home she responded, "It was very unfashionable for women to work in those days. So I thought mail order was a wonderful thing I could do out of the house, stay home, change diapers, do the whole thing."

Vernon's approach was similar to that of Margaret Thatcher, Golda Meir, and Estée Lauder. She decided to raise her kids while having a career, except in her case the family was paramount in her life and the business was an ancillary project. Vernon managed both but not without a price. Her first marriage became a casualty of her attempt to do both simultaneously. The Hochbergs had two boys, David and Fred, before she and Sam were divorced in 1969. She told *USA Weekend* in 1986, "I really loved my first husband. If we hadn't worked together, I think we'd probably still be married." Vernon's two sons appear to have survived the experience quite well. Vernon has traveled extensively with both David and Fred Hochberg as business associates. Fred, the heir apparent, left the business in 1993 to pursue a life in politics, leaving her younger son, David, as the head of communications for the company. He evidently does not have aspirations to lead the firm like his brother, Fred.

Vernon married Robert Katz in 1970 and they stayed married until 1990. When she divorced Katz she obviously concluded that the company was her lifetime passion and changed her name from Lillian Katz to Lillian Vernon. It appears that Vernon has decided that the company is more enduring than other relationships and now founder and company are inseparable in both name and spirit. Her professional and personal lives included having two marriages and two sons coincident with building the dominant company in the mail-order business. The family certainly suffered during the time Vernon fulfilled the triple role of mother, wife, and chief executive. No one can have two masters, especially simultaneously. Lillian appears to have been one of the more successful woman who raised a family while growing a business. Most other women have not been so successful.

Life Crisis

Vernon and her Jewish family were forced to flee anti-Semitic Germany in the mid-thirties and move to Holland for a short period prior to relocating permanently to New York City in 1937. This appears to have been more of a crisis for her parents than for Vernon but on closer observation such dramatic changes during the formative stages of a young girl's life are very traumatic. Young Lillian was faced with learning two new languages, two new cultures, and the loss of friends and familiar surroundings at a very impressionable age. The move from Germany to Holland to America took place when Lillian was between the ages of four and ten. Such transience at a critical developmental period in a child's life imprints her with unexpected life-long abilities. A child faced with unknown and foreign environments learns to cope with the unfamiliar and becomes armed with self-sufficiency when pioneering. Vernon learned to survive new cultures, languages, and schools. She was unknowingly being groomed in the precise experiences required of all innovators and entrepreneurs: building a strong tolerance for ambiguity. This early training was certainly a negative at the time but ultimately armed Vernon with enormous character strengths as an adult. Vernon's early transience was invaluable experience to draw on when she faced crises virtually every day while developing her company.

Vernon was a teenager when her older brother, Fred, was killed in World War II. She doesn't discuss this tragic event, which indicates it is still a traumatic memory for her. Such experiences have been found to be predictive or potentially causal in great achievement. As discussed earlier in this work Ilya Prigogine says that we reach a "bifurcation point" in any great crisis and then evolve to a higher state of being. He says, "Many seeming systems of *breakdown,* are actually harbingers of *breakthrough.*" It appears that part of Vernon's tremendous drive and focus to succeed were precipitated by both her early transience and her brother's untimely death. Research on both male and female creative visionaries indicates that the most critical period of life for impacting the behavior of an individual is between the ages of five and twelve. This is the exact period during which Vernon was facing the traumatic experience of moving from Germany to Holland to the United States. She survived the experience but her fearless persona and passionate commitment to perfection had to have emanated from her early experiences with trauma and transience.

Internally Empowered Entrepreneurial Success

This internally empowered entrepreneur is the consummate businesswoman who has used an enterprising capitalistic spirit to make her way to the top of the business world. Vernon's own well-defined formula for success is based on ten tips as follows:

Lillian's Tips for Success

1. Make time for yourself and your family.
2. Surround yourself with the best people possible.
3. Be open to new ideas and better ways to do things.
4. Be prepared to take risks.
5. Like what you do and like what you sell.
6. Don't dwell on your mistakes or setbacks—but instead learn and grow from them and then move on. Never let your mistakes defeat or discourage you.
7. Don't try to do it all—delegate!
8. Don't grow too fast without the proper systems and people in place to handle it.
9. Don't be afraid of computer technology that can help make your business more efficient.
10. Don't spend more money than you have—set realistic budgets and stick to them. Keep your debts manageable.

Lillian Vernon sells 90 percent of her products to women, which in 1993 amounted to 35,000 orders each day. She markets gift, household, gardening, decorative, and children's products in twenty different catalogs. Over 141 million of these catalogs were mailed to customers during 1993. Vernon's unique style of empowered independence built through hard work and perseverance made this possible. A testimony to her self-confidence is Vernon's offer of a full rebate to any dissatisfied customer for up to ten years. That is her way of showing that satisfaction is always guaranteed at Lillian Vernon. This philosophy could only have come from an entrepreneur who had an inviolable belief in her product and her ability. You will never find such a program in a bureaucratic organization because it does not have such faith in itself or its products. That is the style that has made Lillian Vernon a nonpareil business leader.

Summary

The consummate female entrepreneur that is Lillian Vernon has been awarded five honorary doctorates based on her phenomenal success in the world of business. Her Promethean spirit is what has led her to such lofty heights. She is the first to admit that she never imagined such success in 1951 while sitting at her kitchen table trying to make money for groceries. She had a dream and has been eminently successful implementing that dream. Vernon's 1993 holdings in her company give some credence to how those who pursue their dreams can be rewarded. Vernon's net worth based on 1993 stock prices is in the $100 million range. Not bad for a mom-and-pop start-up operation designed to supplement a husband's salary and provide domestic help in the house. Vernon used her intuitive vision of what average women wanted to buy, offered unique products competitors were not prepared to provide, and then merchandised them with an unheard-of 100 percent guarantee. When coupled with an entrepreneurial flair, this shows a woman of true creative genius. Lillian Vernon is the quintessential role model for any young woman aspiring to achieve in a dynamic world.

Lillian Menasche Vernon
CEO of Lillian Vernon—Queen of Catalogs
b. March 18, 1928, Leipzig, Germany

Dominant trait: Internally empowered entrepreneur

Religion: Jewish, not devout

Mottos: "I never sell anything I won't have in my own home"; "Make the most of every opportunity."

Philosophy: "I never let my mistakes or setbacks defeat or distract me, but I learn from them and move forward in a positive way"; "Don't be afraid to get your hands dirty."

Nickname: Queen of Catalogs

Creation/innovation: Founded largest gift catalog company in the world; products personalized for free; 10-year money-back guarantee

Products/contributions: In 1993 circulated 141 million catalogs averaging 108 pages featuring 700 products. These generated $173 million in revenue.

Success: Built company from scratch through two different husbands and outlasted the likes of Sears and Sharper Image catalog firms. Largest co. founded by woman on American Stock Exchange

Self-description: "I make quick decisions. I take chances relying on what I consider my 'Golden Gut.' . . . I know everything that is going on."

Birth order: First-born daughter; brother three years older

Childhood transience: Moved from Leipzig, Germany, to Holland at age 5 and to New York at age 10

Father's occupation: Father owned a manufacturing business

Mentors: Father and Estée Lauder

Childhood upbringing: Worked from age 14 as movie theater usherette at 10 cents an hour and candy shop sales clerk, which formed her image of work: "I realized then that work could and should be a pleasant and enjoyable experience." Read a lot. Permissive upbringing.

Formal education: Started in Germany, then Holland, then New York City. Three years at New York University in psychology

Life Crises: Family forced to flee the Nazis and move to U.S. Brother killed in WWII while she was teenager.

Marriages/liaisons: Married Sam Hochberg, a lingerie merchant; divorced 1969; remarried to Robert Katz, a Lucite manufacturer; divorced 1990 and took Vernon as surname

---

Risk-taking: "Be prepared to take risks"; "Decision-making at Lillian Vernon has always been— and continues to be—entrepreneurial"; "I take chances relying on my 'Golden Gut.' "

Temperament: Extroverted-Intuitive-Thinking-Judger—Promethean Temperament

Behavior: Prefers "different" (innovator style) of behavior; intuitive; tough; quick temper; competitive; impatient; confident; strong work ethic

Career vs. family: Working mother and entrepreneur through two marriages. Two sons, David and Fred Hochberg, both of whom have worked for their mother

Self-esteem: Her definition of her success: "I was an immigrant, so I had the desire to fit in and contribute to and become a part of this society."

Hobbies: Reading, movies, plays, and the opera

Heroes: Movie stars when young and Estée Lauder

Honors: Director of 14 organizations; five honorary doctorates and myriad "Woman of the Year" and entrepreneurial awards

19

Linda Wachner—"Type A" Workaholic

Vision is the art of seeing things invisible.

—Jonathan Swift

We must be the change we see in the world.

—Mohandes K. Gandhi

Linda Wachner has accomplished what many young girls only dream about. She has been able to realize her childhood dream while still very young. Her dramatic success is due to an obsessive drive, an indefatigable spirit, and a "Type A" work ethic. She has persevered in the face of enormous odds and is a well-respected corporate leader in a field dominated by males. Very few women ever make it as far as the executive suite in a *Fortune* 500 company, let alone control and dominate the organization as she does. Wachner took over a hundred-year-old firm through determination, perseverance, and her own unique blend of focus and drive. These traits were instilled in Wachner when she was eleven years old, encased in a full body cast. At that time she vowed one day to run her own company. Wachner not only realized her dream but her company, Warnaco, just happens to be the largest firm of its kind.

Wachner made it to the very top with little help. She had a dream and worked diligently for its realization. She has left a lot of corpses in her wake, most of whom never knew what hit them as she moved with lightninglike speed in reaching her objective. This driven woman worships price/earnings ratios, earnings per share, EBIT (her mascot frog symbolizes this acronym of "earnings before income tax"), and return on investment. These are the sacrosanct barometers by which Wachner measures success, and everyone who works for her knows it.

Fortune magazine (June 15, 1992) called Linda, "America's most successful businesswoman." Her $3 million annual base salary is indicative of the value

361

362 PROFILES OF FEMALE GENIUS

her board of directors places on her. Wachner's total compensation in 1991 approached $23 million based on stock grants and other perquisites. This "Type A" executive is the first woman ever to capture a company in a hostile takeover, turn it around, and take it public. As CEO of Warnaco—the largest *Fortune* 500 company run by a female—Wachner successfully cut the company's debt and boosted its stock price by 75 percent. She bet $10 million of her own money on the venture and this willingness to put her money on the table as risk capital has been reflected in her personal holdings, totalling $72 million in 1993. Wachner certainly qualifies as a creative genius for having started as a lowly brassiere buyer and working her way to the very top of her industry. And she did it by age forty.

Personal Life History

Linda Joy Wachner was born on February 3, 1946, to older parents in Forest Hills, New York. Her father, Herman, was a New York City fur salesman; her mother, Shirley, a housewife. Linda was the second-born child but raised as an only child since her sister was eighteen years older and was out of the house during Linda's upbringing. Linda was at the leading edge of the baby-boom generation and raised as a fifties child with doting and permissive parents. She says they treated her as an adult very early in life (Margaret Mead said the same of her parents). Wachner's life in the nuclear family generation was unique due to older Jewish parents who instilled in her the invaluable gift of self-esteem. Being an only child of older parents caused Wachner to spend a great deal of time alone or with adults. The result was a very self-sufficient person who does not need to rely on anyone else for moral support. Wachner's parents endowed her with a strong self-esteem by telling her how wonderful she was and how she could do no wrong. She believed to such a degree that by the time she went away to college, "our roles were reversed. I became their surrogate parent, their support system."

When Wachner was eleven a boy at school pulled a chair out from under her. This accident was to change her life. "As a result of that accident I needed corrective spinal surgery and remained in a body cast until age thirteen." At home from the hospital Wachner was immobile for almost two years. She said of the experience: "I was alone, with nothing to do except focus on tomorrow and not know when it would come. Sometimes, when I'm very tired, I still dream about that silver traction triangle hanging over my head" (*Working Woman,* 1992).

Wachner has been a driven woman since this early experience: "I have an unrelenting need to do the right thing—to be as close to a goal as possible." Wachner went on to graduate from high school at age sixteen and attended

Buffalo State College, where she majored in business administration. Wachner's work ethic was apparent in college as she worked at New York City department stores during every college break. She remembers, "I sold in every department there was," giving her the background for her future career path. Wachner was very active in extracurricular activities while in college. She also worked as a proctor at exams, graded papers, and worked in the dean's office. Wachner played tennis and skied, which has become a life-long passion. Linda graduated with a bachelor's in business in 1966 at age twenty and embarked on her destiny in the retail clothing industry. She began her career on her home turf in New York City and set out to realize her childhood dream of owning her own company.

Professional Background

Wachner started where all great creative visionaries must begin—at the bottom. She was hired as a buyer for Associated Merchandising in New York at ninety dollars a week. Her beginning title of "assistant market representative" meant she was a glorified "gofer" in the parlance of business management. One of Wachner's first jobs was researching customers on the floor of the store. This was invaluable experience that she has never forgotten. It is where the action is, the critical point of purchase. That training has been indelibly imprinted on Wachner and today she still insists on feedback from the store floor from every one of her managers. Wachner refined her technique of grilling customers and sales clerks in this first job, where she learned to find out "What's selling today?" and "Why?" and "Why are you buying that dress?" and "What product would you prefer?"

Wachner moved halfway across the United States to accept a promotion at Houston's Foley's Department stores in 1967. She made this move to become an assistant buyer. Once again she spent most of her time cruising the store floors finding out what people were buying and became an expert on customer needs and wants during the following year and a half with the company. Macy's hired Wachner in 1969 as the brassiere and girdle buyer and she returned once more to New York City. Wachner's reputation as a woman on the move was growing as she never hesitated to take on any new position, no matter the location, as long as it was an advancement toward her ultimate goal. Wachner had already realized one of her initial goals. At age twenty-two she was one of the youngest buyers, for Macy's flagship department store on 34th Street in Manhattan. Wachner built her expertise in the garment industry during her five-year stint with Macy's between 1969 and 1974.

During her Macy's days Linda met her husband, Seymour Applebaum, on a flight from Miami to New York. He was playing gin rummy across the aisle from Wachner and at some point, in her inimitable style, she told him, "That's the wrong card." Applebaum ignored her advice and she admitted later that she knew nothing about the game. The incident sparked a relationship that ended in marriage. Applebaum became Wachner's mentor and she still speaks of him with uncommon reverence. "My husband was the first person who told me that I could achieve whatever I set my mind to, and I believed him." Applebaum encouraged Wachner's career ambitions and she moved on to Warnaco for a three-year stay, from 1974 to 1977. Wachner first cracked the proverbial glass ceiling at Warnaco. In 1975 she was named the first female vice president in the company's hundred-year history. She was told by the president of Warnaco on being given the promotion, "You got this [promotion] and you shouldn't expect too much more" (*Working Woman,* 1992). He was subtly telling Wachner that she was a token female executive and would not be promoted further. This type of thinking was not in Wachner's vocabulary, and just eleven years later she would enact her own subtle revenge by becoming CEO and chairman of the company via a hostile takeover.

At Warnaco Wachner met Mary Wells, chairman of the advertising company handling the Warner account. Wells had made a meteoric rise from copywriter to the top of Madison Avenue, and was a logical role model for Wachner. Wells was "very bright," tough, and very aggressive, the very same traits that characterized Wachner. Wells became Wachner's female business mentor and Wachner remembers her as "one of the first shining stars in my life, one of the first to believe in me." And believe she did. Wells introduced Wachner to David Mahoney, the chairman of Norton Simon, the parent company of Max Factor. In 1979 Mahoney hired Wachner, then thirty-three, as president of Max Factor's U.S. division, headquartered in Los Angeles. It was an unusually young age for any executive of a multimillion dollar enterprise, especially considering that Wachner had no prior experience as a president. This was to prove a key move in Wachner's trek to the top of her industry. She admits that this was her real break into the fast-track corporate world. Wachner says, "A lot of people have given me a lot of breaks, but when David Mahoney made me president of the U.S. division of Max Factor, that was the biggest." This was to be a monumental challenge for the thirty-three-year-old Wachner. Max Factor was losing about $16 million a year and was staffed by an entrenched group of "good old boys." Wachner was able to stem the hemorrhaging in her first year and was able to produce a $5 million operating profit in her second. She then duplicated the feat with Max Factor worldwide, turning around a losing situation to profitability within two years. The company introduced a new fragrance, Le Jardin de Max Factor, which won three Fragrance Foundation awards in 1984. Wachner accomplished this with a hard-nosed, no-frills approach to a management that had been steeped in perks and a self-preservation mentality. Wachner became known as the "hatchet lady," as she used mass firings to break up the "good old boys club."

It was at Max Factor that Linda started her "Do It Now" notebooks approach to management. She insists that every executive keep a spiral notebook—like those used in high school—to record both problems and opportunities. Her "Do It Now" symbol is inscribed in large letters on the cover. "Do It Now" became the company motto, emblazoned on memo pads everywhere. Bill Finklestein, controller at Max Factor, said of her style, "Working for Wachner is like working for a start-up: It's as if somebody just set up a circus tent." Wachner's ability to function with the mentality of a start-up company is the reason she is in this book with the other great start-up creative visionaries. During this period Wachner acquired her reputation as a tough taskmaster and control freak. Wachner is not deterred by being described as totally focused on the bottom line and not sensitive to personal criticism. She has been called "magnificent" by one group and "absolutely the worst manager I have ever encountered" (*Fortune,* 1986) by another. One male casualty of her management style says, "I just couldn't take it." Another says, "She has a lot of the characteristics of a hard-driving male boss," adding, "Do people resent her? Yes. But people respect her. She's an executive, not a woman or a man" (*Fortune,* 1992). Other women executives are not so kind. According to one, "She knows the business back and forth. But she's impatient—and she has a longshoreman's mouth." Sounds like the description of a tough male boss.

Wachner says of her Max Factor time, "If you have to get a company turned around before it bleeds to death, you have to have a certain posture in the way you go about things. I'm tough but I'm fair." Not everyone thought so, especially many of the good old boys who bit the dust during her turbulent regime. Wachner's style was one of total control. She asked for results and if they were not forthcoming the individual responsible was gone.

Wachner's time at Max Factor gave her the track record needed to attract venture capital to back her in her own operation, which, after all, was her life-long dream. She had been grooming herself to operate her "own" company and by 1984 the time was right. Wachner approached her boss at Max Factor and received a go-ahead to raise the money to buy the operation she was running. But the board of directors was shocked when she returned with $280 million from a New York investment firm. They changed their minds about allowing her to buy the firm. Wachner responded by resigning. She set out to find her own operation to buy via a leveraged buyout.

Wachner put together a $905 million buyout package with another investment banking firm and set out to buy Revlon. The deal was virtually complete when Ronald Perlman of Pantry Pride stepped forward and bought Revlon for $1.8 billion. Wachner was not deterred, however. She convinced the investment banking firm Drexel Burnum Lambert to back her offer for Warnaco. Warnaco was the hundred-year-old firm she had worked for previously as their token female vice president. She was successful in arranging a hostile takeover of this old-line firm for $550 million, $500 million of which was debt. It was not the kind of leverage for the faint of heart, although no one ever accused Wachner of timidity.

Wachner's takeover was unprecedented. It was the first time in history that a *Fortune* 500 firm was acquired in an unfriendly takeover by a female. It was not without risk, however: Wachner personally staked everything she had ($10 million) in acquiring 770,000 shares in the company with a prearranged agreement to purchase an additional 1.3 million shares at $4.66 per share at a future date. When asked by Christine Donahue of *Ms.* magazine (1987) about her decision to buy Warnaco, Wachner said, "I risked everything I had to buy this company. I put my money down on the line." Then she added, "It proves you *can* go home again."

Wachner took the company private and increased sales by 30 percent, profits by 145 percent, and meticulously cut the debt by 40 percent during her next five years at the helm. In October 1991 she took the company public again at $20 per share and it has since risen to $35 a share, making Wachner's big gamble a profitable one. She had gambled her total life's savings with her 10 percent stake in the company and by 1993 her net worth was in the range of $100 million. Warnaco pays Linda $3 million annually to perform her own unique form of magic. She has no family and freely admits that the company is her family. When *Cosmopolitan* queried her about her personal life in 1990, Wachner said, "It's very hard to meet people with the patience to understand that my business comes first."

Wachner has become the Jewish mother hovering over Warnaco's products and personnel. The company's products include an intimate apparel line constituting 60 percent of sales, men's wear products (32 percent of sales), and a number of retail outlet stores accounting for the remaining 8 percent of sales revenues. The intimate apparel brands are easily recognizable, including Valentino, Scaasi, Ungaro, Bob Mackie, Blanche, and Fruit of the Loom clothing items and Warner & Olga brassieres. The men's wear lines include Christian Dior, Hathaway shirts, Chaps, Golden Bear (Jack Nicklaus) sportswear, Puritan, and Valentino. The company makes private-label products for Victoria's Secret in the amount of $30 million a year, in addition to a Wal-Mart manufacturing agreement for many of their private branded garments.

Wachner achieved her life's ambition of owning and operating her own *Fortune* 500 company at the very young age of forty-five. She is only one of three women CEOs heading *Fortune* 500 firms, the others being Mary Kay Ash (featured in this work), and Katherine Graham of the *Washington Post,* who inherited her position. Wachner's next goal is to "be able to buy a Warner's bra every place I can buy a Coke." This demanding workaholic is tough but fair and her stockholders love her style as she never equivocates about what is important—the EBIT. When Wachner was in that body cast as a very young girl she had made herself a promise that one day she would be ferried across the Triboro Bridge in her own Cadillac instead of that ambulance. She has lived to see that promise come to fruition and then some. She could now buy the limousine company if she were so inclined.

Temperament: Intuitive-Thinking

Wachner is the prototypical "Type A" personality. She is the classic "control freak" who needs total control over her environment. It appears Wachner's early childhood infirmity and loneliness built in her an unsatiable craving to achieve. Her self-esteem seems to be inextricably tied to her success in business. She has an obsession to win at any cost, and she exudes the classic "rushing sickness" found in this type of personality—fast talking, walking, eating, and working. Patience is not one of Wachner's redeeming qualities. She has a very short attention span and a short fuse when it comes to incompetent subordinates. Wachner is the type who feels guilty going on vacation or even watching television. She "multitasks," tending to read a magazine while watching a movie or working on budgets while sitting on the beach. Wachner is intolerant of mediocrity or failure in others and appears to be in a hurry when she is sitting still.

Wachner attempts to keep her work at the office, but in her inimitable fashion has trouble leaving the office. She says, "I don't bring work home anymore. I stay here until I get it done. . . . The problem is that sometimes I don't leave the office." Wachner is not into small talk and avoids nonproductive conversations. Like other "Type A" personalities, Wachner has an obsession with winning: success is in the score not the play! Many males with Wachner's type of personality have been labeled "megalomaniacs on a mission." Wachner qualifies for this description in most respects.

Wachner is an extroverted-intuitive-thinking-judger on the Myers-Briggs personality typology. She has a Promethean temperament and a field-marshall-type behavior, which is how the psychologists metaphorically describe this temperament type. It is an apt description of Wachner. She has an intuitive feel for what is right in new products even though she certainly operates her business by the numbers. She is an extrovert and lives her life in a structured manner, needing to make decisions without procrastination. Wachner's perception of the world is a macro one, as she sees the forest for the trees and has an intuitive flair. Her style is "thinking" in contrast to "feeling," which is most prevalent in females as a group. Wachner's axiom, "Do it now," is testimony to her belief in closure as a business style.

Wachner is sensitive to the needs and possibilities in new ventures and enjoys climbing new mountains. Her exercise passion, skiing, gives a clue to

her thrill-seeking nature. Wachner has also taken flying lessons, another testimony to her higher-than-normal risk-taking propensity. Sitting in her Manhattan suite of offices one would not see a downhill skier or pilot in Linda
Wachner. This imperious and demanding big-city CEO lives her life aggressively
both personally and professionally. She has an aggressive, competitive, and
risk-taking nature not often found in female executives. These traits have helped
her succeed in a field dominated by males. She is often insensitive to the feelings
of others as she is devoted to superior execution and the bottom line. Wachner
says, "I know I push very hard, but I don't push anyone harder than I push
myself." Even so, Wachner has a soft side and a certain sensitivity to women's
issues that belie her tough exterior. She has implemented an expense account
deduction for her female employees for child-care when they have to work
late. That is unheard of in other, less strict corporate organizations. Wachner's
personality can be summarized as a Promethean temperament with a special
proclivity for the numbers and a "Type A" work ethic that would fatigue the
hardiest of souls.

Family versus Career

Wachner is an example of a female visionary who places career over all else.
She sacrificed having children for her profession and has not found another
male willing to share her with Warnaco since her husband died in 1983. Wachner
married Seymour Applebaum at age twenty-seven, when he was fifty-nine. He
became her father figure, mentor, lover, and confidant. Their relationship was
strangely similar to Maria Callas's relationship with a father-like husband. Applebaum was thirty-one years older and Wachner says, "I felt like we were fighting
for his life the whole time." He finally died at age seventy-one in 1983.

Wachner has some regret over her decision not to have a family. Her
husband was in ill health for much of their marriage. Wachner says, "He was
in and out of the hospital with heart problems. I thought at the time it would
be wrong to bring a child into the world with one parent ill. My vision was
wrong—I'd be better off having the child now." She rationalized her decision
to forego motherhood to *Working Woman* in 1992, "I don't think I would
have had the time to raise a child and deal with the quality of male chauvinism
I was dealing with then."

Wachner summed up her philosophy of what comes first in her life to
Cosmopolitan in June 1990, "I think I have made the company my family."
She went on to explain how work is her passion. She sleeps very little and
maintains an energy level that leaves little chance for male companionship.
Wachner's only rule is to take off Thanksgiving and Christmas to go skiing.
She tells all new companions, "Business comes first." Wachner is not a wall-

flower, however. When asked out for dinner she says, "A lot of men have called and asked me to dinner and have found that I've said yes, and they've found that if I like them, I'll fly across the country for the dinner. If I suspect that someone doesn't have a sense of humor, though, I'm not interested." That is the spirit of a committed female power broker who has no qualms about the "personal" versus the "professional" aspects of her life. The professional wins every time.

Life Crisis

Wachner found herself afflicted with a spinal deformation at the age of eleven from a school accident. When in a body cast for almost two years she didn't think she would ever walk again. Wachner says, "The focus I have today comes from when I was sick. When you want to walk again, you learn to focus on that with all your might, and you don't stop until you do it." After interviewing her in 1992, Maggie Mahar of *Working Woman* concluded, "Like most extraordinarily successful individuals, Linda Wachner succeeded not because she wanted to, not because she hoped to, but because she felt she had to." There is certainly evidence that Wachner has been driven by some magical force ever since that period in her life. She has an energy beyond compare. Other executives have given up trying to keep up with her nonstop, whirlwind pace. Wachner is the prototypical example of the obsessively driven visionary often found in the true creative geniuses of the world.

After Wachner's childhood crisis everything else pales in comparison. However, her familial relationships have not fared well by the fates. Her whole being is integrated into work especially since she found herself alone in the world. She lost her husband after only twelve years of marriage in 1983. She lost her father when she was twenty-three; her only sibling, Barbara, in 1981; and finally her mother in 1987. Out of adversity, resolve. In Wachner's words: "When I wasn't able to walk, I used to make these little vows to myself: 'Oh, if I could walk, I know I would never get tired. I know I could do more.' It's definitely a psychological thing" (*Cosmopolitan,* June 1990).

"Type A" Success

This workaholic visionary has achieved enormous success based on an internal drive to achieve. She vowed to never slow down or get tired during those tormented months when she was constrained to a cast and she has never forgotten that pledge. She is obsessively driven to succeed and never allows feelings or adversaries to get in the way of where she is going. Wachner's style has made her some bitter enemies along the way to becoming a successful executive and a rich woman. *Fortune* magazine (June 1992) called her "America's Most Successful Businesswoman," then went on to describe her relentless drive to the top over the bodies of many male executives. One former executive said, "A lot of people have been run over by Linda. She will do anything, *just anything,* to get to the bottom line." Wachner's first boss at Associated Merchandising Corp. sums up her style: "She gets right to the point, and I think her frankness scares people."

Wachner told *Working Woman* in 1992 that women who are focused have an edge over men. She says, "As men grow older, they grow more rigid. As women grow older they become more flexible." Wachner believes more women can reach an exalted position of power if they stay focused and do not falter in the face of adversity. She feels women are hung up on personal approval, which keeps them from making the tough decisions:

> Young women are frightened; they don't have the clear role definition that men have from childhood. But women are able to roll with more punches, and because of their great flexibility, they can breathe fresh air into a stodgy environment. If they took advantage of that, they'd get a lot further. (*Working Woman,* May 1992)

Linda Wachner has been self-sufficient most of her life because she was raised as the only child of elderly parents and treated like an adult. A permissive upbringing groomed her to believe in herself and built a strong self-esteem and confidence. These qualities have become her ally in becoming a competitive leader with the self-confidence to play with the "big boys" on their own turf. Wachner's success has been achieved with an elegance and style all her own. Her aggressive and impatient workaholic behavior have made her a match for any man who has crossed her path. These traits have made her eminently successful and made her the consummate creative genius who showed that a woman can get to the top using the same mentality that men have used for years.

Summary

Linda Wachner's impact on the world of business has been nothing short of sensational. Every job she has undertaken has been executed with panache and perfection. Linda even excelled in the entry-level positions of her youth. Her focus has been her forte and her work ethic, which includes working on holidays and weekends, is beyond reason for most individuals. Wachner's success has allowed her many of the perks of the rich. Wachner is an avid skier who owns a contemporary glass house in Aspen, Colorado. Wachner also has homes in Los Angeles and New York, which she uses sparingly. She skis with oilman Marvin Davis and Helen Gurley Brown and socializes with Barbara Walters. She admits to an unusual work schedule but is often insensitive to other executives' inability to match her boundless energy. She says, "I have enormous energy. I'm a morning person and an afternoon person and an evening person. And I will stay up for two or three days in a row to get it done." That is staying power and the ingredient of true creative genius in the likeness of Thomas Edison and Soichiro Honda, both of whom preached perspiration over inspiration.

Wachner's $3 million annual compensation makes her one of America's highest-paid executives and *the* highest paid female executive anywhere. Wachner's total 1991 compensation of $23 million wowed most Wall Street executives. Wachner has made it to the top of what once would have been referred to as the "good old boys club." No one dares make such a reference to Wachner, however, as she commands the utmost respect from the male power elite in *Fortune* 500 circles. Wachner has made it through the glass ceiling without any mortal wounds. She has weathered a few cuts and scrapes from the experience, but it has left her undaunted in the pursuit of her goals and aspirations for Warnaco. Wachner has used a simple acronym, "Do it now," as her inspirational motivation for workforces raised on Parkinson's Law of "Work expands to fill the time allotted." Wachner's approach has caused Parkinson's accolytes to find either shrinks or new jobs.

Wachner built her experience and résumé from within the walls of corporate America and then had the temerity to go out and acquire her own firm by putting $10 million of her own money on the line. For this *Ms.* magazine named her "Woman of the Year" for 1986. Wachner's accomplishments speak for themselves and Linda Wachner certainly qualifies as one of the true creative geniuses who have changed the way America thinks about female leaders.

Linda Joy Wachner
CEO and Chairwoman—Warnaco Group, Inc.
b. February 3, 1946, Forrest Hills, N.Y.

Dominant trait: "Type A" workaholic

Religion: Jewish, not devout

Mottos: "Do It Now"; frog her mascot for "EBIT—Earnings Before Income Tax"

Philosophy: "I want to make Warner's the Coca Cola of the bra business"; "I really value loyalty, decency, teamwork, innovativeness, stick-to-it-iveness, and I can-do-it-ism."

Nicknames: Princess of Pay, Workaholic Linda, Fire and Ice

Products/contributions: Sells one of every three bras in U.S. Warner's, Olga, Valentino, Speedo, Bob Mackie, Fruit of the Loom, Christian Dior, Hathaway, Jack Nicklaus, Chaps, and Victoria's Secret private labels

Successes: President of Max Factor age 33; first woman ever to acquire a *Fortune* 500 company in hostile takeover, turn it around, and take it public all by age forty. Highest-paid female executive. Largest public company run by female.

Self-description: "I have an unrelenting need to do the right thing—to be as close to a goal as possible"; "I'm fair and I'm demanding."

Birth order: Second born, sister eighteen years older, raised as only child

Childhood transience: Little movement but lonely and unhappy

Father's occupation: New York City fur salesman

Mentors: "My husband [Seymour Applebaum] taught me to hold on to my dream." Mary Wells, Madison Avenue executive, was "one of the first shining stars in my life, one of the first to believe in me."

Childhood upbringing: Raised by older parents who treated her as an adult, generating self-sufficiency

Formal education: Buffalo State College business administration degree, 1966, at age 20

Life crisis: At age 11 she thought she would never walk again; in body cast for 1.5 yrs.

Marriages/liaisons: Married Seymour Applebaum at age 27; he was 59. Applebaum died in 1983.

Risk-taking: Bet all $10 million of her savings on Warnaco. Avid skier

Temperament: Extroverted-intuitive-thinking-judger—driven to achieve

Behavior: Aggressive, impatient, workaholic, and "Type AAA" behavior

Career vs. family: Sacrificed children and all relationships for career

Self-esteem: Built in childhood. "The focus I have today comes from when I was sick. . . . I knew if I could walk, I would never get tired."

Hobbies: Skiing, tennis, golf, work—not necessarily in that order

Heroes: Mary Wells

Honors: "America's Most Successful Businesswoman," *Fortune,* 1992. *Ms.* magazine's "Woman of Year," 1986.

20

Oprah Winfrey—Persuasive Charismatic

Don't aim for success—the more you aim at it and make it a target, the more you're going to miss it. For success, like happiness, cannot be pursued; it must ensue.

—Victor Frankl, *Paradoxical Intention*

There is a limit to the development of the intellect but none to that of the heart.

—Mohandas K. Gandhi

Oprah Winfrey is "Everywoman." She has that unique persona which attracts her to women and men of all creeds, races, nationalities, and ages. Eighty-year-old great-grandmothers love and idolize her while their fifty-year-old daughters are daily addicts of her Oprah Winfrey therapy hour. She is the heroine and mentor of thirty-year-olds with weight and marriage problems. Husbands and fathers tune in to get advice on their relationship problems both at home and work. Rape and abuse victims identify with Oprah as someone who has experienced their problems and has gone on to make it to the very top. She is their heroine and role model. Women in their twenties admire her ability to moderate controversial subjects with aplomb. She is the consummate mentor for black teenagers, who see her as the ultimate role model for success. Her audience has no ethnic, gender, educational, or age bounds. Each day an estimated fourteen million viewers tune in to the "Oprah Winfrey Show," a full 55 percent more viewers than its closest competitor. She is seen in 99 percent of America's homes and sixty-four countries generating $170 million in annual revenues. Winfrey's ratings are greater than all three network morning shows combined. That is her power.

Winfrey's friend Maya Angelou calls her "America's most accessible and honest psychiatrist." Angelou has portrayed Winfrey as having the trait most characteristic of all creative genius, "She goes where the fearful will not tread. . . . She is one of our Roadmakers." Winfrey's ability to go where others fear is almost mystical. She intuitively knows a person's area of vulnerability and has a unique ability to tap into what the audience really wants to hear about an individual. She has the talent and patience to listen attentively to "brutes, bigots, and bagmen" without judgment or revealing her own emotional feelings.

Winfrey has a unique talent to communicate without monotony, titillate without offending, motivate without moralizing, and educate without preaching. Only Oprah could ask an adult film star on her show, "Don't you ever get sore?" and get audience approval ratings. Winfrey's charisma and sensitivity are contagious. This talent allows her to do shows dealing with subjects that would be verboten elsewhere. On one show dealing with penis size she blurted out, "Bring home a big one to mama." Try that Kathy Lee, or Phil Donahue. Winfrey's frankness and sincerity are unique qualities in a profession that neither admires or condones such qualities. Her empathy with viewing audiences allows her to address issues others would not even consider.

Winfrey's dominance of her medium is such that she can make an author an overnight success as she did with Marianne Williamson and her book *A Return to Love* (1992). On Tuesday, February 4, 1992, Williamson appeared on Winfrey's show. Thirty-five thousand copies of the book were sold on that one day alone. Within eight days the publisher confirms three hundred thousand book sales resulting from that one TV appearance. That is unprecedented in the history of the book business, where the average hardcover book sells under ten thousand copies. In July 1993 the appearance of Deepak Chopra had a similar effect on the sales of his new book *Ageless Body, Timeless Mind.*

"Oprah" viewers include prostitutes desiring solace, bored housewives seeking knowledge and excitement, old ladies in retirement homes hoping for titillation, construction workers interested in the female perspective, lonely divorcees looking for mates, abused women seeking direction, alternative lifestylers searching for understanding, and intellectuals hunting for information. No other show has such a broad-based spectrum of interest or viewers. Only Winfrey could pull it off. She has changed the world of TV talk shows more than any other single person in history. For this and her other unique talents she qualifies as a creative visionary.

Oprah Winfrey is the first woman in history to own and produce her own talk show. In 1988 she was voted the International Radio and Television Society's "Broadcaster of the Year"—the youngest recipient and the first African-American woman ever to be given the award in its twenty-five-year history. *Good Housekeeping*'s 1992 poll for the "Most Admired Woman" ranked Winfrey third behind Barbara Bush and Mother Teresa. A 1993 poll from an aviation research firm asked a group what famous person they would most like to share an airplane seat with. Winfrey ranked number one ahead of President or Hillary Clinton, Arnold Schwarzenegger, Ross Perot and other notables. (Madonna tied with Boris Yelstin, who doesn't even speak English.) Winfrey was the recipient of the ultimate rags-to-riches recognition, the Horatio Alger Award, in 1993. The *Washington Times* sums up the Oprah mystique: "This phenomenon can't be reduced simply into words like *charisma* or *star quality*. Something much more profound is going on!"

Personal Life History

Winfrey was born on January 26, 1954 in Kosciusko, Mississippi, the first of three illegitimate children by her mother, Vernita, who was just eighteen at the time. Her parents intended her name to be Orpah, after Ruth's sister-in-law in the Bible, but the midwife transposed the second two letters on the birth certificate, and she has one of the world's most original names. At the time of her birth Winfrey's father, Vernon Winfrey, was in the army and stationed out of state. Her mother moved to Milwaukee to work as a cleaning lady, leaving Oprah on a farm to be reared by her maternal grandmother, a strict disciplinarian. Oprah called her grandmother "momma," since the elderly woman was the only real mother she knew. Her grandmother became Oprah's first real role model in life.

As a child Oprah didn't wear shoes for years. She didn't receive her first dress until entering school. The isolated farm setting forced Oprah to create her own entertainment. She became friends with the animals and found solace in books. There was no television and Winfrey says her grandmother gave her one of the greatest gifts she ever received, teaching her to read and write by age two and a half. This precocious child made her first speech even earlier, addressing the congregation of a rural church on the topic "Jesus rose on Easter Day." The parishioners were in awe and some thought her gifted. This early success was not lost on the impressionable Oprah. Her self-esteem was being molded by positive reinforcement from special adults. This particular event sparked her first dreams of becoming a missionary or preacher. Later, a fourth grade teacher, Mrs. Denvors (an early role model), inspired her to become a teacher.

Winfrey says, "I grew up loving books. . . . It was a way to escape to another person's life." When her grandmother enrolled Oprah in kindergarten, she promptly wrote a note to the kindergarten teacher pointing out in no uncertain terms that she belonged in the first grade. The astonished teacher promoted her. After completing that academic year, Oprah skipped directly to the third grade. It was an early indication of enormous potential for this lonely Mississippi girl. Oprah remembers her stern grandmother as her first important role model, "I am what I am today because of my grandmother:

my strength, my sense of reasoning, everything, all of that, was set by the time I was six years old. I basically am no different now from what I was when I was six years old."

Oprah's mother sent for her to live in a Milwaukee ghetto with her half-brother and sister at age six. She continued public speaking, reciting poetry at black social clubs and church teas, where she became known as "the little speaker." These experiences would leave an indelible impression on the psyche of a little girl looking for an escape to a better world. She told Lyn Tornabee of *Woman's Day,* "I don't know why, but somewhere in my spirit, I always knew I was going to be exactly where I am." (This is a repeated finding among the gifted.) Winfrey spent two years with her mother before being sent back south to Nashville to live with her recently married father. This ambitious little girl continued to lose herself in the fantasyland of books. She told *Good Housekeeping* in 1991, "Books showed me there were possibilities in life, that there were actually people like me living in a world, I could not only aspire to but attain. . . . Reading gave me hope. For me it was the open door." While in Milwaukee, she said, "I would hide in the closet and read by flashlight. Otherwise, others made fun of me thinking I was trying to be 'somebody.' I was." At twelve years of age she was paid $500 to speak at a church. That night she told her dad she wanted to earn her living by being paid to talk, and added, "I told my daddy then and there that I planned to be very famous." Oprah started a diary to record her dreams.

Oprah's mother had legal custody of her, so when she finally married, she left her father to live in Milwaukee with her new family. The Milwaukee ghetto environment was a tragedy. Oprah was raped at age nine by her nineteen-year-old cousin. He bought her an ice cream as a bribe to keep her quiet. Then two other relatives sexually molested her. Winfrey broke down on one of her early shows and acknowledged this early sexual abuse while embracing one of her guests who had had a similar experience. The trusted men in Oprah's life were the ones who took advantage of her, instilling both guilt and confusion. Additionally, she had been a vagabond child with no roots to give her stability. Oprah spent six years in Mississippi with her grandmother, two in Milwaukee with her mother, two in Nashville with her father, and one year back in Milwaukee with her mother. She was now destined to spend the next five in Nashville where her stable and disciplined father would give her the mentoring she needed.

Oprah became a delinquent at age thirteen in Milwaukee. Her lack of parental supervision and direction had taken its toll. She became rebellious, stole money from her mother, and once ran away from home. She spotted Aretha Franklin getting out of a limousine and convinced the singer that she was abandoned and needed "a hundred dollars to get home to Ohio" (Waldron, 1987). Her verbal talents, which were destined to make her millions, brought her the money to hole up for three days in a Milwaukee hotel. When the money ran out, she went to her minister. He took her home to an irate mother who sent her off to a juvenile detention center. Fortunately for Oprah, there were not enough beds and she was sent to live once again with her father and stepmother, Zelma, in Nashville.

Oprah landed in Nashville at age fourteen. She was also pregnant. The child was born prematurely and died shortly after. Winfrey told Randy Banner of the *New York Daily News* (September 7, 1986), "My father saved my life." Vernon Winfrey was a barber at the time, a respectable member of the community and the Nashville City Council. Winfrey told *Good Housekeeping,* "My father turned my life around by insisting I be more than I was and by believing I could be more. His love of learning showed me the right way." Vernon insisted that Oprah add five new words to her vocabulary every day or she forfeited dinner. The ever-talented Oprah became a straight-A student. At fifteen she was selected to speak in California to church groups and upon seeing the Hollywood Parade of Stars said, "One day, I'm going to put my own star among those stars" (Waldron, 1987). Oprah embarked on that journey by presiding over the high school council, joining the drama club, and distinguishing herself in both oratory and debate. At sixteen she won the Elks Club oratorical contest, which guaranteed her a scholarship at Tennessee State University. She was invited to the White House by President Nixon as the representative of Youth in Nashville and represented East High as an Outstanding Teenager of America. Winfrey would later say it was her dad's influence that made her. "It's because of him. . . . I am where I am today."

Winfrey then started making inroads into a show business career. She was crowned Miss Fire Prevention by radio station WVOL at age seventeen. She was the first black to win this contest. The station disc jockey, John Heidelberg, saw her talent and hired her during her senior year in high school to read weekend newscasts. She was good, and earned a hundred dollars a week. Winfrey's verbal talents were finally paying off. By age seventeen the "little speaker" was sent to Stanford University for her winning dramatic interpretation of *Jubilee.*

Winfrey was named Miss Black Nashville and Miss Tennessee as a freshman at Tennessee State, where she majored in speech and drama. In 1971 she was a contestant in the Miss Black America Pageant. Then her first big break came when the local CBS television station, WTVF-TV, offered her a job. She turned it down twice, before a speech teacher reminded her that a job offer from CBS-TV was the reason most people went to college. She accepted the job during her sophomore year and became the first black woman to serve as coanchor on the Nashville evening news. She was just nineteen. In her inimitable style she told *Cosmopolitan* in 1986, "Sure I was a token. But, honey, I was one happy token."

Winfrey was scared to death during her first days as a television news anchor. She told herself "I'll just pretend I'm Barbara Walters," and it worked. Walters became a professional mentor for her. Winfrey's father, however, was still the boss, and a strict disciplinarian. Winfrey said later, "I was the only news anchor in the country who had to be home by midnight." However, she was earning $15,000 a year while a junior in college. Winfrey became an effective reporter and was as candid then as now. When assigned to do a story in a segregated section of town she walked up to introduce herself to a shop owner, only to be met with, "We don't shake hands with niggers down here." Winfrey's response: "I'll bet the niggers are glad." Prior to graduation, in 1976, Winfrey was offered her big chance as a Baltimore reporter and co-anchor on the six o'clock news for WJZ-TV. Winfrey accepted and was on her way to the big time.

Professional Background

Oprah began her new job at the ABC affiliate in Baltimore on April Fools Day 1976. At twenty-two she was the first female anchor of a Baltimore TV station. The station had its own ideas about the appropriate image for Winfrey. They tried new hairdos and clothes, explaining, "Your hair is too thick, your nose too wide, and your chin's too big." Winfrey was devastated when all her hair fell out—a violent reaction from the hair treatment chemicals. Never at a loss for words Winfrey said, "You learn a lot about yourself when you're bald." She turned to food for solace and spent a great deal of time alone. The whole experience turned out to be an opportunity for self-discovery. Winfrey realized she would not be the next Diana Ross (Ross had been her show business idol for years)—"My hips would never ever be like Diana Ross's hips and I had better just be Oprah."

Oprah's strength has always been her unique ability to empathize with virtually everyone. When reporting emotionally disturbing news stories, she often had to fight back tears. The station management told her to toughen up. Her strength had become her weakness—as it is in everyone, although few are aware of it. Hypersensitivity is Winfrey's weakness, and her frailties hurt her efforts to become a tough news reporter. Fortunately for America's viewers, she never really was able to change her style.

The station management was not pleased with the performance for which she was hired. Winfrey had been slotted into the evening one-hour news à la her heroine Barbara Walters. This turned out to be the saddest time in Winfrey's life. The job did not work out; she was just not right for the news position. Winfrey was fired from her job after nine months. She was then assigned morning news broadcasts and "cut-ins" for ABC's "Good Morning America." Her on-air charisma overshadowed her reporting skills. The station decided she would cohost with Richard Sher on "Baltimore Is Talking"—a morning talk show similar to the current Regis and Kathy Lee show. At the end of her first day, Winfrey concluded, "I came off the air, and I knew that was what I was supposed to do. It just felt like breathing. It was the most natural process for me." For the next seven years Winfrey and Sher tackled topics ranging from divorce to child rearing, siamese twins, and the Ku Klux Klan. The show was a monumental success. Unfortunately, Winfrey's personal life was not. It was in a shambles. Winfrey even reached the point of contemplating suicide. However, twelve cities picked up the "Baltimore Is Talking" show because of its high ratings—ratings higher than the "Phil Donahue Show." This prompted a Chicago ABC affiliate, WLS-TV, to take notice.

Dennis Swanson of WLS hired both Oprah and her producer to take over "A.M. Chicago," which was last in the ratings for its time slot. "My first day in Chicago, September 4, 1983, I set foot in this city, and just walking down the street, it was like roots, like the motherland. I knew I belonged here." Brutally honest, Winfrey asked Swanson if her being black would be an issue for "A.M. Chicago." Dennis said, "I don't care if you are green. All I want to do is win. I am in the business of winning and I want you to go for it." Winfrey signed a four-year contract for $200,000 a year. She had finally made the big time and was not yet thirty.

One month after Winfrey's debut as "A.M. Chicago's" new host, the program recorded its strongest ratings in years. Phil Donahue coincidentally moved his show from Chicago to New York and the pundits blamed Winfrey. She was more realistic: "Marlo, not me, made him move." Donahue was known as the Mr. Mom of daytime TV and Winfrey immediately replaced him as Ms. Therapist. She hit Chicago television ratings like a missile exploding. *Variety* reported, " 'A.M. Chicago,' with its new host, Oprah Winfrey, has increased its rating and share by more than 50 percent from a year ago and in the process has put a severe dent in the New York–bound 'Donahue' show."

In 1987 *People* magazine said, "Oprah has a mind as quick as any in television, yes, Carson and Letterman included." Winfrey was fast becoming the best friend of housewives throughout America. Her show was an enigma of success. One day she would have Donnie and Marie Osmond, the next day a transvestite. She explained her ability to listen passionately to views opposite of hers as, "I don't try to change people. I try to expose them for what they are." She had wanted to be a teacher when in the fourth grade and found solace in the fact that she was teaching every day to a national audience of concerned listeners. "I considered my TV job as teacher and facilitator to my viewers." Winfrey's ability to deal with kooks and alternative lifestyle subjects has made her realize, "We are all responsible for ourselves, our victories and our defeats." Winfrey had become "Everywoman." She loved every minute of it, and so did her viewers.

Winfrey continued to gain weight, and was up to 190 pounds. It became a subject on many programs, made more topical by her ever-changing diets. Her lack of a steady mate also become topical. She never lost her sense of humor about her weight or her lack of a permanent relationship, however, prompting her to say on air one day, "Mr. Right is on his way, but he's in Africa, walking." Winfrey tended to wear her personal life on her set as part of the programming. Her philosophy in both was, "We go to the heart of the matter, we go for the absolute gut." Most talk show hosts are prim and proper, with an unnatural formality. Winfrey characterizes them as "behaving themselves." She does not, but she is real. Winfrey's magic is her brutal honesty and off-the-wall candor. She admits to never thinking about a question prior to posing it. It is not always a safe approach but sure to be interesting.

Winfrey's two professional mentors are Maya Angelou, author of *I Know Why the Caged Bird Sings,* and Barbara Walters, the incomparable television interviewer. Winfrey says of Walters, "I think without her none of us would be here. She's a pioneer and she paved the way for the rest of us." Winfrey has interviewed both of her mentors and felt uncomfortable with each saying, "I'm not really good with people. . . . I'm enamored with." *Newsweek* once gave her some critically timed national coverage that enhanced her career. The story described her as "nearly two hundred pounds of Mississippi-bred black womanhood, brassy, earthy, street smart, and soulful." Winfrey did not like the crass description, but admitted it opened a lot of doors for her.

In 1985, Quincy Jones discovered Winfrey while watching TV in his Chicago hotel room. He was producing the movie version of Alice Walker's *The Color Purple* and was looking for someone to play Sophia. Winfrey had no acting experience other than college, but he selected her for the job. The movie was released in December 1985 to rave reviews. Winfrey was hailed by movie critic Gene Siskel, who described her portrayal as "shockingly good." He went on to say, "She exudes basic honesty in her role of this desperate black woman." Winfrey's lawyer was negotiating with Warner Studios to get her more money for the part, and the ever-candid Winfrey said, "Jeff, I'd do it for nothing —please, please don't ask for any more money!" He said, "You're not doing it for free" (*Working Woman,* 1992).

Winfrey received both Oscar and Golden Globe nominations for her role in the movie. She also received the Woman of Achievement Award from the National Association of Women in June 1986 for her sensitive portrayal. Winfrey's success led to a part in the film version of Richard Wright's *Native Son* in 1986. She was cast as a mother in the film, which was not as well received. Winfrey admits it was difficult identifying with a mother when at thirty-two she had little experience with the institution. Her movie success helped the "Oprah Winfrey Show." It skyrocketed in popularity in the wake of her Oscar nomination for *The Color Purple.* On September 8, 1986, King World put the "Oprah Winfrey Show" into syndication in a record 138 cities. This projected to $125 million in profits for the 1987–88 season. This coup immediately made Winfrey the highest-paid performer in show business. She signed a new, five-year contract with King World in late December 1986. By 1993 the show had expanded to an unprecedented 198 U.S. markets (99 percent of the country) and 64 foreign markets including Japan, Norway, Saudi Arabia, New Zealand, and the Netherlands.

Winfrey became a business entrepreneur and CEO in October 1988 when she formed Harpo productions ("Oprah" spelled backwards) and purchased a state-of-the-art, 100,000-square-foot production studio in Chicago—a cool $20 million investment. She was only the third woman in history behind Mary Pickford and Lucille Ball to own and produce her own show. Winfrey was the first African-American to own her own entertainment production company. She produces all of her shows in this studio in addition to various TV specials such as *The Women of Brewster Place.* The production company has an aggressive schedule of feature documentaries planned for the coming years. Winfrey manages eighty-six people and says, "I run the company on instinct, I'm an instinct player, an instinct actor, and I use it to guide me in business." Winfrey signs every check and manages the company with little or no administrative staff.

By 1993 revenues had risen to $100 million for the "Oprah Winfrey Show," of which Oprah's take was $52 million. Winfrey led all entertainers in earnings for 1992–93, according to *Forbes* (September 1993) with $98 million in earnings. (She beat out Stephen Spielberg by $26 million.) Winfrey arrives at work at 6:00 A.M. Monday through Wednesday, where she works out in the gym prior to getting ready for her 9:00 A.M. taping. She spends an hour in business meetings before her second taping at 11:00 A.M. The rest of the day is spent in meetings and approving new projects. Weekends are spent relaxing on her 160-acre Indiana farm, where she reviews new scripts and relaxes with Stedman Graham, her live-in fiancé. She produced a TV movie at Harpo which aired November 1993 called *There Are No Children Here,* based on an inner-city single mother with Oprah playing the lead role. She characterized herself in this role telling the media, "I am the perfect example of someone who came up from zip. I mean zippola, Mrs. Outhouse herself here." That is why she is in this book. She took nothing and made it into something wonderful.

Winfrey the entrepreneur opened a Chicago restaurant with the unusual name The Eccentric in 1991. She is constantly busy with charity events on child abuse and creating new documentaries for Harpo to produce. Winfrey's full-time job is her daily show, which is now the highest-rated talk show in television history, according to Nielsen ratings. When knowledgeable TV producers discuss ratings they refer to the "Oprah effect." CBS News anchor Dan Rather said of Winfrey's huge influence relative to his nightly news program,

"The Oprah factor is enormous. . . . The humbling thing about being in one of these anchor positions is that if you give me Oprah as a lead-in . . . I'll win for you" (*New York Times,* June 1, 1992).

Winfrey's success has given her the ability to buy some toys. She became a millionaire by the age of thirty-two and bought herself an $800,000 apartment as a present. She became the highest-paid entertainer in show business in 1987 and bought herself a 160-acre Indiana farm. In 1988 Winfrey purchased her own production company and opened her Chicago restaurant. More recently, she impulsively purchased an 85-acre ranch near the slopes of Telluride, Colorado, including a nearby guest house, for a total cost of $4.3 million. Other extravagant acquisitions include a Challenger 601-3A jet with a $1.4 million operating cost, four homes, and a new mansion under construction near Santa Fe, New Mexico. Winfrey is one of the most successful business-women in history ranking with Lucille Ball and Madonna. As CEO of Harpo she has only one advisor, her longtime lawyer and partner Jeffrey Jacobs. Jacobs says, "Oprah owns her own show and controls her own money. There's no board of directors, no committees. Every final decision is hers." Jacobs says she still signs every check for the operation and performs the normal executive functions of any other big time corporate executive. What drives Winfrey to do this is not dissimilar to the other women in this work. They demand complete control, which makes them true creative geniuses.

Temperament: Intuitive-Feeling

Winfrey is very extroverted, intuitive, and feeling. She is left-handed, which authenticates her dominant right-brain—intuitive—thinking style. Winfrey's keen sense of what people are thinking (an almost extrasensory power) allows her to ask just the right question to extract the most pertinent information from her subjects. This unique ability has made Winfrey the preeminent talk show host in the world.

Winfrey has a strong sense of self and is resilient and self-sufficient, unafraid of new unknown situations. These traits were formed by her early transience and loneliness. A recap of Winfrey's multiple moves and abrupt relocations gives credence to her self-sufficiency and resilience. She lived in a rural agrarian environment for six years, nurtured by an authoritarian grandmother. She was lonely and discovered books as solace. They developed her keen sense of adventure and macro-vision of life. Then Winfrey's self-assurance and coping skills were honed when faced with adjusting to various new cultures, schools, teachers, and friends. Moving from a quiet rural farm environment to a Milwaukee ghetto was both disruptive and foreboding. Winfrey found herself under the care of a less than nurturing mother who was more absent than present. Winfrey was in Milwaukee less than two years before moving once again at age eight to Nashville, under the strong-willed tutelage of a caring father. This experience was completely opposite from that of Milwaukee. Then, suddenly, within a year, Winfrey was whisked back to the Milwaukee ghetto, where all kinds of traumatic experiences occurred. After a year of torment and rebellion, she was moved back to Nashville, where her father and stepmother gave her the stability she wanted and needed.

Winfrey had made five major moves to three alien surroundings in six years before age thirteen. Think about the imprinting on an impressionable child going from an authoritarian grandmother to an absent mother to a powerful father back to her mother and back again to her father. In between Winfrey was abused, raped, ran away from home, and became the unwed mother of a baby who died. All of the moves included new schools, friends, cultures, and different types of parental influences. No wonder Winfrey has a resilient and fearless persona, capable of operating by her wits in novel circumstances without fear of failure. Winfrey's insecurities have made her an overachiever and an obsessive perfectionist.

Winfrey's early speaking talents earned her positive feedback from influential adults. They told her she was "special," "gifted," and "precocious," which made her believe she was meant to achieve great things. She also received monetary reinforcement, having earned $500 for a church speech at age twelve. Articulate communication was imprinted on Winfrey's unconscious at a very young age. She lived to fulfill that "little speaker" image and was conditioned to perform to adult expectations. Winfrey knew she was brighter than most of her friends and relatives and intuitively knew she had special talents. (It appears she is one of the brightest women in this book.)

Both her grandmother and her father instilled in Winfrey a goal-oriented mentality. It molded her into a classic overachiever. At age fourteen her father took her to the library every two weeks to select books. She not only had to read them but also write a book report on each. This was in addition to working as a clerk in his retail store next to his barber shop. Winfrey continued in this structured, goal-oriented life into college, when she began setting her own goals and objectives. Janet Burch, a Nashville psychologist who chaperoned Winfrey at the Miss Black America Pageant, said, "I have never seen anybody who wanted to do well as much as Oprah did. She used to talk about things, like how one day she was going to be very, very, very wealthy. . . . She believed it. People say, I'd like to be wealthy. Oprah said, I'm going to be wealthy." That was the positive mentality which manifested itself in a self-imposed optimism.

Winfrey's personality is best characterized by her persuasive persona. She has a unique ability to convince people to bare their souls to the world. This ability comes to her naturally because she is willing to bare her own soul, a fact that is readily apparent to her subjects and viewers. In business "she's very controlling" according to Armstrong Williams, her fiance's business partner. He adds, "To deal with Oprah, you've got to be a strong man, because she's a strong woman." Winfrey's exceptional sensitivity to the feelings of others is communicated in her on-air personality. This personality type is classified by psychologists as an Apollonian or "catalyst" temperament. These personality types are "enthusiastic optimists and admirers of integrity," according to psychologist David Keirsey. They are the ones most likely to "draw out the best in people." Winfrey surely fits this scientific definition of her temperament. Her enormous empathy makes her a superb persuader.

Family versus Career

Winfrey has continually postponed marriage in an obvious attempt to make sure she does not make a mistake. She has experienced a series of unsatisfactory relationships on her way to the top, which now make it difficult for her to consummate a good one. It appears Winfrey is worried too much about the potential for failure. Her fear of failure is more the reason she has not married before 40 than her lack of love for her fiance Stedman Graham, her steady for six years and fiance since November 6, 1992. Winfrey told *TV Guide* in 1990, "You know Joseph Campbell said that marriage is really the sacrificing of the ego for the relationship. When I'm ready to put myself in that position I will." The long-term commitment part of marriage has been the only reason for her delay: she has seen too many broken marriages to risk having one of her own. Early in their relationship Winfrey said she wouldn't marry Stedman because she "couldn't imagine putting him—or anyone else—ahead of her career." That is no longer the case, but she is not inclined to follow Madonna's strategy of having a child while still single. She says, "I would never have children without marriage. . . . I recall all to well what it's like to be an illegitimate child." Winfrey is more concerned about committing to a permanent relationship that may not work than to its impact on her career. Winfrey puts her unique relationship with Stedman in context joking, "Lots of people want to ride with you in the limo. But you want someone who'll help you catch the bus," Stedman is Winfrey's bus buddy.

In Baltimore, Winfrey told the press, "People think because I'm in television I have this great social life. Let me tell you, I can count on my fingers the number of dates I've had in the four years I've been in Baltimore, and that includes the ones I paid for." She told the press that she began taking on extra assignments in Baltimore so she didn't have to face the negativity of a social life. Then she says she went on eating binges to satisfy her libidinal energy. Relationships were virtually nonexistent at this time in her life. Winfrey became depressed and spent a great deal of time in bed. Her depression reached its zenith on September 8, 1981, when she attempted suicide when her beau at the time, William Bubba Taylor, refused to marry her.

Winfrey now admits to internalizing the guilt of her early abuse. She has always blamed herself for the heinous acts of others, which made her incapable of managing a relationship that could materialize into anything permanent. Stedman Graham was different. "He is the first man I have ever known who truly wants me to be not only the best I can be, but *all* I can be." But Winfrey adds, "Frankly, a piece of paper legalizing what Stedman and I have together couldn't make it any better than it already is. So, unless we decided to have children, it wouldn't bother me if we never got married." As usual, Winfrey bared her soul when asked about children in her future:

> But do I want a child of my own? Sometimes I think, yes, I do want to have that experience, and other times I must admit having a child is not a deep yearning at this time. Maybe I'm afraid. Raising a child is such serious business. You have to be emotionally mature and responsible, and I'm not sure I'm describing me when I say that, at least not yet. But I'm getting there. (*Good Housekeeping,* 1991)

Life Crisis

Winfrey's early life was one continual bout with trauma and crisis. She was an illegitimate child and left by both parents to be raised by a hard-core grandmother. Then at age nine she was sexually abused by a male relative, only to be molested by two other relatives while living in the Milwaukee ghetto. When Winfrey talked Aretha Franklin into funding one of her soirees it pushed her mother over the edge and she tried to have Oprah placed in a juvenile detention center. The girl had reached the bottom. Her life of abuse and molestation had taken its toll. She found herself pregnant at age fourteen and gave birth to a premature baby who lived just a short while. Recovery from such devastating experiences has been understandably slow. It took over twenty years before Winfrey revealed her abuse in front of a TV audience on one of her broadcasts. These crises have scarred Winfrey for life, but in all bad there is some good. Winfrey's crises and abuse have armed her with tremendous amounts of personal energy and made her fearless. She now is dedicated to wiping out child abuse and is adamant about making the world a better place.

Winfrey's various adult crises have centered around her depression over her weight problems and her inability to end bad relationships. Winfrey's 1981 attempt at suicide occurred when both of these factors coincided to bring her to the lowest emotional point in her adult life. Once again Winfrey had a revelation that turned the bad situation into a positive force. She says, "I realized there was no difference between me and an abused woman who has to go to a shelter, except I could stay home. It was emotional abuse, which happens to women who stay in relationships that do not allow them to be all that they can be. You're not getting knocked around physically, but in terms of your ability to soar, your wings are clipped." This low point in her life catapulted Winfrey upward. Since then her rise has been unhindered. Winfrey had reached the very bottom and from that perspective the view is clearer for some reason. When you are that far down no risk seems very great.

All of these crises have impacted Winfrey. They are despicable experiences for anyone to endure, but even worse for a young child. Even so, the experiences appear to have had some power to energize Winfrey toward reaching greater heights of achievement than would otherwise have been possible. Remember the super learning that takes place in such tramautic situations. It was in this state that Winfrey must have told herself "I will overcome and be the best I can be" in order to make herself feel worthy and to overcome the guilt of her abuse.

Persuasive Persona and Success

Winfrey has used her magnetic charm and personal charisma to open doors since she was two. Her persuasive persona has taken her from a Mississippi farm, where she was without shoes, to the top of the entertainment world. As a young child she dreamed of earning a living through her speaking ability. Her dream has come true and she is now Cinderella living in her television castle. Like virtually all super successful visionaries, Winfrey was not driven by money! She says, "I'm not impressed by money. . . . Now that I have all the *things* I once thought would make me happy, they have little meaning for me. Experience, and not just a little heartache, has taught me money buys convenience and conveniences. (Waldron, 1987)

Winfrey is a renegade because she breaks all the traditional rules of her medium, but invariably she leaves the audience laughing and caring. That is a unique talent not often found in any endeavor, let alone in the dog-eat-dog world of show business. This charismatic woman has such persuasive powers that she can command a huge audience wherever she goes. She is an enigma in the entertainment industry, where her magnetic attraction is "sensitivity" and "empathy," not singing or dancing. Winfrey's vulnerability is contagious, and her empathy is almost mystical. She has an unusual sense of what people are thinking and what audiences want to know.

This charismatic woman is the greatest saleswoman in television history. She can persuade people to do or say almost anything on national television.

A rare talent. Winfrey has no secrets and has the exceptional ability to ferret out everyone else's deepest and darkest secrets. Since most people are only as sick as their secrets, Winfrey, contrary to her own belief, is the sanest person in the universe because her personal closet is an open book. Her keen sense of integrity forces her to tell all without hesitation. A frequent guest on her show, Victoria Secunda, says, "She is emotionally available to people. I think her great appeal is that she can be vulnerable like the rest of us."

Winfrey's rags-to-riches story is deserving of the Horatio Alger Award she won in 1993. Alger sold four hundred million books about immigrants discovering the great American dream. Winfrey is the ideal example of such stories. Her simple vulnerability makes her real, and her "realness" appeals to the heartland of America. This quality has made Winfrey into the most universally loved woman ever to hit television. The fact that she is African-American makes that an exceptional accomplishment. Winfrey has the charisma of Golda Meir and Mary Kay Ash. No other contemporary woman seems to have had the same degree of magnetism as these three. Oprah's charisma has made her the most watched woman in television history, and that makes her a creative genius of the first order.

Summary

Winfrey is America's "Everywoman," performing her magic daily in what she fondly calls her "ministry." Winfrey's mystique is inspirational and this "cheerleader for women" is proactive in a spiritual way. Oprah made speeches before she could write and earned money before she went to school. Her childhood precocity has made her nonpareil in the talk show industry. She dominates her field like no other person in the history of the medium, including Steve Allen, Jack Paar, and Johnny Carson. Winfrey's 1993 earnings of $52 million is a gauge of her success, and her estimated $250 million net worth before turning forty is astonishing. To be the youngest recipient ever of the Broadcaster of the Year Award is an awesome achievement.

All this has not come without a price, however. Winfrey has sacrificed a traditional life with husband and children, but these sacrifices might well be charged off to her childhood abuse and not to her overt decision to place career above family. However, if Winfrey had opted for the family approach earlier in life, there is no doubt she would not have achieved so much so fast.

Winfrey received a great deal of flack from the media over the cancellation of her autobiography, due out in September of 1993. Supposedly her fiance, Stedman Graham, had convinced her that such a complete and compromising disclosure of her innermost secrets was not in the best interest of their marriage.

She had already signed prebook autographs at a Miami book convention announcing a September release date. Graham's position was, "You can't do this! You're dredging up all the unhappy moments of your past when I want us to focus on the future! I won't stand by and watch you reveal your soul to every person in America while we're trying to start a new life together" (Bly, 1993). He was probably right, but Winfrey's style and her success have always been to let it all hang out. Her success in every venture and in every endeavor, both personal and professional, has been based on total honesty and integrity. She relies primarily on instinct and a "gut" feel for what is right, which she usually is.

Winfrey's battle of the bulge is known to every one of her viewers. She has long since given up dieting because she finally came to the realization that her weight was a function of factors beyond food. In a moment of candor she told Alan Ebert of *Good Housekeeping* in 1991, "I now understand my eating and weight gains are symptoms of underlying emotional problems that dieting won't cure. Beneath my added poundage are buried feelings and my fear of feeling whatever they may be. . . . I know if I could just allow myself to get past the fear and feel whatever that pain is, I would finally be free of it, and the weight, because I would be free of the need to protect myself." According to biographer Bly (1993), Winfrey recently spent $142,000 to lose sixty-five pounds.

In August 1993 Winfrey completed a half marathon (thirteen miles) in San Diego, finishing in two hours and sixteen minutes—an hour behind the winner. This accomplishment took her five months of intense training and she lost fifty pounds in the process. At the finish line Winfrey commented, "People told me running would be fun. When I first started training, I said, 'What's fun about this?' But today was a lot of fun. That last mile was tough, but the goal was to finish." When asked why she is now into running, Winfrey said, "I decided a long time ago I have to be healthy by the time I'm forty." January 29, 1994, she turned forty and was in that elusive size 9 dress once again. This highly focused woman had won her biggest battle.

Winfrey is one of the wealthiest and most powerful women in America. She is also America's alter ego, loved, admired, and worshipped by her daily TV audience. Contrary to her television persona, she is an accomplished CEO of her own company and deserves everything she earns because she did it the old-fashioned way: she earned it! Winfrey did so with a uniquely persuasive persona, not by stepping on and over bodies on her way to the top. Testimony to Winfrey's charismatic appeal is found in her devoted staff at Harpo. Longtime producer Mary Kay Clinton said, "I would take a bullet for her," a typical response from those closest to her. Winfrey is a true creative genius who changes the world for the better every single day through television.

Oprah Winfrey

Talk show hostess, actress, CEO of Harpo Studios

b. Jan. 29, 1954, Kosciusko, Mississippi

Dominant trait: Persuasive Persona

Religion: Methodist

Mottos: "I just want to be the best person I can be" (diary entry at age 15; she still believes it philosophically); "I believe in excellence"; "I move with the flow and take life's clues. Let the universe handle the details."

Philosophy: "Uplift—Encourage—Empower!"; "I think we are defined by the way we treat ourselves and treat other people"; "Success is about being honest, not only in your work but in your life"; "We are all responsible for ourselves."

Nicknames: Everywoman, Conscience of Our Times, America's psychiatrist

Creation/innovation: First national black talk-show hostess. First woman in history to own and produce her own talk show.

Products/contributions: Harpo Studios, "The Oprah Winfrey Show," accomplished actress

Successes: Top talk show in history of TV. Nominated for Academy Award, *The Color Purple.* Highest-paid entertainer in TV: $52 million income in 1993.

Self-description: "I intend to do and have it all. I want to have a movie career, a TV career, a talk-show career. . . . I believe in my own possibilities."

Birth order: First-born illegitimate daughter, younger half-sister and half-brother

Childhood transience: Grandmother for 6 yrs., to mother for 2 yrs., to father for 2 yrs., back to mother, and back to father.

Father's occupation: Barber, grocery store owner, and deacon of church; city councilman

Mentors: Father, Vernon; 4th grade teacher, Mrs. Denvors; Barbara Walters; and Maya Angelou. "When my father took me, it changed the course of my life. He saved me."

Childhood upbringing: Raised by authoritarian grandmother. Raped and abused by male relatives and mother's boyfriends. Books became redemption.

Formal education: Taught herself to read and write before age 3. Skipped kindergarten and second grade. Honor student in high school and won full scholarship for oratory to Tennessee State. Degree in drama, 1987.

Life crisis: Illegitimate child, raped by 19-year-old cousin at age 9, abused by trusted relatives. Pregnant at 14. Attempted suicide in Baltimore, 1981.

Marriages/liaisons: Dysfunctional relationships until meeting Stedman Graham. Engaged November 1992.

Risk-taking: Motivated by insecurities. Chicago restaurant called "Eccentric" tells the story

Temperament: Extroverted-intuitive-feeling-perceiver—Apollonian (Catalyst)

Behavior: Persuasive perfectionist, workaholic, high integrity, and generous to a fault

Career vs. family: Sacrificed marriage, relationships, and children for career

Self-esteem: Built in childhood by adults giving positive feedback on verbal acuity

Hobbies: Reading and child-abuse projects. 160-acre Indiana farm and 85-acre Telluride, Colo., ranch. Marathons at age 39.

Heroes: Diana Ross as teenager, Barbara Walters and Maya Angelou as adult

Honors: 1993 Horatio Alger Award. Youngest recipient of Broadcaster of Year Award. *Good Housekeeping* "Most Admired Woman Award," 1992.

21

Promethean Women

I would prefer to be interviewed as an entrepreneur rather than as a "lady" entrepreneur. . . . They buy our stock based on earnings per share. . . . That's the ultimate report card on equality.

—Sandra Kurtzig, *Ask Computers*

Woman, the feminine, must not allow herself to perish in the holocaust that marks the demise of patriarchy.

—Alix Pirani

Successful entrepreneurs, innovators and creative geniuses are unique individuals. They are hypomanic and driven visionaries who are extremely comfortable with ambiguity. Change and risk are their fortes. Optimism pervades their personal and professional lives. They have an imposing self-image that gives them the confidence to defy the establishment. This appears to have evolved out of their upbringing and early parental influences. In fact, their achievements appear to have sprung from early visions and fantasies from their youth. Howard Gardner in *Creative Minds* (1993) found that great creative work often originates in childhood. He said, "Creative geniuses tend to return to the conceptual world of childhood," a finding based on his study of Pablo Picasso, Albert Einstein, Martha Graham, and other great creators.

The women in this book were not that different from the men Gardner studied. These women exhibited many of the traits found in those men, which leads to the conclusion that reaching the very top of most fields is performance- rather than gender-based. These women were definitely performance-driven, which differentiates them from average women who are more satisfied operating in traditional female roles and not driven to risk, sacrifice family life, etc., for their entrepreneurial dream.

393

Promethean Spirited Women

These thirteen women were creative, innovative, and entrepreneurial wunderkinds. They not only made it through the proverbial glass ceiling, they redefined its boundaries. Many crises in their lives appear to have been powerful factors in their success and apparently armed them with unusual amounts of psychic energy and drive. It made them into workaholics, driving them to overachieve. They were supreme optimists and confident beyond all reason. Many variables influence everyone's behavior and success. These variables cover many known and unknown conditioning factors both genetic (nature) and environmental (nurture). The data found in the lives of these great women indicate that many of the necessary behavior characteristics for creative genius are formed in their interaction with family, teachers, siblings, and other key influencers in their lives (see figure 15). Serendipity did play a role but not any more than their early influences, which appear to have instilled in them an obsession for winning. They always saw the big picture.

Nature or Nurture?

I believe creative geniuses are bred not born and that the Mozarts of the world are an aberration not the rule for any great creative endeavor. The creative and entrepreneurial women in this work received their visionary behavior characteristics not from some genetic luck of the draw but from their own experiences in coping with a dynamic changing world. These critical traits are: self-confidence, comfort with ambiguity and risk-taking, a renegade behavior, "Type A" work ethic, intuitive vision, heuristic learning skills, and an obsessive will. While anyone can possess these seven traits in greater or lesser degree, these women acquired them via experiential influences and other intrinsic factors. These traits are detailed in figure 15 and include: Unique birth order, strong parental role models and mentors, permissive family environments, frequent transience, self-employed parents, early crises, and intelligence. The above behavior characteristics and their apparent causal factors are the subject of this book. It appears it was these factors which formed the strong Promethean temperaments found in these women. These particular characteristics were not evident in their youth but only became apparent as they matured, often after they had experienced some truly memorable success. This appears to indicate that women with *impossible* dreams do have the greatest chance to achieve *improbable* fame and fortune.

The enormous success achieved by these women can be summed up in their behavior characteristics which were formed in their interactions with family and the world. In other words, high intelligence was not a material factor

Figure 15

What Makes Female Genius Tick?

Masters of Their Own Destiny—Extrinsic Factors

Seven Behavior Characteristics of Female Creative Genius

1. *Self-Confidence*—An awesome self-image and self-esteem

2. *Risk-Taking and Comfort with Ambiguity*—Highly competitive natures. Willing to bet it all for their dreams.

3. *Renegade Behavior*—Divergent nontraditionalists who break the rules without remorse.

4. *Workaholics*—"Type A" work ethic with high energy—indefatigable

5. *Intuitive Vision*—Majority (10 of 13) have intuitive-thinking temperaments; 9 of 13 are extroverts

6. *Obsessive Wills*—Highly focused and driven to succeed at any cost. Many are obsessive-compulsive or manic-depressive personalities.

7. *Heuristic Learners*—Compulsive seekers of knowledge and truth.

Luck of the Draw—Intrinsic Factors

Family and Experiential Influences

1. *Birth Order*—11 of 13 raised as first-borns creating need for perfection and achievement.

2. *Strong Parental Role Models/Mentors*—Father most influential followed by female role models at home and in school which taught coping skills. Single-sex schooling a factor.

3. *Permissive Family Environment*—Built self-considence, risk-taking, and fearlessness

4. *Frequent Transience*—All but one moved often as children with five changing countries. This taught them to cope with unknown/foreign environments, independence, and self-sufficiency.

5. *Self-Employed Parents*—All but one had self-employed fathers (Mary Kay), which demonstrated early that secure employment in a big organization is not necessary. Instilled entrepreneurial spirit to strike out in new foreign environments.

6. *Early Crises*—Five lost family members; six had close brushes with death, imprinting them with a fearless demeanor and a desperate resolve to achieve. Resiliency resulted.

7. *Intelligence*—All bright with IQs between 120 and 140; none brilliant

in their great success but they would not have made it to the top if they were not bright. They did have slightly above-average intelligence and were raised in home environments conducive to building a self-esteem and temperament capable of great achievement. These women were not prodigies although it appears that their families in many cases treated them as such, telling them they were special and precocious. They believed.

All of these women were lucky to have had strong role models early in their lives and female mentors during the formative stages of their development. Most were groomed to be leaders in tolerant homes where they were allowed to err without ridicule and were taught to be self-reliant. Early transience, self-employed fathers, and crises helped them learn independence and how to cope in unknown and foreign environments. Their unhappiness forced them to find solace in books and other escapes that gave them larger-than-life heroines to emulate. All of these factors contributed to their success. As in everything in life, truth is not black or white. Both life and truth are shades of gray. Likewise, creative genius is a combination of many variables working in concert and resulting in a uniquely molded character that is best suited for innovation, entrepreneurship, and creativity.

The following two general definitions represent portraits or profiles in summary form of an average female creative genius. There are certainly exceptions to both definitions, but they represent a generalized description of the creative visionary.

Summary Definition of Female Creative Genius

Intrinsic Genetic Profile

First-born female with slightly above-average intelligence who had a self-employed father as the dominant influence in her life. Her parents were permissive allowing a nonjudgmental outlet for her inquisitiveness. Frequent moves or extensive travel has taught her to cope with unknown foreign environments. Lonely or unhappy as a child, she lost herself in books. She faced an early crisis that imprinted her with resilience and drive. Strong female role models or heroines or all-girl schools were a positive influence.

Extrinsic Personality Profile

An obsessively driven, intuitive-thinking Promethean spirit who has a renegade mentality and is comfortable with ambiguity and risk-taking. She has an awesome self-esteem which empowers her to be independent and self-reliant. Because of her excessive energy and work ethic her peers label her "workaholic," and an optimistic "will-to-power" attitude gives her a unique charismatic persona that attracts numerous disciples who assist her in her maniacal drive to the top. Formal education is not a material factor in her success.

Internal versus External Influences on Creativity

A European Jungian psychologist offers an interesting perspective on this internal versus external facet of women's creativity. Psychotherapist Alix Pirani wrote *The Absent Father—Crisis and Creativity* (1988) as a mythological metaphor on modern day female creativity. She suggests that the myth of Danae and Perseus from Greek mythology can be used to define the methodology for harnessing creative drive. She paints a picture of the patriarchy (established, male-dominated society) as the limiting factor for all female growth and innovation. She maintains that this barrier to creativity can only be overcome via methodical destruction of patriarchy.

Using her metaphor relative to female creativity we would find Perseus destroying the establishment and patriarchal value systems. The mythological character Perseus (a creative, right-brain hero) slays Medusa (patriarchal, left-brain establishment) in order to release Pegasus (consummate creative genius), the winged horse. Pegasus is synonymous with universal creativity or a "spiritual imagination." The Greek god Zeus was Perseus's absent father, who had seduced his mother, Danae, in a shower of golden rain. Pirani describes how the hero (Perseus—our internal strength) can kill lethargy (Medusa—our unconscious fear of failure) and release the internal fantasy (Pegasus—innovation and imagination). In Pirani's words: "Perseus becomes a reluctant destroyer of the corrupt patriarch and an ally of the benign feminine; but he slays the poisonous feminine, the Medusa, and from her beheaded body is born Pegasus, symbol of liberated spiritual imagination."

Pirani contends that this myth is appropriately twentieth century in nature, as it defines our evolutionary need to destroy the Medusas of the establishment and release Pegasus, our contemporary growth potential and opportunity. I concur with this mythological analogy for the creative future of humanity. The thirteen creative geniuses in this work had the fundamental spirit of a Perseus and were constantly faced with destroying their nemesis—the anticreative Medusa. Those women who are unable to overcome their nemesis (patriarchy) never make it to the top, as they are systematically destroyed by their Medusa.

Modern Promethean Woman as World Leader

Hillary Rodham Clinton and Tipper Gore, baby-boomer wives of the president
and vice president of the United States, are the first set of executive wives
to have graduate degrees. This is a sign of our changing times and it sets
the stage for women's destiny in the future leadership of the United States.
Kim Campbell was elected by her party in 1993 as the first prime minister
in the history of Canadian politics. Though not long in office because she
was hobbled by the political legacy of her predecessor, Campbell joined females
at the helm in Dominica (Eugenia Charles), Iceland (Vigdis Finnbogadottir),
Netherland Antilles (Maria Liberia-Peters), and Nicaragua (Violeta Chamorro).
Carol Gilligan of Harvard University predicted the emergence of women in
great political positions and this movement has begun to gain momentum.
Gloria Steinem and many others worked to make it a reality and maybe the
patriarchy is now weakening its hold on the top leadership positions. Recent
elections in the United States would lead one to this conclusion.

I believe that the feminine skills found in overachieving females are the
ones best suited to lead nations. We are in an era of change and the only
individuals qualified to deal with a dynamic world are those with a dynamic
nature. These visionary women have the behavioral traits ideally suited for
combating adversarial relationships between nations and societies. Diane
McGuiness of Stanford University recently said, "Women are communicators
and men are takers of action." In the world of politics at the millennium it
is preferable to have someone talk about fighting rather than actually fighting,
or more poignantly, to discuss pushing the "red" button rather than actually
pushing it. Women do not have the same level of testosterone running through
their systems, thus their tendencies for aggression are far less than the average
male. A woman will negotiate rather than intimidate and will talk with her
adversaries rather than attacking them.

Creative geniuses are intent on destroying the status quo, which is not
the same as destroying one's enemies. Aggression is not consistent with innovation
and creativity, even though the creative minds of the world tend to be mavericks
willing to violate the status quo in order to create the new. Pioneering right-
brain, intuitive reasoning is highly correlated to creative genius, and women
with these qualities are the Promethean spirits destined to lead our organizations
and nations. They tend to have macro-vision and a long-range perspective,
strong traits for dealing with major issues in a rational, logical manner. It
is this type of female who will make a great President of the United States
in our near future.

But how do these women differ from men?

Visualization versus Verbalization Skills

Males have been shown to be better at tasks requiring visual-spatial skills (maps and interrelationships) while females are better at tasks requiring language and communication skills (verbalizing). However, the female's communication skill, like most other strengths, can become her greatest weakness if not constrained. Women excel in language proficiency, and studies have shown them to be six times more inclined to sing in tune than males. Women are far more sensitive to relationships than men, as pointed out by Carol Gilligan in *In a Different Voice* (1982): "Masculinity is defined through separation while femininity is defined through attachment." In other words, males tend to be frightened by intimacy and commitments and women tend to be threatened by the lack of intimacy and commitment. Women fear separation and nonintimacy and males find it appealing. Women are better at bonding, men are better at independence.

Paradoxical Intention: Don't Be Too Smart

The female creative genius has a reality map that gives her permission to pioneer in unknown areas, and she often succeeds because she does not know too much. In other words, she is not too smart about what can or cannot be accomplished. This is another way of saying that she has eliminated her ego in pursuit of her life's goal. With the ego removed, talent can take over and lead an individual toward success. Allowing the "Golden Gut" to take over, to use Lillian Vernon's vernacular, increases the chances for success in most ventures in life. Allowing the ego to get in the way tends to inhibit achievement. Victor Frankl, the psychotherapist who survived Auschwitz, refers to this concept as "paradoxical intention." He found that "fear brings about that which one is afraid of, and hyperintention makes impossible what one wishes." More simply defined, this theory states, "Trying too hard is counterproductive to ultimate success." Setting goals is important, but once set they should be ignored in lieu of the variable critical to successful performance. An example is setting a goal to win a tennis match. Once set, the goal should be forgotten and all energies directed at hitting the necessary strokes to win. If you think about winning, you cannot win because your ego gets in the way of your body. You can only win by *not* thinking about winning, and concentrating on the strokes essential for winning. This idea is simple but effective.

The above logic demonstrates that we become, not what we consciously wish to become in life but what we unconsciously believe our destiny in life to be. That is, we need to relax our conscious minds enough to allow our unconscious minds the freedom to explore new and unknown territory. Howard Gardner, in his book *Creating Minds* (1993), found that "too much time and

experience thinking in a certain way can prove uncongenial in any innovation."
He says "It is a particular combination of youth and maturity that allows
the most revolutionary work to take place." Psychologist Dean Simonton in
Scientific Genius (1988) says that too much knowledge is a "self-defeating aspect
of creativity." Creative genius means removing the ego and acknowledging your
ignorance in order to master the unknown.

Holistic Mentality and Creative Accomplishment

The ability to operate holistically with all our faculties, right and left brain,
conscious and unconscious, mind and body, is critical to the creative process.
Margaret Mead is the consummate example of this strategem. Her parents
never sent her to a formal school until she was a teenager because they wanted
her trained in experiential activities like the arts, music, and poetry—i.e., using
her hands as well as her mind. Jean Houston tested Mead as an adult and
said of her early training, "Dualisms were discouraged; she was trained to
accept unity of mind and body, thinking and feeling." This talent, according
to Houston, allowed Mead to "move in and out of her unconscious with ease."
Those with this ability to tap the power of the unconscious are destined to
become the great creative geniuses of the world because they are able to replace
distinctive details of the conscious with imaginative possibilities from the
unconscious.

Mead was unique, but we can all utilize our internal (unconscious) belief
systems to assist in our daily performance. The important thing is to insure
that our unconscious imprintings are positive and desirable images. If they
are not, it is critical that we change our internal scripting to fit a positive
model of our optimal best interest just as all of these women did via positive
imprinting. As the old adage says, "Be careful of your life goals, you might
just achieve them." Creative, visionary women like Margaret Mead have a
programmed, unconscious tape that tells them to be limitless in their pursuits.
Mead lived her life fulfilling her childhood image of herself and had a unique
and holistic attitude toward life. She had a reality map totally open to acceptance
of whatever came along. Women with this mentality are destined to travel
along divergent paths and not be deterred by their conscious needs for survival.
This is the ability found in most of the thirteen women in this book. They
were able to actualize their childhood dreams of success into great achievements
in business, entertainment, and politics.

The ability to operate holistically—utilizing both left and right brain mentalities—into a well-rounded personality is critical to the creative process. Women
must search for unfulfilled societal needs that happen to match their internally
programmed movies. This will give them the greatest chance for success as

creative and innovative women. These thirteen women had the unique ability to tap their internal resources, their dreams and fantasies, while resisting all external distractions. They never allowed their quantitative minds to get in the way of their qualitative images. Our unconscious can be an evolving, ever improving source of imaginative power. Unfortunately for most people it becomes a fixed resource which is reinforced in its existing state.

Power Shifts: Male to Female

Alvin Toffler in *Power Shift* (1990) makes a cogent argument for the origins of power in our "future shock" world. He describes the ancient mentality where physical power was the dominant means to achieving power. This was later supplanted by financial power during the Industrial Revolution, which has recently evolved into knowledge power, spurred on by the computer revolution. Because of the nature of physical or muscle power, males were dominant during the time of tribal cultures, where the strong prevailed over the weak. Men controlled the industrial base and thus continued to reign when muscle power was replaced by financial power. Men began as the hunters, women the nurturers; then men became the workers and women the housekeepers. As we near the second millennium, anyone with knowledge power can acquire both physical and financial power. Therefore, women can now become equal as never before, since they can have the same power as men in the world of business, politics, humanities, and entertainment.

Dorothy Cantor and Toni Bernay in *Women in Power* (1992)—a study of Diane Feinstein, Pat Schroeder, Barbara Boxer, and other recent female victors in the political wars of 1992—have found that power has become more evenly distributed, especially in careers where knowledge has been critical to success. This has contributed to the parity found in the recent elections in Texas, California, and Canada where women have dominated the top jobs. In Cantor and Bernay's study women in power were found to be highly educated, often in all-girl schools. This group of highly successful politicians represented more than ten times the national average for women attending all-female schools. These female political superstars evidently reached the top because of powerful role models with whom they interacted in all-girl schools. Single-sex schooling and the role-model influence were also found to be abnormally high for the thirteen visionary women in this work. An example is Margaret Thatcher, who attended no school with a male until she reached law school.

Beauty and Physical Attractiveness

In research on more than a hundred male entrepreneurs hair, nails, or color of clothes were never mentioned as important in their drive to the top. In a similar number of women studied, I found no instance where these factors were *not* discussed. Even the supposedly androgynous Iron Lady was worried over her hair and the color of her dresses. She admitted on U.S. television that she was willing to give up precious sleep, even when it meant only an hour and a half a night, in order to look good. Ted Turner could not have cared less about his appearance. Whether feminists like it or not women and men are different and approach life differently in respect to their physical looks. Warren Farrell in *Why Men Are the Way They Are!* (1986) found that "just as careers give men power, so beauty gives women power." Farrell was the only man elected three times to the board of the National Organization of Women in New York City and he makes a strong case for women being driven to achieve prominence due to their obsession with beauty and physical attractiveness. Warren makes the point that women seek security and romance in their relationships while men pursue their careers and sex at the expense of all else. The consensus is that women bargain their intimacy for security and men bargain their commitments to get sex.

A number of the women in this volume were accused of using their femininity to reach their goals. Golda Meir, Madonna, and Gloria Steinem were accused of this most often. Steinem was often castigated by her sisters because she was attractive. She was known in the sixties as the "pinup girl of the intelligentsia." Steinem didn't encourage this femme fatale image, but it did assist her in achieving many of her goals. Most observers are convinced she consciously or unconsciously used her physical assets to accomplish many of her goals. Meir was accused of the same thing by her political adversaries because she had actually gained mainly political appointments from men with whom she had affairs. Mary Kay Ash acknowledges using her appearance to distract men when walking into a room. She says "I make a point of looking as pretty as possible and acting as feminine as possible and I keep my mouth shut until I really know what I'm talking about" (*Self-Made Women,* 1991).

Verbal acuity, knowledge power, and beauty are three distinct areas where the women in this book have excelled. All were highly verbal: in fact, they were off the scale in this respect. They were all bright and knew more about their field of expertise than anyone. All were attractive and charismatic. They were sensuous women who knew how to open doors and did so when they needed to. These women reached the very top of their fields and achieved beyond the ordinary by staying within their given areas of expertise and knowledge. They did not attempt to move into high-tech skill areas (e.g., math and science), where men often have the edge. They did not attempt to excel in areas requiring great financial or technological skill. All of them made their marks in business, politics, entertainment, and humanities. Five of them revolutionized the world of business: Mary Kay Ash, Liz Claiborne, Estée Lauder, Lillian Vernon, and Linda Wachner. Margaret Thatcher and Golda Meir were political visionaries, while Maria Callas, Jane Fonda, Madonna, and Oprah Winfrey dominated the entertainment industry. And the remaining two—Ayn Rand and Gloria Steinem—utilized their humanitarian skills to alter societal values and ethics.

Gender-Dominant Skills

Gender appears to have little bearing on creative achievement. Hypomania, competitiveness, risk-taking propensity, and a keen intuitive vision have been found to be the critical variables in both men and women who have achieved great success. Both genders demonstrate these particular traits although to different degrees. Women are more methodical than men and are more prone to analyzing the ramifications of their decisions. They also live less on the edge and their aggressiveness is more verbal than physical. The following lists some other interesting factors:

POLITICAL AND VERBAL

As previously discussed, females are better at *verbal* and *communication* tasks than males. It is apparent that many of the successful women in history have utilized this skill to overcome their adversaries. Catherine the Great used persuasive communication and charisma in conquering a nation indoctrinated by Peter the Great in the use of physical force. Margaret Mead was precociously verbal, and Mother Teresa saved millions based on her ability to attract funding for her great cause. Golda Meir was an inspirational and captivating speaker. Her biographer, Ralph Martin, in his book *Golda* (1988), comments that Meir could move people to tears when speaking. Her long-time political adversary, David Ben-Gurion, characterized her verbal skills after hearing her speak to the British just prior to Israel's statehood: "I trembled at her daring words. Her speech shook the convention. She spoke with genius, assertively, bitterly, with hurt, sensibly."

Margaret Thatcher had a similar ability when debating or speaking in a group. She used her extensive knowledge of a subject and put it into a philosophical perspective that could be understood by the masses. Thatcher's refusal to back down in any confrontation gave her much support from the males in Parliament. She refused to be thought of in the stereotypical female way as weak and submissive. She always resorted to a combative, never-back-down attitude in debate. Consequently, both Thatcher and Meir were labeled intransigent by their enemies and friends. They were strong-willed and articulate women who used the verbal gifts of their gender to reach the pinnacle of their chosen fields. Mary Kay Ash so mesmerized her female beauty consultants that they were in a frenzy to just touch her and would cry when she spoke.

In 1993 an unprecedented number of females reached the very top of the political world in leadership positions formally held by men. Barbara Boxer and Diane Feinstein wrested senatorial seats from men in California, the first time two females represented our largest state; Janet Reno became the first female attorney general of the United States; Kim Campbell became the first female prime minister of Canada; Kay Bailey Hutchison was elected senator from Texas; Tansu Ciller became the first female prime minister of Turkey; and Ruth Bader Ginsburg was appointed to the U.S. Supreme Court, making her only the second woman appointed to that body.

NURTURING SPIRITS

Women throughout history have been recognized for their nurturing natures giving them unique strengths as: *protectors* of their children, *securers* of the family nest, and *stabilizers* of social and organizational systems. Their strengths turned into weakness when it came to creative and entrepreneurial endeavors: the above positive traits of motherhood and wifedom are counterproductive relative to professional pioneering. The above traits tend to condition a person to become risk-averse, which is incompatible with creative breakthroughs. Even though these factors are counterproductive for business ventures, they are invaluable qualities for the political arena, thus the success of Catherine the Great, Mother Teresa, Golda Meir, Margaret Thatcher, and Gloria Steinem.

BEAUTY

Beauty and physical attraction are critically important to most females. Catherine the Great told Voltaire when he reproached her for her sexual dalliances, "I am absolutely faithful. To whom? To beauty of course. Beauty alone attracts me." Most women are groomed from birth to revere these attributes. Women discover quite early in life that their success is often a function of their physical approval, so they strive to seek approval via their hair, grooming, dress, and attractiveness. Margaret Thatcher was considered a bit asexual by most observers, but even the Iron Lady was forever concerned about her looks and her hair. All of our female subjects were sensitive to the beauty factor: in fact, eight of the thirteen either sold beauty products (Mary Kay Ash, Estée Lauder, Liz Claiborne, Lillian Vernon, and Linda Wachner) or needed beauty to perform (Maria Callas, Jane Fonda, and Madonna).

Jane Fonda said it best when asked why she entered the fitness video-tape industry. "There wasn't much about business I did understand. . . . It came to me like a bolt of lightning, the way my best ideas usually do, that the one thing I really do know about is being healthy, being fit." Then she added "For twenty-five years I went to dance classes. I saw many women like me who took the rigorous training, not to become professional dancers, but because they wanted to reshape their bodies." *Video Review* commented on Fonda's success in an arena she admittedly knew nothing about: "Jane Fonda is the biggest single success factor of the entire video business." Fonda made beauty her business and did it better than anyone else.

Women understand and appreciate beauty and appearance far better than most men. In *The Beauty Myth* Naomi Wolf states that women are "strongly dissatisfied" with their looks and men are "very satisfied" with theirs. Warren Farrell, in *Why Men Are the Way They Are,* found that women learn very early that the path to success in life is through their physical and sexual attraction. Consequently they spend an inordinate amount of time pursuing beauty and indulging in whatever it takes to achieve it. It makes sense then that women seeking great success should do what they know best. Estée Lauder, Mary Kay Ash, and Liz Claiborne followed their basic instincts in this area and founded great empires based on cosmetics, skin care, and women's career clothing.

Forbes magazine (June 1988) profiled Liz Claiborne as the first woman to recognize that women's fashion was not art but a part of life. "Claiborne was the first of this breed of woman designer to realize that, by designing clothes she herself appreciated, she would be designing clothes that women everywhere would like." Lillian Vernon often said the same thing about her dominance in the catalog industry. She purchased items that she personally wanted to own and she turned out to be correct in over 90 percent of the cases. These women recognized their areas of expertise and rose to the very top of their industries without knowing anything special about business to get there. They knew their specialty—in this case beauty—and that knowledge carried them to the top.

ENTERTAINMENT

Communication skills and beauty skills are never more evident than in show business. Attractive communication is the essence of the entertainment industry and women are typically better suited to this endeavor than men. Oprah Winfrey outpaced Phil Donahue in the TV ratings race for daytime talk shows in her first year and has penetrated 99 percent of American households. Within a decade Madonna surpassed the Beatles in all-time successive single hit songs. Maria Callas became the equal of Caruso and has been called the greatest diva of the twentieth century, not for her voice, but because of her dominant stage presence and theatrical skills. Jane Fonda excelled in the theater, movies, videos, and various fitness businesses. She has won two Academy Awards for her acting skills, but she revolutionized the videotape industry with her fitness tapes and books. This field appears especially conducive to females desirous of excelling as innovators and creators.

HUMANITIES

No man would have been accepted into the jungle homes of Samoa and New Guinea and allowed to speak to the teenage daughters of the natives about their reproductive and sexual proclivities. Margaret Mead not only accomplished this feat, she did so during her mid-twenties, when she actually looked more like a teenager herself than a future world-acclaimed anthropologist. Mead utilized her social consciousness to dissect the cultures of various societies. Mother Teresa did the same in her life's work of helping the poor and dying in India. She started in Calcutta and has since been highly successful in spreading her message throughout the world.

Ayn Rand, Gloria Steinem, and Jane Fonda personify females with a social consciousness desirous of changing the world. The first two spent their lives in social commentary; Fonda's efforts have been more fleeting. These macro-vision women cared about what was happening to society and decided to change it through knowledge, the power of the press, and the written word. Our societal and ethical systems have been significantly altered because of the presence of these women. Both Ayn Rand and Gloria Steinem used their unique understanding of human nature and the interrelationships between human beings and society to make their mark in the world. Both sacrificed their maternal instincts for the realization of their dreams. Fonda was the only social activist with her own press agent, but she has mellowed on most issues and is now devoted to ecological and world health matters.

Ayn Rand created the philosophy of objectivism based on the "art of selfishness"—an antibureaucratic credo of enlightened self-interest. She devoted her life to free enterprise for everyone, personally or professionally. Gloria Steinem founded many organizations devoted to the equality of women in society. In doing so she became the alter ego of a whole female generation. No man could ever have filled her role or achieved what she has. She was the right person at the right time with the right talents to bring about critical changes in women's rights. Steinem was willing to sacrifice everything for her dreams and as shown in the monetary rewards chart (Fig. 17) later in this chapter, she received little or no compensation in relation to her contributions. Among these women she is the least successful financially, though money was never important to her. Steinem labored over the abuse, intolerance, and inequality in society and found herself later in life with little to show for her efforts other than the satisfaction of making important headway toward female justice, which is its own reward.

Gender-Based Differences*

Each of our women was successful in her given field because she dared to be different. As a group, these women were able to harness their tremendous energies around their female strengths and use them to change the world for the better. These women always preferred to negotiate rather than instigate. They were tolerant rather than judgmental and they nurtured instead of being contentious. They verbalized rather than criticized and communicated rather than dictated. These female traits made them successes. However, they had the same obsession with performance as that found in men, and, surprisingly, they were willing to sacrifice their families and mates for their professions. This male behavior is often credited to the fact that males do not have the same degree of nurturing spirit as females. But the females in this work were very malelike in their willingness to sacrifice everything for their goals.

Men and women are different, even if they are great creative geniuses. One of the most obvious differences is based on the way men and women view the world. I am convinced the Anita Hill/Judge Thomas debacle had more to do with gender differences in relational values and attitudes than it had to do with any overt discrimination. Each of these adversaries saw the same issues from his or her own unique perspective based on years of conditioning and gender differences. Research on creative genius has shown that men need to look important while woman need to look good. To men success is power, and to women success is a strong relationship. Women prefer to communicate; men prefer to intimidate. Women seek interpersonal approval; men seek interpersonal dominance. Women are sensitive to others' feelings; men are sensitive to their egos. Women give sex to get romance; men give romance to get sex. Women will discuss controversy; men will avoid controversy. These differences indicate that men and women approach life from far different perspectives. Even so, it appears from the research on female creative genius that these thirteen women were more like their male counterparts than they were different. In fact, our subjects had more in common with male creative visionaries than with the average female.

As a group the women were nicer, the men more crass. The men made more money as a group. The women were more spiritual and thus not so inclined to have sexual dalliances. Both were far healthier than the average

---

*See *Profiles of Genius* (1993)

population with the men less inclined to obesity than the women. Both groups had excessive work ethics. The men were more frivolous and therefore had more fun, whereas the women were inclined to be more serious. Both were far more driven than the average population. The women reached the top at a much older age mainly due to their childbearing responsibilities. Both were more attractive and charismatic than persons found in the gender generally.

The bottom line is that both groups had the critically important variables in common. Both had common personality traits, which manifested themselves in hard work, competitiveness, high risk-taking, and an obsession with their ideas. These are the variables that make a creative genius. Figure 16 is a comparative analysis of the genders relative to creative genius.

Aggression (males) versus communication (females). When a male and female are faced with a major confrontation, each responds in a dramatically different way. The male responds by either immediately striking out (punching the adversary in the nose) or withdrawing and repressing his aggressive urges (Seyle's fight or flight syndrome). The female virtually never strikes out in aggression. She will communicate to resolve the conflict. In other words, the female resorts to her strength, communication, in order to resolve conflict; the male resorts to his strength—fighting or fleeing. The male response is either *aggression or submission,* and the female's is *communication* (often to the chagrin of the male).

Communication is preferable in business, as well as social and political venues, making the female more suited emotionally in these settings. This type of behavior also makes the female less qualified for front-line combat action in the military. The above example is why males have completely dominated third-world societies, where physical power predominates. In contemporary societies, where knowledge and communication are more important, the females are destined to rise to positions of power.

Testosterone. Gender-based differences are definitely a function of testosterone. This hormone is found in much greater amounts in men than women and in the greatest amounts in risk-taking, aggressive, and competitive males who reach the top. In fact, the "Big T" factor was found to be one of the most common character traits in male creative genius. The women in this book were very aggressive and competitive and took greater risks than the average female. It is apparent that if tested, they would have exhibited a higher than normal testosterone level. This makes these women different from the so-called average female, and more like the average male. Even with theoretically higher-than-normal testosterone levels, these women were less competitive, risk-oriented, and aggressive than the males studied, and they were far less libidinally driven. Madonna, Meir, Mead, and Fonda are notable exceptions. A total of thirteen of each were studied (see *Profiles of Genius,* 1993, for detail on the males). These twenty-six men and women represent a small but eminent sampling of

Figure 16

Male and Female Success Variables

Variables	Male	Female
Age to success	Younger (77% under 35)	Older (30% under 35)
Built billion-dollar operation	10 (77%)	3 (23%)
Net worth of a billion	5 (38%)	1 (8%)
College degree	6 (46%)	5 (38%)
Family economic status: rich/poor	5 (38%)/3 (23%)	1 (8%)/4 (31%)
First-born	9 (77%)	6 (46%)
Major influence	Mother	Father
Visualization	Spatial	Verbal
Multiple Marriages	7 (54%)	5 (38%)
Religious	Not very—3 (23%)	More devout—5 (38%)
Risk-Taking: Business/Personal	Awesome/high (7 flew/raced)	Guarded/Low
Self-employed fathers	13 (100%)	11 (85%)
Intuitive-thinking temperament	13 (100%)	9 (69%)

great entrepreneurs, innovators, and creative leaders in the world.

First-born and self-employed fathers. Being first-born was not quite as important in the women as in the men. Only one of the men was not the first-born male, while just half of the women were. However, five of the women were raised like the first-born, mitigating the differences. Having a self-employed father was not quite as prevalent for the women: all of the men had self-employed fathers, while all but two of the women had fathers who were self-employed or were entrepreneurs.

Feminism/chauvinism. All the females studied were avid promoters of equality and free enterprise for women but only one was a feminist (Gloria Steinem), and many of them actually had disdain for militant feminists. They were for equality in pay, opportunity, and treatment. Mary Kay Ash actually started her firm for the express purpose of providing a vehicle for career women because of her own unfortunate experiences with discrimination. Yet Ash disliked the feminist movement because of what she thought were its belligerent, anti-feminine attitudes. Most of these women decried the fact that the media were constantly badgering them to make an issue out of their enormous success as a female. Lillian Vernon says, "I would prefer to be interviewed as an entrepreneur, rather than a 'lady' entrepreneur." Margaret Thatcher told the

Daily Mirror, "I don't notice that I'm a woman. I regard myself as the prime minister," and she told the *Times,* "The feminists have become far too strident and have done damage to the cause of women by making us out to be something we're not. You get on because you have the right talents." Golda Meir iterated this view in her biography: "I never had sympathy for the women's organizations as such. . . . Teaching girls various trades is more important than women's rights." Ayn Rand was a life-long antifeminist. She said, "Living for someone else's values is terrible." She saw many women's libbers as attempting to get something for nothing, which was foreign to her objectivist philosophy. Even Tipper Gore on Valentine's Day, 1994, told *U.S.A. Today,* "I still subscribe to it [feminism] in terms of legalities—equal pay for equal work—but in terms of your life, I've dismissed a lot of it as unworkable."

The males studied in my earlier volume were egomaniacs and competitive macho types in many ways but were seldom found to discriminate against females. The dominant and often macho methods of these men were at times interpreted otherwise, but they were not chauvinistic, just autocratic. They broke most of the rules of business but never with malice.

Sex drive. High libidinal drive was far more prevalent among the male visionaries than among the females. The thirteen men had fifty-three children, or an average of four each: four of these men were extremely prolific with ten, nine, seven, and seven children each. The thirteen women had a total of only fourteen children and almost half of our female geniuses (six) had no children. In other words, the women sacrificed parenting for their professions. The thirteen men had a total of twenty-six marriages between them for an average of two each. The women had a total of eighteen marriages between them for an average of a little more than one. Two women (Steinem and Winfrey) never married. In other words, the women sacrificed their relationships more than the men. The incidence of promiscuity was far greater in the men than in the women. Half of the men were promiscuous. It appears that only a few of the women would qualify as promiscuous.

Financial success. It is difficult to rank the degree of success attained by each gender. The men made the most money but the women attained higher stations for longer periods of time (see figure 17). In other words, the women had a greater societal impact and the men more of a monetary impact. Although Estée Lauder's fortune is estimated in the $5 billion area by *Fortune* magazine, making her an equal to any of the males studied with the possible exception of Bill Gates, Oprah Winfrey's $52 million annual earnings are higher than any of the men's. Eight of the thirteen women have accumulated in excess of $100 million, which is not an easy task. By any measure these women have been enormously successful financially.

Formal education. Six of the men and five of the women were college educated. However, the men were more technically inclined and the women

Figure 17

Financial Success of Female Visionaries

Individual	Career Path	Accomplishment	Financial Success
Mary Kay Ash	Business	Mary Kay Cosmetics; revolutionized skin care	Hundreds of millions
Maria Callas	Entertainment	Top diva in the world	$100 thousand annually at peak; multimillion-dollar estate
Liz Claiborne	Business	Liz Claiborne, Inc.; dominates women's fashion	Hundreds of millions
Jane Fonda	Entertainment	Academy Awards, top book and videotape producer	$60–80 million
Estée Lauder	Business	Estée Lauder Cosmetics	$5.2 billion (*Forbes,* 1992)
Madonna	Entertainment	16 successive top singles (broke Beatles' record)	$100 Million
Margaret Mead	Humanities	World's most famous anthropologist	Affluent
Golda Meir	Politics	Prime minister of Israel, key to creation of Israeli state	Subsistence living
Ayn Rand	Humanities	Mother of philosophical novel; created objectivist philosophy	Affluent
Gloria Steinem	Humanities	Leading American feminist; founder of *Ms.* magazine	Subsistence living
Mother Teresa	Humanities	Founded Missionaries of Charity (1950); won Nobel Peace Prize (1979)	Subsistence Living
Margaret Thatcher	Politics	First female prime minister of Great Britain; longest term in office in twentieth century	Affluent
Lillian Vernon	Business	Queen of the direct-mail catalog business	$100 million
Linda Wachner	Business	CEO of largest *Fortune* 500 company at age forty	$100 million
Oprah Winfrey	Entertainment	Most-loved, most-watched, and highest-paid entertainer	$250+ million

more inclined toward the liberal arts. The men did not use their educations in their creative endeavors and would have had the same degree of success without their educational pedigrees. Only one of the five women with college degrees (Margaret Thatcher) had a technical education. The women tended to use their formal educations in their creative endeavor more than the men. Eight of the women and seven of the men did not finish college. All were extremely knowledgeable if not the preeminent individuals, in their field, even though they had little or no formal education.

Personality types. All thirteen of the male creative visionaries had Promethean temperaments (intuitive-thinking personality style of behavior as measured by Myers-Briggs). Nine of the thirteen women had an intuitive-thinking style. This is extraordinary since 75 percent of American females have a preference for "feeling" not "thinking" in their decision-making preference. Additionally, eleven of the thirteen women were strong intuitors on that personality scale, which is critical to any great creative or innovative endeavor. They saw the forest instead of just the trees to become successful visionaries. Although they were not as statistically likely to be Promethean as the men, they were far more likely to be Promethan in temperament than the average female.

Relational attitudes of behavior. Male and female visionaries handle relationships differently. It is probably the most significant difference between the sexes. Male visionaries were found to be more ego-driven and focused on their individual accomplishments, while the women were more relationship-driven and focused on their ability to perform within the system or firm. Males tended to value the intrarelationships, where they could exercise their competitive drives in order to better accomplish their objectives. Females valued the interrelationships, where they could exercise their communicative and nurturing skills in accomplishing their objectives.

Age of successful breakthrough. The thirteen females reached the top at a much older age than their male counterparts. One of the reasons for this difference was due to professional paths that were more career- than product-based innovations. Careers take significantly longer to materialize than products. Another material factor was the multirole responsibility of women: they more often functioned as wives, mothers, and professionals. Note the two individuals who selected politics as their career path were much older when they reached the top. This is understandable since politics demands a much longer incubation period than other professions. Consequently, Meir and Thatcher tend to skew the findings, although six of these women (Callas, Fonda, Madonna, Steinem, Wachner, and Vernon) reached the top of their professions before their fortieth birthdays (see figure 18). Nine of the thirteen men studied reached the top under the age of forty and none had to wait until age fifty to reach the top. Four of the women were over fifty before reaching their peak. Over 77 percent of the men had made it by age thirty-five and only 30 percent of the women had made it by that age.

Figure 18

Age of Peak Success of Female Visionaries

Individual	Career Path	Age Started	Age at Peak
Mary Kay Ash	Business	52	60s
Maria Callas	Entertainment	16	30
Liz Claiborne	Business	47	50s
Jane Fonda	Entertainment	28	30s
Estée Lauder	Business	38	50s
Madonna	Entertainment	20	20s
Golda Meir	Politics	25	70
Ayn Rand	Humanities	37	40s
Gloria Steinem	Humanities	35	40s
Margaret Thatcher	Politics	33	50s
Linda Wachner	Business	20	40
Lillian Vernon	Business	23	50
Oprah Winfrey	Entertainment	21	30s

Religion and Creativity

These women were not so much religious as spiritual. They preferred to create dogma than observe it. The women were far more religious than the men. The males studied were mostly agnostic or nonreligious (nine of thirteen were not religious). The women were far more likely to have a denominational affiliation they took somewhat seriously, as nine of the thirteen followed some kind of faith (see figure 19). Only Ayn Rand of the thirteen women was a devout and vocal atheist. Most of the others were middle of the road religiously, with the exception of Mary Kay Ash, who is a devout Southern Baptist.

Based on the findings it appears that religion is not an important variable in creative genius. Religion seems to have given the women in this book the strength to continue during the crises they all encountered in their march to the top. Almost all were spiritual, but they never allowed their spirituality to interfere with their drive toward an ultimate goal. Many were superstitious and even mystical at times. Both Madonna and Callas had experiences bordering on the occult. Madonna was convinced that Elvis Presley died on her birthday for some special reason. On turning nineteen on August 16, 1977, when Presley

Figure 19

Religious Preference of Female Visionaries

Individual	Career Path	Religious Affiliation
Mary Kay Ash	Business	Devout Southern Baptist
Maria Callas	Entertainment	Devout Greek Orthodox
Liz Claiborne	Business	Roman Catholic
Jane Fonda	Entertainment	Spiritual but not religious
Estée Lauder	Business	Jewish
Madonna	Entertainment	Roman Catholic/agnostic
Golda Meir	Politics	Nonorthodox Jewish
Ayn Rand	Humanities	Atheist
Gloria Steinem	Humanities	Not religious
Margaret Thatcher	Politics	Methodist
Linda Wachner	Business	Jewish
Lillian Vernon	Business	Jewish
Oprah Winfrey	Entertainment	Methodist

died, she said, "His soul has gone into me and has given me the power to perform" (Anderson, 1991). Madonna also felt she had precognitive powers: she was blown away when Sandra Bernhard came on stage in Greenwich Village and recited a dream about surviving WWIII with her. Madonna immediately raced backstage to meet her as she had had the same dream and felt it was an omen that they should meet and begin a strong relationship. Maria Callas believed in tarot cards and astrology. She had been told by a fortuneteller that she would die quite young, and she believed it. She died unexpectedly at age fifty-four almost in a possible self-fulfilling prophecy or synchronicity according to Carl Jung.

Greek Mythological Heroines

These creative visionary women were mythological in the sense that they envisioned themselves as omnipotent beings. Their internalized images were epic and heroic. They seemed to innately know their destinies. They believed it was their fate to reach the top, so they never questioned their "divine right" to the throne. These dreams became their conscious realities which were ultimately transformed into inviolable self-esteem. It was this extraordinary self-esteem which helped these women become great leaders, heroines, and politicians. Their unconscious need to achieve led them to unprecedented heights. Most admitted to this inner knowledge much later in life.

These visionaries can appropriately be described as metaphorical goddesses. Athena is the mythological Greek goddess of wisdom and warfare; she would make an ideal patron saint for these women. They were bright and aggressive women, possessing the persona of an Athena. These visionaries invariably set out to change the world with no other weapons than an Athenalike self-confidence bred through marvelous self-esteem and spawned by an amazing self-image. They often donned the persona of warriors fighting the establishment to fulfill childhood dreams. The Perseus myth is a prophetic metaphor for looking at the success of these thirteen women. In this myth, Athena helped Perseus slay the monster Medusa (an analogy for the establishment that resists change). Perseus (the female innovator) is therefore the creative destroyer who fights and kills patriarchal systems (Medusa). She does this to release Pegasus (enlightenment) who represents creativity and innovation. These thirteen women were Athenas who changed the world by destroying old-fashioned dogmatic ways and bringing enlightenment to their fields of endeavor.

Success Tips

The conclusions from this research would indicate that *any female with slightly above-average intelligence and health can achieve greatness.* It is evident that certain regimens and thinking are critical to the process of great creative and entrepreneurial success. These factors are summarized in figure 20.

Summary

Female creative genius is synonymous with a strong self-esteem and self-confidence coupled with a right-brain-driven intuitive spirit and a manic energy to succeed. Ironically, the trait of self-confidence is what Mary Kay Ash considers to be the most lacking in all females. "If you would ask me what is the common denominator among women, I would have to say it's a lack of confidence in their own God-given ability. They don't believe in themselves." Mary Kay is the prototypical example of a woman who exudes confidence, as did the other women we have discussed. They all believed in themselves and their destinies to the point that they were able to ignore all dissenting arguments against their chances for success.

These women were more inclined to take intellectual and economic risks

Figure 20

Success Tips for Aspiring Female Innovators

Select One of Your Unique Traits. Pick one personal talent or innate ability which separates you from the pack. Use it in formulating your new venture. (Fonda knew fitness and exercise; Winfrey loved to talk.)

Pursue Your Passionate Dream. Select one idea or passion which you cherish more than anything else in the world and go for it. It should be an emotional, spiritual, passionate dream. (Ash selected a business for women, by women, with women.)

Bet the Farm. Be prepared to sacrifice everything for the fruition of your dream or idea.

Ignore all Experts. Never listen to an expert who will always know all the reasons why your idea has no merit.

Start Small. Build on your dream as you would a foundation for a house. Focus on one success and build on it. Build one, then ten, then millions. Attempting to start big almost always ends in disaster.

See the Big Picture. Macro-vision and a long-term view keeps you in perspective and highly focused on the ultimate goal.

Work Hard. Perspiration is endemic to all great success. Be prepared for seven-day, eighty-hour weeks in the formative stages of your enterprise.

Seek Consummate Knowledge. Learn more about what you are doing than anyone in the world. Seek truth and knowledge. Use trial-and-error techniques to eliminate the errors encountered in your endeavor.

Be Different. Visionaries are mavericks because they violate traditional norms, which is the catalyst of all great enterprise. Go where others fear to tread. You will be alone but truly innovative.

Obsessive People Overachieve. Driven individuals find a way to overcome the obstacles encountered on the road to great achievement.

Optimism Builds Character. A positive attitude is critical to the creative process. It builds personal self-esteem and the necessary belief to attract the followers needed to achieve all great ventures.

Persevere. Persistence prevails. Never give up and success will follow.

than would the average female. They never hesitated to go where others feared to tread even when they were scorned for daring to defy the establishment. They were constantly faced with new and unknown environments and death-defying crises as children. These experiences programmed them to cope and survive in foreign habitats. Our female visionaries were willing to destroy the present order of things in their march to the top of their fields. Ironically, three of these successful women—all entertainers (Madonna, Oprah, and Fonda)—violated their traditional image of "frivolous press idols" by operating as chief executive officers of multimillion dollar enterprises. They were the "boss" in every definition of the word. These women had a unique ability to master whatever was needed at the time to continue on the path to their Elysian Fields.

These female creative geniuses had similar behavior characteristics and drives to the male visionaries studied, but were different in other ways. They did not take risks with the same reckless abandon as a Ted Turner, a Nolan Bushnell, or a Bill Lear, and were not as aggressively competitive in their management styles as the male visionaries. In their personal acquisitions—their "adult toys"—they had the same predilections as the men. Madonna paid an extra $2.5 million for a Miami Beach estate because she "wanted it," and in her words, "I do what I want." Oprah wanted an eighty-five-acre ranch near a ski resort, so she bought it for $4.3 million—she doesn't even ski. Most men wouldn't have been quite that frivolous, although most of the visionaries studied were. The ever-conservative Liz Claiborne owns three estates and Estée Lauder has chalets in Europe, Palm Beach, and New York.

These women were at ease with risks, competition, and a killing work schedule. They had a higher propensity for these qualities than the average female—a fact that contributed to their success—but they were not as energized by these qualities as the men. Golda Meir, Liz Claiborne, Margaret Thatcher, Lillian Vernon, Linda Wachner, Madonna, Jane Fonda, Ayn Rand, and Oprah Winfrey have operating styles that can be characterized as malelike. They usually place their career above their family priorities and are tough taskmasters as chief executive officers. In fact, most of these women were incensed when feminist issues were raised as a factor in their success or in their operating styles. They insisted that their success was based on their own talent and were reluctant to have anyone suggest that their femininity had anything to do with their rise. I would concur with their assertions. These women made it to the top because of their talent, personal empowerment, and work ethic—not their gender. Often they succeeded in spite of their gender.

The "universal female creative genius" can be defined as follows: A focused female who is armed with enormous self-confidence probably due to being the first-born female (or being the most venerated); who was blessed with a strong, self-employed father who was her early role-model; whose permissive parents educated her in a single-gender school or boarding school where she met some strong female role models or mentors; who experienced some earth-shattering crisis that was not overly dysfunctional to her development; who was imprinted with a Promethean—intuitive-thinking—temperament and a renegade behavior allowing her to pioneer, ignore the experts, and take inordinate risks; who was always comfortable with ambiguity and the new.

All thirteen women had most of the above qualities and traits. They were not born richer, smarter, prettier, or better connected than most women in the world. They were dealt a hand of cards not different from most, but they almost certainly played it better. They were willing to aggressively pursue their dreams, and the world is a far better place because they did. They are truly the consummate female visionaries of this or any other era. They molded impossible dreams into improbable success.

Figure 21

Most, Greatest, and Best of Females Visionaries

Richest	Estée Lauder
Poorest	Gloria Steinem
Brightest	Ayn Rand, Madonna, and Oprah Winfrey
Highest sex drive	Golda Meir and Madonna
Best dressed	Estée Lauder
Worse dressed	Golda Meir
Most famous	Madonna
Best adjusted	Margaret Thatcher and Lillian Vernon
Worst adjusted	Maria Callas
Most religious	Mary Kay Ash
Least Religious	Ayn Rand
Highest risk-taker	Madonna and Golda Meir
Lowest risk-taker	Margaret Thatcher
Most loved	Oprah Winfrey and Mary Kay Ash
Most hated	Madonna and Jane Fonda
Most driven	Linda Wachner
Most talented	Maria Callas and Jane Fonda
Nicest	Liz Claiborne
Most rebellious	Madonna
Most Charismatic	Golda Meir and Mary Kay Ash
Highest paid	Linda Wachner
Hardest working	Margaret Thatcher
Highest self-esteem	Lillian Vernon
Highest social consciousness	Gloria Steinem and Jane Fonda
Greatest impact on world—20th century	Margaret Thatcher
Greatest impact on world—21st century	Ayn Rand

Figure 22

Inhibiting Factors for Female Entrepreneurs
"Their Strengths become their Weaknesses"

Nurturing Natures
Females tend to be nicer than males and strive to maintain relationships at all costs, which becomes counterproductive to the entrepreneurial process. Studies have shown that women will stop playing the game if it threatens any valued relationships. Men would never allow any relationship to interfere with winning the game.

Verbal Acuity
Females are far more adept at verbalization than men, who are better at spatial relationships. Women's ability to talk can open many doors but will often close the doors even faster when they either talk too much or it interferes with the progression of business.

Noncompetitive
Women have been trained to win by being submissive and accommodating. Congeniality is their strength and they envision competitive achievement as counter to their femininity. Men, in contrast, value competitive achievement and resist committed intimacy. Intimacy is craved by the female which often makes the female fair game in a highly competitive business.

Pygmalion Syndrome
Women value relational compatibility so much they often attempt to change their associates to be more like them, which to their thinking is the road to a more secure relationship. It is counterproductive to the process as they waste valuable energy building relationships while their competitors are building products and networks.

Risk-Aversity
Female leaders have an internal need to secure their personnel and organizations against potential failure; thus they often resist new high-risk opportunities which could adversely impact their ability to survive. They are more "care-taking" than "risk-taking" and therefore not willing to "live on the edge," which is where all great innovation takes place.

Generalists Not Specialists
The brains of females have been shown to be more "generalized," males more "specialized." Therefore, women tend to see the longer macro-view of new opportunities and tend to work on philosophic projects rather than on specific product innovations. All of their successes tend to take longer and involve political or large female organizational environments.

Coolidge Effect (Scientific term for male promiscuity)
Males are gregarious socially and sexually and adapt to changing partners positively. Women prefer building strong committed relationships in a monogamous fashion. The male approach is more compatible with a dynamic, changing society, especially in the world of innovation and entrepreneurship. Entrepreneurial women need to avoid resisting change.

Compassionate and Cooperative
Women are nicer than men in general because they strive to build long-lasting relationships, while men live in perpetual fear of commitment to permanent relationships. In highly competitive environments normally found in the world of entrepreneurship "nice people do finish last." Entrepreneurial women should keep their compassion in proper perspective.

In conclusion, women and men are different. Women have a holistic and intuitive macro-vision view of the creative process. Men have a more narrow and specialized orientation to innovation. In other words, women use a more generalized mentality in creating products or ideas while men utilize a more specialized approach to idea and product creation. Men deal with problem resolution quantitatively, women qualitatively. Women are care-focused and tend to build relationships in order to achieve their goals. Men are more justice-focused and self-centered in achieving goals. Women are visual, men spatial. Women nurture, men lecture. Women make emotionally based decisions, men rationally based decisions. Men competitively attack problems; women tend to be cooperative. Women strive for power through a subtle use of their feminine qualities. Men strive for power through physical performance and actions. Women like to negotiate; men prefer to intimidate. Men resolve confrontation through aggression and will fight. Women are more nurturing, preferring to resolve conflict by talk. Men generally have an ego-oriented view of the world, while women see a more compassionate big picture. Eminent women reach the top using the identical methods, business tactics, and traits found in great men; it is only their personal approach that is uniquely different.

Females are different from men in that they use relationships in pursuing great entrepreneurial achievement. The women in this book started with generalized concepts, which led to specific product achievements—a direct contrast to the successful men studied. Mary Kay Ash embarked on the larger concept of an "idealized" female company, but ended up revolutionizing distribution of unique beauty products. Jane Fonda decided to improve the female fitness market and ended up selling more videotapes than any other person in history. Estée Lauder wanted to enhance beauty and became the queen of a cosmetics empire. Ayn Rand espoused a capitalistic philosophy (Objectivism) and her writing made her into a great novelist. The men studied began with specific product innovations, which turned into generalized accomplishments in their industries. Consider Ted Turner's CNN, which was created as a 24-hour news network and ended up skrinking the world into the proverbial global village. Howard Head's oversized tennis racket innovation was aimed at improving his tennis game (an ego invention), but it revolutionized the game of tennis. The Bic pen was invented to meet the mass-market needs for a 19-cent ballpoint pen, but it spawned the throw-away culture. Men prefer to invent, women to refine.

Feminine insight opened many doors for these women in their trek to the top. They tapped unique female qualities (visual/verbal acuity) to get through that elusive glass ceiling. Many feminists find fault with a woman using her feminine talents and endowments to achieve success. However, subjugating the feminine mystique is counterproductive to creative and innovative success. We should utilize all of our attributes and talented women should be prepared to use their feminie qualities just as men use their spatial and analytical talents. Mary Kay Ash made charismatic entrances into a room in order to attract attention until she could demonstrate her management talents with the males in the room. It worked, and she should be proud of her eminent success. This is the essence of the creative process. These exceptional women mimicked Ash's approach and used their female talents with elegance, style, and panache, and thereby reached the top of their fields in the process. They achieved power by using their intuitive skills and the world is better off for their enormous contributions.

References

General References

Aburdeen, Patricia, and John Naisbitt. 1992. *Megatrends for Women.* New York: Villard Books.

Alexander, John. 1989. *Catherine the Great.* New York: Oxford Press.

Amabile, Teresa. 1989. *Growing Up Creative—Nurturing a Lifetime of Creativity.* New York: Crown Publishing.

Barzun, Jaques. Summer 1989. "The Paradoxes of Creativity." *The American Scholar,* p. 337.

Benbow, Camilla, and Julian Stanley. December 1980. "Sex Differences in Mathematical Ability: Fact or Artifact?" *Science.*

Block, Jeff. August 1992. "The Richest Women in America." *Ladies Home Journal,* p. 120

Boorstin, Daniel. 1992. *The Creators.* New York: Random House.

Cantor, Dorothy, and Toni Bernay. 1992. *Women in Power—The Secrets of Leadership.* New York: Houghton-Mifflin.

Cappon, Daniel. May/June 1993. "The Anatomy of Intuition." *Psychology Today,* p. 41

Current Biography Yearbook
    Liz Claiborne Ortenberg (1989), p. 110.
    Maria Callas (1956), p. 98.
    Jane Fonda (1986), p. 139.
    Indira Ghandi (1966), p. 114.
    Billy Jean King (1987), p. 225.
    Frances Lear (1991), p. 357.
    Estée Lauder (1986), p. 296.
    Madonna [Madonna Louise Veronica Ciccone], (1986). p. 328.
    Margaret Mead (1951), p. 421.

Golda Meir (1970), p. 284.
Sandra Day O'Connor (1982), pp. 297–301.
Ayn Rand (1982), p. 331.
Sally Ride (1983), p. 318.
Patricia Schroeder (1978), p. 367.
Gloria Steinem (1988), p. 542.
Margaret Thatcher (1989), p. 567.
Mother Teresa (1973), p. 403.
Barbara Walters (1971), p. 432.
Oprah Winfrey (1987), p. 610.

Farrell, W. 1986. *Why Men Are the Way They Are.* New York: McGraw-Hill.

Ferguson, Marilyn. 1976. *The Aquarian Conspiracy.* Los Angeles: J. P. Tarcher.

Forbes. October 1992. "*Forbes* Richest 400 People in America," p. 90.

Fucini, Joseph and Suzy. 1985. *Entrepreneurs—The Men and Women behind Famous Brand Names and How They Made It.* Boston: G. K. Hall.

Gardner, Howard. 1993. *Creative Minds.* New York: HarperCollins.

Ghiselin, Brewster. 1952. *The Creative Process.* Berkeley, Calif.: Berkeley Press.

Gilligan, Carol. 1982. *In a Different Voice: Psychological Theory and Women's Development.* Boston: Harvard University Press.

Goleman, Daniel, Paul Kaufman, and Ray Michael. 1992. *The Creative Spirit.* New York: Dutton.

Herschmann, D., and J. Lieb. 1988. *The Key to Genius.* Buffalo, N.Y.: Prometheus Books.

Hirsh, Sandra, and Jean Kummerow. 1989. *Life Types.* New York: Warner.

Hutchison, Michael. 1990. *The Anatomy of Sex and Power.* New York: Morrow.

Johnson, Robert. 1986. *Inner Work—Using Dreams and Active Imagination for Personal Growth.* San Francisco: Harper.

Jung, Carl. 1976. *The Portable Jung.* New York: Penguin.

Keirsey, David. 1987. *Portraits of Temperament—Personality Types.* Del Mar, Calif.: Prometheus Nemises.

Keirsey, D., and M. Bates. 1984. *Please Understand Me.* Del Mar, Calif.: Prometheus Nemises.

Kroeger, Otto, and Janet Thuesen. 1992. *Type Talk at Work.* New York: Delacorte Press.

Lear, Frances. 1992. *The Second Seduction.* New York: Harper.

Leman, Kenneth. 1985. *The Birth Order Book.* New York: Dell.

MacKinnon, David. 1965. "Personality and the Realiziation of Creative Potential." *American Psychologist,* pp. 273–81.

Mahar, Maggie. October 1992. "No Bull Advice" [article on Jane Bryant Quinn, the Dr. Spock of Personal Finance]. *Working Woman.*

Oppenheimer, Jerry. 1990. *Barbara Walters.* New York: St. Martin's Press.

Ornstein, Robert. 1986. *The Psychology of Consciousness.* New York: Penguin Books.

Pearsall, Paul. 1993. *Making Miracles.* New York: Avon Books.

People. August, 30, 1993. "Flush Femmes." Oprah, Madonna, and Fonda personal net worths discussed.

Silver, David. 1985. *Entrepreneurial Megabucks—The 100 Greatest Entrepreneurs of the Last 25 Years.* New York: John Wiley and Sons.

Storr, Anthony. 1993. *The Dynamics of Creation.* New York: Ballantine Books.

Taylor, I, and J. Gretzels. 1975. *Perspectives in Creativity.* Chicago.

Toffler, Alvin. 1990. *Power Shift.* New York: Bantam Books.

Troyat, Henry. 1980. *Catherine the Great.* New York: Berkley Books.

Mary Kay Ash

Ash, Mary Kay. 1987. *Mary Kay.* New York: Harper and Row.

———. 1984. *Mary Kay on People Management.* New York: Warner Books.

Conger, Jay. 1989. *The Charismatic Leader.* San Francisco: Jossey-Bass.

Entrepreneurial Woman. June 1991. "Role Model Mary Kay Ash," p. 36.

Fucini, Joseph and Suzy. 1985. *Entrepreneurs.* Boston: G. K. Hall, p. 96.

Gudeman, Janice. 1991. "Interview: Mary Kay Ash." *Challenge,* no. 43, pp. 13–17.

Jennings, Diane. 1987. *Self Made Women.* Dallas, Tex.: Taylor Publishing.

McMurran, Kristin. July 29, 1985. "Mary Kay Ash Bio," p. 57.

Shook, Robert. 1980. *The Entrepreneurs.* New York: Harper and Row.

Silver, A. David. 1985. *Entrepreneurial Megabucks.* New York: John Wiley and Sons, p. 143.

Sobel and Sicilia. 1986. *The Entrepreneurs.* "Mary Kay Ash—The Pink Cadillac Approach," p. 38.

Wiley, Kim. June 1983. "Cold Cream and Hard Cash." *Savvy,* p. 36.

Maria Callas

Callas, Evangelia. 1960. *My Daughter Maria Callas.* New York: Fleet.

Callas, Jackie. 1989. *Sisters.* New York: St. Martin's Press.

Callas, Maria, and Anita Pensotti. January and February 1957. "Memoirs." *Oggi.*

Hamilton, David. 1987. "Maria Callas." *Metropolitan Opera Encyclopedia.* New York: Simon and Schuster, p. 62.

Hamilton, Mary. 1990. "Maria Callas." *A-Z of Opera.* Facts On File.

Jellinek, George. 1960. *Callas.* New York: Ziff-Davis Publishing.

Lowe, David A. 1986. *Callas—As They Saw Her.* New York: Ungar Publishing.
Meneghini, Giovanni Battista. 1982. *My Wife Maria Callas.* New York: Farrar Straus Giroux.
Remy, Pierre-Jean. 1978. *Maria Callas A Tribute.* New York: St. Martin's Press.
Stanicoff, Nadia. 1987. *Maria Callas Remembered.* New York: E. P. Dutton.
Stassinopoulas, Arianna. 1981. *Maria Callas: The Woman Behind the Legend.* New York: Simon and Schuster.

Liz Claiborne

Better, Nancy. April 1992. "The Secret of Liz Claiborne's Success." *Working Woman,* p. 68.
Business Week. September 17, 1990. "Liz Claiborne Without Liz: Steady as She Goes," p. 70.
Ciampi, Thomas. May 8, 1991. "Liz Claiborne: A $2 Billion Phenomenon." *Women's Wear Daily,* pp. 7–9.
Ettorre, Barbara. July, 6, 1980. "Working Woman's Dressmaker." *New York Times,* p. 7.
Guzzardi, Walter. March 12, 1990. "The National Business Hall of Fame." *Fortune,* p. 118.
Hoffer, William. August 1987. "Businesswomen: Equal But Different." *Nations Business,* p. 46.
Hoover, G., A. Cambell, and P. Spain. 1991. "Liz Claiborne" in *Profiles of Over 500 Corporations.* Emoryville, Calif.: Publishers Group West, p. 336.
Jaffe, Thomas. September 2, 1991. "Fashionable Cash." *Forbes,* p. 332.
Loomis, Carol. April 24, 1989. "Secrets of the Superstars." *Fortune.*
Moskowitz, M., R. Levering, and M. Katz. 1990. *Everybody's Business—Liz Claiborne.* New York: Bantam, p. 93.
Morris, Michele. June 1988. "The Wizard of the Working Woman's Wardrobe." *Working Woman,* pp. 74–80.
Ms. (Nov. 1986). "Liz Claiborne," p. 50.
Sellers, Patricia. January 5, 1987. "The Rag Trade's Reluctant Revolutionary." *Fortune,* p. 36.
Silver, David. 1985. *Entrepreneurial Megabucks.* New York: John Wiley, pp. 339–41.

Jane Fonda

Adler, Jerry. February 1991. "Jane and Ted's Excellent Adventure." *Esquire,* p. 68.

Anderson, Christopher. 1990. *Citizen Jane.* New York: Dell Publishing.

Collins, Nancy. September 1993. "Prime Time Live" interview. Subject: "Why Did You Leave Moviemaking?"

Davidson, Bill. 1990. *Jane Fonda—An Intimate Biography.* New York: Dutton.

Kaplan, J. February 1985. "Fonda—Fit After Forty." *Vogue,* p. 374.

Landrum, G. 1993. *Profiles of Genius.* Buffalo, N.Y.: Prometheus Books.

Mitullo-Martin, Julia. February 20, 1984. "The Business Education of Jane Fonda." *Fortune,* p. 128.

Orth, M. February 1984. "Driving Passions of Jane Fonda." *Vogue,* p. 350.

Painton, Priscilla. January 6, 1992. "The Taming of Ted Turner." *Time,* p. 34.

Estée Lauder

Hoover, G., A. Cambell, and P. Spain. 1991. "Estée Lauder" in *Profiles of Over 500 Corporations.* Emoryville, Calif.: Publishers Group West, p. 227.

Israel, Lee. 1985. *Estée Lauder—Beyond the Magic.* New York: Macmillan Publishing.

Lauder, Estée. 1985. *Estée—A Success Story.* New York: Random House.

Moskowitz, M., R. Levering, and M. Katz. 1990. *Everybody's Business—Estée Lauder.* Bantam, p. 158.

Madonna

Anderson, Christopher. 1991. *Madonna.* New York: Dell.

Bego, Mark. 1992. *Madonna—Blonde Ambition.* New York: Harmony Books.

Goodman, Fred. December 1991. "Madonna and Oprah—And the Companies They Keep." *Working Woman,* p. 52

Greenberg, Keith. 1986. *Madonna.* Minneapolis, Minn.: Lerner Publications.

Gunderson, Edna. October 9, 1992. "Stage Image No Indication of True Self." *USA Today,* pp. 1–2D.

Madonna. 1992. *Sex.* New York: Time Warner.

Meisel, Steven. November 1992. "Entertainment—Sex Tips from Madonna." *Glamour,* p. 186.

———. October 1992. "Madonna in Wonderland." *Vanity Fair,* p. 206.

Sessume, Kevin. April 1990. "White Heat." *Vanity Fair,* p. 143.

Sexton, Adam. 1993. *Desperately Seeking Madonna.* New York: Dell.

Schifrin, Mathew, and Peter Newcomb. October 1, 1990. "A Brain for Sin and a Bod for Business." *Forbes*, p. 162.

Thompson, Douglas. 1992. *Madonna—The Unauthorized Biography*. New York: Leisure Books.

Margaret Mead

Howard, June. 1984. *Margaret Mead*. New York: Simon and Schuster.

Mead, Margaret. 1972. *Blackberry Winter—My Earlier Years*. New York: Morrow.

Golda Meir

Mann, Peggy. 1971. *Golda*. New York: Coward, McCann and Geoghehan.

Martin, Ralph. 1988. *Golda*. New York: Scribner and Sons.

Meir, Golda. 1975. *My Life*. New York: Putnam.

Ayn Rand

Branden, Barbara. 1986. *The Passion of Ayn Rand—A Biography*. New York: Doubleday.

Branden, Nathaniel. 1989. *Judgement Day—My Years with Ayn Rand*. Boston: Houghton-Mifflin.

Branden, Nathaniel and Barbara. 1962. *Who Is Ayn Rand?* New York: Random House.

"Contemporary Literary Criticism." 1975. CLC-3 Ayn Rand. p. 423.

Rand, Ayn. 1957. *Atlas Shrugged*. New York: Signet.

———. 1961. *For the New Intellectual*. New York: Signet.

———. 1982. *Philosophy: Who Needs It?* New York: Signet.

———. 1993. *The Objectivist Newsletters—1962 through 1965*. Oceanside, Calif.: Second Reanaissance Books.

———. 1993. *The Objectivist Newsletters—1966 through 1971*. Oceanside, Calif.: Second Reanaissance Books.

———. 1993. *The Ayn Rand Newsletters—1971 through 1976*. Oceanside, Calif.: Second Renaissance Books.

Toffler, Alvin. March 1964. "*Playboy* Interview: Ayn Rand." *Playboy*.

Gloria Steinem

Anderson, Walter. 1989. "Gloria Steinem Talks About Risk." *Cosmopolitan,* p. 60.

Barthel, Joan. March 1984. "The Glorious Triumphs of Gloria Steinem." *Cosmopolitan,* pp. 217–19.

Harper's Bazaar. September 1983. "The 10 Most Influential Women in America."

Henry, Sondra, and Emily Taitz. 1987. *One Woman's Power—A Biography of Gloria Steinem.* Minneapolis, Minn.: Dillon Press.

Levitt, Leonard. October 1971. "She—The Awesome Power of Gloria Steinem." *Esquire,* p. 87.

McCall's. January 1972. "Woman of the Year—Gloria Steinem," pp. 67–69.

Steinem, Gloria. 1983. *Outrageous Acts and Everday Rebellions.* New York: Holt, Rinehart and Winston.

———. November/December 1991. "Self-Esteem." *Ms.,* p. 25.

———. 1992. *Revolution from Within—A Book of Self-Esteem.* Boston: Little, Brown.

Mother Teresa

Mother Teresa. 1985. *My Life for the Poor.* New York: Harper and Row.

Muggeridge, Malcolm. 1971. *Something Beautiful for God.* New York: Harper and Row.

Royle, Roger, and Gary Woods. 1992. *Mother Teresa—A Life in Pictures.* New York: Harper Collins Publishing.

Tames, Richard. 1989. *Mother Teresa.* New York: Franklin Watts.

Margaret Thatcher

C-SPAN. December 15, 1993, Television interview with Margaret Thatcher.

Garfinkle, Bernard. 1985. *Thatcher.* New York: Chelsea House.

Murray, Patricia. 1980. *Margaret Thatcher.* Great Britain: W. and J. Mackay Ltd.

Newhouse, John. February 10, 1986. "Thatcher." *The New Yorker.*

Ogden, Chris. 1990. *Maggie—An Intimate Portrait of a Woman in Power.* New York: Simon and Schuster.

Young, Hugo. 1989. *The Iron Lady.* New York: The Noonday Press.

Lillian Vernon

American Management Association. May 1993. "Lillian Vernon Focuses on Customers." *Management Review*, p. 22.

Barrett, Mary. September 26–28, 1986. "Look What Lillian Has Wrapped Up." *USA Weekend*, p. 4.

Coleman, Lisa. August 17, 1992. "I Went Out and Did It." *Forbes*, p. 102.

Fierman, Jaclyn. January 1, 1990. "The Year's 25 Most Fascinating Business People." *Fortune*, p. 65.

Finney, Martha. February 1987. "The Treasure of Her Company—Lillian Katz." *Nations Business*, p. 73.

Jennings, Diane. 1987. *Self Made Women*. Dallas, Tex.: Taylor Publishing.

Wilkinson, Stephan. June 1986. "The Maestro of Merchandise—Lillian Katz." *Working Woman*, p. 62.

Younger, Joseph. September 1988. "Lillian Katz—The Queen of the Catalogs." *Piedmont Airlines*, p. 44.

Linda Wachner

Caminiti, Susan. June 15, 1992. "America's Most Successful Businesswoman." *Fortune*, p. 102.

Donahue, Christine. January 1987. "Linda Wachner." *Ms.*, p. 78.

Fortune. December 14, 1992. "Leaders of Corporate Change—Linda Wachner," p. 105.

Leinster, Colin, and John Newport. January 6, 1986. "The Would-Be Queen of Revlon's Beauty Business." *Fortune*, p. 76.

Mahar, Maggie. May 1992. "The Measure of Success." *Working Woman*, p. 70.

McElwaine, Sandra. June 1990. "*Cosmo* Talks to Linda Wachner." *Cosmopolitan*, p. 146.

Oprah Winfrey

Angelou, Maya. January/February 1989. "Oprah Winfrey." *Ms.*, p. 88.

Casey, Kathryn. November 1992. "The Mystery of Oprah." *Ladies Home Journal*, p. 186.

Cohen, Roger. August 12, 1990. "What Publishers Will Do." *The New York Times*.

Ebert, Alan. September 1991. "Oprah Winfrey Talks Openly about Oprah." *Good Housekeeping*.

Essence. June 1991. "Oprah Body and Soul," p. 46.

Forbes. September 1993. "America's 40 Highest Paid Entertainers."

Goodman, Fred. December 1991. "Madonna and Oprah—And the Companies They Keep." *Working Woman,* p. 52.

People. September 7, 1992. "Not Scared Not Silent," p. 48.

———. November 23, 1992. "Her Man Stedman," p. 132.

Randolph, Laura. October 1993. "Oprah Opens Up About Weight, Her Wedding, and Why She Withheld the Book." *Ebony,* p. 130.

Rogers, Jackie. September 1993. "Understanding Oprah." *Redbook,* p. 91.

Waldron, Robert. 1987. *Oprah.* New York: St. Martin's Paperbacks.

USA Today. November 9, 1992. "Oprah's Steady to Be Her Hubby," p 2D.

Index

433